Law and Time

Research on law's relationship with time has flourished over the past decade. This edited collection aims to put law and time scholarship into wider context, advancing conversations on time and temporalities between socio-legal scholars, anthropologists, sociologists, geographers and historians. Through a diverse range of contributions, the collection explores how legal modalities of time emerge and have effects within wider clusters of social and political action. Themes include: law's diverse roles in maintaining linear historicist models of time; law's participation in the materialisation of times; and the unsteady effects of temporal pluralism and polytemporalities in law. De-naturalising the 'time' in law and time scholarship, this collection positions time as something that can be enacted and materialised as well as experienced, with distinct implications for questions of social justice.

Siân M. Beynon-Jones is a Lecturer in Sociology at the University of York.

Emily Grabham is Professor of Law at Kent Law School, University of Kent.

Part of the
SOCIAL JUSTICE
series

For more information about the series and details of previous and forthcoming titles, see https://www.routledge.com/Social-Justice/book-series/RCSOCJ

A GlassHouse book

Law and Time

Edited by
Siân M. Beynon-Jones
and Emily Grabham

Routledge
Taylor & Francis Group
a GlassHouse book

First published 2019
by Routledge
2 Park Square, Milton Park, Abingdon, Oxon OX14 4RN

and by Routledge
52 Vanderbilt Avenue, New York, NY 10017

First issued in paperback 2020

a GlassHouse book

Routledge is an imprint of the Taylor & Francis Group, an informa business

British Library Cataloguing-in-Publication Data
A catalogue record for this book is available from the British Library

Library of Congress Cataloging-in-Publication Data
Names: Grabham, Emily, editor. | Beynon-Jones, Siân Maeve, editor.
Title: Law and time/Emily Grabham and Siân Beynon-Jones.
Description: Abingdon, Oxon; New York, NY: Routledge, 2018. |
Series: Social justice
Identifiers: LCCN 2018009158 | ISBN 9780415792219 (hardback)
Subjects: LCSH: Time (Law)–Social aspects.
Classification: LCC K579.T5 L39 2018 | DDC 340/.11–dc23
LC record available at https://lccn.loc.gov/2018009158

ISBN 13: 978-0-367-66530-2 (pbk)
ISBN 13: 978-0-415-79221-9 (hbk)

Typeset in Galliard
by Integra Software Services Pvt. Ltd.

Contents

Contributors

Philip Ashton is Associate Professor of Urban Planning and Policy at UIC. His research and practice focus on the restructuring of US retail finance, with a consistent interest in how minority borrowers and neighbourhoods have fared in the 'new financial marketplace'. This has translated into research projects on subprime mortgage lending and the racialisation of credit risk, the foreclosure crisis and its governance and the role of investment banks and infrastructure funds in producing the growing market for urban infrastructure assets. He is currently working on a book project on fraud and discrimination litigation against large subprime mortgage lenders.

Siân M. Beynon-Jones is a Lecturer in Sociology at the University of York. Her research is situated at the intersection of feminist theory, Science and Technology Studies and medical sociology. She has published on issues of time and regulation within abortion practice and in relation to the governance of the futures of innovative biomedical technologies. Recently her research has focused on women's lived experiences of the temporalities of pregnancy and abortion and the ways in which such experiences intersect with, and challenge, regulatory assumptions about the meaning of 'time' in this context.

Kevin Birth is a professor of anthropology at Queens College of the City University of New York. He studies cultural concepts of time in relationship to cognition and has conducted ethnographic research in Trinidad and on the current leap second controversy. His publications and presentations cover a wide ranging array of topics including chronobiology and globalisation, comparative calendars, timekeeping in Roman Britain, culture and memory, cognitive neuroscience, early modern clocks and ideas about roosters in the Middle Ages. He is the author of three books: *Any Time is Trinidad Time* (University Press of Florida), *Bacchanalian Sentiments* (Duke University Press Objects of Time (Palgrave Macmillan) and, most recently, *Time Blind* (Palgrave Macmillan).

Emilie Cloatre is Professor of Law at Kent Law School. Her research interests are mainly focused on the intersection between law and 'science in society debates', in particular, law and medicine. She is currently Principal Investigator on a Wellcome Trust Investigator Award (2017–2022) entitled 'Law, Knowledges and the Making of Modern Healthcare: Regulating alternative and traditional medicines in contemporary contexts'. Her publications include *Pills for the Poorest: An Exploration of TRIPS and Access to Medicines in Sub-Saharan African* (Palgrave McMillan, 2013 – awarded the 2014 Hart Socio-Legal Book prize) and *Knowledge, Technology and Law* (Routledge, 2014, with Martyn Pickersgill).

Máiréad Enright is a Senior Lecturer in Law at the University of Birmingham. Máiréad's research interests include critical legal theory, law and religion, reproductive justice and the politics of private law. She has published interdisciplinary articles on law in journals including the *Journal of Law & Society, Social & Legal Studies, International Journal of Law in Context* and the *Modern Law Review*. Her current work focuses on the politics of reproductive rights in Ireland as these concern access to abortion and reparations for obstetric violence.

Emily Grabham is Professor of Law at Kent Law School, University of Kent. Emily's research interests include law and time, labour law and feminist legal theory. She pursues an interdisciplinary approach to legal studies, drawing on methods and perspectives from feminist legal theory, social anthropology, sociology and Science and Technology Studies. Emily's monograph *Brewing Legal Times: Things, Form and the Enactment of Law* was published by University of Toronto Press in 2016. She has published interdisciplinary articles on law in a wide range of peer reviewed journals including *Economy & Society, Australian Feminist Studies, Body & Society, Social & Legal Studies, Oxford Journal of Legal Studies* and *Canadian Journal of Law & Society.*

Carol Greenhouse is the Arthur W. Marks '19 Professor of Anthropology at Princeton University. Her primary research interests are in the ethnography of law, in particular regarding the experiential – including temporal – dimensions of federal power in the United States and, more generally, interpretive ethnographic questions in relation to state powers in comparative and transnational contexts. Her publications include *The Paradox of Relevance: Ethnography and Citizenship in the United States* and *A Moment's Notice: Time Politics Across Cultures.* She is past president of the Law & Society Association and the American Ethnological Society.

L.J.B. Hayes is a Lecturer in Law at Cardiff University and held the *Journal of Law and Society* Research Fellowship 2013–2016. Her monograph, *Stories of Care: A Labour of Law. Gender and Class at Work* (Palgrave, 2017) connects ethnographic research with doctrinal analysis to argue that care workers are institutionally humiliated by the gendered inadequacy of labour law. She has also published on equal pay, the national minimum wage, covert surveillance in care work, caring labour and austerity, the regulation of working time, vulnerability, migration issues and the right to organise and bargaining collectively.

Mikko Jalas holds a PhD in Organisation and Management from the Aalto University School of Business. He currently has a position as a Professor at the Aalto University School of Arts, Design and Architecture. He has worked on a time use approach to energy consumption as well as on time use rebound-effects and social rhythms. More recently he has worked on renewable energy and energy efficiency technologies in the residential building sector. His research also covers local embedding of renewable energy technologies, self-building activities and consumer empowerment.

Maya John is a History scholar based in the University of Delhi (India) where she is currently teaching. She has published on the evolution of labour law in colonial India, the relationship between caste and the labour market and the question of education in the colonial and post-colonial period. Some of her other research interests include social movements, caste and the history of affirmative action, dynamics of women's participation in the colonial and post-colonial labour market and state formation in India. John is also actively working with unions of domestic workers, nurses, teachers and other sections of the urban workforce.

Sarah Keenan is Senior Lecturer in Law at Birkbeck College. Her research draws on legal geography, feminist and critical race theory to rethink the relationship between membership and ownership, offering new perspectives on a range of social, legal and political issues. Her book *Subversive Property: Law and the Production of Spaces of Belonging* (Routledge, 2015) develops a theory of property as a spatially contingent relation of belonging – a relation that can be understood as a blurring of ownership and membership, but that will only form property when it is 'held up' by the space in and through which it exists, that is, when the wider social processes, structures and networks that constitute space give force to that relation. She is currently researching the relationship between land title registration, time and race.

Sameena Mulla is Associate Professor of Anthropology in the Department of Social and Cultural Sciences at Marquette University. She is the author of *The Violence of Care: Rape Victims, Forensic Nurses, and Sexual Assault Intervention* (New York University Press, 2014), for which she was awarded the 2017 Margaret Mead Award by the American Anthropological Association and the Society for Applied Anthropology. She is co-editor of *Police/Worlds: Studies in Security, Crime and Governance*, a book series at Cornell University Press.

Genevieve Renard Painter is an Assistant Professor at Concordia University. She earned her PhD in Jurisprudence and Social Policy from the University of California, Berkeley. She holds degrees in common and civil law (BCL/LLB) from McGill University. A member of the Quebec bar, she has practised in aboriginal and constitutional law and has worked as an advocate for several human rights organisations.

Sinéad Ring is a Senior Lecturer at Kent Law School, University of Kent where she teaches the Law of Evidence. Her research interests lie in the area of political and legal responses to historical gendered violence.

Jenny Rinkinen is a Senior Research Associate at the DEMAND Centre (Dynamics of Energy, Mobility and Demand) at Lancaster University. Her research interests include broadly the dynamics of energy demand and questions of temporality and materiality in theories of social practice.

Antti Silvast is a Postdoctoral Researcher in the Department of Anthropology at the University of Durham, researching the energy infrastructure, Energy Systems Integration and whole systems modelling and their implications for the UK. Previous to this, he was postdoctoral researcher in Princeton University's Global Systemic Risk Community and a Research Fellow at the University of Edinburgh. His PhD in sociology is from the University of Helsinki.

Irene van Oorschot is a postdoctoral researcher at the University of Amsterdam on the ERC-funded RaceFaceID research project (principal investigator: Prof. Amade M'charek). There, she concentrates on the legal mobilisation and contestation of forensic research. She recently defended her dissertation *Ways of Case-Making* (with honours). In this book, she concentrates on legal modes of fact- and truth-making and on the performativities of social scientific knowledges. She has published in, among others, *Symbolic Interaction*, the *Journal of Law and Society* and *Social & Legal Studies.* She previously worked as a guest editor at the peer-reviewed Dutch journal *Sociologie* and is currently an editor for *Krisis: Journal of Contemporary Philosophy.*

Acknowledgements

Many people and organisations have contributed to this edited collection coming into being. We would like, in particular, to thank colleagues at the University of York and University of Kent who have provided research guidance and support for this book and for the networks that have sustained it: Sarah Shrive-Morrison and Ed Kirby at York; and Sarah Slowe, Cathy Norman and Sarah Gilkes at Kent.

The Department of Sociology at York and Kent Law School have provided us with rich intellectual and collegial environments in which to pursue this cross-disciplinary adventure.

We would like to thank the Arts and Humanities Research Council for funding the *Regulating Time* network that supported many of the conversations advanced in this book (through grant number AH/M008533/1). Members of the network, which launched in 2015, have contributed wonderful insights, analysis, interest and enthusiasm over the past three years, creating the field of 'law and time' through their academic labour and temporal preoccupations and making this edited collection possible.

The editors and publishing staff at Routledge have been consistently generous with their time and patience and we would like to thank them for sticking with us.

Siân would like to thank Emily for being so understanding and immensely supportive of a corporeal project that was routinely out-of-sync with Law and Time. In turn, Emily would like to thank Siân for her timely, honest and insightful feedback.

Introduction

Emily Grabham and Siân M. Beynon-Jones

Introduction

The intellectual inspiration for this collection has been a flourishing, over recent years, in critical, socio-legal scholarship on law's temporalities. Such scholarship has begun to take seriously time's effects on law and social ordering. Yet legal scholarship also has shown a tendency to naturalise time. As Renisa Mawani puts it: 'law's time has too often been assumed rather than problematized' (Mawani, 2014, p. 69). Through the temporal operation of precedent in common law, commencement dates and sunset clauses in legislation, and even through horizons of time created through legal doctrine and discourse (e.g. constitutional originalism, foreseeability in tort), law has proved to be particularly open for temporal analysis. And whilst socio-legal scholarship has been adept at delineating the subjectivities, institutional arrangements and cultural expectations that shape legal engagements more generally, Mawani's argument is that much of this research has relegated time to a role as the background or container for social action or, at most, as a subjective experience that shifts depending on one's social or historical positioning. As she puts it: 'time is often assumed to exist as though it were a natural phenomenon, unfolding effortlessly and inconspicuously as the backdrop to social and political life' (Mawani, 2014, p. 70). The approach has been to overlook law's production of time, instead exteriorising time as something distinct from law itself (Mawani, 2014, p. 71). This continued attachment to the idea of time as a container for social life has been maintained alongside the law and geography movement's very well-established commitment to following the co-production of law with space, place and jurisdiction, denaturalising law and following the co-articulation of temporalities with spatial mechanisms (Braverman et al., 2014; Mawani, 2014; Valverde, 2015). It has also survived the curiosity about time that anthropologists – including legal anthropologists – have brought to the study of social ordering (Engel, 1990; Fabian, 2014; Greenhouse, 2014, 1996; Richland, 2013, 2008) and scholars of history have brought to periodisation (e.g. Davis, 2008) and historical time (Koselleck, 1985).[1]

In bringing together this collection on law's relationship with time, our concern has been to register an increasing commitment among scholars across disciplines to shift such patterns of engagement. Our own research over the past few years has been preoccupied with the question of law's temporalities, drawing on a range of critical resources to investigate, through empirical research, the co-production of legal and temporal norms, subjectivities and political ontologies. In our related efforts to create an interdisciplinary network of scholars working on law and time,[2] we have noted a distinct openness to questions of law, regulation and legality from social sciences and humanities scholars working on temporality, on the one hand (e.g. Adkins, 2012; Amoore, 2013; de Goede, 2015; Mitropoulos, 2012; Opitz et al., 2015), and an incisive conceptual and methodological interdisciplinarity among critical and socio-legal scholars, on the other (e.g. Cooper, 2013; Cornell, 1990; Craven et al., 2006; Douglas, 2011; Fitzpatrick, 2013; Keenan, 2014; Philippopoulos-Mihalopoulos, 2013; Valverde, 2015; van Marle, 2003). Critical approaches to linear time and attention to law's shaping of time in diverse forms and through multiple techniques have animated research across disciplines. We hope that the present collection will highlight these shared concerns, fostering the cross-fertilisation of ideas and methods and further developing conversations on law and time between socio-legal scholars, anthropologists, sociologists, geographers, historians and others.

Our contribution is to hone in on questions of the 'making of time' through a focus on law, time's knotted relationship with matter, material processes and technologies. Attempts to understand time and change in the study of social life have been preoccupied by Newtonian continuity, what Karen Barad terms a 'tidy affair' in which: '(e)ffects follow causes end on end and each particle takes its preordained place with each tick of the clock' (Barad, 2007, p. 233). Within this story, time is eternal and non-material ('Matter is discrete but time is continuous', Barad, 2007, p. 233) and, moreover, the status of time as distinct from nature and matter is foundational of objective views of the world. Regular, eternal, container time has played a significant role in constituting scientific objectivity, yet these ideas of time and objectivity can be refigured (Barad, 2007, p. 233). For example, the advent of quantum physics disturbs the notion of container time and its associated objectivity. Time's crumpling and fluid qualities work beyond strictly linear approach to objects, events, human action and history (Serres and Latour, 1995), replacing the 'rolling unravelling stasis' of Newtonian physics with dynamic processes of mattering (Barad, 2007, p. 233).

In registering the call to move beyond notions of time as always naturally linear, containing of social action and progressive, we are interested in developing approaches to time that explore law's ambivalent, yet constitutive, roles in broader social and political processes of temporal ordering and in forming distinct temporal ontologies. If time can be plural and non-linear – if it can consist of 'polytemporalities' (Haraway, 2016) or 'chimneys of thunderous acceleration' (Serres and Latour, 1995, p. 57); if, crucially, time can be a participant or an effect in processes of social and material formation and not always the driver (Barad, 2007) – then we might investigate how law participates in the creation of temporal ontologies just as much as reflecting on how law itself is shaped by dominant temporal assumptions.

Setting aside the notion of linear container time is associated with assaults on received notions of objectivity by the so-called 'ontological turn' in social theory

(Barad, 2007; Mol, 2003), challenging distinctions common to modern thought between the natural world and human social action, between cause and effect and between discourse and matter (Haraway, 1991) that sustain an idea of time as exterior and exceptional (e.g. Latour, 1993). Refiguring time has been central to black quantum futurism (Phillips, 2015) and feminist new materialism (Coole and Frost, 2010), as much as it has animated studies broadly collected under the term 'actor network theory' and in wider social theory. Richard Tutton advocates conceptualising the future as an 'entanglement of matter and meaning' and 'enacted through particular material-discursive practices' (Tutton, 2017, pp. 485, 488). It is thereby possible to understand many temporalities as being created through mutual articulations between matter and meaning: as materialised, in other words (Tutton, 2017) in a move that brings time closer, denaturalising it along the way. For those interested in law, such an approach brings with it the potential for a multidirectional process of co-production between law, temporalities and other elements of social and political life (Valverde, 2015).

In particular, we would like to view law in creative juxtaposition with time's unsteady contingency on processes of mattering: what Barad terms the 'making/marking' of time through 'lively' processes of 'enfolding' (Barad, 2007, p. 181). As such, we are interested in 'praxiographic' accounts of law and time (Grabham, 2016, following Mol, 2003), which open up unexpected alignments, as well as non-linear movements and which follow law's relationship with material and political intra-actions (Davies, 2017; Philippopoulos-Mihalopoulos, 2014; Pottage, 2014). Our argument, then, is for an approach to law, regulation and time that conceives of time (just as much as law) as made or co-produced, not pre-existing and separate, and which is engaged in dialogue with concepts of time emerging across disciplines.

Making time across disciplines

In this section, we signpost such conceptual trajectories by highlighting the incredible breadth of current work on time and temporality across disciplines, before going on to introduce the key themes arising from the collection as a whole in the section that follows. Rather than attempting to provide an exhaustive review of literatures on time, our aim is to trace lines of enquiry that might be productive for thinking about law within cross- or interdisciplinary studies of time and temporality. The task of articulating current or important literatures on time comes with significant risk of losing one's coordinates along the way. Yet curating encounters between disciplines requires a degree of journeying, straying away from received disciplinary commitments before re-engaging with new and stranger perspectives. This is part of our commitment to connecting up conversations about law's temporalities and time's legal manifestations.

Our journeying has shown us that scholars working on questions of time and legality have an increasingly rich range of resources on which to draw. Feminist and postcolonial thought has long been significant for challenging linear time and developmental historicism by dismantling apparently 'natural', homogenous or teleological concepts of time. Historicism tends not only to foundationalise development as a driver of social progress and history, but also to reassert the idea that development is linked to time elapsing in linear mode. This form of linearity can be violently excluding of those who do not or cannot fit within the historico-developmental project. As Máiréad Enright puts it, writing in this collection: '(h)omogeneity enables a radical break with the past – there are no important stragglers' (this collection, p. 48). Identifying such temporal homogeneity and writing against it has been the task of a wide range of scholars. For example, Julia Kristeva's feminist intervention *Women's Time* poses a specifically female mode of temporality, characterised by repetition (through cycles and gestation), eternity; a form of monumental time that resides outside of linear time with 'no cleavage or escape', which is 'all-encompassing and infinite like imaginary space' (Kristeva et al., 1981, p. 16). Kristeva juxtaposes this with the time of history, the teleology of which, she argues, is masculine, civilisational and obsessional (Kristeva et al., 1981, p. 18). More recent reflections on normative gender and sexuality have taken up the challenge of understanding how social, sexual and economic arrangements are intertwined with powerful ideals of the life course. Feminist and queer scholarship has proposed approaches based on 'queer counter-historiography' (Freeman, 2011, 2005) and 'queer rationalism' (Power, 2009) to counter dominant modes of temporal organisation attached to productivism and development. Debates about the progressive potential of queer futures (Muñoz, 2007) and the centrality of 'reproductive futurism' to wider models of political rationality (Edelman, 2004) have explored how hetero-normative temporalities underpin exclusionary political horizons. Research on diverse queer and transgender experiences of time now complicates the epistemological primacy of sexed linear development and its associated social and cultural milestones (Conley, 2008; Dinshaw et al., 2007; Fisher et al., 2017; Halberstam, 2005; Jaime, 2017; Keeling, 2009). Feminist theories of non-chronological time (Barad, 2015; Walker, 2014), hope (Coleman and Ferreday, 2011) and crip analysis of futurity (Kafer, 2013) all articulate radical temporal alternatives.

In such accounts, materiality and material relations are often enormously significant and contribute to queering our understanding of corporeality. For example, Siân Beynon-Jones found that women's narratives of conception not only started at points much earlier than she had expected but described something more complex than a discrete point in time. 'Becoming pregnant' was a 'bodily state that emerge(d) over an extended time period, in relation to multiple, inextricable, socio-material processes with varying temporal rhythms', even as many women described their transition from non-pregnant to pregnant embodiment as a shocking and disruptive moment (Beynon-Jones, 2017, pp. 840–1). Surprisingly, women's accounts often gave hormonal contraception a central role in the process of becoming pregnant, suggesting that what others understand as the gestational time of the foetus is experienced by women instead as a more knotty and socially complex temporality, mediated through encounters with contraceptive technologies and heterosexuality and reaching further 'back in time'.

Allowing the strangeness of time to come to the surface is therefore not only empirically useful but also politically significant. This has been a recurrent theme within studies of colonialism, in which historicism and Enlightenment universalism have been critiqued for figuring colonial subjects and projects as 'behind' modern time (Chakrabarty, 2009; Scott, 2014, 2004). As Dipesh Chakrabarty puts it: 'Historicism is what made modernity or capitalism look not simply global but rather as something that became global over time, by originating in one place (Europe) and then spreading outside it' (Chakrabarty, 2009, p. 7). Posing Europe as the 'site of first occurrence' perpetuates a 'not yet' orientation to the colonies, relegating them to anachronism, archaism or other forms of out-of-time-ness. Chakrabarty notes that this 'not yetness' has been answered by the 'now' demands of national independence movements, which have essentially pluralised time by centring as political agents people who would otherwise have been deemed 'archaic'. By contrast, David Scott, writing about the failed Granada revolution of 1979, evokes what is for some, a pervasive temporal 'afterness' of postcolonial and postsocialist time (Scott, 2014, p. 21). This is a time or lived temporality in which, a moment of revolution having been and gone, generations have become stranded in the present. Here, in the aftermath of a longed-for event – a revolution, which also, in anticipation, played its own strong role in configuring temporal horizons – the present equates to ruined time and brings with it the task of responding to a loss of political hope (Scott, 2014, p. 71).[3]

Recent work on race and racialisation has approached linear time slightly differently. As in critiques of colonial time, scholars have noted an 'epistemological grammar' of advancement and backwardness that positions white subjects within a future-oriented paradigm of modernity and relegates non-white subjects to times and timeframes outside modernity (El-Enany, 2016; Gilmore, 2002; Smith and Vasudevan, 2017). Yet studies of race in critical geography, in particular, have emphasised how present biopolitical projects intrinsically rely on, and construct, future imaginaries (Smith and Vasudevan, 2017, p. 211). For example, as Shiloh Krupars and Nadine Ehlers have shown, biomedical racial targeting explicitly aimed at increasing the wellness of black subjects and populations ultimately re-enacts race through 'death-expectant' logics of intervention (Krupar and Ehlers, 2017, p. 233). Scholars have also noted, however, the dangers for non-white subjects of jettisoning practices of looking forward. Cultural theorist Jose Muñoz has argued in favour of maintaining practices of hope alongside temporal critique: 'It is important not to hand over futurity to normative white reproductive futurity' (Muñoz, 2007, p. 365).

Critiques of historicism, future-making, and linear time are necessary for unmooring essentialist knowledge practices that maintain colonial orders or particular configurations of gender, sexuality and race as 'timeless', 'modern' or 'advanced'. Yet these critiques have also emerged in conversation with cross-disciplinary research in areas such as finance; economic policy; science, technology and innovation; environmental policy; and security, for example, which focuses on the role of time in complex governing assemblages.[4] Such work is extremely wide-ranging, encompassing topics as diverse as the analysis of risk (Amoore, 2004; Beck, 1992; O'Malley, 2004); crisis (Bryant, 2016; Cooper and Konings, 2015; Dowling and Harvie, 2014), environmental time (Adam, 1998); expectations and the construction of the future (Adam and Groves, 2007; Borup et al., 2006; Brown et al., 2000); speculation (de Goede, 2015, 2012); austerity times (Gray, 2016; Knight and Stewart, 2017); and pre-emption (Anderson, 2010; de Goede and Amoore, 2008). Feminist enquiries into the new economy have noted the far-reaching consequences of thinking through post-Fordist time and the temporalities of financial crisis, as well as engaging with alternative economic and community structures (Adkins, 2012; Cooper, 2012; Gibson, 2015; Sharma, 2014). Speed has also been a focus: critical studies have analysed the construction of urgency (Olson, 2015), cultural and political logics of speeding up and slowing down (Sharma, 2014) and the apparent acceleration of social life through technical and legal innovations (Francot and Mommers, 2017; Rosa, 2013; Wacjman, 2015). In turn, slowness has been investigated through concepts of 'slow traumas' (Alexandrakis, 2016), the 'slow violence' of environmental devastation and the aftermath of war (Nixon, 2011), for example, as well as the pre-figurative potential of 'slow' research (Berg and Seeber, 2016) and design (Pschetz et al., 2016).

Within this work as a whole, governance strategies are seen responding to, or anticipating, apparently urgent, overwhelming social dilemmas and their associated consequences: the catastrophe of climate change, for example, or the distributed, unpredictable threat of terrorism. Actors and organisations ranging from national governments to incipient activist networks mobilise terms such as emergency, premeditation, pre-emption, precaution, anticipation and resilience, articulating divergent positions on unknown yet near and soon-to-be experienced worlds. The term 'emergency', for example, emphasises a current and usually limited process of disruption or harm, which has the 'quality of unpredictable, rapid change and the time of a turning point' and which is for that reason difficult to map or anticipate (Anderson, 2017, p. 465). Whilst much scholarship has figured emergency in terms of exceptionality, specifically the 'state of exception' theorised in Agamben's work on sovereignty and the suspension of the legal order, other strands of thinking articulate emergency as a quality of a breakdown between apparently 'normal' and 'abnormal' events, consequent on increasingly connected social relationships, such that 'emergency' is a result of a kind of radical contingency (Adey et al., 2015). A range of future-oriented stances is rooted in the logic of taking action even before emergencies can unfold (Adey et al., 2015). By contrast, 'premeditation' describes a set of imaginative processes exceeding risk management in their capacity to speculate and plan for worst-case scenarios (de Goede and Amoore, 2008; Grusin, 2010). Security processes visualising a field of past or ongoing transactions, financial and otherwise (e.g. transport), can reframe security governance temporalities by enabling 'pre-emptive' measures that acknowledge 'that which can never be captured' (de Goede and Amoore, 2008, p. 179). This augurs a tactics of power that works by eschewing control in the face of uncertainty. Most recently, developments in cyberspace security that aim for 'resilience' adopt the apparent intrinsic 'grace' of systems themselves in an attempt to create evolving responses to complex and distributed emergencies (Simon and Goede, 2015).

Reacting to such a 'turbulent field' (Adey et al., 2015, p. 8), governance responses to the largest of large-scale social problems are characterised by a form of workable urgency, which relies on a constructed notion of 'real time' to link both threats and responses on the same heuristic scale. The 'actionable future' is therefore often built on an apprehension that 'total threats' – threats that are pressing, large-scale and irreversible – are amenable to intervention through a specific set of governance arts and techniques (de Goede and Randalls, 2009). Concepts such as emergency imply faith in action and are hence particularly well-suited not just to organising immediate responses but also to helping to instantiate new political movements, addressing, for example, climate change (Adey et al., 2015) or the endemic violence of structural racism (Anderson, 2017). The scale and unpredictability of the threat adds to a sense that any government or wider social action should happen immediately after or even in advance of the anticipated harms. As de Goede and Randalls put it: '(B)oth the threat of terrorist annihilation and climate change can be articulated in terms of simultaneous uncertainty *and* catastrophe, incalculability and potential apocalypse' (de Goede and Randalls, 2009, p. 864).

Such developments are not confined to the field of state action. New articulations of risk – or risk 'in the mode of possibility rather than strict probability' as Louise Amoore has put it – resonate between the scenario planning and modelling tools used in management consultancy, on the one hand, and anticipatory state security practices, on the other (Amoore, 2013, p. 10). Moving away from reliance on strict probability, this 'politics of possibility' instead works on the 'inductive incorporation of suspicion, imagination and pre-emption' into public and commercial systems (Amoore, 2013, p. 10). Such diffuse and decentred temporal stances can be contrasted with epistemologies of what Tutton would call 'great future change' (Tutton, 2017, p. 478), such as the 'anthropocene', in which the era of human impact on the Earth's atmosphere is positioned as a distinct geological era, with attendant social and political implications. These are world-level, definitive, human-led temporal epochs that not only situate human action – 'the time we live in' – within a much vaster time of 'nature' and 'environment' but also reconfigure that larger time based on human agency and effects.

In the context of this focus on human-led temporalities, Donna Haraway has argued for an approach to nature and time that challenges the human exceptionalism and individualism found in mainstream political economy (Haraway, 2016, p. 57). In her most recent book *Staying with the Trouble* (2016), Haraway radically reframes teleological approaches to human history, arguing instead for a polytemporal and indeterminate concept of multispecies 'worlding' (Haraway, 2016, p. 11). Channeling human exceptionalism into our epochal understandings of humans and 'nature' through concepts like the 'anthropocene', Haraway argues, leads to a complex mix of cynicism and self-fulfilling predictions in which, she states, 'both technotheocratic geoengineering fixes and wallowing in despair seem to coinfect any possible common imagination' (Haraway, 2016, p. 56). Haraway's aim, by contrast, is to imagine a new type of multi-species flourishing, a 'nonarrogant collaboration with all those in the muddle' (Haraway, 2016, p. 56). Hence her need to reconfigure how we understand and act with time.

Haraway's concept of the 'Chthulucene' is a polytemporality and 'timeplace' that resists dating (Haraway, 2016, p. 51) as well as – arguably – linearity and which refers to the trouble we need to take and learn to live with in living and dying on a damaged earth (Haraway, 2016, p. 2). As she puts it:

> The unfinished Chthulucene must collect up the trash of the Anthropocene, the exterminism of the Capitolocene, and chipping and shredding and layering like a mad gardener, make a much hotter compost pile for still possible pasts, presents, and futures.
>
> (Haraway, 2016, p. 57)

The Chthulucene emerges from Haraway's commitment to feminist science fiction, speculative fabulation and string figures, all of which, she argues, need each other. Taken together, 'SF' is a type of nonlinear and anti-foundational figuring and method (Haraway, 2016, pp. 3,12) through which analytic threads can be followed, made, picked up and dropped in a process of 'becoming-with each other' (Haraway, 2016, p. 3). SF, in other words, is a form of speculative temporal making that challenges abstract futurism and advocates the situated material-semiotics of 'staying with the trouble' (Haraway, 2016, p. 4).

This conception of a disaggregated conceptual-material compost pile of temporalities is hugely productive for thinking about dilemmas occasioned by the economic and social politics of ecological devastation, but it is also generative in thinking about the politics and materialities of time more widely. As a form of temporal figuring, the SF concept of the Chthulucene provides a pragmatic politics of time, oriented to the 'muddle' and thoughtful about the stakes of action as it relates to temporal worlds. The approach we aim to cultivate through this collection is likewise one of 'staying with the trouble'. We interpret this as a mode of engagement that is grounded in empirical analyses of the messy ontologies of law, legality and time. Inspired by Haraway and many others cited here, we tend towards the refusal of large-scale abstract temporal norms, following instead the socio-material practices by which times are made and unmade.

Making time and law across disciplines

As we have indicated, then, critiques of linear time and historicism have much to offer critical legal analyses of time and temporality, as have cross-disciplinary literatures that account for time-related interventions or epistemologies within wider social and governmental processes or visionary propositions that trace new temporal horizons and modes of action. These literatures often readily follow legal techniques and knowledges as elements within clustered social and governmental dynamics. Yet because their scope of analysis is necessarily multidirectional, they much less often trace law's specific role in proffering distinctive temporal mechanisms or ontologies. The present collection is motivated by an enquiry into what focusing on law can tell us about the otherwise opaque temporal modes of governance in these and other time-related conversations. Many of the chapters take up this challenge, creating a fine-grained analysis of how legal times are made and outlining how this might add to current inter- and cross-disciplinary enquiries into time and temporality.

We have ordered the chapters by topic. The collection begins with four chapters broadly collected under the heading of social time (Greenhouse; Enright; Ashton; Ring), before moving on to consider post/colonial times (Painter; Cloatre; Keenan), the politics of labour time (John; Hayes), technologies and infrastructures of time (Birth; Silvast et al.) and, finally, topologies of time (Van Oorschot; Mulla).

The first group of chapters we have gathered under the heading of 'Social time: Courts, litigation and public authority'. All of the contributions in this group consider variations on what Carol Greenhouse identifies, in conversation with Durkheim, as 'social time', focusing on the homogenous, unifying or powerful notions of time arising from patterned legal and political interventions and tracing their effects on constructions of solidarity and collective interest, and on marginalised populations. As Greenhouse argues powerfully: 'Social time belongs to politics before it belongs to nature' (Chapter 1). The concept of social time – a way of tracing the power dynamics of shared time – provides an essential vantage point for understanding the political ontologies driving law's temporal workings. By what means does time become shared? What roles do legal processes play in this? Focusing on, among other things, the role of courts in responding to widespread social harm or contested claims for political authority, these chapters follow myriad legal technicalities and epistemologies attaching to litigation on social 'problems', as well as their socio-temporal effects.

In *The long sudden death of Antonin Scalia* (Chapter 1), Carol Greenhouse defines social time not as coordinated time-keeping as much as a powerful means of setting the conditions and limits of agency (see also Greenhouse, 2014, 1996). Writing in conversation with Kantorowicz, Durkheim and Weber, Greenhouse works through an illuminating case study from 2016 in which the Republicans blocked the Obama administration's replacement for Justice Antonin Scalia in the US Supreme Court, thereby creating an 'empty seat'. Focusing on the Republican action as an attempt to 're-set the time', Greenhouse provides a fascinating theorisation of high office as what she terms an 'infrastructure of social time', achieved through the artificial personhood of 'office' that has modulated the changing relationship between mortal humans and immortal corporate bodies since twelfth- and thirteenth-century corporation and which is dependent on the affect of the collectivity. The emptiness of the seat in Greenhouse's study resonates productively with Nadine El-Enany's analysis of the 'un-seating' of Lutfur Rahman from his position as mayor of Tower Hamlets in London in 2015 by a court judgment finding him guilty of 'undue spiritual influence' under the Representation of the People Act 1983 (El-Enany, 2016).[5] In both cases, the occupation – and lack of occupation or removal – of a seat of 'high office' becomes a moment for struggles over authority and agency that raise urgent questions over the political stakes, and the constitution, of shared time. Considering the empty seat following Scalia's death, Greenhouse argues, therefore involves reflecting on the 'contested solidarities' (Chapter 1) of social time.

Social time is often mapped onto the time of the nation, and in Máiréad Enright's chapter *'No. I won't go back': National time, trauma, and legacies of symphysiotomy in Ireland* (Chapter 2), we see the Irish state's construction of a homogenous national time that refuses to acknowledge the endemic gendered harm of pelvic surgery performed on women during childbirth from the 1940s to the 1980s. Enright traces in detail the legal techniques and temporal ontologies used by Fine Gael governments to construct this as a 'legacy issue' left over from a previous era of religious nationhood, against the ongoing activism of groups such as Survivors of Symphysiotomy (SOS). Calls on law and legal rationality have come from many angles: from the official Walsh report, through to representations by SOS to the UN Human Rights Committee, through to the establishment of a state redress scheme in the face of increasing litigation against the government by survivors. Enright notes, in particular, the state's use of time-compressing legal devices to deter women from continuing with litigation over or alongside the redress scheme, including the continued insistence on a 2-year statute of limitations for litigation and a 20-day time limit for applying to the scheme. Resonating with recent feminist thinking on the productive possibilities of 'closure' relating to widespread sexual violence (Knop and Riles, 2016; Welsh, 2017), Enright's contribution instead allows space for the temporalities of women's embodied experience to endure by writing trauma back into what would otherwise be a national, secular, story of progress. She concludes: 'In its inescapable embodiment, symphysiotomy reveals homogenous national time as something essentially political, precariously assembled, wrought in pain; as something that could be otherwise' (this collection, p. 50).

Philip Ashton's contribution, *Time-spaces of adjudication in the US subprime mortgage crisis* (Chapter 3), shifts our analysis from legal engagement with embodied harm to economic exploitation. In 2007, borrowers in the US issued private civil fraud claims for unjust enrichment and criminal enterprise in the Federal District court for Southern California against Countrywide Home Loans and affiliates on the basis of highly damaging 'hybrid' adjustable rate mortgages. These claims were intended to constitute a class action but failed the relevant legal tests of civil procedure on the basis, broadly speaking, that the plaintiffs could not establish that they had been harmed in a common manner due to Countrywide's own complex business model. Ashton shows that the jurisdiction of private law claims and their attachment to the individual circumstances of plaintiffs created time-spaces of legal rationality that could not admit a finding of widespread harm. As he puts it: 'It is within these time-spaces of adjudication that we find law's (in)capacity to speak to historically and spatially specific configurations of social power' (this collection, p. 79). Further litigation by 10 state Attorneys General against Countrywide for threatening the health and welfare of state citizens was quickly settled. But, instead of rescinding the mortgages, the mandated technique was to modify the mortgage contract to make it more likely that the borrower could stay in their home, with the effect that any uncertainty about the future was transferred back onto borrowers. One of Ashton's key contributions, among many others, is to define and emphasise the significance of time-spaces of adjudication and contracting in our attempts to understand contemporary financial dynamics of precarity and indebtedness.

The final chapter in this cluster is Sinéad Ring's *On delay' and duration: Law's temporal orders in historical child sex abuse cases* (Chapter 4). This chapter picks up the theme of the temporalizing effects of litigation, this time in the context of widespread allegations of childhood sexual abuse reported in Ireland many years after the acts were alleged to have happened. Whereas in 1992 a delay of one day was deemed too long to allow a prosecution to proceed, Ring charts the development in the late 1990s and early 2000s of a 'new' type of delay jurisprudence by the Irish Superior Courts in response to fears that allowing long periods of elapsed time to obviate legal claims would prevent meaningful legal and wider social responses to the abuse. This jurisprudence, however, imposed linear legal timeframes on non-linear experiences and re-asserted problematic myths about the role of criminal justice and the 'untrustworthy' rape victim. In contrast to the linear model of time enunciated through the jurisprudence, Ring proffers a Bergsonian understanding of time as duration as a means of recuperating the non-linear experiences of those who have survived abuse. More specifically, by understanding otherwise linear operations of precedent through the notion of duration, she argues convincingly that it is possible to return to observe and follow law's own recursivity and to remain open to unpredictable legal futures.

The second cluster of chapters, 'Post/colonial times', turns to colonial legal techniques of time. Scholarship on the workings of time in colonial law has been growing and includes, for example, analysis of the significance of emergency powers and the concept of emergency to colonial rule in India (Hussain, 2009), the temporal techniques of racialisation that went into the construction of citizenship categories such as 'Indian settler' in early twentieth-century South Africa (Mawani, 2014), the rendering of indigenous subjects as 'out of synch with legal, liberal, secular chronological time' through testimonial practices in colonial inquiries in contemporary Canada (Murdocca, 2017, p. 129) and the making of Hopi sovereign time through indigenous governance practices such as the tribal court of the Hopi Indian Nation (Richland, 2008). The present collection contributes specific insights to this literature by following how colonial legal-temporal techniques have underpinned enduring and widespread knowledge practices for example in biomedicine (Cloatre) and land title registration (Keenan), paying attention in particular to the role of narrative and language in legal techniques of dispossession (Painter).

Genevieve Painter's chapter, '*Give us his name': Time, law and language in a settler colony* (Chapter 5), argues that paying attention to language used in and across legal encounters can help us to understand how temporality and state law underpinned dispossession. Through a rich case study of written records of meetings about the future of the Naas River valley region in British Columbia between leaders of the Nisga'a and Tsimshian leaders and government officials in the nineteenth century, Painter reminds us that 'language and narrative are integral to the law's temporalities' (this collection, p. 109). More specifically, paying attention to the temporality of grammar and narrative helps us understand better how indigenous dispossession was legally achieved, for example through the grammar of 'setting aside' the land and the use of the word 'commencing', which performatively created a reserve. Painter's study analyses the plural temporalities existing within the negotiations and their associated records and the many ways in which these reflected a civilisational European temporality, which positioned indigenous peoples behind the time of the whites. These temporalities existed alongside the temporalities of indigenous negotiators – including the times of human lifetimes, family lineages, memory and taking care of the land for children. Painter's chapter ends with the moment when the chiefs present at the meetings laughed at being told that the land belonged to the Queen and not the Indians, asking who was the chief that gave away the land. As Painter puts it: 'The law's jurisdiction wells up as it speaks' (this collection, p. 124). In this way, paying attention to narrative and grammar helps us analyse the emergent temporalities of colonial jurisdiction.

In *Traditional medicines, law, and the (dis)ordering of temporalities* (Chapter 6), Emilie Cloatre focuses on how biomedicine has constituted itself as modern and forward-looking in contradistinction to the temporalities associated with alternative and traditional medicines. Cloatre's analysis of biomedicine's preoccupation with modernity investigates a type of forward-looking that resonates with research on more dystopian temporal thinking in recent global health initiatives: the catastrophism of anti-microbial resistance interventions, for example (Brown and Nettleton, 2017). In particular, Cloatre argues that biomedicine has founded itself on a myth of linear development from an ancestral past, through to scientific knowledge and progress, with an associated break from 'pre-existing' therapeutic interventions. Law has often enabled these moves towards modernity in contradistinction to 'traditional' practices, and indeed law and medicine as powerful institutions have enabled exclusion and violence, biomedicine having been a key method of colonialism through its role in denouncing existing health practices and enabling new forms of population management. As Cloatre aims to explore through detailed multisite fieldwork, this is now complicated by changing attitudes to alternative medicines in contemporary postcolonial contexts such as Ghana, where efforts are being made to regulate the field of traditional medicine in a situation in which the biomedical system is poorly resourced. What Cloatre terms 'choreographies of legitimacy' (this collection, p. 141). re-open questions of modernity in biomedicine, in ways that range from engaging with pre-colonial health practices (Widmer, 2010) to pluralising medical interventions in Western states.

Sarah Keenan's chapter, *Making land liquid: on time and title registration* (Chapter 7), shifts the focus to land law and its associated temporal orientations and time-related mechanisms. Based on detailed analysis across four case studies – England and Wales, the Torrens system in Australia, land title registration in the Global South in conjunction with the World Bank and other international financial institutions and the Mortgage Electronic Registration System in the United States – Keenan argues that land title registries create a temporal disjuncture between the titles themselves and the land to which they relate. As she convincingly argues, land title systems developed through colonial experimentation over what was understood to be 'new' land, for example in Australia, and have had the effect of creating future-oriented legal title where previously title was tethered to the histories of the land. This has been achieved in large part through legal concepts and technicalities, such as the mirror principle, which registration systems have inaugurated. Keenan argues that land registries replace the 'slices of time' strung over generations found in previous methods of establishing title with staccato-like slices of time detached from past in an effort to ease marketability. She develops the concept of 'out of synch' to register the timely effects of a colonially developed practice, showing how registration erases multiple temporalities and histories lived on and through the land.

The third set of chapters, 'The politics of labour time', focuses on labour regulation's oppressive and dissonant temporalities. Labour time has long been a focus for engagements with Marxist theories of political economy (e.g. Negri, 1991; Postone, 1996; Weeks, 2011). Some theorists of post-Fordism have more recently proposed that the time of labour is being reoriented from a temporal logic of 'retroactivity' to 'futurity' for example (Adkins, 2008), with attendant implications for analysing changing configurations of social reproduction (Adkins, 2009; Vora, 2012; Waldby and Cooper, 2010). Labour scholars have approached vastly uneven lived experiences of work through concepts such as 'power chronographies' (Sharma, 2014), 'remaindering' (Tadiar, 2012) and 'contingent labour' (Peck and Theodore, 2012) to register time's multiple roles in generating conditions of dispossession. Alongside this work, socio-legal scholars and labour historians have focused in depth on how contract law and contracting practices, colonial law and contemporary legislative interventions have constructed temporal epistemologies of labour, which have, in turn, affected experiences of labour within and outside formal paid work (Conaghan, 2006; Rose, 2017; Sinha, 2014; Zbyszewska, 2016). In conversation with such work, this section features contributions by Maya John and L.J.B. Hayes, which unpack legal interventions into workers' experiences of labour time through factories legislation, contracting practices and electronic monitoring, creating novel interpretations of law's role in temporal ordering along the way.

Picking up on the focus on colonial law from the previous section, Maya John's chapter, *Regulating the 'half-timer' in colonial India: Factory legislation, its anomalies, and resistance* (Chapter 8), retraces the creation and articulation of the concept of the 'half-timer' in colonial Indian factories legislation. John's study resonates with other legal histories of colonial labour, such as Nitin

Sinha's work on river boatmen, which focuses on how contracting practices evolved in response to environmental demands, weather and flooding, creating a pragmatic legal approach to 'delay' (Sinha, 2014). Shifting the analysis from contracting to legislation, however, John registers myriad social and political dynamics surrounding the creation of the 'half-timer' status for child labourers: shifting relationships between colonial metropolitan employer lobbies in Lancashire and Manchester, who were concerned to limit the competitiveness of the Bombay cotton textile industry; the Arbuthnot Commission and its successors; and uneven attempts to provide education for child factory workers. Child labourers, as John notes, attempted to fight back against harsh employment and contracting practices, aiming along the way to reclaim a semblance of rest and non-work time – what John terms 'abstract passage of time' (this collection, p.163) through demands for wages, rest periods and through strikes.

With L.J.B. Hayes's chapter, *Work-time technology and unpaid labour in paid care work* (Chapter 9), we move to the contemporary regulation of paid care work. Hayes undertook ethnographic research with homecare workers based in the south of England to understand changing conditions of work, and experiences of working time, within this marketised sector. She found workers employed on very low wages, widespread adoption of zero hours contracts and the use of telephone-based electronic monitoring to track workers' arrivals and departures from each homecare appointment. In particular, Hayes focuses on the inter-relationship between what she understands, in novel terms, to be two equivalent technologies – zero hours contracts and telephone monitoring – in limiting careworkers' pay, thereby creating savings for the private companies that held the contracts to provide care. Working with E.P. Thompson's analysis of time, Hayes argues that telephone monitoring 're-engineered clock-time' through care work by allowing companies to monitor the precise time spent on caring for a client and cutting out transport and other transition time between appointments from the pay period. As such, as Hayes puts it, both zero hours contracts and telephone monitoring have become technologies of time, altering how time has materialised through labour and law.

Hayes's insights about the conceptual potential of understanding contracts in relationship with, or as, temporal technologies provide a bridge to the fourth and penultimate set of chapters: 'Technologies and infrastructures of time'. As we have already seen, a wide range of work across disciplines explores the role of technological innovation in the fabrication of new temporal ontologies. Concerns about the making and unmaking of innovation times are perhaps best known from Science and Technology Studies (STS) and in particular, the sociology of expectations (Borup et al., 2006; Brown et al., 2000). In these accounts, material-discursive relations are enormously significant: expectations emerge through future-oriented embodied engagements with technologies as much as through policy and legal discourse (Brown and Kraft, 2006; Tutton, 2017). Individual and collective expectations about technology and technological change also often coordinate between groups of actors and scales of organisation, easing, prompting or thwarting responses to emergent socio-technical dilemmas (e.g. Beynon-Jones and Brown, 2011; Brown and Kraft, 2006). In the context of this literature, contributions by Kevin Birth, on the one hand, and by Antti Silvast, Miko Jalas and Jenni Rinkinen, on the other, provide distinctive routes into understanding the co-production of law and regulation with time politics and infrastructural deliberations.

Kevin Birth focuses on global timescale pluralism through a case study of international deliberations over the regulation of the leap second. In *Standards in the shadows for everyone to see: The supranational regulation of time and the concern over temporal pluralism* (Chapter 10), Birth denaturalises clock time and its associated tethering to law, highlighting many sources of 'timescale pluralism' (this collection, p. 196) along the way, including divergent standards based on local solar time, satellite navigation, radio communication and weights and measures standards. Birth juxtaposes these standards with universal (or rather, universalising) timescales such as Coordinated Universal Time (UTC), which is based on the measurement of seconds using atomic clocks and used to regulate other clocks and the international markets. As such, his chapter works in dialogue with 'critical horology' research, which engages in experimental design for transformative clocks (Bastian, 2016). However, Birth's concern is to bring to light the oddities of UTC, based as it is on a mixture of the Gregorian calendar and 24-hour days, the result not of linear scientific development but colonial dominance and shifting power relations, and non-scalable from the smallest unit to the largest unit. Within this strange mixture, debates over the leap second assume importance in resolving the problem of uneven day length in the context of ongoing challenges to the eurocentrism of UTC by countries such as China. As Birth notes, the effort put in by time metrologists to establish an accurate measure for time are often not followed by courts and legislators, who tend not to enquire as to the reliability of their time source. His finding that what has been termed the 'legal traceability of time' (Levine, 2001) historically served not the legal system itself directly, but instead those concerned about legal interventions, provides us with new insights into the role of time metrology within law more broadly.

Birth's chapter in large part focuses on political debates over infrastructures of time measurement. Picking up this theme, Antti Silvast, Miko Jalas and Jenny Rinkinen trace multiple shifting temporal ontologies within energy law and governance in Finland in their contribution: *Energy governance, risk, and temporality: the construction of energy time through law and regulation* (Chapter 11). As we have already seen, work across politics, geography and sociology traces how governance works in and through collaborative and/or dominant modes of time instantiated through systems and infrastructures, shaping behaviours and temporal knowledges as innovations unfold. With this in mind, Silvast et al. focus on the more mundane side of large-scale anticipatory government action: that aimed at securing energy provision through diverse means, including, not least, through shifting legally supported temporal stances of anticipation and resilience, as well as the incorporation of alternative temporalities such as prior preparedness.

The next cluster of chapters takes us from a topic or theme to a temporal orientation: 'Topologies of law and time'. Topologies of time will be familiar to those who have engaged with the work of Barad or Serres and the final two chapters in the collection, by Irene van Oorschot and Sameena Mulla, provide a springboard for legal scholars to the alternative approach to time these thinkers proffer. Michel Serres, in particular, has challenged modern notions of developmental, historical time by proposing that the past is not out of date (Serres and Latour, 1995, p. 48). He argues that what moderns believe to be progress since thinkers such as Lucretius, for example, is no more than the result of a trick we play with time such that we always place ourselves at the summit of time (the spatial equivalent would be in the middle of the universe) (Serres and Latour, 1995, p. 44). Serres introduces an alternative way of understanding time beyond succession. As he puts it, time percolates or flows in turbulent ways. It is this that allows him to put the thought of Lucretius and modern theories of fluid dynamics 'in the same neighbourhood' (Serres and Latour, 1995, p. 57). Such a move away from geometric regularity in time arises from Serres's 'non-metrical' or 'topological' approach, which he explains through the well-cited example of the crumpled handkerchief:

> If you take a handkerchief and spread it out in order to iron it, you can see in it certain fixed distances and proximities. If you sketch a circle in one area, you can mark out nearby points and measure far-off distances. Then take the same handkerchief and crumple it, by putting it in your pocket. Two distant points suddenly are close, even superimposed.
>
> (Serres and Latour, 1995, p. 60)

Within Science and Technology Studies, the topological approach has assisted investigations into the crumpled temporalities of objects. As Amade M'charek's work on race and DNA reference sequencing argues, objects are not timeless and motionless, but rather can be understood as folded, encompassing and enacting layers of history that can strike back unexpectedly (M'charek, 2014).

Irene van Oorschot's chapter, *Doing times, doing truths: The legal case file as folded object* (Chapter 12), takes up the challenge of thinking law's times topologically. Van Oorschot undertook ethnographic research in a Dutch criminal court dealing with simple, non-exceptional cases with the intention of approaching judging as a set of human and non-human practices. As part of this research, she followed around 15 cases, reading the case file and attending relevant court sessions and meetings. In reflecting on this research, van Oorschot focuses on the case file itself, what she terms a 'recalcitrant legal actor' and its role within Dutch criminal procedure in effectively gathering multiple temporalities in the service of creating legal truth. Drawing on M'charek's concept of the 'folded object', van Oorschot argues that legal case files mediate 'epistemic access to "what really happened"' (this collection, p. 231), anticipating their own future and creating areas of visibility and opaqueness in service of its legal rationality. As she puts it: 'By folding, ordering, and sorting different temporalities, the case file is, however, both what allows procedure and facts to be 'kept apart' as much as it presents the possibility of such temporal interferences, and with these, the undoing or unmaking of a case' (this collection, p. 244).

Sameena Mulla's contribution, *Topological time, law, and subjectivity: a description in five folds* (Chapter 13), also works through law's topological effects, asking in particular how topological time can help in understanding law's relationship with violence. By placing Mulla at the end of an arrangement of chapters that began with 'social time', we aim to re-emphasise the often shocking and extensively exclusionary effects of temporal ordering. Mulla's own research has been into forensic interventions in cases of sexual assault in the US, in which, as she puts it: 'divergent configurations of space and time mark the nexus of clinic and courtroom, reshaping the relationship of care to investigation, and projects of healing to projects of justice' (this collection, p. 247). Once again, tracing time as topology is a means of following how legal rationalities travel through encounters, institutions and forms of engagement. Mulla's reflective essay weaves together three temporal modalities – forensic time, criminal time, and biographical time – through accounts of her own experience of nearly drowning, research on forensics and in conversation with Pradeep Jeganathan's work on the role of checkpoints in Sri Lanka in anticipating violence.

Drawing on the same passages from the conversation between Serres and Latour on the 'crumpled handkerchief' as we have cited earlier, Mulla points out that in describing topological time Serres was also engaged in disputing a concept of time as succession that was inherently violent, being fundamentally about war. As Chakrabarty has shown, the trick of succession, being temporal, spatial and political, is closely linked with imperialist expansion (Chakrabarty, 2009), yet linear time's conceptual stickiness makes it hard to rethink. Indeed, Bruno Latour picks up on such a difficulty in his conversations with Serres, if from a very different angle:

> BL It's obvious to us moderns that, as we advance in time, each successive stage outstrips the preceding one.
> MS But that's not *time*.
> BL That's what you need to explain to me – why this passage of time is not time.
> MS That's not time, only a simple line . . . It's not even a line, but a trajectory of the race for first place – in school, in the Olympic Games, for the Nobel Prize. This isn't time, but a simple competition – once again, war. Why replace temporality, duration, with a quarrel?
>
> (Serres and Latour, 1995, p. 49)

Within modern universal time, within a struggle to gain a foothold at the summit of progress, proposing that one stage or period has been succeeded by another involves feats of destruction and contestation: warring, quarreling. By arguing that these processes are not about the inherent qualities of time, as such, Serres also replaces an over-emphasis on naturalised succession in our understanding of linearity with politics and struggle. Mulla picks up on this, noting Serres's membership of the war generation. For her, topological time helps us to understand not only the confluence of time and space, but in relation to law specifically, it is suited to the task of accounting for legal subjectivities shaped by violence.

Encountering legal times

The chapters gathered in this edited collection, then, investigate a range of legal knowledge and techniques for their temporal effects. Legally regulated high office – the human instantiation of legal decision-making in the judge for example – supports the infrastructure of shared time (Greenhouse). The very definition of time is contested legally through international legal struggles over coordinated time that are mediated through patchy technical advances (Birth). Legal precedent, as it unrolls through litigation, creates time-spaces of adjudication by analogising between cases (Ashton). Time limits, debates over statutes of limitations and rules of criminal procedure instantiate practical and epistemological barriers for state action relating to endemic gendered harm (Enright). Contracts and contracting practices modulate the relationship between constructed legal spheres of private and public responsibility, emerging as clusters of temporalizing action in the world of work (Hayes, John) and – through mortgages and efforts to restructure them – in the world of home ownership (Ashton), with oppressive social effects. Criminal procedure instantiates and shapes concepts of delay in historic sex abuse cases (Ring) and creates case files as folded legal objects that crumple together multiple times and places (van Oorschot). Forensic procedure creates boundaries between care and investigation (Mulla). Legal prohibitions on alternative medicines construct biomedicine as 'modern' and the knowledge practices of colonised others as archaic (Cloatre). Registration conjures disjuncture and temporal dissonance between land and its title, overwriting pre-existing techniques that fostered an uneven linearity (Keenan) and access to land itself is underpinned by, among other legal techniques, the temporality of narrative and grammar (Painter). In turn, legislation shapes energy infrastructures temporally (Silvast et al.) and creates temporally defined categories of child workers (half-timers) to defuse trade rivalries (John).

These contributions not only advance interdisciplinary studies of time and temporal regulation in their chosen areas, but show, in detail, how legal modalities of time emerge and have effects within wider clusters of social and political action. Specifically, as we describe below, they demonstrate: (1) law's diverse roles in maintaining linear historicist models of time; (2) law's participation in the materialisation of times; and (3) the unsteady effects of temporal pluralism and 'polytemporalities' in law. In these ways, the studies contained in this collection serve to de-naturalise the 'time' in law and time scholarship, instead positioning time as something that can be enacted and materialised.

First, then, it is clear that many contributors share the goal of examining and undermining the presumption of external linear time in the historicist mode. Developmental, universal, linear time, however inconsistent and diversely achieved, provides foundational challenges for contemporary interdisciplinary scholarship on law, time and temporalities and the futures, pasts and presents with which we grapple (see also Johns, 2016). It is not just that historicism and linear time do not represent the widest range of temporal possibilities in social life; rather, the idea of time as a container holding natural processes and social interactions is under significant critique across the chapters in the present collection. Many of the technical means by which law works have the effect of instantiating an orientation to a constructed past, present, or future in linear or teleological form, and several chapters engage with linear, monumental time, providing fresh insights along the way into law's collaborative role in its production (e.g. Greenhouse, Enright, Painter, Ring, Keenan). For example, Greenhouse's work on social time brings to the fore the role of power and authority in enunciating politics as time itself. Time results from power and agency and is shared, collective and contested. Orientations to a future or a past – for example attempts to reset the time of succession on the US Supreme Court – are not the result of social adjustments to an external temporality but always instead the materialisation of political struggle by other means. The very notion of high office, Greenhouse shows us, is an unsteady attempt to settle the juxtaposition of mortality and the need for succession through the exercise of public authority. As such, we might view linear arrangements in law and politics – concepts of succession in office, for example – as the materialisation of social struggle, as much as we understand them as disciplinary techniques.

Law's linearity and forward moving teleology, it is often argued, are achieved as a result of one of the archetypal modes of Western law: the common law's reliance on precedent and its own understanding of its capacity to generate certain stances towards history (Parker, 2015, 2011). Common law certainly jurisdictionalises time (or temporalizes jurisdiction), as Ashton shows, but law also works to make stark 'cuts' in time, attempting to move social debate 'forward' in the face of historic harm through the workings of common law doctrine (Ring), as well as creating a fore-shortened and self-referential future through legal innovations such as land title registration (Keenan). It is perhaps law's performative nature that is especially difficult to grapple with, as Painter indicates: the self-instantiating effects of colonial land acquisition and title can only be understood via speech act theory and attention to grammar and narrative.

The construction of a social issue as a 'legacy' from a now outdated past (Enright) can also be seen to have been secured through legal tactics as much as anything else. Being out of, behind or in between times is a temporality worthy of legal analysis, as Cloatre's unpicking of the modern times of biomedicine and its connections with law shows. Criticising the legal construction of stasis or out of time-ness within assumptions of linear national time can help to keep alive multiple alternative narratives and experiences. David Scott argues eloquently that: '(t)he past's leavings haunt the present, even if inchoately like the distant sound of indecipherable thunder' (Scott, 2014, p. 96). Yet as Enright, Ashton, Ring and Cloatre all show, the ongoing effects of widespread social harm are not often inchoate, even though they do haunt the present. Instead, social injustice is often constructed as 'out of time' with linear norms, but experienced as near at hand, physically experienced in the body and structured through law.

Working beyond linear time requires understanding it as created, real, yet non-definitive of time more broadly. As such, the second theme we would like to highlight is the potential for understanding legal temporalities as materially entangled and dependent on the particularities and contingencies of legal objects and subjects.[6] As we have seen, many currents of sociological thought provide space for understanding temporality in material terms. Actor-network theories emphasise the 'sorting' of times in a move that aims to dislodge time from the background of social life and instead trace its emergence as a result of interrelationships of human and non-human actants (Latour, 1993, p. 76). Within an agential realist account, furthermore (Barad, 2007), linear time can be one result among many performative human-social-material intra-actions. As such, it is possible to understand temporalities – including legal temporalities – as emerging from subjective experiences and socio-material practices (e.g. Grabham, 2016).

Several chapters in the collection pick up on this theme, developing new and distinctive approaches to the analysis of both law and of time. For example, telephone-based electronic monitoring systems are seen to interact with zero hours contracts to foreshorten pay for homecare workers (Hayes) and land registration systems, managed now through large electronic databases produce the forward, out-of-synch orientation of dis-embedded title (Keenan). Energy infrastructure is legislated, managed and built through temporal horizons of prior preparedness and resilience (Silvast et al.). Legal objects – or objects that have become legal – themselves enact crumpled temporal horizons, ranging from the collapsed temporalities of case files in criminal legal proceedings (van Oorschot) to international debates over the leap second, which evolve in dialogue with new technological developments in time metrology (Birth). Two chapters directly engage with the task of thinking legal temporalities topologically, allowing for an approach to legal-material culture that is based on the unsteady temporalities of chaos theory and proximity rather than the regular geometric time of Euclidean thought (Mulla; van Oorschot). Taken together, we hope these chapters provide inspiration for further productive reflections on law's materialisation of time and temporalities.

The final theme that connects the contributions is that of the plurality of legal temporalities. Social science literature, and interdisciplinary scholarship in law, traces multiple experiences and enactments of temporalities across legal fields (e.g. Benda-Beckmann, 2014; Benda-Beckmann and Benda-Beckmann, 2014; Griffiths, 2014) showing how plural legal temporalities can co-exist and interact. For example, drawing on ethnographic research on the regulation of fisheries in the Canadian Maritimes, Melanie Wiber has explored the temporal dissonance occurring between various levels of environmental and fisheries regulation, from local to national. She proposes that temporal pluralism and temporal dissonance can be understood through using ideas of 'syncopated rhythms' to analyse changes in tempo between fishermen's daily livelihoods and governance practices (Wiber, 2014). Contributing to this literature, the present collection encourages a focus on understanding how plural legal temporalities come to be materially shaped, for example, by distinct legal technologies or via apparently non-legal interventions, in a similar vein to Haraway's insistence on a polytemporal account of 'worlding'. Furthermore, as the contributions make clear, it can be useful not only to follow these plural temporal orders but also to understand what happens when they interact (or not) with one another in producing new ontologies. This involves analysing apparently homogenous temporal orders (Enright; Cloatre) as potentially fragile and most probably hiding a multiplicity of dissonant stories. It also requires describing and accounting for the moments when apparently unified or linear narratives break down, and the means by which this breaking down happens (Painter), evidencing alternative stories and worldviews. We might name the clash between temporal orders as a disjuncture or being 'out of synch' (Keenan), 'hesitant' or 'out of joint'.[7] Other temporal genres that we have already met along the way might themselves inevitably reference a plurality of times: the delay of whose time against what time, for example (Ring), a half-timer as opposed to a full-timer (John), the time-spaces of equity as juxtaposed with the time-spaces of criminal law in responses to mortgage claims in the US (Ashton). Ultimately, what the contributions to this collection point to, in various ways, is the productive potential of what Haraway would term 'staying with the trouble': acknowledging multiple dissonant temporalities, refusing easy either/or options when it comes to time, and instead grappling with the contradictions of the 'at-the-same-timeness' of many social conflicts and dynamics (Haraway, 2016).

Concluding remarks

As we conclude this introduction, we would like to note that analysing the 'making' of legal temporalities, if anything, only intensifies our accountability and responsibility to act in and on the world in ways that work towards social justice. The chapters collected together here can help to prompt fresh theorising of law's participation in establishing normative, exclusionary and even fatal patterns of living with and engaging with others. All the contributions in some way touch on the politics of exclusion, disenfranchisement or oppression, whether through analysing subprime mortgages, land title, zero hours contracts, symphysiotomy, child sex abuse, forensic responses to sexual violence, the construction of criminal cases, alternative medicines, the provision of energy or the politics of high office, for example. Yet what emerges, we hope, is the possibility of a pragmatic legal politics of time, inspired by Haraway's work on the Chthulucene, in which the task of thinking beyond linear temporalities involves following the uneven consequences of questioning radical futures, and understanding the stakes of creating emancipatory non-linear or subversive alternatives. Such an approach prompts an intensified focus on questions of ethics and action that reach beyond notions of developmental progress, allowing us to acknowledge stasis, for example and refusing foundational moves towards enacting complex social harm as 'legacy' (Enright, this volume). Instead, what many of these chapters call for is something akin to what Jack

Halberstam has offered as the pedagogic value of failure as a means of establishing reparative thinking and practices (Halberstam, 2011; Shahani, 2013).

The work of establishing alternative temporal orientations is often grounded in practices of doing time otherwise, as much as it results from critique and analysis. Writing about the promise of black quantum futurism (BQF), which draws on quantum physics, futurist thought and conceptions of time and space from black/African traditions, Rasheedah Phillips notes that BQF practitioners consciously work to subvert chronological time (Phillips, 2015, p. 12). BQF is hence an intentional set of practices as well as an alternative theory of time. Furthermore, Rebecca Coleman has proposed an 'inventive feminist theory', which emphasises the performativity of feminist interventions in describing and acting on our worlds (Coleman, 2014, p. 42). Conscious practices of subversion and invention bring to mind what Barad would call an ethico-onto-epistemology (Barad, 2007, p. 185) or an ethical politics of practice, knowledge and many-species 'worlding' (Haraway, 2016). In destabilising ontologies of natural, linear time, we are left with the question of what to do next and asking and answering this question must be grounded in specific empirical analyses that facilitate grounded responses. Haraway might term such interventions 'speculative fabulations' of time, in which we conceive new futures and temporal orientations as much as following or researching them, and in which we reflect on our roles, as scholars, in creating times as much as we study them.

Our argument here is that studying legal temporalities should involve understanding how times as well as laws and legal knowledges are constituted; how they come to matter. This type of analysis does not merely trace the discursive production of time but instead understands temporal ontologies as materialised and enacted through legal as well as other means, with attendant ethical implications (Loewen Walker, 2014). When we perceive matter and time unfolding in a mutual process, the question of ethics exists at every moment or stage:

> In an important sense, in a breathtakingly intimate sense, touching, sensing, is what matter does, or rather, what matter is: matter is condensations of responses, of response-ability … Matter is a matter of untimely and uncanny intimacy, condensations of beings and times.
>
> (Barad, 2015, pp. 401–402)

As an object of study, then, it is clear that the analysis of law yields distinct routes into understanding time more broadly and the current collection aims to clarify and develop this. Yet our proposal involves more than bringing law into the picture. Instead, drawing on the chapters collected here, we suggest that studying the variegated means by which law and time materialise and developing a consciousness of the temporal genres that law helps to create are important ways of registering and working with what Barad would term the 'call to respond and be responsible' (Barad, 2007, p. 182) by uncovering and acting on law's timely response-abilities.

Notes

1 As David Engel put it, writing in 1990 about analysing time in studies of courts and litigation across cultures: 'That certain fundamental social concepts will be altered or transformed over time (including the concept of time itself) should ... be a source of interest rather than despair' (Engel, 1990, p. 336).
2 This is the AHRC-funded network Regulating Time: New Perspectives on Regulation, Law, and Temporalities: https://www.kent.ac.uk/law/time/.
3 As Scott puts it, the collapse of the Grenada revolution: '[S]ignalled ... a collapse of the very conditions of a generation's experience of political time, an organization of time in which past-present-future were connected in a chain of progressive succession so that the past gave way to future in uniform and unfailing rhythms of dialectical overcoming' (Scott, 2014, p. 108).
4 These explorations of powerful temporal concepts, norms and assemblages have been inspired by concepts of time found in the work of sociologists Pierre Bourdieu (Bourdieu, 2000) and Henri Lefebvre (Lefebvre, 2004), for example, and the philosophy of Karen Barad (Barad, 2007), Henri Bergson (Bergson, 2008, 2007), Rosi Braidotti (Braidotti, 2002), Gilles Deleuze (Deleuze, 2004), Elizabeth Grosz (Grosz, 2005, 1999), Donna Haraway (Haraway, 2016, 1991) and Michel Serres (Serres and Latour, 1995), among others.
5 As Nadine El-Enany has shown, the Lutfur Rahman judgment simultaneously racialised and temporalised Rahman's Muslim supporters in the area as 'backwards', indicating the extent to which racial legal categories in the UK continue to be created through temporalizing moves (El-Enany, 2016). See further: Nadine El-Enany (2017), 'Racial and Spatial Injustices in the Tower Hamlets Coup' in Emma Patchett and Sarah Keenan (Eds.), *Spatial Justice and Diaspora*, Eastbourne: Counterpress, 134–144; http://criticallegalthinking.com/2015/05/16/why-muslims-cant-trust-the-legal-system/.
6 See also, for example, Parfitt (2018); Ros Williams: *Blood in the Archive: The Anticipatory Logic of Umbilical Cord Blood Collection*, paper delivered at the *Diagnosing Legal Temporalities* workshop, University of Kent, 2015 (see Williams, 2018); Iwan Morus: *Time Out: Telegraphing the Victorian Future*, paper delivered at the *Time, Regulation and Technoscience workshop, University of York, 2016*. For details of these events, see the Regulating Time network website (fn 2 above).
7 See also Sonal Makhija: *Temporality of Law and Waiting*, paper delivered at the 2016 conference *The New Legal Temporalities? Discipline and Resistance across Domains of Time*, University of Kent; Ruth Fletcher *Hesitation and Appointment Time on the Abortion Trail*, paper delivered at *New Legal Temporalities* conference 2016.

Bibliography

Adam, B. (1998). *Timescapes of Modernity: The Environment and Invisible Hazards.* Routledge.

Adam, B. and Groves, C. (2007). *Future Matters: Action, Knowledge, Ethics.* Brill.

Adey, P., Anderson, B., Graham, S., Adey, P., Anderson, B. and Graham, S. (2015). Introduction: Governing Emergencies: Beyond Exceptionality. *Theory Cult. Soc.*, 32, pp. 3–17.

Adkins, L. (2012). Out of Work or Out of Time? Rethinking Labor after the Financial Crisis. *South Atl. Q.*, 111, pp. 621–641.

Adkins, L. (2009). Feminism after Measure. *Fem. Theory, 10*, pp. 323–339.

Adkins, L. (2008). From Retroactivation to Futurity: The End of the Sexual Contract? *Nord. J. Fem. Gend. Res.*, 16, pp.182–201.

Alexandrakis, O. (2016). Transformative Connections: Trauma, Cooperative Horizons, and Emerging Political Topographies in Athens, Greece. *Hist. Anthropol.*, 27, pp. 32–44.

Amoore, L. (2013). *The Politics of Possibility: Risk and Security Beyond Probability.* Duke University Press.

Amoore, L. (2004). Risk, Reward and Discipline at Work. *Econ. Soc.*, 33, pp. 174–196.

Anderson, B. (2017). Emergency Futures: Exception, Urgency, Interval, Hope. *Sociol. Rev.*, 65, pp. 463–477.

Anderson, B. (2010). Preemption, Precaution, Preparedness: Anticipatory Action and Future Geographies. *Prog. Hum. Geogr.*, 34, pp. 777–798.

Barad, K. (2015). TransMaterialities Trans*/Matter/Realities and Queer Political Imaginings. *GLQ J. Lesbian Gay Stud.*, 21, pp. 387–422.

Barad, K. (2007). *Meeting the Universe Halfway: Quantum Physics and the Entanglement of Matter and Meaning.* Duke University Press.

Bastian, M. (2016). Liberating Clocks: Developing a Critical Horology to Rethink the Potential of Clock Time. *New Form.* forthcoming. [remaining info here?]

Beck, U. (1992). *Risk Society: Towards a New Modernity.* Sage.

Benda-Beckmann, K. von (2014). Trust and the Temporalities of Law. *J. Leg. Plur. Unoff. Law*, 46, pp. 1–17.

Benda-Beckmann, F. von and Benda-Beckmann, K. von (2014). Temporalities in Property Relations under a Plural Legal Order: Minangkabau Revisited. *J. Leg. Plur. Unoff.*, Law 46, pp. 18–36.

Berg, M. and Seeber, B. (2016). *Slow Professor: Challenging the Culture of Speed in the Academy.* University of Toronto Press.

Bergson, H. (2008). *Time and Free Will: An Essay on the Immediate Data of Consciousness.* Cosimo, Inc.

Bergson, H. (2007). *Matter and Memory.* Lightning Source.

Beynon-Jones, S.M. (2017). Gestating Times: Women's Accounts of the Temporalities of Pregnancies that End in Abortion in England. *Sociology of Health and Illness.*, 39, pp. 832–846.

Beynon-Jones, S.M. and Brown, N. (2011). Time, Timing and Narrative at the Interface between UK Technoscience and Policy. *Sci. Public Policy*, 38, pp. 639–648.

Borup, M., Brown, N., Konrad, K. and Van Lente, H. (2006). The Sociology of Expectations in Science and Technology. *Technol. Anal. Strateg. Manag.*, 18, pp. 285–298.

Bourdieu, P. (2000). *Pascalian Meditations.* Polity Press.

Braidotti, R. (2002). *Metamorphoses: Towards a Materialist Theory of Becoming.* Wiley.

Braverman, I., Blomley, N. and Delaney, D. (Eds.). (2014). *The Expanding Spaces of Law: A Timely Legal Geography.* Stanford University Press.

Brown, N. and Kraft, A. (2006). Blood Ties: Banking the Stem Cell Promise. *Technol. Anal. Strateg. Manag.*, 18, pp. 313–327.

Brown, N. and Nettleton, S. (2017). There is Worse to Come': The Biopolitics of Traumatism in Antimicrobial Resistance (AMR). *Sociol. Rev.*, 65, pp. 493–508.

Brown, N., Rappert, B. and Webster, A. (2000). *Contested Futures: A Sociology of Prospective Techno-Science.* Ashgate, Aldershot; Burlington, VT.

Bryant, R. (2016). On Critical Times: Return, Repetition, and the Uncanny Present. *Hist. Anthropol.*, 27, pp. 19–31.

Chakrabarty, D. (2009). *Provincializing Europe: Postcolonial Thought and Historical Difference.* Princeton University Press.

Coleman, R. (2014). Inventive Feminist Theory: Representation, Materiality and Intensive Time. *Women Cult. Rev.*, 25, pp. 27–45.

Coleman, R. and Ferreday, D. (Eds.). (2011). *Hope and Feminist Theory*. Routledge.

Conaghan, J.A.F. (2006). Time to Dream: Flexibility, Families and Working Time. in *Precarious Work, Women and the New Economy: The Challenge to Legal Norms*. Hart Publishing, pp. 101–129.

Conley, R. (2008). 'At the Time She Was a Man': The Temporal Dimension of Identity Construction. *PoLAR Polit. Leg. Anthropol. Rev.*, 31, pp. 28–47.

Coole, D. and Frost, S. (2010). *New Materialisms: Ontology, Agency, and Politics*. Duke University Press.

Cooper, D. (2013). Time against Time: Normative Temporalities and the Failure of Community Labour in Local Exchange Trading Schemes. *Time Soc.*, 22, pp. 31–54.

Cooper, M. (2012). Workfare, Familyfare, Godfare: Transforming Contingency into Necessity. *South Atl. Q.*, 111, pp. 643–661.

Cooper, M. and Konings, M. (2015). Contingency and Foundation: Rethinking Money, Debt, and Finance after the Crisis. *South Atl. Q.*, 114, pp. 239–250.

Cornell, D. (1990). Time, Deconstruction, and the Challenge to Legal Positivism: The Call for Judicial Responsibility. *Yale J. Law Humanit.*, 2, p. 267.

Craven, M., Fitzmaurice, M. and Vogiatzi, M. (Eds.) 2006. *Time, History and International Law*. Brill.

Davies, M. (2017). *Law Unlimited: Materialism, Pluralism and Legal Theory, Social Justice*. Routledge.

Davis, K. (2008). *Periodization and Sovereignty: How Ideas of Feudalism and Secularization Govern the Politics of Time*. University of Pennsylvania Press.

de Goede, M. (2015). Speculative Values and Courtroom Contestations. *South Atl. Q.*, 114, pp. 355–375.

de Goede, M. (2012). *Speculative Security: The Politics of Pursuing Terrorist Monies*. University of Minnesota Press.

de Goede, M. and Amoore, L. (2008). Transactions after 9/11: The Banal Face of the Preemptive Strike. *Trans. Inst. Br. Geogr.*, 33, pp. 173–185.

de Goede, M. and Randalls, S. (2009). Precaution, Preemption: Arts and Technologies of the Actionable Future. *Environ. Plan. Soc. Space*, 27, pp. 859–878.

Deleuze, G. (2004). *Difference and Repetition*. A&C Black.

Dinshaw, C., Edelman, L., Ferguson, R.A., Freccero, C., Freeman, E., Halberstam, J., Jagose, A., Nealon, C. and Hoang, N.T. (2007). Theorizing Queer Temporalities. *GLQ J. Lesbian Gay Stud.*, 13, pp. 177–195.

Douglas, S. (2011). Between Constitutional Mo(nu)ments: Memorialising Past, Present and Future at the District Six Museum and Constitution Hill. *Law Crit.*, 22, pp. 171–187.

Dowling, E. and Harvie, D. (2014). Harnessing the Social: State, Crisis and (Big) Society. *Sociology*, 48, pp. 869–886.

Edelman, L. (2004). *No Future: Queer Theory and the Death Drive*. Duke University Press.

El-Enany, N. (2016). *'The Body that Loses its Chair': Law, Temporalities and the Racialised Subject*. Pap. File Author.

Engel, D.M. (1990). Litigation across Space and Time: Courts, Conflict, and Social Change. *Law Soc. Rev.*, 24, p. 333.

Fabian, J. (2014). *Time and the Other: How Anthropology Makes Its Object, With a New Postscript by the Author*. Columbia University Press.

Fisher, S.D.E., Phillips, R. and Katri, I.H. (2017). Introduction: Trans Temporalities. *Somatechnics*, 7, pp. 1–15.

Fitzpatrick, P. (2013). Marking Time: Temporality and the Imperial Cast of Occidental Law. *Birkbeck Law Rev.*, 1.

Francot, L. and Mommers, S. (2017). Picking up the Pace – Legal Slowness and the Authority of the Judiciary in the Acceleration Society (a Dutch Case Study). *Int. J. Leg. Prof.*, 24, pp. 275–293.

Freeman, E. (2011). *Time Binds: Queer Temporalities, Queer Histories.* Duke University Press.

Freeman, E. (2005). Time Binds, or Erotohistoriography. *Soc. Text*, 23, pp. 57–68.

Gibson, K. (2015). Temporal Belongings Interview Series.

Gilmore, R.W. (2002). Fatal Couplings of Power and Difference: Notes on Racism and Geography. *Prof. Geogr.*, 54, pp. 15–24.

Grabham, E. (2016). *Brewing Legal Times: Things, Form and the Enactment of Law.* University of Toronto Press.

Gray, L.E. (2016). Registering Protest: Voice, Precarity, and Return in Crisis Portugal. *Hist. Anthropol.*, 27, pp. 60–73.

Greenhouse, C.J. (2014). Time's up, Timed out: Reflections on Social Time and Legal Pluralism. *J. Leg. Plur. Unoff. Law*, 46, pp. 141–153.

Greenhouse, C.J. (1996). *A Moment's Notice: Time Politics across Cultures.* Cornell University Press.

Griffiths, A. (2014). Embodied Histories: Exploring Law's Temporality in Relation to Land in Botswana. *J. Leg. Plur. Unoff. Law*, 46, pp. 37–59.

Grosz, E.A. (2005). *Time Travels: Feminism, Nature, Power.* Duke University Press.

Grosz, E.A. (1999). *Becomings: Explorations in Time, Memory, and Futures.* Cornell University Press.

Grusin, R. (2010). *Premediation: Affect and Mediality After 9/11.* Palgrave Macmillan, London; New York.

Halberstam, J. (2011). *The Queer Art of Failure.* Duke University Press.

Halberstam, J. (2005). *In a Queer Time and Place : Transgender Bodies, Subcultural Lives/Sexual Cultures.* New York University Press.

Haraway, D.J. (2016). *Staying with the Trouble: Making Kin in the Chthulucene.* Duke University Press, Durham, NC; London.

Haraway, D.J. (1991). *Simians, Cyborgs, and Women: The Reinvention of Nature.* Free Association Books.

Hussain, N. (2009). *The Jurisprudence of Emergency: Colonialism and the Rule of Law.* University of Michigan Press.

Jaime, K. (2017). 'Chasing Rainbows' Black Cracker and Queer, Trans Afrofuturity. *TSQ Transgender Stud. Q.*, 4, pp. 208–218.

Kafer, A. (2013). *Feminist, Queer, Crip.* Indiana University Press.

Keeling, K. (2009). LOOKING FOR M—Queer Temporality, Black Political Possibility, and Poetry from the Future. *GLQ J. Lesbian Gay Stud.*, 15, pp. 565–582.

Keenan, S. (2014). *Subversive Property: Law and the Production of Spaces of Belonging, Social Justice.* Routledge.

Knight, D.M. and Stewart, C., (2017). *Ethnographies of Austerity: Temporality, Crisis and Affect in Southern Europe.* Routledge.

Knop, K. and Riles, A. (2016). Space, Time and Historical Injustice: A Feminist Conflict-of-Laws Approach to the 'Comfort Women' Settlement (SSRN Scholarly Paper No. ID 2886588). *Social Science Research Network*, Rochester, NY.

Johns, F. (2016). The Temporal Rivalries of Human Rights. *Indiana Journal of Global Legal Studies*, 23 (1), 39–60.

Koselleck, R. (1985). *Futures Past: On the Semantics of Historical Time.* Columbia University Press.

Kristeva, J., Jardine, A. and Blake, H. (1981). Women's Time. *Signs*, 7, pp. 13–35.
Krupar, S. and Ehlers, N. (2017). Biofutures: Race and the Governance of Health. *Environ. Plan. Soc. Space*, 35, pp. 222–240.
Latour, B. (1993). *We Have Never Been Modern.* Harvard University Press.
Lefebvre, H. (2004). *Rhythmanalysis: Space, Time and Everyday Life.* Bloomsbury Academic.
Levine, J. (2001). GPS and the Legal Traceability of Time. *GPS World*, January, pp. 52–57.
Loewen Walker, R. (2014). The Living Present as a Materialist Feminist Temporality. *Women: A Cultural Review*, 25:1, pp. 46–61.
Mawani, R. (2014). Law as Temporality: Colonial Politics and Indian Settlers. *Irvine Law Rev.*, 4, pp. 65–96.
M'charek, A. (2014). Race, Time and Folded Objects: The HeLa Error. *Theory Cult. Soc.*, 31, pp. 29–56.
Mitropoulos, A. (2012). The Time of the Contract: Insurance, Contingency, and the Arrangement of Risk. *South Atl. Q.*, 111, pp. 763–781.
Mol, A. (2003). *The Body Multiple: Ontology in Medical Practice.* Duke University Press.
Muñoz, J.E. (2007). CRUISING THE TOILET LeRoi Jones/Amiri Baraka, Radical Black Traditions, and Queer Futurity. *GLQ J. Lesbian Gay Stud.*, 13, pp. 353–367.
Murdocca, C. (2017). 'A Matter of Time and a Matter of Place': Colonial Inquiries and the Politics of Testimony. *Law Cult. Humanit.*, 13, pp. 123–144.
Negri, A. (1991). *Marx Beyond Marx: Lessons on the Grundrisse.* Autonomedia.
Nixon, R. (2011). *Slow Violence and the Environmentalism of the Poor.* Harvard University Press.
Olson, E. (2015). Geography and Ethics I: Waiting and Urgency. *Prog. Hum. Geogr.*, 39, pp. 517–526.
O'Malley, P. (2004). *Risk, Uncertainty and Government.* Routledge, London; Portland, OR.
Opitz, S., Tellmann, U., Adey, P., Anderson, B. and Graham, S. (2015). Future Emergencies: Temporal Politics in Law and Economy. *Theory Cult. Soc.*, 32, pp. 107–129.
Parfitt, R.S. (2018). Fascism, Imperialism and International Law: An Arch Met a Motorway and the Rest Is History. 31 *Leiden Journal of International Law* (forthcoming in issue 3).
Parker, K.M. (2015). Response: The Politeness of History. *Law Soc. Inq.*, 40, pp. 264–269.
Parker, K.M. (2011). *Common Law, History, and Democracy in America, 1790–1900: Legal Thought before Modernism.* Cambridge University Press.
Peck, J. and Theodore, N. (2012). Politicizing Contingent Work: Countering Neoliberal Labor Market Regulation … from the Bottom Up? *South Atl. Q.*, 111, pp. 741–761.
Philippopoulos-Mihalopoulos, A. (2014). Critical Autopoiesis and the Materiality of Law. *Int. J. Semiot. Law – Rev. Int. Sémiot. Jurid.*, 27, pp. 389–418.
Philippopoulos-Mihalopoulos, A. (2013). Atmospheres of Law: Senses, Affects, Lawscapes. *Emot. Space Soc.*, 7, pp. 35–44.
Phillips, R. (Ed.). (2015). *Black Quantum Futurism: Theory & Practice.* The Afrofuturist Affair/House of Future Sciences Books.
Postone, M. (1996). *Time, Labor, and Social Domination: A Reinterpretation of Marx's Critical Theory.* Cambridge University Press.
Pottage, A. (2014). Law after Anthropology: Object and Technique in Roman Law. *Theory Cult. Soc.*, 31, pp. 147–166.
Power, N. (2009). Non-Reproductive Futurism: Ranciere's Rational Equality against Edelman's Body Apolitic. *borderlands*, 8.
Pschetz, L., Bastian, M. and Speed, C. (2016). *Temporal Design: Looking at Time as Social Coordination.* Design+Research+Society.

Richland, J.B. (2013). Perpetuities Against Rules: Law, Ethnography and the Irresolution of Inheritance. *Law Cult. Humanit.*, 8, pp. 433–447.

Richland, J.B. (2008). Sovereign Time, Storied Moments: The Temporalities of Law, Tradition, and Ethnography in Hopi Tribal Court. *PoLAR Polit. Leg. Anthropol. Rev.*, 31, pp. 8–27.

Rosa, H. (2013). *Social Acceleration: A New Theory of Modernity*. Columbia University Press.

Rose, E. (2017). Workplace Temporalities: A Time Based Critique of the Flexible Working Provisions. *Ind. Law J.*, 46, pp. 245–267.

Scott, D. (2014). *Omens of Aversity: Tragedy, Time, Memory, Justice*. Duke University Press.

Scott, D. (2004). *Conscripts of Modernity: The Tragedy of Colonial Enlightenment*. Duke University Press.

Serres, M. and Latour, B. (1995). *Conversations on Science, Culture, and Time*. University of Michigan Press.

Shahani, N. (2013). The Future Is Queer Stuff Critical Utopianism and Its Discontents. *GLQ J. Lesbian Gay Stud.*, 19, pp. 545–558.

Sharma, S. (2014). *In the Meantime: Temporality and Cultural Politics*. Duke University Press, Durham, NC; London.

Simon, S. and Goede, M. de. (2015). Cybersecurity, Bureaucratic Vitalism and European Emergency. *Theory Cult. Soc.*, 32, pp. 79–106.

Sinha, N. (2014). Contract, Work, and Resistance: Boatmen in Early Colonial Eastern India, 1760s–1850s. *Int. Rev. Soc. Hist.*, 59, pp. 11–43.

Smith, S. and Vasudevan, P. (2017). Race, Biopolitics, and the Future: Introduction to the Special Section. *Environ. Plan. Soc. Space*, 35, pp. 210–221.

Tadiar, N.X.M. (2012). Life-Times in Fate Playing. *South Atl. Q.*, 111, pp. 783–802.

Tutton, R. (2017). Wicked Futures: Meaning, Matter and the Sociology of the Future. *Sociol. Rev.*, 65, pp. 478–492.

Valverde, M. (2015). *Chronotopes of Law: Jurisdiction, Scale and Governance, Social Justice*. Routledge.

van Marle, K. (2003). Law's Time, Particularity and Slowness. *South Afr. J. Hum. Rights*, 19, pp. 239–255.

Vora, K. (2012). Limits of 'Labor': Accounting for Affect and the Biological in Transnational Surrogacy and Service Work. *South Atl. Q.*, 111, pp. 681–700.

Wacjman, J. (2015). *Pressed for Time: The Acceleration of Life in Digital Capitalism*. University of Chicago Press.

Waldby, C. and Cooper, M. (2010). From Reproductive Work to Regenerative Labour. The Female Body and the Stem Cell Industries. *Fem. Theory*, 11, 3–22.

Walker, R.L. (2014). The Living Present as a Materialist Feminist Temporality. *Women Cult. Rev.*, 25, pp. 46–61.

Weeks, K. (2011). *The Problem with Work: Feminism, Marxism, Antiwork Politics, and Postwork Imaginaries*. Duke University Press.

Welsh, L. (2017). The Role of Law in Temporal Reasoning: An Interview with Annelise Riles. *Fem. Leg. Stud.*, 1–7.

Wiber, M.G. (2014). Syncopated Rhythms? Temporal Patterns in Natural Resource Management. *J. Leg. Plur. Unoff. Law*, 46, pp. 123–140.

Widmer, A. (2010). Native Medical Practitioners, Temporality, and Nascent Biomedical Citizenship in the New Hebrides. *PoLAR Polit. Leg. Anthropol. Rev.*, 33, pp. 57–80.

Williams, R. (2018). Bloody Infrastructures! Exploring Challenges in Cord Blood Collection Maintenance. *Technology Analysis & Strategic Management*, 30(4), pp. 473–483.

Zbyszewska, A. (2016). *Gendering European Working Time Regimes*. Cambridge University Press.

1 The long sudden death of Antonin Scalia

Carol J. Greenhouse, Princeton University

The double theme of time and regulation is both inviting and challenging. It is inviting, in recalling the implication of shared time in Emile Durkheim's idea of *social time* (Durkheim, 2012, 10–11). It is challenging, too, since shared time raises the question of whether it is shared equally. Once we think of time as social rather than natural, it precludes neither claims of ownership nor asymmetries of distribution. Social time belongs to politics before it belongs to nature, and there are potentially high stakes in understanding it as "a true social institution" (Durkheim, *id.*, 11, n. 6) in which issues of power and inequality are as relevant as in any other institutional context. Political authority works power not just *in* time, but *as* time – in the process remixing the subjects and objects of regulation. This volume's concerns with regulating time are thus particularly relevant – urgent even – to understanding certain forms of political crisis in democratic states. In this chapter, the remixing involves the United States Supreme Court, President Obama, and the Republican caucus in the U.S. Congress.

For Durkheim, the visibility of the social in law (in *Division of Labor in Society*) and in time (in *Elementary Forms*) are two sides of the same question, as to how a society sustains its own collectivity as necessary and sufficient to its ethical credibility. That question points to various kinds of risk that are easily overlooked. But, in fact, anyone's assurance that the times are on their side might be misplaced, to their peril. Miscalculation is always a risk, for at least two reasons. First of all, social time is never sole or total (by Durkheim's definition, social time is concerned with difference across what he calls civilizations), but it functions *as if* it were. That *as if* is not the work of time, but rather the solidarity for which social time is a contingent expression or sign. Second, for this very reason, in times of political or social crisis – as I suggest below – social time can be seriously off. Theorizing the materiality of what she calls "legal times", Emily Grabham proposes that:

> Human action does not exist within time, but instead generates temporalities, including legal temporalities, in specific assemblages of other human and nonhuman actors ... I ask what our understanding of law and time might look like if we followed things as well as people, if we allowed objects to open access to new worlds, and if we paid attention to the agentic

potential of, for example, matter, metals, and particles, and not merely conscious human behaviour.

(Grabham, 2017, 6)

Grabham's question is suggestive, since it pushes us to be agnostic about what represents what in the regulatory apparatus of time – and, more fundamentally, to consider agency ahead of representation. This is a constructive provocation to suspend the commonplace assumption that social time is itself wholly temporal, a proxy for whatever real time is (or is imagined to be).[1] That provocation quickly runs up against, and corrects, a reception tradition that conflates time and social time. That tradition is widespread, in spite of Durkheim's explanation that social time is not "my" time, or some natural time. That distinction tends to be lost, for example, in anthropological readings that render social time in either managerial terms, ahead of social activity (coordinating it), or semiotic terms, following social activity (representing it).[2] Under the logic of such readings, social time can never be off. It is always the right time, by definition – its continuous recursivity assured *in time* and *on time*.

Thinking about the transitive materiality of law and time unsettles that assurance, since time (like material objects) can be designed and built, consumed or unexpectedly moved, delivered late, broken, appropriated by others or made subject to contested ownership claims, or go missing altogether. Grabham's key image is "brewing" – referring to a percolation of ingredients that produces a new substance. Holding onto such material imagery enables us to consider that social time is not first and foremost (or somehow automatically) a technology for time-keeping or representing. Rather, it sets the limiting conditions of agency – different limits in different circumstances, including but not limited to different temporal orthodoxies.[3]

These reflections are prologue to what follows. I begin with a case study of sorts – based on a recent and ongoing story from the front pages of the U.S. newspapers. It is in some ways about a material object – the seat on the United States Supreme Court bench that was (and remains) vacated unexpectedly with the sudden death of Justice Antonin Scalia. But the very materiality of the seat, its arrangement of planes, conjures its composition of *social* surfaces as social time – i.e., the interrelations of the late Justice, the Court, and beyond. Social time is in question, as events unfolded around a concerted partisan political effort to reset the times – a tactical reset that would clear the seat's title, so to speak, and secure it for the future.[4] The extremity of that tactic sets the theme for the second part of the chapter – an engagement with interpretive resources from three classic social theory texts, selected for their explicit address to problems of succession. The third part of the chapter returns to the problem of shared time in relation to contemporary states in the throes of democratic crisis.

I

Antonin Scalia, Senior Associate Justice of the United States Supreme Court, died unexpectedly while on a hunting vacation with a group of 35 friends at a west Texas ranch resort, sometime in the night of February 12–13, 2016.[5] He was 79. Cibolo Creek Ranch – some 30,000 acres in a remote area south of

Marfa, TX – is a private luxury resort. The remoteness made for some complications of a heartbreakingly practical sort. The coroner – many miles away – certified his death by natural causes by telephone, as allowed by Texas law (Moravec, Horwitz, and Markon, 2016; see also Martin and Contreras, 2016), and the public announcement was delayed (ultimately made by Chief Justice John Roberts on February 13). There was some initial uncertainty and a brief ugly tussle over who should have custody of the body (the county sheriff or federal officials). I will skip those details. In the end, a team of U.S. Marshals and Supreme Court Police escorted his body back to Washington, D.C., on Sunday morning, February 14.

Within hours of the death, and well before the body arrived in Washington, Senator Mitch McConnell (R-KY), majority leader of the U.S. Senate, made a public statement of his view that Justice Scalia's successor should be named by President Obama's successor, and that it would be wrong to do otherwise (Landler and Baker, 2016) – posting to his Facebook page: "The American people should have a voice in the selection of their next Supreme Court Justice. Therefore, this vacancy should not be filled until we have a new President" (McConnell, 2016).

Developments in the course of the day quickly confirmed that this was not just McConnell's view, as Senate Republicans and most Republican candidates for the presidency declared their blanket opposition to whomever the president might nominate. But their pledge was not just opposition to the eventual nominee. The Republican position coalesced around a lockstep refusal to hold hearings on the nominee, or even to receive him or her in the round of courtesy calls that is customary in the lead-up to Senate Judiciary Committee hearings. Weekend news reporters struggled to keep to their own commemorative conventions, Scalia's smiling portrait the backdrop on every channel, as the political story unwound.

Scalia's death came a full nine months before the election and 11 months until the next inauguration in January, 2017 – an unprecedently long vacancy, if Republicans did not yield. In response to McConnell's statement, Harry Reid (D-NV), minority leader of the Senate, said: "Failing to fill this vacancy would be a shameful abdication of one of the Senate's most essential constitutional responsibilities" (Landler and Baker, 2016). Republicans tried to resist the "unprecedented" part – claiming that it would be highly unusual for a Supreme Court confirmation to occur in the last year of a presidential administration. Statistically, they might have been correct, since most vacancies on the Court occur as planned retirements, and the odds of a justice dying in office in the last year of a presidency are mathematically slim.[6] But Harry Reid was correct on the substance. Justice Kennedy was confirmed in the final year of the George H. W. Bush presidency in 1988, and, in any case, the Republicans were not talking about rejecting the president's nominee; rather, they were refusing to acknowledge the president's – *this* president's – authority to make the nomination. This was indeed unprecedented (Liptak, 2016b; Kar and Mazzone, 2016; New York Times, 2016). Meanwhile, President Obama confirmed his intention to proceed (Landler, 2016). All of this happened before Scalia's body was back in Washington.

Shock was an objective response to these events, in my view. But, for the sake of argument, I grant that there is a case to be made otherwise, as partisan antagonism was already shocking in the Congress and between the legislative and executive branches. Mitch McConnell had long since pledged his commitment to making the Obama administration a failed presidency (on the occasion of Obama's first inauguration in 2008),[7] and for eight years led an obstructionist Republican caucus (as Senate Majority Leader since 2015). Moreover, within their own circles, conservatives had staked out something like this strategy long before Justice Scalia died, touting the virtues of leaving a seat open for a term "or two" for the sake of preserving a conservative majority on the Court.[8] But even the commentators who took that position did not go so far as to challenge outright a president's authority to make a nomination. Especially now that shock has become routine in the U.S. political environment, it may be difficult for readers to recapture the lurching sense of being on new ground as the Republicans' policy of obstruction against President Obama reached this new pitch. But a sense of shock is analytically useful, even if it is not an emotion all readers share.

Indeed, it was more than the obstruction or the "don't give an inch" partisanship that was unsettling in this instance. It was the Senate's preemption of executive authority and the subordination of the Supreme Court's constitutional authority to be a national court – something like a floor giving way under the most fundamental tenets of the separation of powers in the U.S.[9] The Republicans were almost casual in their explicit disregard for President Obama's legitimacy *as president*. It was that delegitimation that weaponized their tactic, while concealing it in populist wraps.[10]

As might be clear already, I believe the Republican efforts to normalize the state of affairs as fulfilling a democratic imperative are not credible; their particular targeting of President Obama and the claimed erasure of his mandate gives this away. It was Senator Grassley (R-IA), chair of the Senate Judiciary Committee, who got to the heart of that matter, expressing the view that the 2014 midterm elections, which had returned a Republican majority to the Congress, had effectively overturned President Obama's reelection in 2012: "People spoke in the midterm election [in 2014], and [Obama] came out on the short end of that. In America, a democracy, you have to accept the judgment of the voters" (Ibid.).

Later in the spring, when Donald Trump, by then the presumptive Republican nominee, faltered at the polls, political debate briefly shifted to the question of allowing a lame duck appointment – some Republicans conceding that by then the people would have spoken (and, in the process, giving away their expectation that the president-elect would be Hillary Clinton) (Herszenhorn, 2016). But McConnell was steadfast, refusing to allow hearings on any Obama nominee.[11] These developments are evidence that it was not (as McConnell initially claimed) that the last year of a presidency was too late for a nomination. It was the Republicans' view (as Grassley explained) that divided government made the president's authority moot. But not just the president's authority – only *this* president's authority (as McConnell's subsequent position indicated).

By mid-March, when President Obama nominated Merrick Garland, it was clear that for Republican leadership, the seat had become more valuable empty than filled. Indeed, McConnell's intransigence proved to be prescient as an effective tactic in the 2016 presidential election, as it made the Court a campaign issue, giving conservatives and other voters opposed to abortion a reason to rally behind Trump, given his campaign pledge to nominate a successor in Scalia's tradition. He won the election with strong majorities among white Catholic and evangelical voters (Smith and Martínez, 2016). The Senate subsequently confirmed the new administration's nominee, putting Neil Gorsuch on the Court as Associate Justice.

The rest of this chapter focuses on what the Scalia story might reveal, in more general terms, about what high office is made of, as an infrastructure of social time.

II

Since Tocqueville's *Democracy in America*, the United States has always been marked out as an exception, compared to European states with parliamentary systems. In the U.S., these brackets tend to be erased in a generalized notion of modernity, but they are relevant to the story. Since the nineteenth century, refrains in this regard have included the lack of a distinction between civil servants and politicians, the role of money in American politics and, more fundamentally, a democracy that sets no checks on the powers of the majority. Max Weber, whose theory of bureaucratic authority still dominates our understandings of modern institutions of government (and to whom I will return later), marked out these and other exceptions in references to what he called the "American case".[12] The popularization of neoliberalism in moral terms (as free choice, for example) has set up a horizon of comparability on which the U.S. exception is by now a difference of degree rather than of kind.[13] Be that as it may, we may reasonably ask whether in the current milieu political democracy has become more effective as a means of managing governability through processes of qualification than as a means of distributing and sharing power across self-constituted political communities.[14] Thinking about that empty seat as a materialization of social time underscores the contested claims to its ownership (and, in this case, the incommensurability of those claims). Thinking about social time from the standpoint of the regulatory apparatuses associated with it makes visible little remarked (or unremarked) processes that sustain the public value of high office – by which I mean high office as affirmation of the public's value.

Anticipating what follows, those processes constitute high office as a form of artificial personhood independent of the incumbent, and this accounts in part for the labile qualities of the empty seat that made it available for political contest. Disembedded as political apparatus, the empty seat was twice valuable, as trophy and future control. The seat is not just the symbol or shade of the late Justice; it is also materially integral to the office of justice in an institution that claims permanent value. This three-sidedness (institution, office, incumbent) is material – as is evident in the practical problems that followed on the death of Justice Scalia.

The dynamic materiality of the seat gives rise to a host of interpretive problems, such as anticipated by J.G.A. Pocock:

> [W]hen a change in a society's self-awareness has become at all widely disseminated, that society's styles of thinking and acting have been irreversibly altered. There may still be much in its traditions of behavior which has not emerged into consciousness and perhaps never will; what has changed, however, is its mode of being and becoming conscious of itself and its existence in time, and once this has happened a society is no longer what it was.
>
> (Pocock, 1989, 239)

It is Pocock's reference to a shift in the "mode of being and becoming in time" that I take as an opening to the next part of this discussion.

In what follows, I lean on three classic works – by Kantorowicz, Durkheim and Weber – as resources for thinking through what mode of being and becoming in time the Scalia story might entail. I have chosen these particular works for their centrality to modern sociological understandings of succession to high office – respectively as a problem of theology, symbolic representation, and state organization. In each case, however, I read them against the grain, to pick up on elements of the works that speak as much to their own political environments as they do that of their stated subjects. In those moments of uncontainability, they are suggestive (reflexively and critically) in the here and now. Their implication, read alongside the story of the empty seat, offers particular insight into the vulnerability of democratic states to rupture not from below, as Tocqueville and others feared, but from above.

The King's One Body

In *The King's Two Bodies*, Ernst Kantorowicz details the history of the relation between office and incumbent as the solution to a problem of continuity that absorbed medieval thinkers when they thought about time (Kantorowicz, 1997). In his chapter on twelfth and thirteenth century corporations, he explains that the very meaning of continuity transformed at that time, as time – canonically established as a finite segment of eternity – now came to represent the infinity of life (Kantorowicz, 274):

> Time … became a vivifying element, a symbol of endless duration, of Life. To be sure, not the individual life was immortal; but immortal was the life of the genera and species which the mortal individual represented. Time now became the symbol of the eternal continuity and immortality of the great collective called the human race, of the species of man, of the seminal powers, of the forces of germination.
>
> (Kantorowicz, 277)

This new paradigm was not made from a simple inversion of terms, since eternity still belonged to God – and therefore forcing a distinction between immortality and eternity. Over time, the solution to this problem apparently involved foregrounding a third kind of time, the aevum. This mediating third term was the time of the angels – which, like humans, were created as individuals, but unlike humans, were immortal (Kantorowicz, 281). Kantorowicz explains that this third term opened a symbolic space wherein people could be mortal and, at the same time, like angels, members of an immortal humanity, a "permanent present" (to borrow from Pottage, 2004, 264).[15] For Kantorowicz, the secularization of the aevum was part and parcel of the development of the idea of the corporation – a permanent association of mortal individuals.[16] In this way, the corporation involved a fictional personhood, and among its expressions was the idea of office – itself a legal fiction that conjoined a mortal individual to an immortal corporate body. The analogy between office and angels lay in the individuality of their fictional personhood but also in the irreducibility of that personhood to the identity of an actual person (Kantorowicz, 282). Kantorowicz makes this connection specifically in relation to judicial bodies (in the double sense of that term):

> [T]he personified collectives of the jurists, which were juristically immortal species, displayed all the features otherwise attributed to angels; for the legal "fictitious persons" were, in fact, pure actualizations and thus appeared like the next of kin of the angelic fictions ... The de-individualized fictitious persons of the lawyers, therefore, necessarily resembled the angels, and the jurists themselves recognized that there was some similarity between their abstractions and the angelic beings.
>
> (Ibid.)

Kantorowicz's analysis is suggestive in pointing to *office* as an idea that calls for separate attention beyond the modern convention of equating office with *role*. I find it useful to consider the relevance of that formulation in relation to the Scalia story, since it suggests that the importance of continuity of office may be less its provision for institutional operations (i.e., by supplying a steady succession of mortal occupants), than its materialization of corporate claims to authority and value in relation to which the office itself is obviously important but in some ways incidental.

If office refers to the permanence of a corporation, specifying the corporation becomes essential. That is the core question in the dispute over the empty seat. In our story, "the people" are invoked by McConnell and others in his caucus, but *only* those "people" who voted for the Republican majority. Their only actionable corporate claim is for the Senate Republicans themselves. The exclusion of the minority party (and enfolding the elected president and Democratic voters into that same disparaged category)[17] resonates with another part of Kantorowicz's analysis, as he explains how the medieval corporation confronted its problem of leadership – the problem being the contradiction between corporate (i.e., collective) personhood and the singularity of its leader or head. He tells us that the medieval solution to this problem took the form of a novel idea: a "one-man corporation" – someone whose corporate form was conceived in time (i.e., in a series of predecessors and successors), rather than in a common social location (i.e., among present contemporaries) (Kantorowicz, 312).

Linear time thus became a new way of organizing the plurality of corporateness and overcoming the contradiction between collectivity and distinction within the corporate body. This is the analytical value of preserving some sense of shock in the events. In the Scalia story, the contest is precisely over the corporate body, as the empty seat does not void the office but – in the politics of the day – *does* void the idea of a permanent public that in theory sustains the value of the office. Even if the seat is empty, in other words, the office endures, and continues to refer to a public (conceived as a corporate body) that is the source of its permanence and value. The relation of office and corporate body is akin to property and title – an analogy I borrow from Keenan (2016).[18] The judicial relation to the corporate body is ritually suppressed in the United States, where it seems that the distinction between incumbent and office took precedence over the connection between office and public. Be that as it may, that third side – even if ritually occluded – obviates a political need for a public rite of inauguration for justices; the public is (theoretically) accounted for in the very idea of the judiciary.[19] The absence of that rite in the judicial context (for the time being) is as crucial to the symbolic separation-of-powers infrastructure of U.S. democracy in its idealized form as are the very public rites of the presidential inauguration.

To put this differently, although we conventionally render office and incumbent as a binarism, Kantorowicz – thinking in shared time, and alert to the contradictions of naturalizing the authority of public officials – encourages us to keep in view the hidden third term, i.e., the legal fiction of the permanent corporate body of which office is a part. I want to emphasize that in his argument it is the *corporate quality* of the people, i.e., the priority of their own constitutive authority as a collectivity (not an aggregation of constituents) that sustains that symbolic association. The story of the empty seat thus underscores the importance of attending closely to the shape-shifting slipperiness of the corporate referent in that context, as it was moved around from nation to party.[20] This brings us a step closer to the larger context of our discussion. Anthropological literature was once filled with discussion over just such symbolic associations and elaborations under the rubric of totemism (see, especially, Durkheim, 2012; Frazer, 2015; Lévi-Strauss, 1964).

Office as collective representation

Totemism was classically considered by anthropologists of the nineteenth and early twentieth century to be the symbolic expression of clan identity – cult for some, solidarity for others, somewhere between politics and religion. Totemism is shared time par excellence – shared over time and across located communities. Claude Lévi-Strauss long since reminds us that the totemism of these early anthropologists leaned far too heavily on the functions of totems as charters for social organization. It was a sort of hysteria, he says – their hysteria – saying more about their anxiety to preserve a line between civilization and savagery through law and religion than with the reality of how people without social science intellectualize their collective relations (Lévi-Strauss, 1). So I am not about to suggest a direct analogy between totemism and the Republican quest for a worthy successor for Scalia, any more than I would present the Republicans as direct heirs to medieval philosophers. But literature on totemism contains hints that (as Lévi-Strauss also suggests) the authors were thinking not just of their ethnographic cases, but also of dilemmas of leadership, solidarity and affect known to them from their own political anxieties as citizens. It is those contemporary anxieties that make this body of work interesting for our purposes.

In *Elementary Forms of Religious Life*, Emile Durkheim couched his novel idea of social time in an extensive discussion of totemism, based on then-available literature on aboriginal Australia, Native America, and Polynesia. Durkheim understood totemism as a broad rubric for a certain type of expressive need:

> [If]the Australian is so strongly inclined to represent his totem, it is in order not [i.e., it is not in order] to have a portrait of it before his eyes which would constantly renew the sensation of it; it is . . . because *he feels the need* of representing the idea which he forms of it by means of material and external signs, no matter what these signs may be.
>
> (Durkheim, 127)

For North Americans, he writes, the totem itself – a material object – is "always surrounded with a sort of religious halo" (Durkheim, 125; emphasis added). To this, Durkheim quickly adds that the symbolic object representing the totem is not sacred in itself; it is sacred along with "the beings of the totemic species and the members of the clan (Durkheim, 130)."[21] Indeed, he concludes, "each individual has a double nature: two beings coexist within him, a man and an animal" (Durkheim, 134).

The double nature Durkheim finds in totemism echoes what has been discussed already, regarding the double nature of the king at the end of Kantorowicz's book. It also echoes the discourse of nationalism emergent at that time, as the French state centralized and standardized public administration to the detriment of provincial cultural communities and the diversity of their particular traditions of authority. While it might seem that Durkheim draws on modern citizenship to explain the logic of the totem, it is also the case that what he understands of the logic of totemism makes citizenship thinkable in a new way, as the *office* of the person in relation to the corporate body of the nation. Indeed, he might as well have written: "Each individual has a double nature: two beings coexist within him, a citizen and a person." The contemporary resonance of this formulation presses hard on the question – again – of "which corporation?" Durkheim asks this very question himself: "[T]he totem is before all a symbol, a material expression of something else. But of what?"

Continuing the passage, he answers the question this way:

> [The totemic representation] expresses and symbolizes two different sorts of things. In the first place, it is the outward and visible form of what we have called the totemic principle or god. But it is also the symbol of the determined society called the clan. *It is its flag; it is the sign by which each clan distinguishes itself from the others, the visible mark of its personality* ... The god of the clan, the totemic principle, can therefore be nothing else than the clan itself, personified and represented to the imagination under the visible form of the animal or vegetable which serves as totem.
>
> (Durkheim, 206; emphasis added)

And as he conjures up for himself the personality of the corporate group, Durkheim slips into the first-person plural, specifying the cultural and political labor in his world (no longer aboriginal Australia only, but a radical rhetorical "we" in shared time) that sustains the plausibility of the corporate claim on which the aura of the leader depends:

> But a god is not merely an authority upon whom we depend; it is a force upon which our strength relies. The man who has obeyed his god and who, for this reason, believes the god is with him, approaches the world with confidence and with the feeling of an increased energy ... For the collective force is not entirely outside of us; it does not act upon us wholly from without; but rather, since society cannot exist except in and through individual consciousnesses, this force must also penetrate us and organize itself within us; it thus becomes an integral part of our being and by that very fact this is elevated and magnified.
>
> (Durkheim, 209–210)

His illustrative example on this point underscores the extent to which individuality may lose its boundaries – for better or for worse – in the ecstatic "frisson" (his term) (Durkheim, 190) of the moment, rendering the collective itself not only unstable but objectively undecidable:

> There are occasions when this strengthening and vivifying action of society is especially apparent. In the midst of an assembly animated by a common passion, we become susceptible of acts and sentiments of which we are incapable when reduced to our own forces; and when the assembly is dissolved and when, finding ourselves alone again, we fall back to our ordinary level, we are then able to measure the height to which we have been raised above ourselves. History abounds in examples of this sort.
>
> (Ibid.)

And just in case his readers have missed the contemporaneity of his allusion, he adds lines that are readily legible today: "[I]n the present day just as much as in the past, *we see society constantly creating sacred things out of ordinary ones. If it happens to fall in love with a man and if it thinks it has found in him the principal aspirations that move it, as well as the means of satisfying them, this man will be raised above the others and, as it were, deified.* Opinion will invest him with a majesty exactly analogous to that protecting the gods (Durkheim, 212–213)."

Note that Durkheim is talking about the quasi-apotheosis of an individual in a way that flips his account, making it about the politics of his own time. Reflecting back from these lines, his example highlights the extent to which the value of anyone's citizenship is indeterminate in real time, as that value derives not from one's personhood or even from one's rights, but from the affective charge of the corporate group upon which it is contingent.

Durkheim refers to this affective charge as a force – a force that he compares to an electrical current, connecting internal and external worlds. In his account, the sensation of that current is (at least at first) pleasurable, but it is also dangerous. After all, he has just described a scenario in which collective representation becomes the condition of its own antithesis as the crowd deifies a leader from a place beyond their own conscious self-interests, and outside of any accountability or apparent alternative, since it is by definition not rational. Weber, too, in passing allusions, finds a limiting condition of bureaucratic rationality in thrill – the thrill of pleasing one's superior, a desire that consumes bureaucratic rationality from within (Weber, 1978: 941–955). This brings us full circle.

III

To recap: Kantorowicz's analysis usefully draws attention away from the question of who controls the seat to the more theoretically interesting question of the source and nature of the corporate claims on which legitimate control depends. The partisan contest over Scalia's successor involved competing claims on this point. As noted earlier, the Republicans under McConnell made the seat the attribute of their party; the Democrats claimed it instead for the nation. This is a major difference, evident in the first instance in the fact that the Republicans pledged a new Scalia, whereas President Obama had put forward a moderate in Judge Garland. But from a broader perspective, the difference is also apparent in the fact that the new administration – fulfilling campaign pledges – has reversed Obama-era legislation and regulations and pledged to dismantle or reduce federal agencies associated with environmental protection and social services.

Having drawn on Kantorowicz's analysis of kingship to highlight the Republican blockage as an anti-democratic assault from within the government, we turned to the related issue in a reading of Durkheim that points to the frailty of collective representations. Durkheim's account of totemism - albeit written in a discourse of ethnology – suggests the extent to which the risk of anti-democratic assault from within the democratic process is inherent wherever the symbolic representation of the collectivity becomes a cynical proxy for the public itself. Seen from that standpoint, contemporary conditions – including major private investment in electoral campaigns, intensive mediatization, branding and profound participation deficits – point to the vulnerability of democracy from within the state itself. While the success of the Trump candidacy goes beyond the scope of this paper, the exclusionary force of its populism is relevant. I reject the commonplace claim that he has a mandate based on the voice he is said to have given to an alienated segment of the electorate, since – following the reasoning of this chapter, and leaving aside the inconsistencies in his policy positions – his power appears to owe more to his capture of the Republican Party and his repeated demonstrations of the futility of opposition.

I conclude by revisiting the idea of force as a modality of shared time. Durkheim and Weber use the same term – force – in parallel ways: Durkheim to hold onto the distinction between personal and collective judgment, and Weber to reckon with the moral ambiguity of the modern state.[22] Neither is writing straightforwardly as description, any more than Kantorowicz is speaking in his own voice when he writes of the sacredness of kings. Rather, they are anchoring their social science to a hermeneutics of justice – inflected differently for each of them, but in common predicated on their recognition of history, ethnology and political sociology as commitments to shared time, on the side of the public.

Whether it is read as desire or as armed coercion, Weber's reference to the visceral force of domination within the state is familiar to any student of social science:

> [F]orce is certainly not the normal or the only means of the state – nobody says that – but force is a means specific to the state. Today the relation between the state and violence is an especially intimate one. In the past, the most varied institutions – beginning with the sib – have known the use of physical force as quite normal. Today, however, we have to say that a state is a human community that (successfully) claims the monopoly of the legitimate use of physical force within a given territory.
>
> (Weber, 1946: 1)

This passage is usually read as a comment on the state's monopoly of violence. More precisely, it is about the claim to monopolize legitimate violence. This is an important distinction, as it makes the immortal community of the state contingent on that claim's truth value. For our purposes, then, the significance of this passage is less the state's claim to monopolize access to the means of violence on the part of state agents, than it is the state's claim to monopolize the ends of violence. These become prominent not only in outwardly directed militarism or domestic policing, but also, crucially, within the government itself as state institutions contract around their internal contests over the instruments of power.

This brings us back to the Republican gambit for (in effect) a one-party state, and the shock of what this reveals of the vulnerability of democracy to antidemocratic struggles within its own core institutions. There is no reason to think of this as a uniquely U.S. story, given that the interests, identities, and institutions at its core are transnational in various ways.[23] The participation deficit is pervasive, and the neoliberalization of government and global capital everywhere, in diverse ways, tends to widen the gap between nationalist and "globalist" constituencies, as well as between national and local political constituencies – correspondingly raising the stakes in intragovernmental battles between national legislatures and executives. Xenophobia and nativism are powerful projects in such scenarios, particularly in contexts in which citizenship has been popularized in a consumerist discourse that occludes its own exclusions.

Such circumstances of democratic unease may put the status of the public in doubt, but *social time* retains critical theoretical valence as a way of thinking through (and working through) solidarity as an ethical principle foundational to the human sciences. Social time works through relations of solidarity more surely than it can be claimed to *represent* solidarity – since relations may be contested and temporally diverse whereas the claim to representation would necessarily presuppose a fixed prior entity. The empty seat invites an analysis of social time in the former sense (contested solidarities), drawing attention to the question – a political question – of how the office it represents acknowledges its relation to a specific corporate body. Thinking in shared time makes visible and comparable the ways social bodies are bent, moved, consigned and stretched in the riptides of political antagonism.[24] As Pocock suggests in the passage quoted at the outset, and subsequent events in the current milieu have confirmed, radical transformation does not necessarily announce itself, but is discoverable after the fact in what can be the shock of learning the time.

Notes

1 See Bastian 2018.
2 On Durkheim's distinction between social and personal time, see Greenhouse 2014; on the anthropology of social time, see especially Gell 1992 and Munn 1992.
3 On agency and temporal form, see Greenhouse 1996: especially Part I.
4 The allusion to title is inspired by Sarah Keenan; see note 38, *infra*.
5 For full coverage and an obituary, see Liptak 2016a.
6 On justices' deaths in office, see Nurik 2016.
7 On McConnell's strategy of opposition to President Obama and his policy of obstruction since 2009, see MacGillis 2016.
8 "Presidencies last four to eight years. A Supreme Court appointment can last three decades . . . The inconvenience of one or more terms at the Supreme Court with fewer than nine justices—even through an intervening midterm election—pales in comparison with the repercussions of making a bad selection. It's worth the fight, and worth the wait" (Barnett and Blackman, 2015).
9 For an analytical overview of U.S. federal separation of powers from a comparative constitutional perspective (England, France, and Germany), see Zoller 2008.
10 There were also consequences for the Court. The Court continues to function when there is a vacancy, but a tie vote returns the case to the court below, without decision, reverting to the lower court's ruling. For an overview of the Court's 2015–16 term and the impact of Justice Scalia's absence, see Liptak 2016b. The Court deadlocked in two major cases – one supporting public unions, and the other in effect overturning President Obama's executive order deferring deportation for certain categories of undocumented immigrants.
11 Conservative organizations invested millions of dollars in mobilizing the grassroots to pressure senators in their home districts during the spring recess (Wegman, 2016).

12 Weber (1978: 1452) includes the United States presidential elections in his discussion of plebiscite by "the masses" (rather than parliament) as a path to "caesarism."
13 Weber argues that the very aspiration to equate political order with moral order precludes both (1946: 24).
14 On the discursive compression of politics and economy in democracies, see Polanyi 1957: especially Part II.
15 The context of Pottage's discussion of *aevum* (as "permanent present") is his analysis of bioethics regulation – but nonetheless suggestive with respect to this essay. In particular, he points to the discursive construction of "intergenerational equity", and to the occlusion of risk and uncertainty in a discourse of "variation" within "an enduring species form" (Pottage, 2004: 264). I am grateful to Emily Grabham for pointing me to this reference.
16 I am grateful to Riccardo Baldissone for his differentiation between immortality and permanence in this context.
17 My thanks to Nadine El-Enany for pointing out the metonymic relation of the African American president to African American electorates in this logic.
18 Keenan analyzes the shift from possession- to registration-based title (the Torrens system) from the standpoint of their different temporalities – possession reflecting "histories and relations with the land" and registration occluding those histories in favor of clear title in future perpetuity (Keenan, 2016, p. 1).
19 Elsewhere, I have written on the absence of public ritual at the installation of Supreme Court justices (Greenhouse, 1989). See also Peralta 2016. Justice Scalia's casket rested at the Supreme Court for a period prior to his funeral mass at the Basilica of the National Shrine of the Immaculate Conception, the largest Roman Catholic church in North America (National Shrine, 2016). President Obama was widely rebuked in the conservative press for not attending the funeral (Vice-President Biden and Mrs. Biden did attend). He and Mrs. Obama did pay their respects to the family and members of the Court at the Great Hall. Of the seven justices who died in office over the past seventy years, presidents have attended four of those funerals (Nurik, 2016).
20 The reference to slipperiness acknowledges my debt to Abrams' formulation of "the slippery concreteness of the state" (1988).
21 Lévi-Strauss (1964: 64, 78) is highly critical of the classic association of totems with clans as too narrow, and also too narrowly fixed on animals and other material objects (intangible elements such as wind and disease can also serve as clan symbols, but this criticism does not weaken the suggestiveness of Durkheim's formulation for our purposes.
22 For examples, see Durkheim 1912: 26; Weber, Protestant Ethic, ch. 5. In these examples (among others), the idea of force subsumes the sensation of obligation and domination, but not necessarily physical coercion.
23 Nadine El-Enany (n.d.) provides a surprisingly sharp parallel, in the concerted (and successful) effort to empty the seat of Britain's first Muslim mayor by recall. Her analysis illuminates the precarity of political mandates in the narrow institutional sense against the political heft of more broadly seated racial and religious exclusions.
24 I borrow the image of stretched bodies from Lalor (n.d.): "Queer bodies are therefore stretched between international, transnational and domestic legal frameworks and the resulting spatio-temporal imaginaries that these frameworks conjure."

Bibliography

Abrams, P. (1988). Notes on the difficulty of studying the state (1977). *Journal of Historical Sociology*, 1(1), pp. 58–89.

Barnett, R. E. and Blackman, J. (September 14, 2015). The next justices: A guide for GOP candidates on how to fill court vacancies. *The Weekly Standard*. September 14, 2015.

Electronic document: http://www.weeklystandard.com/the-next-justices/article/1024728.

Bastian, M. (2018). Liberating clocks: Developing a critical horology to rethink the potential of clock time. *New Formations: A Journal of Culture/Theory/Politics*, 92, pp. 41–55. Electronic document: http://www.research.ed.ac.uk/portal/files/27947571/Bastian_Liberating_clocks_final_accepted_version.pdf.

Durkheim, E. (2012 [1915, 1912]). *Elementary Forms of the Religious Life*. Trans. Joseph Ward Swain. London: George Allen & Unwin (Project Gutenberg). Electronic document: http://www.gutenberg.org/files/41360/41360-h/41360-h.htm#FNanchor_213_213.

El-Enany, N. (n.d.). *The Body that Loses its Chair*. Law, temporalities and the racialised subject. Unpublished manuscript on file with author; cited with permission.

Frazer, J. G. (2015 [1887]). *Totemism*. Cambridge: Harvard University Press.

Gell, A. (1992) *The Anthropology of Time: Cultural Constructions of Temporal Maps and Images*. Oxford: Berg.Grabham, E. (2017). *Brewing Legal Times: Things, Form, and the Enactment of* Law. Toronto: University of Toronto Press.

Greenhouse, C. (1989). Just in time: Temporality and the cultural legitimation of law. *Yale Law Journal*, 98(8), pp. 1631–1651.

———. (1996). *A Moment's Notice: Time Politics Across Cultures*. Ithaca, NY: Cornell University Press.

———. (2014) Time's up, timed out: Reflections on social time and legal pluralism. *Journal of Legal Pluralism and Unofficial Law*, 46(1), pp. 141–153.

Herszenhorn, D. M. (2016). Merrick Garland visits Capitol as G.O.P. digs in. *New York Times*. March 17, 2016. Electronic document: http://www.nytimes.com/2016/03/18/us/politics/obama-supreme-court-senate.html.

Kantorowicz, E. H. (1997 [1957]). *The King's Two Bodies: A Study in Medieval Political Theology*. Princeton: Princeton University Press.

Kar, R. B. and Mazzone, J. (2016). Essay – The Garland affair: What history and the Constitution *really* say about President Obama's powers to appoint a Replacement for Justice Scalia. *New York University Law Review*, 91, pp. 53–114. Electronic document: http://www.nyulawreview.org/sites/default/files/%20NYULawReviewOnline-91-Kar-Mazzone.pdf.

Keenan, S. (2016). Smoke, curtains and mirrors: The production of race through time and title registration. *Law & Critique*, 28(1), pp. 87–108.

Lalor, K. (n.d.). Encountering the past: LGBTI rights and contested histories. Unpublished paper on file with author; cited with permission.

Landler, M. (2016). Obama to nominate Scalia replacement over Republicans' objections. *New York Times*. February 13, 2016. Electronic document: http://www.nytimes.com/2016/02/14/us/politics/obama-to-nominate-scalia-successor-over-republicans-objections.html?ref=liveblog.

Landler, M. and Baker, P. (2016). Battle begins over naming next justice. *New York Times*. February 13, 2016. Electronic document: http://www.nytimes.com/2016/02/14/us/politics/battle-begins-over-naming-next-justice.html?ref=liveblog.

Lévi-Strauss, C. (1964). *Totemism*. Trans. Rodney Needham. London: Merlin Press.

Liptak, A. (2016a). Antonin Scalia, Justice on the Supreme Court, dies at 79. *New York Times*. February 13, 2016. Electronic document: http://www.nytimes.com/2016/02/14/us/antonin-scalia-death.html?_r=0.

———. (2016b). Sidebar: Study calls snub of Obama's Supreme Court pick unprecedented. *New York Times*. June 13, 2016. Electronic document: http://www.nytimes.com/2016/06/14/us/politics/obama-supreme-court-merrick-garland.html?action=click&content

Collection=us&module=NextInCollection&region=Footer&pgtype=article&version=newsevent&rref=collection%2Fnews-event%2Fsupreme-court-nomination-2016.

———.(2016c). The right-wing Supreme Court that wasn't. *New York Times*. June 28, 2016. Electronic document: http://www.nytimes.com/2016/06/29/us/politics/supreme-court-term.html.

MacGillis, A. (2016). Sunday Review – news analysis – Why is Mitch McConnell picking this fight? *New York Times*. February 19, 2016. Electronic document: http://www.nytimes.com/2016/02/21/opinion/sunday/why-is-mitch-mcconnell-picking-this-fight.html?_r=0.

Martin, G. and Contreras, G. (2016). U.S. Supreme Court Justice Antonin Scalia found dead at West Texas Ranch. *My San Antonio*. 2/16/16. Electronic document: http://www.mysanantonio.com/news/us-world/article/Senior-Associate-Justice-Antonin-Scalia-found-6828930.php.

McConnell, M. (2016). Facebook post: https://www.facebook.com/mitchmcconnell/posts/1021148581257166.

Moravec, E. R., Horwitz, S. and Markon, J. (2016). The death of Antonin Scalia: Chaos, confusion, and conflicting reports. *New York Times*. February 14, 2016. Electronic document: https://www.washingtonpost.com/politics/texas-tv-station-scalia-died-of-a-heart-attack/2016/02/14/938e2170-d332-11e5-9823-02b905009f99_story.html.

Munn, N. (1992). The cultural anthropology of time: A critical essay. *Annual Review of Anthropology*, 2, pp.93–123.

National Shrine. Electronic document: http://www.nationalshrine.com/site/c.osJRKVPBJnH/b.4719297/k.BF65/Home.htm.

New York Times. (2016). How long does it take to confirm a Supreme Court nominee? *New York Times*. Electronic document: http://www.nytimes.com/interactive/2016/02/13/us/how-long-does-it-take-to-confirm-a-supreme-court-nominee.html.

Nurik, C. (2016).Ask Factcheck: Obama's funeral attendance. March 17, 2016. Electronic document: http://www.factcheck.org/2016/03/obamas-funeral-attendance/.

Peralta, E. (2016). America: In photos: A short history of official funerals for Supreme Court justices. *National Public Radio*. February 16, 2016. Electronic document:http://www.npr.org/sections/thetwo-way/2016/02/16/466938198/in-photos-a-short-history-of-official-funerals-for-supreme-court-justices.

Pocock, J. G. A. (1989 [1960]). *Politics, Language & Time: Essays on Political Thought and History*. Chicago: University of Chicago Press.

Polanyi, K. (1957 [1944]). *The Great Transformation: The Political and Economic Origins of Our Time*. Boston, MA: Beacon Press.

Pottage, A. (2004). *Our Original Inheritance in Alain Pottage and Martha Mundy*, eds. Law, Anthropology, and the Construction of the Social, pp. 249–285. Cambridge: Cambridge University Press.

Smith, G. A. and Martinez, J. (2016). Pew Research Center – Fact tank: How the faithful voted: A preliminary 2016 analysis. November 9, 2016. Electronic document: http://pewrsr.ch/2fSNWBY.

Weber, M. (1930 [1905]). *The Protestant Ethic and the Spirit of Capitalism. Trans. Talcott Parsons and Anthony Giddens*. London and Boston, MA: Unwin Hyman. Electronic document: https://www.marxists.org/reference/archive/weber/protestant-ethic/ch05.htm.

———. (1946). Politics as a vocation *in* H. H. Gerth and C. Wright Mills Trans. and ed.), *From Max Weber: Essays in Sociology*, pp. 77–128, New York: Oxford University Press.

Electronic document: http://anthropos-lab.net/wp/wp-content/uploads/2011/12/Weber-Politics-as-a-Vocation.pdf.

———. (1978). *Economy and Society: An Outline of Interpretive Sociology.* G. Roth and C. Wittich, eds. E. Fischoff, G. Gerth, A. M. Henderson, F. Kolegar,C. Wright Mills, T. Parsons, M. Rheinstein, G. Roth, E. Shils and C. Wittich, trans. Berkeley: University of California Press.

Wegman, P. (2016). Reinforced by grassroots, Senate Republicans hold line on Supreme Court nomination. *The Daily Signal.* April 4, 2016. Electronic document: http://dailysignal.com/2016/04/04/reinforced-by-grassroots-senate-republicans-hold-line-on-supreme-court-nomination/.

Zoller, E. (2008). *Introduction to Public Law: A Comparative Study.* Amsterdam: Martinus Nijhoff Publishers.

Acknowledgments

I am grateful to Emily Grabham and Siân Beynon-Jones, organizers of the conference on "The New Legal Temporalities? Discipline and Resistance across Domains of Time" at the University of Kent, Canterbury, for generous intellectual hospitality and collegial engagement with an earlier version of this chapter. In that same context, I gratefully acknowledge the contributions of Michelle Bastian, Nadine El-Enany, Sarah Keenan and Kay Lalor. An early version of the paper benefitted from discussion with fellows and staff of the Program in Law and Public Affairs at Princeton. Any errors remain entirely my own.

2 'No. I won't go back'

National time, trauma and legacies of symphysiotomy in Ireland[1]

Máiréad Enright,[2] University of Birmingham

Part of the common sense of the contemporary Irish state is the understanding that we are living in new times: that Ireland has decisively emerged from a past in which church and state power were so tightly intertwined as to be indistinguishable from one another. State responses to gendered religious institutional abuse are crucial to this common sense. Governments point to a public reckoning with a twentieth century history of widespread, systemic and long-lasting abuses in Catholic-run institutions, embodied in cases, judicial and other inquiries, and reports. These 'legacy issues'[3] include the child abuse in religious-run reformatory and industrial schools (Ryan Report, 2009)[4] and in Catholic primary schools (*O'Keeffe v. Ireland*, 2014);[5] church officials' failure to protect children from abuse by parish priests (Ferns Report, 2005 and the Murphy Reports on Dublin 2009 and Cloyne 2011)[6,7]; the incarceration of women in Magdalene Laundries (McAleese Report, 2013); and the maltreatment of unmarried mothers (Luddy, 2011); the fatal neglect of some babies and the forced adoption of others in religious-run 'mother and baby homes' (Mother and Baby Homes Commission, ongoing). Although these institutions were religious-run, their activities fell within the scope of government responsibility; they reflected the formal and informal (Killian, 2015) outsourcing of particular coercive biopolitical functions to a church eager to discipline citizens' sexual and reproductive lives.[8]

This chapter takes the government response to Survivors of Symphysiotomy as an exemplary 'legacy issue'. Survivors of Symphysiotomy (SOS) is the leading advocacy group for elderly Irish women who were subjected to symphysiotomy,[9] a childbirth operation which cuts or tears the *symphysis pubis*, a ligament at the front of the pelvis. It was revived as an elective surgery in Ireland in the 1940s, when it had long died out as a non-emergency practice elsewhere in the developed world, and was practised in some places into the 1980s. Symphysiotomy and its aftermath were often intensely painful.[10] Many women report lifelong incontinence, chronic pain and walking difficulties.[11] Others report depression, post-traumatic stress disorder, sexual dysfunction[12] and damage to family life as a result of ongoing disability.[13] Both SOS and the state accept that symphysiotomy's peculiar Irish history cannot be understood apart from its religious dimensions. However, symphysiotomy's defenders present it as a minor operation, independently justifiable in medical terms, rarely wrongful as such. By contrast, SOS construct it as a form of historical religiously motivated institutionalised obstetric violence, with long-lasting consequences, and directed, like the others mentioned above, at women's sexual and reproductive lives. They argue, and the state has accepted, that doctors generally did not seek women's consent to symphysiotomy.[14] The state had a legal obligation to prevent this treatment[15] and now must investigate it and provide appropriate remedies. The state steadfastly refuses to do so. These women aspire, nevertheless, to make themselves heard; to be, in Felman's vibrantly temporal terms, 'actively and sovereignly reborn from a kind of social death into a new life'(Felman, 2001). 'We might be in our 70s and 80s, but we want the truth. Someone has to say, these operations should never have been done. ... You wouldn't do it to a cow' (Cahill, 2014).

This chapter argues that government responses to SOS are an iteration of an emerging effort to establish and police the boundaries of 'homogenous national time'. The politics of national time underpin and sustain discourses of responsibility for historical abuse. They enable the state to corral certain historicised abuses within a distinct regulatory space and accordingly to achieve 'closure'; limiting the state's responsibility to investigate those abuses or compensate those who suffered them. The first section of this chapter introduces Irish discourses of homogenous national time. The state imagines its history in linear terms, neatly divided into religious past and secular present. Within this imaginary, injuries such as symphysiotomy become 'legacy issues'; leftovers from a different time. I use the idea of legacy to unsettle national time, exposing it as a precarious assemblage wrought out of multiple contradictory timings. There is no clear line between past and present, with symphysiotomy occupying a natural place on one side or the other. Rather, symphysiotomy is implicated in a contested passage of time.

In the chapter's second section, I explore these contestations by drawing out the contrasting histories of symphysiotomy articulated in the government-commissioned Walsh Report, and in the testimonies of SOS's members. Walsh is the official history of symphysiotomy, produced instead of a public inquiry, and the foundation of a subsequent, restrictive, symphysiotomy redress scheme. Walsh naturalises the religious dimensions of symphysiotomy and simultaneously reconstructs it as a legitimate and dignified medical practice. I then locate SOS as irritating the temporal project in Walsh; drawing out their embodied exposure of its contradictions and exclusions. In the third section, introducing the operations of law, I examine the state's policy of inhibiting women's access to the courts, in favour of enforcing 'closure' through a contractual and bureaucratic state redress scheme based on Walsh. Law is doggedly instrumentalised to prevent the transmission of disruptive testimonies and to contain their drag on national time. The state invests remarkable energies in this process. In the final section, I set out the affective stakes for the state of preserving homogenous national time. I turn here to theories of trauma, particularly to Lyotard's idea of the 'double blow', to explain the state's reluctance to engage with symphysiotomy's legacies. I locate the trauma in the unresolved collapse of the state's old relationship with religion as origin of law. Read in this way, national time exceeds political and legal agency. Its threads are also held together by affect surpassing any deliberate settlement. The state's legal manoeuvres then look less like marginal techniques of already settled national time, than a frantic effort to suppress a foundational failure; a violent incapacity.

Ireland, closure and homogenous national time

In the last six years, Fine Gael governments have responded to a range of historical institutional abuses. In doing so, they have cast themselves as founders of a new secular national time, on behalf of the national 'we', which can determine the limits of responsibility for the past. The Ireland of the past, they tell us, was an 'evil' (Donnelly and Inglis, 2010) 'cruel pitiless'[16] collective that used religious institutions to isolate and contain undesirable subjects (Kenny, 2016) Today's Ireland, however, is a changed secular and more authentically Catholic (Sutton, 2012) society; one that is no longer 'morally subservient'[17] to religious power; that cherishes its women (Crowley and Kitchin, 2008); that acknowledges past exclusions as wrongs[18] and seeks to repair them. The national time imagined here is Walter Benjamin's 'empty time'; filled in with the belief in inevitable national progress (Benjamin, 2015). Apologising to women who had been incarcerated in Magdalen Laundries, the Taoiseach, Enda Kenny, said:

> Today we live in a very different Ireland with a very different consciousness [*sic*] awareness – an Ireland where we have more empathy insight heart. We do so because at last we are learning those terrible lessons. We do because at last we are giving up our secrets. We do because in naming and addressing the wrong, as is happening today, we are trying to make sure we quarantine such abject behaviour to our past and eradicate it from Ireland's present and Ireland's future.[19]

The appeal to that unitary 'we' invokes homogenous national time (Anderson, 2006): the nation, as Benedict Anderson elaborates, is presented as 'a solid community moving steadily down (or up) history'(ibid 26) in the same ways and with the same consequences for all. Homogeneity enables a radical break with the past – there are no important stragglers. The triumphant state 'heralds a new dawn'.[20] There is little attempt to examine the ongoing impacts of past abuse[21] or to consider whether the motivations and systems that enabled that abuse have persisted, despite secularisation and social change (Simpson et al., 2014). With these distinctions between times firmly established, the state tells us its primary role is to seek 'closure'.[22] 'Closure' here suggests neatly divided time; periods hang together 'like the beads of a rosary'.[23] The culpable past does not leak into the innocent present. As such, 'closure' signifies a limit to responsibility and accountability – an installation of boundaries between the present state and the wrongdoing of the past; boundaries that are all the more tenuous when we recall that the injuries to be addressed took place within living memory.

As Latour writes, time appears to be a natural resource, passing smoothly under its own irreversible forward momentum (Latour, 2013). For the government, the time of the nation 'passes as if it were really abolishing the past behind it. They all take themselves for Attila, in whose footsteps no grass grows back' (Latour, 2012). But the linear upward transition from one period of national time to the next is not smooth or inevitable. There is a clue in the catch-all governmental term for historical institutional abuses; 'legacy issue'. The word 'legacy' is used carelessly without elaboration; the suggestion is of loose ends that remain at the end of a transition from past to present already almost completed. But legacy is both something transmitted or inherited, perhaps unexpectedly, from the past and something to be bequeathed to live on in the future. Legacies do not only signify death or ending, but the task of carrying on and working through (Haddad, 2013). The nation-state can only continue 'its existence one more turn', gain substance and last in time, because subjects take it up again and again, inheriting from previous occasions.[24] As Derrida wrote, inheritance is always a task, '[a]n inheritance is never gathered together, it is never one with itself ... One must filter, sift, criticize, one must sort out several different possibilities that inhabit the same injunction' (Derrida, 1994). All legacies are divisible and we must choose how we interpret them; how to grapple with their divisions. The impossibility of truly homogenous national time becomes apparent when we read it together with this idea of legacy; to borrow again from Latour, '[w]hat passes is not a stable fixture but a whole moving assemblage of disconnected parts'.[25] Moreover, it is inherently heterogeneous, made up of clusters of different – national, historical, local and personal – timings (Radstone, 2007). Time's passing depends on interpretation; the application of official histories, and legal mechanisms that elevate those histories above competitors and suppress contradictions where necessary. Each cluster of timings is necessarily a locus of alterity and provocation (Simon, 2014). The stable, coherent passage of homogenous national time requires disentanglement, re-combination and binding together of a multiplicity of inherited threads. The combination could always be otherwise. As such, the construction of homogenous national time raises questions of emphasis, representation,[26] assimilation (Allen, 2008) and memorialisation[27] exceeding any simple 'closure'. As an assemblage, national time is never a fixed arrangement. Rather it is always in process, across multiple sites of struggle.

Even a brief initial consideration of SOS's position discloses it as a complex irritant to homogenous national time. This account from one survivor shows the difficulty of encompassing symphysiotomy even within personal linear time, much less distributing it across a neat timeline with clear divisions between past and present. The time of symphysiotomy is simultaneously the time of memory, of future worry, of permanent wounding, of everyday coping, of foreclosed youth and early motherhood:

> I cope with it every day ... you just live with the repercussions, the pain ... [the incontinence] ... I was so sore, I was limping the day I went to see the

> consultant – some winters, and some summers, it would be bad . . . But I'm strong, I'm not going to let it get the better of me. I'm on an anti-depressant . . . You wouldn't do it to a cow, would you? . . . I am still bereaved for that first fortnight in the hospital. I will never get over that . . . You'd see the older women, crippled, in pain all the time, and you'd ask yourself, is that my lot? But you still have to get on with life.[28]

That symphysiotomy is clearly embodied; visibly anchored and retained in elderly women's failing flesh and bones, contains much of its challenge to homogenous national time. SOS, to borrow from Bradiotti, straddles 'time zones' (Braidotti, 2011). Elizabeth Povinelli uses 'carnality' to describe how disciplinary discourses materialise in flesh; these women hold in their aging bodies the signs and marks of past governmental interventions in reproduction. Their injuries are a 'physical mattering forth' of injuries they would attribute to the state (Povinelli, 2006). Their flesh, however, is not reducible to what was done to them in the past'; it is somehow unruly (ibid 30). For example, SOS's appeal to an embodied time of birth and reproduction that is presumptively common to all women carries significant political potential.[29] SOS's demands for reparation clearly resonate with contemporary Irish reproductive rights campaigns; particularly around abortion and maternal death, which focus on the continuing co-imbrication of religion and obstetrics in Ireland.[30] That connection might suggest, in Homi Bhabha's language, the possibility a 'time-lag' (Bhabha, 2012); SOS's appearance threatens to slow down the progress of the nation state, producing a moment of disunity or delay which makes visible the past, impels and projects it, by lending it the quickness of the present. In the process, it reveals the continuities and common gestures that would bind present and past if only they could be encountered in a shared idiom. In its inescapable embodiment, symphysiotomy reveals homogenous national time as something essentially political, precariously assembled, wrought in pain; as something that could be otherwise. 'Closure' requires the state to address and suppress the irritant minor times of symphysiotomy.

Walsh: Suppressing women's times

The state-commissioned Walsh Report (Walsh, 2014), written by a medical historian, has become the definitive official history of symphysiotomy in Ireland from 1944–1987. The state has repeatedly used this report to defend itself against SOS's campaign domestically and in various international fora.[31] For SOS, symphysiotomy as practised in Ireland was a human rights abuse, borne of a particular intermeshing of medical practice and religious belief. SOS's campaign depends on an intermeshing of religion and reproductive medicine, so that symphysiotomy is both obstetric violence *and* religious practice. SOS argues that Catholic activist doctors,[32] working in hospitals that pursued a Catholic ethos,[33] revived and developed symphysiotomy in the 1940s in an attempt to adapt medical practice to Catholic reproductive imperatives. Observant Catholic women who needed one C-section were considered likely to need several. Doctors were concerned that women in this position would try to avoid future repeat sections and so would use artificial contraception to limit their pregnancies.[34] Artificial contraception was illegal for much of the period in which symphysiotomy was practised in Ireland and senior Catholic doctors supported the continuation of this ban. They deliberately deployed symphysiotomy in an attempt to avoid the necessity for the first Caesarean or for 'prophylactic' reasons;[35] to facilitate multiple future vaginal births by permanently widening the pelvis.[36] In subsequent decades, doctors experimented unsuccessfully with symphysiotomy, in an attempt to broaden the range of circumstances in which it could be employed.[37] In so doing, they subjected women to unnecessarily painful and dangerous labour.[38] The Irish elective symphysiotomy, on SOS's account, was a hybrid practice; only explicable by reference to conservative religious belief and delegitimised by its religious underpinnings.

Walsh recuperates symphysiotomy within a universalistic medical narrative, recognisable and transmissible to the present.[39] The report acknowledges symphysiotomy's religious context, but naturalises the religion of the past as a static feature of the clinical landscape, rather than as a dynamic aspect of medical decision-making. Walsh examines symphysiotomy from an 'historic distance'. While it acknowledges that this distance 'should not excuse unacceptable behaviour', it insists that the Irish practice of symphysiotomy can only be assessed according to the accepted standards of the time[40] and understood within the context of Ireland's exceptional historical relationship to Catholicism.[41] Walsh finds that symphysiotomy as practised in Ireland was generally a clinically acceptable operation, developed, refined and revised by a small but prominent group of Irish obstetricians, who vigorously defended it despite external criticism.[42] Doctors did not appreciate the morbidity associated with symphysiotomy by comparison with C-section or did not consider it important to conduct follow-up studies on patients that would have disclosed its long-term effects.[43] They eventually discarded it as new techniques for 'active management of labour' were developed.[44] For Walsh, failure to obtain women's consent to symphysiotomy is a side-effect of essentially benign medical paternalism.[45] Walsh concludes that the only objectionable symphysiotomies were those performed after Caesarean section because these were clearly non-emergency procedures that did not fit the rationale the proponents of symphysiotomy had established through reputable scientific channels; that of facilitating imminent birth.[46] Other symphysiotomies were justifiable as rare emergency response to specific forms of pelvic difficulty in labour[47] in cases where C-section was considered too dangerous or otherwise unacceptable. On the Walsh account, C-sections were considered dangerous or unacceptable in Ireland when they might not have been so considered elsewhere because, for the bulk of the period in which symphysiotomy was practised in Ireland, hospitals followed a rigid Catholic ethos (Earner-Byrne, 2007 and 2010). More importantly, law, following Catholic teaching, forbade contraception and this law could not be transgressed or made otherwise.[48] This position was cemented by lay people's 'willing acceptance' of legal precept.

Women were thus 'slaves to fertility';[49] their lives marked by a 'deep and unquestioning' acceptance of a 'startling level' of external interference.[50] That being the case, women were prone to multiple repeat pregnancies,[51] which doctors believed rendered C-section unsafe by comparison to symphysiotomy. As the Minister for Health summarised, symphysiotomy was 'a clinical response to the limitation *imposed* by specifically Catholic religious and ideological circumstances'.[52] Religious influence here is naturalised; presented as general, sweeping and monolithic – religious power is located in an external 'public apparatus', 'a tacit and unchallenged decree'.

Walsh presents religion as an impenetrable structure, separable from agency in the past, and outside the scope of present responsibility. However, the Walsh account forgets women's burgeoning resistance to church teaching on birth control,[53] particularly from the 1960's onwards. Walsh also downplays the suggestion that the doctors who developed symphysiotomy were an activist minority. Some doctors assisted their patients in obtaining contraception or at least did not practise medicine on the basis that women should not choose to obtain it.[54] In addition, most doctors performed C-sections where they used symphysiotomy.[55] I do not mean to suggest here that C-section is inherently superior to symphysiotomy – women continue to protest the non-consensual imposition of C-sections in Ireland today.[56] Rather, I want to suggest that a plurality of responses to the religious status quo was possible. Walsh, in avoiding these matters, splits the religion of the past from religious subjects' agency; things could not have been otherwise. Religion becomes simultaneously medicine's outside and its past.

By contrast with the enfleshed history advanced by SOS, Walsh is disembodied. It successfully neutralises religious power by disconnecting it from and subordinating it to medical reason. It locates symphysiotomy in the universal, ahistoricised progressive time of scientific development; as a necessary response to religious circumstances since overcome. Walsh is constructed from a range of historical medical literature and hospital statistics.[57] It did not examine personal medical records.[58] It only drew on a small number of survivors' testimony[59] because members of SOS boycotted the interviews. They did this to protest a draft report, published in 2012, which established the report's main conclusions before survivors were consulted (Hennessy, 2013). Whether or not this could have been helped, Walsh, accordingly, adopts a top-down medical systemic framing of symphysiotomy, in which the operation is understood primarily in terms of management of populations of pregnant women and enhancement of medical knowledge. There is, of course, a rich feminist literature charting how deference to gynaecological and obstetric reasoning is secured by suppressing and downplaying women's embodied experience of medical interventions.[60] Materials prepared by SOS for submission to the UN Committee Against Torture are littered with vivid and immediate memories of symphysiotomy:

> The smell of it, the anaesthetic, I couldn't breathe. It was a miracle I was alive. I was left so long in labour, I'd have been alright if they did a

> [Caesarean] section [in the beginning], it wouldn't have been so bad ... I'd like them [the doctors] to go through it, to see how it felt. I didn't want to live ... I can still feel the cold of that labour ward today. They didn't say anything about the pelvis, they didn't say anything about the pelvis bone. They left me with half a back.[61]
>
> I fainted with the pain, it was like walking on thorns, the pain and the soreness. I got no help, no, no help whatsoever from them [in hospital] ... [At home], the wound was discharging; there was a terrible smell. I dosed it with Dettol. There was no nurse [to look after me]. I remember, it was the winter, the pain in my back [was so bad], it would be a fine thing to be dead, I thought.[62]

The women who experienced this pain have deeply textured memories of the exercise of religious authority. They recall it not as an abstract monolithic generality, but as a direct, intersubjective practice of power,[63] bound up in the practice of medicine and directed at the justifying and legitimating of pain:

> I normally do a Caesarean section, [the doctor] said, but because you are such a good Catholic, I'll do a symphysiotomy, you're a Catholic family, you'd be expected to have at least ten – if you have a Caesarean, you can only have three. And, as a Catholic, you need to go through the pains of childbirth – if you had a Caesarean, you wouldn't. [64]
>
> [Dr] Feeney came in ... He took off his beige leather gloves and coat – he was after being at Mass ... Feeney was very abrupt. You can have ten children, all normal, he said. Who wants ten children, I said ... They did it without my permission ... I was cut from the navel down ... We were Catholics, but my mother's people were Church of Ireland. Protestants would only have three children, at most.[65]

SOS's testimony provoked the state to produce, via Walsh, a public memory or official history that attempts to restore past and present to equilibrium, in the process de-authorising women's memories. Walsh de-legitimises and displaces ways of knowing about the past which do not fit the state's agenda (Freeman, 2010), in the process denying the economy of violence (Osborne, 1995) that underlies the smooth passage of homogenous national time. Just as collective forgetting (McAlinden, 2013) and destruction of memory[66] enabled the abuse of women and children decades ago, so too women's disruptive stories of that abuse must be muted. This muting continues when women seek an encounter with law.

SOS and the denial of access to law

In July 2014, SOS made representations to the UN Human Rights Committee, during Ireland's periodic examination under the ICCPR. The Committee found that symphysiotomy, as performed in Ireland, breached women's rights under

Article 7 ICCPR in that they were subjected to forced medical experimentation and torture and inhuman and degrading treatment. They were entitled, under Article 2 ICCPR to an investigation of this breach and to an effective remedy. The Committee recommended that Ireland should re-engage symphysiotomy's legacies:

> [I]nitiate a prompt, independent and thorough investigation into cases of symphysiotomy, prosecute and punish the perpetrators ... and provide the survivors of symphysiotomy with an effective remedy for the damage sustained, including fair and adequate compensation and rehabilitation, on an individualized basis.[67]

In July 2014, following publication of Walsh, the state established a non-statutory *ex gratia* redress scheme. The scheme's design drew extensively on Walsh (O'Carroll, 2013). However, it also considered the possibility that women would wish to go to court to contest the Walsh narrative – particularly its finding that symphysiotomies performed otherwise than immediately after a C-section were generally acceptable. By early 2014, 150 members of SOS had begun cases in the High Court, and others intended to commence actions.[68] The courts were considered a last resort. SOS campaigned for a collective settlement of their claims with individualised compensation payments between 250,000 and 400,000 euros each,[69] together with an official government statement of wrongdoing.[70] The redress scheme was administered by a retired judge; Maureen Harding-Clarke. However, it was entirely paper-based, centred on production of medical records rather than personal narrative and provided no opportunity for public reconsideration of the Walsh narrative or individual attention to women's experiences.[71] Neither was any statement of wrongdoing forthcoming from the government. The retired judge, Yvonne Murphy, who designed the scheme, did not cost or explore SOS's proposal or discuss the demand for further public dialogue. She proceeded on the assumption that the state had two options. The first was to prepare to defend High Court actions, on behalf of hospitals. Assuming 10 women succeeded in court, and a significant number of remaining cases were settled, the state would face expenses relating to costs and damages[72] of 95 million euros.[73] The second option was to reduce the number of actions by offering a redress scheme, allowing for much smaller payments than SOS had asked for, with women who had symphysiotomies otherwise than after C-section entitled to between 50,000 and 100,000 euros.[74] This was a significant discount on the amount that many women would be entitled to if successful in court.[75] The cost of such a scheme was estimated at 35 million euros.[76] In the end, the scheme paid out less.[77] SOS members' initially voted to reject the redress scheme, condemning 'paternalistic'[78] government efforts to strip survivors of their legal rights. They described the scheme as an attempt to 'blindfold' women; 'an opaque and close-ended process designed to lure them away from their legal actions'.[79] They perceived similarities in the state's treatment of other institutional abuse survivors.[80] Nevertheless, most members of SOS were among the 563 women who submitted applications for redress and most who received offers under the scheme accepted them.

Only 28 women were still involved in High Court actions at the close of the redress scheme. A handful of cases have made it to hearing. The first, *Kearney*,[81] successful in the High and Supreme Courts, pre-dates the redress scheme's establishment and is a case of post-Caesarean symphysiotomy. Another ended when the claimant died (O'Carroll, 2014), a third settled (O'Carroll, 2015) and a fourth, *Farrell*,[82] lost in the High Court and the Court of Appeal in 2016.[83] There are, of course, several problems with symphysiotomy litigation. First, private litigation individualises harm:[84] cases are decided 'on their own facts', in ways which necessarily occlude the structural dimensions of an evolving decades-long medical practice. Second, it is not possible to litigate the issue of consent because, in the decades since symphysiotomies were routinely practised, memories and records have degraded and key actors have died.[85] Courts will not attempt to determine what a woman was told at the time of her operation. Third, because the consent question is not tried, symphysiotomy is not framed as violence. Instead it is medical negligence; an insufficiency of skill or care or an inappropriate professional response to risk.[86] The court will ask whether the plaintiff's doctor's practice accorded with some school of medical thought at the time. Doctors' open discussion of their trial-and-error experimentation in elite journals and forums is treated as sufficient evidence of controlled and well-regulated practice.[87] That international peers or a majority of Irish colleagues[88] disapproved of the practice is irrelevant, as long as it was not outright condemned.[89] The old legal position on contraception distinguishes Irish obstetrics from its English equivalent.[90] Majority disagreement with a minority school of thought is evidence of medical pluralism, rather than of defective practice.[91] Finally, doctors' failure to appreciate the morbidity associated with symphysiotomy is not condemned, even where they do not appear to have reflected on or studied previous patients' long-term experiences over the preceding 15 years (Khaleeli, 2014) or listened to them when they reported pain and incapacity in the immediate aftermath of the operation. At first blush, then, the courts are a space in which symphysiotomy is again framed as a relatively benign medical practice, to be assessed on the same terms as any other.[92] Religious issues are barely noted, if at all, and women's bodily experience is again subordinated to medical knowledge. Symphysiotomy claims are not incommensurable with prevailing legal forms: they are readily enclosed and summed up in known precedent, pre-structured by them (Adjin-Tettey, 2007). The few decided cases, however, cannot tell us what arguments might have been made if the state's deployment of the redress scheme had been less effective. In addition, these cases' shortcomings do not in themselves legitimate the state's refusal to establish a more expansive public inquiry, as SOS requested. Rather they speak to the limitations of any response to past harm which asks survivors to choose between bureaucratic redress and limited private actions.

Although the courts have been inhospitable to symphysiotomy claims, the state has actively sought to deter symphysiotomy litigation and induce conformity with the aims of the redress scheme. Minister of State Kathleen Lynch observed: 'If someone wants to go to the courts ... there is nothing anyone can do about that; clearly, that is the person's choice.'[93] Nevertheless, the government made use of legal devices that radically compressed the time available for decision-making and for resistance. First, the government rejected proposed legislation that would have lifted the Statute of Limitations in symphysiotomy cases.[94] As a result, women can only succeed in court if they can show that they instituted proceedings within two years of the 'date of knowledge' of their injury. Second, as a condition of accepting a payment under the redress scheme, participants must waive all other legal claims against the state and other potentially culpable bodies.[95] Finally, applicants were initially given just 20 days to apply to the scheme. This time limit for application was extended in 27 cases. Consequently, women who were considering litigation could not wait to assess the outcome of test cases before deciding whether to settle for a redress payment.[96] The decision between redress and litigation became too urgent to resist; the threat of litigation was often extinguished. These deployments of law accelerated the upward movement of national time; preventing it from folding back on itself (Radstone, 2007), keeping challenges in their place.

The application of these legal temporal devices both hastened women's decisions and produced SOS's claims as always 'out of time' for the courts. SOS's litigants had made a claim to be heard individually; to unfold their personal narratives within the official time of law; to access a slow, sovereign time of oral exchange and normative deliberation (Valverde, 2015). As we have seen, the few symphysiotomy judgments achieved have abbreviated and limited women's experience of symphysiotomy, enmeshing them again within totalising medico-legal frames. But the lawsuits, while they were maintained in being, performed a strategic function. The women had successfully suspended their claims within that costly, weighty temporality: insisting on and maintaining litigation in parallel to the state's proposals. The state, however, by invoking a series of technical legal devices, compelled them to recalibrate to its time, and engage with a different, faster, more 'efficient' bureaucratic world (Grabham, 2016).

There is an increasing sense in which Irish governments apply different legal tactics to 'legacy issues' than to claims that have their origins in more recent injuries. The 'legacy issue' is emerging as a distinct set of governmental practices. Limited investigations, followed by *ex gratia* redress schemes have become the hallmark of this government's response to 'legacy issues'. This was the approach taken to the Magdalene women's claims (Enright, 2015) and to survivors of abuse in residential institutions. Similarly, in addressing 'legacy issues' elsewhere, the government has been accused of aggressively discouraging litigation[97] and of facilitating religious perpetrators in evading their financial responsibilities to people who were abused while under their care.[98] The effect of this emergent regime is that an injury cannot be simultaneously the product of Ireland's religious past and a cause of action in the new time of the secular present. On its own account, the government is acting in women's best interests by placing obstacles in the path of litigation (O'Carroll, 2014). It presents them as litigants made vulnerable by old age,[99] whose advisors have exposed them to stress of court appearances and the risk of costs, while exaggerating their chances of success in court.[100] Women are entitled to care and consideration, or at least the public performance of it, but not to contest the terms on which that performance takes place. In 2013, for example, the Minister for Health reported that he had 'listened closely to the testimony of the women [members of SOS]' and been 'moved by them'.[101] Yet, as Matilda Behan, a founder of SOS, noted while reflecting on these encounters: 'I was with [the Minister for Health] before Christmas and told him my story. [H]e said it was [t]errible. But sure that's as far as it goes.'[102] Felman, borrowing from Benjamin, might say that the state makes women 'expressionless' in the present: those 'whom violence has treated in their lives as though they were already dead, those who have been made (in life) without expression, without a voice and without a face' (Felman, 2002). Women's claims are colonised by law, but not open to the opportunities that law might provide for hearing and contestation.

Closure, affect and the 'double blow'

What drives the state's refusal to allow SOS access to law? Elizabeth Freeman notes that certain affects 'inhere in shared timings'.[103] The history of the nation, understood as shared time appears as 'a mirror in which a fragmented, fractious, injured community sees itself as beautiful, coherent, happy' (Christodoulidis and Veitch, 2001; Douzinas, 2012). SOS, by its difficult representations of the past, by its apparent anger and ingratitude, threaten to disfigure the beautiful order which holds the time of the nation together.[104] In order to see itself as beautiful, fractures and injuries must be silenced and forgotten. I want to suggest that the state's response to SOS can be conceptualised as the response of an 'injured' or 'traumatised' community. Before proceeding, I should say that in conceptualising that response as 'traumatised', I do not mean to repeat the state's transferral of women's bodily experiences onto the purportedly homogenous body of the nation.[105] The trauma at play here is not the kind of direct experience of religious violence that survivors of symphysiotomy suffered. Instead, I rely on something akin to Ragland-Sullivan's Lacanian conceptualisation of trauma as 'the appearance of a void in being and knowledge': a brush with the 'real'.[106] Trauma here entails not necessarily a physical wounding, but that some fantasy that enables the cohesion of the nation has been punctured and an emptiness in meaning – an abyss, a chaos – appears in its place.[107] An 'ego-ideal', which combines an idealised self-image with the values of one's parents is lost (Khanna, 2013). National trauma need not be associated with a single overwhelming rupture, but with a gradual progression of events as in contexts of colonialism or occupation (Lloyd, 200). In the Irish context, this trauma might centre on the devastating failure of the legal and constitutional settlement between church and state power. In one of his 'legacy issue' apologies, the Taoiseach gestured to this trauma:

> This is not Rome. Nor is it industrial-school or Magdalene Ireland, where the swish of a soutane smothered conscience and humanity and the swing of a thurible ruled the Irish-Catholic world. This is the 'Republic' of Ireland 2011. A Republic of laws ... of rights and responsibilities ... of proper civic order ... Those who have been abused can take some small comfort in knowing that they belong to a nation, to a democracy where humanity, power, rights, responsibility are enshrined and enacted, always ... always ... for their good. Where the law – their law – as citizens of this country, will always supersede canon laws that have neither legitimacy nor place in the affairs of this country.

The promise of law, as Juliet Rogers writes, is that we shall have its love (Rogers, 2011a) and through that love a certain freedom (Rogers, 2007). Only those who break that law will be brutalised. The new Irish state was built on an ideal of reconciliation of governmental power to religious precept, which promised to create a well-regulated, virtuous, prosperous and presumptively masculine nation.[108] Its terrible failure was apparent throughout the twentieth century in a quotidian experience of physical violence, shame and sacrificial destruction of lives.[109] Memories of symphysiotomy – with their atmosphere of menacing religious institutional power, uncertainty, uncanny absence of care and sudden violence – instantiate that failure. Desires for a particular kind of shared religious life under law entangled the nation-state in its own traumatic wounding (Mbembe, 2915). In intimate and family life, it created direct complicity and experiences of powerlessness between husbands and parents and religious agents of violence.[110] Belief in the good faith of law and religion was duly undone.

In positing this trauma as a route to framing the state's response to symphysiotomy, I am guided by the state's determined suppression of women's efforts to make legal claims around religious power and obstetric violence. Silences, and the mutilations of language and of law, that accompany them, are the 'cryptic enclaves' left behind by trauma (Schwab, 2010). Trauma is unlike any other loss because it is overwhelming; (Herman, 2015) it utterly objectifies the subject,[111] breaching its shields and barriers (Luckhurst, 2013). Trauma confounds and numbs the senses,[112] so that it is not 'fully perceived as it occurs' (Caruth, 1995). Because trauma is not fully perceived, it resists the normal operations of political discourse: we cannot speak of it in the normal scheme of things (Roth, 2013) and we do not remember it as we remember other losses.

Lyotard's notion of trauma as a 'double blow' (Lyotard, 1990) is instructive in understanding the relationship between trauma and suppression of survivor voices. On this reading, trauma does not make its mark at the time.[113] It is not that it is never seen at all, but that it cannot be absorbed and represented at first; it is not seen 'in time'. Because the initial trauma is a shock that cannot be registered or experienced it cannot be made the site of this sort of rebuilding.[114] In the absence of this mourning, the nation becomes melancholically attached to the past traumatic injury. Instead of being re-externalised, the trauma is incorporated by silencings, which displace its core meaning. Silencing here is more than a withholding of facts, a 'being silent about'.[115] Ronell captures the destructive agency at play when she writes of 'the eye that has seen too much and that has blinded itself'.[116] Silencing of aspects of the past, however violent, enables the nation to survive the trauma – self-deception becomes the necessary price of persistence and social unity.[117] Trauma, in this sense, can be said to reconfigure national time. Because it ensures that trauma cannot be communicated as other remembered experiences can, trauma radically disrupts temporal continuity between the present and an aspect of the past.[118] At the same time, trauma is not a simple rupture between past and present because trauma's effects persist as repetitions in the present; more present fact than past wound (Olkowski, 1999). Silencing does not effectively disappear the trauma or sever our attachment to the past. What is silenced, and thus left unencountered, is often ultimately reinscribed and repeated[119] in an effort to recapture a sense of the wholeness taken from us by trauma.[120] Trauma becomes 'indestructible' (Ricoeur, 2009). It continues to intrude into national life.[121]

The 'double blow' frames the relationship between trauma, silence and repetition. The first blow cannot be registered or mourned. But it may return as a second blow – a symptom that makes the first blow known – forcing 'a breach in the flow of time that the imagination – the faculty that synthesises the heterogeneous – normally ensures' (Gressgård, 2013). Some details of the trauma are suddenly made known in breathtaking detail, while others are obscured (Young, 2006; Rogers, 2011b). On the terms of my argument, SOS's testimony to pain and fear and degradation, and their insistence on the origins of that pain – not in the necessary operations of medicine but in the power afforded to religious agents by an enabling state – is the second blow. Their public claims do not enact a new trauma, but belatedly resurrect an older one. They signal the return of something missed the first time, insinuating past injury into the future. That is why they cannot be allowed to access sites of public meaning-making such as litigation. The second blow, although it does not produce shock, produces affect; it commands 'flight' – an effort to leave the scene. The second blow comes back from the (lost) traumatic first; what happened in the past takes effect in the present. National time then forcefully and obviously appears as otherwise than chronological: 'the present is the past and … the past is always present.'[122] The second blow is almost 'incompatible with time'.[123] It makes national time seem 'a bit monstrous, unformed, confusing, confounding', menacing.[124] This upset in time produces a desire in the state to recoil from the unknown, but at the same time the desire to reorder it; to resolve the discrepancy between the time of the first blow and that of the second and 'inscribe them on the line of a single and uniform history':[125]

> The decision to analyse, to write, to historicize is made according to different stakes ... but it is taken, in each case, against this formless mass, and in order to lend it form, a place in space, a moment in temporal succession, a quality in the spectrum of qualifications, representation on the scene of the various imaginaries and sentences.[126]

The second blow signals that something has happened that cannot be managed, but that nevertheless provokes totalising, homogenising responses.-[127] The first blow cannot successfully be neutralised or contained; it will always exceed responses to the second blow. And yet every attempt will be made to sacrifice and suppress it; to close the gap that it has opened in homogenous national time. Lyotard would call this process of silencing a *differend*: The state refuses any encounter between the law of the state that might generate a 'disjuncture of the present with itself' (Chakrabarty, 2009).

This analysis offers some insight into the state's determination to deny SOS access to litigation in favour of a contained redress scheme. Assessment was on the basis of written statements and medical records. Medical records were always preferred to reports from women's current doctors, and discrepancies between these and the women's statements were examined by the scheme's own medical advisors. Where records were not available, scar and radiology evidence was sought (Harding-Clark, 2016). The scheme acknowledged that records were often not available and often not reliable even where they could be found. It also acknowledged that scar evidence and radiography were not definitive, particularly where it was sought to prove the degree of seriousness of a woman's injury.[128] Nevertheless, women were not given an opportunity to be heard orally. Even though the redress scheme's own evidentiary processes showed the incoherence of its mission, what mattered was that the state chose the standard against which women's claims about the past would be measured. In Lyotard's words '[O]ur institutionalised idioms, our verification procedures, our mechanisms for adjudicating truth, [pre-establish] the realities whose truth we then assert' (Schlag, 1998).

SOS members are stripped of the right to testify to the harm done to them or that testimony is stripped of authority (Lyotard, 1988). The violence involved in the suppression of the *differend* becomes apparent when Maureen Harding-Clarke, who had administered the redress scheme, produced a report on its operation. The report was adopted by the government; the Minister for Justice called it 'fair' and 'comprehensive'.[129] Several senior doctors welcomed its conclusions. The report largely re-asserts the Walsh history. Its particular contribution is to support that history, by denying SOS's authority to contest it. It describes women in language that both undermines their engagement with the scheme and their entitlement to characterise their injuries at all. At best, they are patronised as 'suggestive personalities',[130] 'amenable to ... emotional contagion'[131] and subject to 'acquired group memory'[132] developed through involvement in campaigning organisations:

> [I]t is very probable that the combination of a traumatic birth experience and exposure[133] to other women's stories has created a self-convincing confabulation of personal history. Another inference is that the possibility of financial payment has influenced suggestible women and their family members into self-serving adoption and embracing of the experiences described by others or in the media and created psychosomatic conditions.[134]

At worst women are chastised for buying into 'conspiracy theories',[135] for 'unreasonable' reactions, for their anger and disappointment.[136] Harding-Clarke maintained that 185 applicants to the scheme had not been able to prove they had undergone symphysiotomy.[137] She describes those applicants to the scheme who engaged with campaigners in highly problematic language, suggesting that their applications to the scheme bore similar 'lurid' or 'harrowing' motifs gleaned from media reports.[138] The report suggests that some prominent campaigners within SOS who 'have been active in representing themselves as victims in the media'[139] had not undergone symphysiotomies at all. The condemnation of campaigners is underscored by contrast with the report's account of ideal applicants: happy women concerned with family rather than campaigning, who are spending money on 'spoiling themselves', rather than on the amelioration of pain and disability:

> I was ultimately glad that most exaggerated accounts were ignored and compassion was applied to these women who perhaps were influenced by others to make the statements. This led to some of the more pleasurable moments as judicial assessor when I read the warm letters and notes from the women who wrote to me after they received their awards to tell me that they were certainly intent on spoiling themselves a little. Several very happy applicants rang to tell me how they were going to spend their money. One lady was buying a special hat. One applicant lifted my heart when she told me that she had never had any money in her savings account. Now she looked at her bank account every morning, for the sheer pleasure of seeing the amount of money in the account in her own name. One delightful applicant invited me to tea at her house and one wrote a poem of appreciation. Most women who wrote, told me that it gave them huge pleasure to be able to help their children or their grandchildren with their awards.

The Harding-Clarke report, written to justify confining SOS members to the redress scheme which silences those injuries, then condemns them for participating in that scheme in certain disobedient or political ways; for refusing to share in the 'good feeling' of the redress scheme (Ahmed, 2014). The effect is that the scheme has effectively held women's account of the past at bay as 'unthought knowledge';[140] inaccessible but waiting to be known; a 'record that has yet to be made' (Felman and Laub, 2013). The space of the *differend* is an unstable state, signalled by feeling, 'wherein something which must be able to be put into phrases cannot yet be' (Lyotard, 2006); which has no place in the prevailing time. SOS are 'stranded with an unprovable reality' (Ronell, 2005).

Conclusion: Law, unease and national time

In the case of symphysiotomy, national time is worked out over women's bodies, through the violent suppression of their temporal knowledge and experience. SOS is denied the encounter with law demanded and consigned to a slower time of endurance: 'Sometimes I think [the campaign] is dead in the water, then at other times, I think someone should have been made answerable.'[141] That stolid endurance does not imply failure. The radical insight of trauma theory is that the state's violent deployment of law does not necessarily imply a restoration of state sovereignty over that knowledge or its seamless reintegration into the narratives that undergird homogenous national time. SOS's continuing counter-demand for public inquiry is, in Lyotard's terms, a demand for 'anamnesis'; a 'painful process of working through, a work of mourning for attachments and conflicting emotions, loves and terrors associated with [particular] names' (Lyotard, Massumi and Nieslu-chowski, 1988). Whereas history aims to tell what happened, anamnesis 'let's itself be led by the unknown that happened then, by what is unpredictable and invisible in the event ... The past is not sought in order to be established' (Lyotard and Ronan, 1999). Anamnesis might redeem past injury through paying attention to the exclusions of national time, although it cannot repair it (Habermas, 2015). The state is determined to make law unavailable to this process. This discloses a persistent unease and inadequacy at the core of Irish law's relationship with religion and national time. What holds or drives law's relationship to national time in contexts such as these is not the ordered steadiness of progress, but the flight away from an unapproachable past.

Notes

1 Land ... where time is time past.
A palsy of regrets.
No. I won't go back.
My roots are brutal.
Eavan Boland 'Mise Eire'.

2 This chapter was developed as a paper at the Beatrice Baine Reading Group, UC Berkeley, and as part of the ESRC-funded Public Life of Private Law seminar series. Thanks to colleagues for their comments and questions. Thanks also to Marie O'Connor and Ruadhan Mac Aodhan of Survivors of Symphysiotomy (SOS): this paper draws, in particular, on Marie O'Connor, *Bodily Harm: Symphysiotomy and Pubiotomy in Ireland, 1944–92* (Evertype 2011); and on Marie O'Connor and Ruadhan Mac Aodhain, 'Survivors of Symphysiotomy to the UN Committee Against Torture' (2014) 35–40; http://cdn.thejournal.ie/media/2014/03/symphysiotomy-submission-to-uncat-10-march-2014.pdf accessed 14 August 2016, discussed within.

3 See e.g. 'National Report Submitted in Accordance with Paragraph 5 of the Annex to Human Rights Council Resolution 16/21* - Ireland.' 6; http://www.upr.ie/Web

site/UPR/uprweb.nsf/page/DOJL-A97JFV1512120-en/$file/National%20Report %20IE%20Cycle%202.pdf accessed 14 August 2016. Dáil Deb 17 Jul 2014; Dáil Deb 2 Feb 2016; Dáil Deb 14 Aug 2016.

4 'The Commission to Inquire into Child Abuse'; http://childabusecommission.ie/ accessed 2 August 2016. The Commission was chaired first by Ms Justice Mary Laffoy and then by Mr Justice Sean Ryan. See further John Bergin, 'Dysfunctional Organization? Institutional Abuse of Children in Care in Ireland.' (2007) 4 *Journal of Management, Spirituality & Religion* 461.Carol Brennan, 'Trials and Contestations: Ireland's Ryan Commission' in Johanna Sköld and Shurlee Swain (Eds.), *Apologies and the Legacy of Abuse of Children in 'Care'* (Palgrave Macmillan 2015); http://link.springer.com/chapter/10.1057/9781137457554_5 accessed 31 July 2016. Fred Powell and others, 'The Irish Charity Myth, Child Abuse and Human Right,s: Contextualising the Ryan Report into Care Institutions' (2013) 43 *British Journal of Social Work* 7.Sinead Pembroke, 'The Role of Industrial Schools and Control over Child Welfare in Ireland in the Twentieth Century' (2013) 21 *Irish Journal of Sociology* 52.

5 Conor O'Mahony, 'State Liability for Abuse in Primary Schools: Systemic Failure and *O'Keeffe v. Hickey*' (2009) 28 *Irish Educational Studies* 315. James Gallen, 'O'Keeffe v Ireland: The Liability of States for Failure to Provide an Effective System for the Detection and Prevention of Child Sexual Abuse in Education' (2015) 78 *Modern Law Review* 151.

6 The inquiry was chaired by former judge Francis Murphy. ibid.

7 'Commission of Investigation,Dublin Archdiocese, Catholic Diocese of Cloyne'; http://www.dacoi.ie/ accessed 2 August 2016. The inquiries were chaired by former judge Yvonne Murphy.

8 On the Irish church's role as institutionalised moral disciplinarian, see Claire McLoone-Richards, 'Say Nothing! How Pathology within Catholicism Created and Sustained the Institutional Abuse of Children in 20th Century Ireland' (2012) 21 *Child Abuse Review* 394. And Una Crowley and Rob Kitchin, 'Producing "decent Girls": Governmentality and the Moral Geographies of Sexual Conduct in Ireland (1922–1937)' (2008) 15 *Gender, Place & Culture* 355

9 'SOS Ireland – Survivors of Symphysiotomy'; http://symphysiotomyireland.com/ accessed 31 May 2015. The organisation was founded in 2002. It is survivor-led and run on democratic principles. SOS pursues a variety of activities aimed at building solidarity and raising consciousness of the wrongfulness of symphysiotomy among survivors. SOS is often described as one of three patient representative groups; the other two are Patient Focus and Survivors of Symphysiotomy Ltd. These organisations are funded directly by the Health Services Executive (HSE), have a much smaller membership, and tend to adopt policy positions that are antagonistic to those advanced by SOS, suggesting division among survivors where, often, this is not the case. See e.g. 'Symphysiotomy Redress Scheme Criticised' (*RTE.ie*); http://www.rte.ie/news/2014/0911/ 642929-symphysiotomy/ accessed 31 May 2015. For instance, Patient Focus rejected the UN Human Rights Committee's July 2014 criticism of the government's policy on symphysiotomy Laurence Lee, 'Battling Insensitivity over Symphysiotomy' (*Al Jazeera Blogs*, 19 November 2014); http://blogs.aljazeera.com/blog/ europe/battling-insensitivity-over-symphysiotomy accessed 31 May 2015.(see further infra) They also welcomed the redress scheme discussed infra., when SOS have strongly criticised it for the reasons discussed below. Paul Cullen, 'More than 360 Apply for Symphysiotomy Redress Scheme' *Irish Times* (6 December 2014); http://www.irishtimes.com/news/health/more-than-360-apply-for-symphysiotomy-redress-scheme-1.2027914 accessed 31 May 2015.

10 O'Connor and Mac Aodhain (n 1) 9.

11 ibid 11–13.

12 ibid 13.

13 ibid; Irene Jillson, 'Symphysiotomy in Ireland: A Qualitiative Study' (Georgetown University 2012) 16–18; http://www.patientfocus.ie/site/images/uploads/SYMPHYSIOTOMY_IN_IRELAND_By_Irene_Jillson_PhD.pdf accessed 14 August 2016.
14 O'Connor and Mac Aodhain (n 1) 9. Yvonne Murphy, 'Independent Review of Issues Relating to Symphysiotomy' (2014) 21; http://health.gov.ie/wp-content/uploads/2014/07/Scanned-Murphy-report-redacted-version1.pdf accessed 18 August 2016.
15 *Alyne da Silva Pimentel Teixeira (deceased) v. Brazil*, CEDAW, UN Doc CEDAW/C/49/D/17/2008 (2011). See further Juan Méndez, *UN Special Rapporteur on Torture: Report on Abuses in Healthcare Settings* UN Doc. A/HRC/22/53 (2013), 6.
16 'Taoiseach Enda Kenny's Statement on Magdalene Report'. http://static.rasset.ie/documents/news/kenny-magdelene-speech.pdf accessed 3 August 2016.
17 'Taoiseach Enda Kenny's Statement on Magdalene Report' (n 22). On apology as allowing us to feel shame and therefore to feel better, see Ahmed Sara Ahmed, *The Cultural Politics of Emotion* (Routledge 2013) 101–121.
18 'Taoiseach Enda Kenny's Statement on Magdalene Report' (n 22).
19 'Taoiseach Enda Kenny's Statement on Magdalene Report' (n 22).
20 'Taoiseach Enda Kenny's Statement on Magdalene Report' (n 22).
21 'Taoiseach Enda Kenny's Statement on Magdalene Report' (n 22).
22 Paul Michael Garrett, 'A "Catastrophic, Inept, Self-Serving" Church? Re-Examining Three Reports on Child Abuse in the Republic of Ireland' (2013) 24 *Journal of Progressive Human Services* 43. *Kate Kenny, 'Affective Disruption: Walter Benjamin and the "History" of Ireland's Industrial Schools' (2013) 8 Management & Organizational History* 10.
23 Benjamin (n 28).
24 Latour (n 37) 43–44.
25 Latour (n 37) 50.
26 Glynn, Evelyn (n 7) 38. *Erin Costello Wecker, 'Reclaiming Magdalenism or Washing Away Sin: Magdalen Laundries and the Rhetorics of Feminine Silence' (2015) 44 Women's Studies* 264.
27 Glynn, Evelyn (n 7) 37. Fintan Walsh, 'Transforming Shame and Testimonial Performance', *Queer Performance and Contemporary Ireland* (Palgrave Macmillan 2016);http://link.springer.com/chapter/ 10.1057/9781137534507_4 accessed 1 August 2016. Gabriella Calchi-Novati, 'Irish Biopolitics and National (Un)Consciousness: Gerard Mannix Flynn's Public Performances of Inclusion' in Jade Rosina McCutcheon and Barbara Sellers-Young (Eds.), *Embodied Consciousness* (Palgrave Macmillan 2013); http://link.springer.com/chapter/10.1057/9781137320056_10 accessed 1 August 2016. Kate Antosik-Parsons, 'Suppressed Voices: The Suffering and Silencing of Irish Institutional Abuse Survivors in Áine Phillips's Redress Performances' [2014] *Études irlandaises* 137. Sheila McCormick, 'The Darkest Corner: Documenting Institutional Abuse and Its Consequences at the Abbey Theatre' (2012) 20 *Irish Studies Review* 179. Miriam Haughton, 'From Laundries to Labour Camps: Staging Ireland's "Rule of Silence" in Anu Productions' Laundry' (2014) 57 *Modern Drama* 65.
28 Glynn, Evelyn (n 7) 37. Fintan Walsh, 'Transforming Shame and Testimonial Performance', *Queer Performance and Contemporary Ireland* (Palgrave Macmillan 2016);http://link.springer.com/chapter/10.1057/9781137534507_4 accessed 1 August 2016. Gabriella Calchi-Novati, 'Irish Biopolitics and National (Un)Consciousness: Gerard Mannix Flynn's Public Performances of Inclusion' in Jade Rosina McCutcheon and Barbara Sellers-Young (Eds.), *Embodied Consciousness* (Palgrave Macmillan 2013); http://link.springer.com/chapter/10.1057/9781137320056_10

accessed 1 August 2016. Kate Antosik-Parsons, 'Suppressed Voices: The Suffering and Silencing of Irish Institutional Abuse Survivors in Áine Phillips's Redress Performances' [2014] *Études irlandaises* 137. Sheila McCormick, 'The Darkest Corner: Documenting Institutional Abuse and Its Consequences at the Abbey Theatre' (2012) 20 *Irish Studies Review* 179. Miriam Haughton, 'From Laundries to Labour Camps: Staging Ireland's "Rule of Silence" in Anu Productions' Laundry' (2014) 57 *Modern Drama* 65.

29 See e.g. Kristeva, 'Stabat Mater' in Susan Rubin Suleiman (ed.), *The Female Body in Western Culture: Contemporary Perspectives* (Harvard University Press 1986). Early in SOS's campaign, one member insisted that if the Minister for Health, then a woman, 'was in my body even for one day we would have [a political response] the next day'. Eithne Donnellan, 'Group Calls for Cowen to Dismiss Harney' (*The Irish Times*); http://www.irishtimes.com/news/group-calls-for-cowen-to-dismiss-harney-1.624128 accessed 10 April 2017.

30 See for example Amnesty International, 'She Is Not a Criminal: The Impact of Ireland's Abortion Law' 15; https://www.amnesty.org.uk/sites/default/files/she_is_not_a_criminal_report_-_embargoed_09_june.pdf accessed 18 August 2016. 'How and Where Your Baby Is Born – Who Gets to Decide?'; http://aimsireland.ie/how-and-where-your-baby-is-born-who-gets-to-decide/ accessed 20 August 2016.

31 See e.g. 'Additional Responses Following Ireland's Appearance before the Human Rights Committee, July 14–15 2014' (2014) 11; http://tbinternet.ohchr.org/_layouts/treatybodyexternal/Download.aspx? symbolno=INT%2fCCPR%2fAIS%2fIRL%2f17669&Lang=en accessed 14 August 2016. 'National Report Submitted in Accordance with Paragraph 5 of the Annex to Human Rights Council Resolution 16/21* - Ireland.' (n 2) 6. 'CEDAW Response to List of Issues prior to Reporting' (4 July 2016); http://www.upr.ie/Website/ UPR/uprweb.nsf/page/DOJL-ABKLPL165665-en/$file/Response%20to%20CEDAW%20LoI%20-%20DRAFT%20FOR%20CONSULTATION.pdf accessed 14 August 2016. 'Irish Observations on the Report by the Commissioner for Human Rights, Mr. Nils Muiznieks, on His Visit to Ireland'; https://wcd.coe.int/ com.instranet.InstraServlet?command=com.instranet.CmdBlobGet&InstranetImage=2965984&SecMode=1&DocId=2399942&Usage=2 accessed 10 April 2017.

32 O'Connor and Mac Aodhain (n 1) 31.

33 Hospitals in Ireland are of three types: public, voluntary public and private. Voluntary public hospitals were originally private, charitable, religious hospitals; Geraldine Robbins and Irvine Lapsley, 'Irish Voluntary Hospitals: An Examination of a Theory of Voluntary Failure' (2008) 18 *Accounting, Business & Financial History* 61. Although constitutionally independent, voluntary hospitals have been in receipt of various forms of public funding since the 1800s. The Public Hospitals Act 1933 brought voluntary hospitals under state scrutiny in exchange for increased public funding; see further O'Connor and Mac Aodhain (n 1) 21–22. Today the National Maternity Hospital and the Coombe are voluntary public hospitals, owned and managed by non-profit bodies but funded primarily by the state. Historically, the National Maternity Hospital and the Coombe served working class Catholic populations. The National operates under the patronage of the Archbishop of Dublin. Our Lady of Lourdes Drogheda became a public hospital in 1997. From its founding in 1957 until 1997 it was a voluntary public hospital run by the Medical Missionaries of Mary.

34 O'Connor and Mac Aodhain (n 1) 30–31. See Master of the National Maternity Hospital, Alex Spain, quoted in Murphy (n 17) 9.

35 O'Connor and Mac Aodhain (n 1) 8–9.

36 Walsh (n 55) 59. Murphy (n 17) 27–28.

37 O'Connor and Mac Aodhain (n 1) 32.

38 ibid 32–33.

39 Similar criticisms have been made of the McAleese Report into state involvement in the Magdalene laundries: that it excludes survivor testimony while giving ample space to perpetrators to justify their actions. See further Glynn, Evelyn (n 7).
40 Walsh (n 55) 86–87.
41 ibid 74.
42 ibid 26. Murphy (n 17) 12.
43 Walsh (n 55) 101. Murphy (n 17) 12.
44 Walsh (n 55) 80.
45 ibid 84 and 86–87.
46 ibid 60–61. This is also the view of the Institute of Obstetricians and Gynaecologists;'RCPI Walsh Report on Symphysiotomy in Ireland: Statement by the Institute of Obstetricians and Gynaecologists" https://www.rcpi.ie/news/releases/walsh-report-on-symphysiotomy-in-ireland-statement-by-the-institute-of-obstetricians-and-gynaecologists/ accessed 18 August 2016.
47 Walsh (n 16) 62 and 66–67.
48 Walsh (n 55) 19.
49 ibid 20.
50 ibid.
51 ibid 74–76.
52 'Symphysiotomy Not Barbaric- Reilly'; http://www.irishhealth.com/article.html?id=20377 accessed 14 August 2016. Emphasis mine.
53 O'Connor and Mac Aodhain (n 1) 41.
54 Until 1979, under s. 17 of the Criminal Law (Amendment Act) 1935, it was illegal to import or sell contraception, not to prescribe it, use it or supply it otherwise than for sale. The right of married couples to access contraception was recognised in 1973 in the Supreme Court case of *McGee v. AG* [1974] IR 284. From 1979, under the Health (Family Planning) Act 1979 contraceptives were available on prescription for 'bona fide family planning purposes'. In the years between *McGee* and the Act, and for many years afterwards, contraception was available from private organisations that supplied contraceptives to thousands of customers in defiance of the law; Chrystel Hug, *The Politics of Sexual Morality in Ireland* (Springer 2016) 91.
55 O'Connor and Mac Aodhain (n 1) 41.
56 See e.g. *Health Service Executive v. B and Another* [2016] IEHC 605.
57 On the unreliability of official records see e.g. Randall Kune, 'The Stolen Generations in Court: Explaining the Lack of Widespread Successful Litigation by Members of the Stolen Generations' (2011) 30 *University of Tasmania Law Review* 32.
58 Walsh explains that hand searching of individual medical records was outside the report's terms of reference, and would have required the permission of individual patients; Walsh (n 55) 8.
59 ibid 74–76.
60 Jana Sawicki, *Disciplining Foucault: Feminism, Power, and the Body* (Psychology Press, 1991) 76–80. Elizabeth Klaver, *The Body in Medical Culture* (SUNY Press, 2012). Julia Kristeva, *Pouvoirs de L'horreur (English)* (Columbia University Press, 1982). Women, by turn, are denigrated by association with the body; Jennifer Terry and Jacqueline L Urla, *Deviant Bodies: Critical Perspectives on Difference in Science and Popular Culture* (Indiana University Press, 1995) 13. Adriana Cavarero, *For More Than One Voice: Toward a Philosophy of Vocal Expression* (Stanford University Press, 2005) 206.
61 O'Connor and Mac Aodhain (n 1) 15.
62 ibid 16.
63 Jillson (n 16) 21.; O'Connor and Mac Aodhain (n 1) 6.
64 O'Connor and Mac Aodhain (n 1) 26.

65 ibid 6.
66 Glynn, Evelyn (n 7) 34.
67 'Concluding Observations on the Fourth Periodic Report of Ireland' (2014); http://docstore.ohchr.org/ SelfServices/FilesHandler.ashx?enc=6QkG1d%2fPPRi-CAqhKb7yhsieXFSudRZs%2fX1ZaMqUUOS9yIqPEMRvxx26PpQFtwrk%2bhtvbJ1frkLE%2bCPVCm6lW%2bYjfrz7jxiC9GMVvGkvu2UIuUfSqikQb9KM-VoAoKkgSG accessed 14 August 2016. See similarly CEDAW Concluding Observations on the Combined Sixth and Seventh Periodic Reports of Ireland (2017) CEDAW/C/IRL/CO/6-7.
68 'Childbirth Medical Negligence | Medical Negligence Claims in Ireland - Part 2'; http://www.irishmedicalnegligence.ie/news/category/childbirth-medical-negligence/page/2/ accessed 11 August 2016.
69 Murphy (n 17) 18.
70 Dail Debates 26 September 2013. ibid.
71 'The Surgical Symphysiotomy Ex Gratia Payment Scheme: Terms and Conditions' (2014) 20; http://www.payment-scheme.gov.ie/Symphyisotomy/Symphyisotomy.nsf/0/ A8B200BE1D7D9A6880257D89003DDABA/$file/Terms%20of%20The%20Surgical%20Symphysiotomy%20Payment%20Scheme%20-%2010%20Nov%202014.pdf accessed 19 August 2016.
72 The State Claims Agency is responsible for managing the defence of cases in respect of which there is no identifiable occurrence based insurer. 'Clinical Indemnity Scheme | State Claims Agency'; http://stateclaims.ie/about-our-work/clinical-indemnity-scheme/ accessed 18 August 2016. Most hospitals where symphysiotomies were performed either had very limited insurance, or could not trace their insurers for the relevant periods, so that they would seek to recover awards from the State. ibid 31.
73 Murphy (n 17) 50.
74 Connall O Faharta, 'Symphysiotomy Scheme Time Limit "Is Punitive"' (14 November 2014); http://www.irishexaminer.com/ireland/symphysiotomy-scheme-time-limit-is-punitive-297771.html accessed 31 May 2015. A high burden of proof and difficulty in obtaining medical records have meant that most women have obtained the lower payment of 50,000 euros. In April 2015, it was reported that 50 applicants to the scheme had failed to produce the required records. 'Concern over Symphysiotomy Redress Scheme' (*RTE.ie*); http://www.rte.ie/news/2015/0414/694095-concerns-over-symphysiotomy-compensation/ accessed 18 October 2015.
75 A successful claimant in a personal injuries case could expect to obtain 275,000 euros in general damages, with the possibility of recovering special damages in an appropriate case. 'Clinical Indemnity Scheme State Claims Agency' (n 106) 45.
76 Murphy (n 17) 50.
77 Symphyisotomy Payment Scheme, 'Progress Reports – Symphysiotomy Payment Scheme.' (*Symphyisotomy Payment Scheme*) http://www.payment-scheme.gov.ie/Symphyisotomy/Symphyisotomy.nsf/ page/Progress%20Reports-en accessed 18 August 2016.
78 'Symphysiotomy Survivors Reject Offer' (9 December 2013); http://www.irishexaminer.com/ireland/ symphysiotomy-survivors-reject-offer-252056.html accessed 14 August 2016.
79 'Government Accused of Trying to Blindfold Survivors of Symphysiotomy'; http://claredaly.ie/government-accused-of-trying-to-blindfold-survivors-of-symphysiotomy-by-setting-up-an-opaque-and-closed-ended-process/ accessed 14 August 2016.
80 'Survivors of Symphysiotomy Refuse to Enter into a Magdalene Type Redress Scheme'; http://symphysiotomyireland.com/survivors-wont-enter-into-any-magdalene-type-redress-scheme/ accessed 14 August 2016.

81 [2012] IESC 43
82 *Farrell v. Ryan* [2016] IECA 281.
83 *Farrell v. Ryan* [2015] IEHC 275; Mary Carolan, 'Woman Who Had Symphysiotomy Takes Appeal Seen as Test Case' (*The Irish Times*); http://www.irishtimes.com/news/crime-and-law/courts/high-court/woman-who-had-symphysiotomy-takes-appeal-seen-as-test-case-1.2608386 accessed 11 August 2016.
84 Elizabeth Adjin-Tettey, 'Righting Past Wrongs Through Contextualization: Assessing Claims of Aboriginal Survivors of Historical and Institutional Abuses' (2007) 25 *Windsor YB Access Just.* 95. T. Anthony and H.M. van Rijswijk, 'Can the Common Law Adjudicate Historical Suffering?' [2012] *Melbourne University Law Review*; https://opus.lib.uts.edu.au/handle/10453/23348 accessed 9 April 2017.
85 See further *Kearney v. McQuillan* [2006] IEHC 186; *Kearney v. McQuillan* [2012] IEHC 127, [62]
86 *Kearney v. McQuillan* [2010] 3 IR 576 *per* McMenamin J.
87 *Farrell v. Ryan* [2015] IEHC 275, [7.9].
88 *Farrell v. Ryan* [2016] IECA 281 [99].
89 *Farrell v. Ryan* [2016] IECA 281 [122].
90 *Farrell v. Ryan* [2016] IECA 281 [57] [108] – [112] and [147].
91 *Farrell v. Ryan* [2016] IECA 281 [126].
92 *Farrell v. Ryan* [2016] IECA 281 [159].
93 Oireachtas Health Committee, 16 January 2014.
94 Dail Debates, 19 January 2012. 'Smphysiotomy Bill Passed in Irish Parliament' (*BBC News*, 17 April 2013); http://www.bbc.co.uk/news/world-europe-22181867 accessed 31 May 2015; Paul Hyland, 'Survivors of Symphysiotomy Group to Present Petition ahead of Dáil Decision' *TheJournal.ie* (5 April 2013); http://www.thejournal.ie/symphysiotomy-survivors-group-petition-dail-857007-Apr2013/ accessed 31 May 2015. In the Court of the Appeal, Peart J. held that the claim in *Farrell v. Ryan* [2016] IECA 281 was statute-barred.
95 'It is seeking to use these women victims themselves as a means of indemnifying the doctors who carried out those barbaric operations and the religious orders that owned the hospitals where they took place' – Mark Kelly, ICCL 'Groups Claim Symphysiotomy Payment Scheme Violates Human Rights' (*Breaking News*, 9 December 2014); http://www.breakingnews.ie/ireland/groups-claim-symphysiotomy-payment-scheme-violates-human-rights-653895.html accessed 31 May 2015.
96 O Faharta (n 108).
97 'Residential Institutions Redress Board'; http://www.rirb.ie/ accessed 16 August 2016.
98 Monday, November 04 and 2013, 'Lifting the Veil on Orders' €500m Redress Bill Battle' (4 November 2013); http://www.irishexaminer.com/ireland/lifting-the-veil-on-orders-500m-redress-bill-battle-248355.html accessed 16 August 2016. BBC News, 'Magdalene Laundries: Four Religious Orders Refuse to Pay into Fund' (*BBC News*); http://www.bbc.co.uk/news/world-europe-23325716 accessed 16 August 2016.
99 'Government Announces Details of Symphysiotomy Payment Scheme' (*Department of Health, Ireland*, 6 November 2014); http://health.gov.ie/blog/press-release/symphysiotomy-payment-scheme/. O'Carroll, 'U-Turn on Statute of Limitations as Closure Sought for Symphysiotomy Survivors' (n 101).'Statute of Limitations (Amendment) 17 Apr 2013: Dáil Debates'; https://www.kildarestreet.com/debates/?id=2013-04-17a accessed 14 August 2016.
100 Reilly (n 145).
101 O'Carroll, 'U-Turn on Statute of Limitations as Closure Sought for Symphysiotomy Survivors' (n 113).

102 Matilda Behan, a member of SOS quoted at: 'Politicians "Don"t Even Listen to You', Says Symphysiotomy Victim' (*Breaking News*); http://www.breakingnews.ie/ireland/politicians-dont-even-listen-to-you-says-symphysiotomy-victim-633299.html accessed 31 May 2015.
103 Freeman (n 95) xi.
104 Latour (n 38) 73.
105 For a critical account of Irish traumaculture (focusing especially on the Famine) see Carville, Conor, '"Keeping That Wound Green": Irish Studies and Traumaculture' in Shane Alcobia-Murphy (ed.), *What Rough Beasts? Irish and Scottish Studies in the New Millennium* (Cambridge Scholars Publishing, 2008).
106 Ellie Ragland-Sullivan, 'The Psychical Nature of Trauma: Freud's Dora, the Young Homosexual Woman, and the Fort! Da! Paradigm' (2001) 11 *Postmodern Culture* 15; http://muse.jhu.edu/journals/pmc/v011/11.2ragland.html accessed 17 September 2014. See also Schroder; trauma is simply whatever the subject cannot reincorporate into the symbolic order. Jeanne Lorraine Schroeder, *The Four Lacanian Discourses: Or Turning Law Inside Out* (Routledge, 2008) 44.
107 Ragland-Sullivan (n 154) 15.
108 See for example Ruth Fletcher, 'Post-Colonial Fragments: Representations of Abortion in Irish Law and Politics' (2001) 28 *Journal of Law and Society* 568; Siobhan Mullally, 'Debating Reproductive Rights in Ireland' (2005) 27 *Human Rights Quarterly* 78; Barry Collins and Patrick Hanafin, 'Mothers, Maidens and the Myth of Origins in the Irish Constitution' (2001) 12 *Law and Critique* 53; Patrick Hanafin, 'Rewriting Desire: The Construction of Sexual Identity in Literary and Legal Discourse in Postcolonial Ireland' (1998) 7 *Social & Legal Studies* 409; Patrick Hanafin, 'Constitutive Fiction: Postcolonial Constitutionalism in Ireland' (2001) 20 *Penn State International Law Review* 339; Lindsey Earner-Byrne, 'The Rape of Mary M.: A Microhistory of Sexual Violence and Moral Redemption in 1920s Ireland' (2015) 24 *Journal of the History of Sexuality* 75; Ailbhe Smyth, 'Paying Our Disrespects to the Bloody States We're In: Women, Violence, Culture, and the State' (1995) 7 *Journal of Women's History* 190.
109 On religion as requiring that we give ourselves back and up to the other, see Jacques Derrida, *Acts of Religion* (Routledge, 2013) 71.
110 For comments from interviews with husbands, see Jillson (n 16) 22–24.
111 Lloyd (n 157) 23.
112 Lloyd (n 157) 24.
113 On past trauma as the essence of our obligation before the law, see Lyotard (n 171).
114 Khanna (n 156) 22.
115 Schwab (n 164) 11.
116 Avital Ronell and Anne Dufourmantelle, *Fighting Theory* (University of Illinois Press, 2010) 56. See similarly the idea of 'psychic splitting' Schwab (n 164) 21.
117 Ragland-Sullivan (n 173) 13.
118 Roth (n 170) xviii.
119 Roth (n 170) xxvi. Schwab (n 164) 2.
120 Schwab (n 164) 4. See also Juliet Rogers, 'Beyond the Script of Law' (2009) 18 *Griffith Law Review* 269.
121 Freeman (n 95) 8.
122 ibid.
123 Gressgård (n 183).
124 Lyotard (n 171) 17.
125 ibid 16.
126 ibid 17.
127 Gressgård (n 183).

128 See further Midwives for Choice, 'Review of The Surgical Symphysiotomy Ex Gratia Payment Scheme Report'; http://midwivesforchoice.ie/wp-content/uploads/2017/01/MfC-Review-of-Harding-Clark-FINAL.pdf accessed 10 April 2017.
129 Dail Deb Dec 1 2016.
130 Harding-Clark (n 192) 97.
131 ibid.
132 ibid 62.
133 'Some Mistook Problems for Symphysiotomy - Boylan' [2016] RTE.ie; /news/2016/1123/833859-health-symphysiotomy-compensation/ accessed 10 April 2017.
134 Harding-Clark (n 192) 97.
135 ibid 56.
136 ibid 97.
137 ibid 28.
138 ibid 61.
139 ibid 103.
140 Schwab (n 164) 7. See similarly Fiona Barclay, *Writing Postcolonial France: Haunting, Literature, and the Maghreb* (Lexington Books, 2011) xxiii.
141 O'Connor and Mac Aodhain (n 1) 27.

Bibliography

Adjin-Tettey, E. (2007). Righting Past Wrongs Through Contextualization: Assessing Claims of Aboriginal Survivors of Historical and Institutional Abuses. *25 Windsor YB Access Just.*, 95.

Ahmed, S. (2014). The Politics of Good Feeling. *10 Critical Race & Whiteness Studies.*

Allen, T.M. (2008). *A Republic in Time: Temporality and Social Imagination in Nineteenth-Century America.* Univ. of North Carolina Press, 9.

Anderson, B. (2006). *Imagined Communities: Reflections on the Origin and Spread of Nationalism.* Verso, 25, 26.

Barclay, F. (2011). *Writing Postcolonial France: Haunting, Literature, and the Maghreb.* Lexington Books, xxiii.

Benjamin, W. (2015). *Illuminations.* Random House 2015.

Bhabha, H.K. (2012). *The Location of Culture.* Routledge, 364.

Braidotti, R. (2011). *Nomadic Subjects: Embodiment and Sexual Difference in Contemporary Feminist Theory.* Columbia University Press, 4.

Cahill, A. (2014). My Life Was Ruined by Symphysiotomy [online]. Available at: http://www.irishexaminer.com/analysis/my-life-was-ruined-by-symphysiotomy-275544.html [accessed 31 May 2015].

Caruth, C. (1995). *Trauma: Explorations in Memory.* JHU Press, 6.

Chakrabarty, D. (2009). *Provincializing Europe: Postcolonial Thought and Historical Difference.* Princeton University Press, 109.

Christodoulidis, E.A. and Veitch, S. (2001). *Lethe's Law: Justice, Law and Ethics in Reconciliation.* Hart Publishing, 227.

Clough, N., Crowley, U. and Kitchin, R. (2008). Producing "Decent Girls": Governmentality and the Moral Geographies of Sexual Conduct in Ireland (1922–1937). *15 Gender, Place & Culture*, 355.

Collins, B. and Hanafin, P. (2001). Mothers, Maidens and the Myth of Origins in the Irish Constitution. *12 Law and Critique*, 53.

Concern over Symphysiotomy Redress Scheme. (2015). *RTE.ie* [online]. Available at: http://www.rte.ie/news/2015/0414/694095-concerns-over-symphysiotomy-compensation/ [accessed 18 October 2015].

Derrida, J. (1994). *Specters of Marx: The State of the Debt, the Work of Mourning, and the New Internationa*. Psychology Press. 16.

Derrida, J. (2013). *Acts of Religion*. Routledge, 71.

Donnelly, S. and Inglis, T. (2010). The Media and the Catholic Church in Ireland: Reporting Clerical Child Sex Abuse. *25 Journal of Contemporary Religion*, 1.

Douzinas, C. (2012). History Trials: Can Law Decide History? *8 Annual Review of Law and Social Science*, 273.

Earner-Byrne, L. (2007). *Mother and Child: Maternity and Child Welfare in Dublin, 1920s-1960s*. Manchester University Press.

Earner-Byrne, L. (2010). Moral Proscription: The Irish Medical Profession, the Roman Catholic Church and the Prohibition of Birth Control in Twentieth-Century Ireland. In Catherine Cox and Maria Luddy (Eds.), *Cultures of Care in Irish Medical History. 1750–1950*. Palgrave.

Earner-Byrne, L. (2015). The Rape of Mary M.: A Microhistory of Sexual Violence and Moral Redemption in 1920s Ireland. *24 Journal of the History of Sexuality*, 75.

Faharta, C.O. (2014).Symphysiotomy Scheme Time Limit "Is Punitive" [online]. Available at: http://www.irishexaminer.com/ireland/symphysiotomy-scheme-time-limit-is-punitive-297771.html [accessed 31 May 2015].

Felman, S. (2001). Theaters of Justice: Arendt in Jerusalem, the Eichmann Trial, and the Redefinition of Legal Meaning in the Wake of the Holocaust. *27 Critical Inquiry 201*, 231.

Felman, S. (2002). *The Juridical Unconscious: Trials and Traumas in the Twentieth Century*. Harvard University Press, 14.

Felman, S. and Laub, D. (2013). *Testimony: Crises of Witnessing in Literature*, Psychoanalysis *and* History. Routledge, 57.

Fitzgerald, F. (2014). Opening Remarks at Ireland's Appearance before the UN Human Rights Committee on International Convention on Civil and Political Rights [online]. Available at: http://www.justice.ie/en/JELR/Pages/SP14000193 [accessed 31 May 2015].

Fletcher, R. (2001). Post-Colonial Fragments: Representations of Abortion in Irish Law and Politics. *28 Journal of Law and Society*, 568

Freeman, E. (2010). *Time Binds: Queer Temporalities, Queer Histories*. Duke University Press 2010, 10.

Garrett, P.M. (2015). Excavating the Past: Mother and Baby Homes in the Republic of Ireland. *British Journal of Social Work*, bcv116.

Grabham, E. (2016). *Brewing Legal Times: Things, Form, and the Enactment of Law*. University of Toronto Press, 14.

Gressgård, R. (2013). *Multicultural Dialogue: Dilemmas, Paradoxes, Conflicts*. Berghahn.

Habermas, J. (2015). *The Philosophical Discourse of Modernity: Twelve Lectures*. John Wiley & Sons.

Haddad, S. (2013). *Derrida and the Inheritance of Democracy*. Indiana University Press, 33.

Hanafin, P. (1998). Rewriting Desire: The Construction of Sexual Identity in Literary and Legal Discourse in Postcolonial Ireland. *7 Social & Legal Studies*, 409

Hanafin, P. (2001). Constitutive Fiction: Postcolonial Constitutionalism in Ireland. *20 Penn State International Law Review*, 339

Harding-Clark, M. (2016). *The Surgical Symphysiotomy Ex Gratia Payment Scheme Report* [online]. Available at: http://health.gov.ie/wp-content/uploads/2016/11/The-Surgical-Symphysiotomy-Ex-Gratia-Payment-Scheme-Report.pdf [accessed 10 April 2017].

Hennessy, M. (2013). Symphysiotomy Survivors Reject Magdalene Type Redress Scheme *TheJournal.ie* [online]. Available at: http://www.thejournal.ie/symphysiotomy-1018837-Aug2013/ [accessed 31 May 2015].

Herman, J.L. (2015). *Trauma and Recovery: The Aftermath of Violence–From Domestic Abuse to Political Terror*. Basic Books.

Jillson, I. (2012). Symphysiotomy in Ireland: A Qualitiative Study. *Georgetown University*, 16–18. Available at: http://www.patientfocus.ie/site/images/uploads/SYMPHYSIOTOMY_IN_IRELAND_By_Irene_Jillson_PhD.pdf [accessed 14 August 2016].

Kenny, K. (2016). Organizations and Violence: The Child as Abject-Boundary in Ireland's Industrial Schools. *37 Organization Studies*, 939.

Killian, S. (2015). For Lack of Accountability: The Logic of the Price in Ireland's Magdalen Laundries. *43 Accounting, Organizations and Society 17*, 24.

Khaleeli, H. (2014). Symphysiotomy – Ireland's Brutal Alternative to Caesareans. *The Guardian* [online]. Available at: http://www.theguardian.com/lifeandstyle/2014/dec/12/symphysiotomy-irelands-brutal-alternative-to-caesareans.

Khanna, R. (2013). *Dark Continents: Psychoanalysis and Colonialism*. Duke University Press, 84.

Latour, B. (2012). *We Have Never Been Modern*. Harvard University Press, 69.

Latour, B. (2013). What's the Story? In Daniel Robichaud and Francois Cooren (Eds.), *Organization and Organizing: Materiality, Agency and Discourse*. Routledge, 43.

Lloyd, D. (2008). *Irish Times: Temporalities of Modernity*. Field Day Publications, 28

Luckhurst, R. (2013). *The Trauma Question*. Routledge, 3.

Luddy, M. (2011). Unmarried Mothers in Ireland, 1880–1973. *20 Women's History Review*, 109.

Lyotard, J.F. (1988). *Le Différend*. University of Minnesota Press, 5.

Lyotard, J.F. (1990). *Heidegger and 'the Jews'*. University of Minnesota Press, 15.

Lyotard, J.F., Crome, K. and Williams, J. (2006). *The Lyotard Reader and Guide*. Columbia University Press, 104.

Lyotard, J.F., Massumi, B. and Niesluchowski, W.G.J. (1988). Ticket to a New Décor. *Harper's Magazine*. Available at: http://harpers.org/archive/1988/06/ticket-to-a-new-decor/ [accessed 14 August 2016].

Lyotard, J.F. and Ronan, J. (1999). Anamnesis of the Visible 2. *Qui Parle*, 21.

Mbembe, A. (2015). The Colony: Its Guilty Secret and Its Accursed Share in Elleke Boehmer and Stephen Morton (Eds.), *Terror and the Postcolonial* 34. Available at: https://books.google.co.uk/books?hl=en&id=fTykBgAAQBAJ&oi=fnd&pg=PA27&dq=MBEMBE+%22accursed+share%22&ots=aWYY9NbQb5&sig=A5YiLj0xvWujEQQDdH6bONkGLcQ [accessed 25 July 2016].

McAlinden, A. (2013). An Inconvenient Truth: Barriers to Truth Recovery in the Aftermath of Institutional Child Abuse in Ireland. *33 Legal Studies 189*, 209.

Mullally, S. (2005). Debating Reproductive Rights in Ireland. *27 Human Rights Quarterly*, 78.

Murphy, F. (2005). *Ferns Report* [online]. Available at: http://www.lenus.ie/hse/bitstream/10147/560434/2/thefernsreportoctober2005.pdf [accessed 2 August 2016].

Murphy, Y. (2014). *Independent Review of Issues Relating to Symphysiotomy 21* [online]. Available at: http://health.gov.ie/wp-content/uploads/2014/07/Scanned-Murphy-report-redacted-version1.pdf [accessed 18 August 2016].

O'Carroll, S. (2013). 'U-Turn on Statute of Limitations as Closure Sought for Symphysiotomy Survivors' *TheJournal.ie* [online]. Available at: http://www.thejournal.ie/symphysiotomy-3-1193378-Nov2013/ [accessed 31 May 2015]. 'Additional Responses Following Ireland's Appearance before the Human Rights Committee, July 14 –152014' (n 56) 11.

O'Carroll, S. (2014). Woman in Intensive Care Bringing Case against Hospital over 'Unwarranted' Symphysiotomy. *TheJournal.ie* [online]. Available at: http://www.thejournal.ie/symphysiotomy-high-court-1559459-Jul2014/ [accessed 31 May 2015].

O'Carroll, S. (2015). I Am a Symphysiotomy Survivor. I Am Glad It's All Over. *TheJournal.ie* [online]. Available at: http://www.thejournal.ie/symphysiotomy-court-case-coombe-1917295-Feb2015/ [accessed 31 May 2015].

Olkowski, D. (1999). *Gilles Deleuze and the Ruin of Representation.* University of California Press, 110.

Osborne, P. (1995). *The Politics of Time: Modernity and Avant-Garde.* Verso, 141.

Povinelli, E.A. (2006). *The Empire of Love: Toward a Theory of Intimacy, Genealogy, and Carnality.* Duke University Press, 7.

Radstone, S. (2007). *The Sexual Politics of Time: Confession, Nostalgia, Memory.* Routledge, 9.

Redress for Women Resident in Certain Institutions Act, (2015). *Mairead Enright, 'What's Wrong with the Magdalenes Redress Scheme? – Human Rights in Ireland* [online]. Available at: http://humanrights.ie/gender-sexuality-and-the-law/whats-wrong-with-the-magdalenes-redress-scheme/ [accessed 16 August 2016]. *The Trouble with Redress – Symphysiotomy and Other Failures. – Human Rights in Ireland* [online]. Available at: http://humanrights.ie/gender-sexuality-and-the-law/the-trouble-with-redress-symphysiotomy-and-other-failures/ [accessed 16 August 2016].

Ricoeur, P. (2009). *Memory, History, Forgetting.* University of Chicago Press, 445.

Rogers, J. (2007). Who's Your Daddy – A Question of Sovereignty and the Use of Psychoanalysis. 11 *Law Text Culture*, 151.

Rogers, J. (2009). Beyond the Script of Law. *18 Griffith Law Review*, 269.

Rogers, J. (2011a). Nostalgia for a Reconciled Future. *20 Griffith Law Review*, 252.

Rogers, J. (2011b). *The Pure Subject of Torture: Or, Lynndie England Does Not Exist. 35 Australian Feminist Law Journal, 75*, 86.

Ronell, A. (2005). *The Test Drive.* University of Illinois Press, 106.

Ronell, A. and Dufourmantelle, A. (2010). *Fighting Theory.* University of Illinois Press, 56.

Rose, G. (1996). *Mourning Becomes the Law: Philosophy and Representation.* Cambridge University Press, 75.

Roth, M. S. (2013). *Memory, Trauma, and History: Essays on Living with the Past.* Columbia University Press, 92.

Schlag, P. (1998). *Laying Down the Law: Mysticism, Fetishism, and the American Legal Mind.* NYU Press, 63.

Schwab, G. (2010). *Haunting Legacies: Violent Histories and Transgenerational Trauma.* Columbia University Press 2010, 4.

Simon, R. I. (2014). *A Pedagogy of Witnessing: Curatorial Practice and the Pursuit of Social Justice.* SUNY Press, 215.

Simpson, A.V. and others. (2014). Doing Compassion or Doing Discipline? Power Relations and the Magdalene Laundries. *7 Journal of Political Power*, 253.

Smyth, A. (1995). Paying Our Disrespects to the Bloody States We're In: Women, Violence, Culture, and the State. *7 Journal of Women's History*, 190.

Sutton, M. (2012). The Cloyne Report and the Taoiseach's Speech: Towards 'Hibernian Catholicism'? *101 Studies:An Irish Quarterly Review*, 273, 276.

Taoiseach Enda Kenny's Statement on Magdalene Report'. Available at: http://static.rasset.ie/documents/news/kenny-magdelene-speech.pdf [accessed 3 August 2016].

Valverde, M. (2015). *Chronotopes of Law: Jurisdiction, Scale and Governance.* Routledge, 17.

Walsh, O. (2014). *Report on Symphysiotomy in Ireland 1944–1984* [online]. Available at: http://health.gov.ie/wp-content/uploads/2014/07/Final-Final-walsh-Report-on-Symphysiotomy1.pdf [accessed 14 August 2016].

Young, H.B. (2006). *Haunting Capital: Memory, Text and the Black Diasporic Body.* UPNE, 91.

3 Time-spaces of adjudication in the U.S. subprime mortgage crisis

Philip Ashton, University of Illinois at Chicago

Introduction[1]

As accounts of the 2007–2008 global financial crisis have proliferated, time seems everywhere. The speed of finance's turnover has been one notable trope used to understand the production of the crisis and its diffusion from one corner of the financial system – the U.S. subprime mortgage market – into global financial circuits. The speculative techniques used to produce and trade mortgages and other claims against property all decreased turnover time and allowed capital to be reinvested in the expropriation of excess profits with increasing speed, a process Scheuerman (2004) has generally labeled the "social acceleration of time." All mortgages are essentially claims against borrowers' future earning power and/or future housing price appreciation, endowing them with a dimension of *futurity* – an expectation that recurrent monthly payments will generate profits in the future (cf. Commons, 1924). As lenders turned to complex financial instruments such as subprime mortgage-backed securities – which funded the mortgage boom by selling stakes in the interest revenue generated by pools of mortgages – to fund their lending, they spread these expectations into financial portfolios across the globe, setting the stage for losses on those instruments to reverberate well beyond the neighborhoods where those loans were made (French, Leyshon, and Thrift, 2009).

However, speed is not the only temporal register evident in analyses of the crisis. Accounts of emergency interventions have foregrounded questions of temporality inherent in the governance of system-threatening events – for instance, by documenting the "eventfulness" evident in the emergence of crises as emergencies (Anderson, 2016), or by highlighting the forms of calculation mobilized to measure deviance from some anticipated future state of financial stability (Langley, 2014). The extension of crisis management to distressed homeowners, through mortgage modifications that keep them in their homes by shifting their financial obligations into the future, has further highlighted the temporal work of forbearance (Langley, 2009) in inscribing debt as a *perpetual* social relation. Underlying these initiatives are deeper questions about whether the global crisis should be interpreted as some fundamental rupture or transition or whether crises and disruptions are instead a recurring and stable feature of millennial capitalism.

The latter accounts, emanating primarily from cultural economy, economic sociology, and critical geography, have usefully foregrounded the heterogenous arrangements of discursive and non-discursive devices and resources – *apparatuses* – through which the crisis has been governed (Anderson, 2016; Langley, 2014). Just as with time, law is also omnipresent in these accounts. Legal contracts form the very material at stake in the governance of the crisis, whether as assets on bank balance sheets or, in the case of housing policy, as objects whose parameters are open to modification to aid homeowners at risk of foreclosure. The governance of the crisis has also unfolded within a multitude of overtly legal venues: foreclosure proceedings involving insolvent homeowners (Immergluck, 2009), courtroom litigation by investors against allegedly nefarious lenders (de Goede, 2015), administrative law tribunals weighing bank culpability (Dorn, 2011), and rulemaking processes envisioning a stable set of rules governing finance in the future (Ashton and Christophers, 2016).

Yet, the role of law in these accounts often recedes into the background, with scholarly accounts sometimes devolving to "lawless capitalism" (Ramirez, 2014) or a lack of "juridical reason" (Davies, 2016) as characterizations of the crisis and its governance. Riles (2011) notes that this inattention to law partially mirrors practitioners' own perspectives on legal work within finance, which, in the example of derivative markets, demotes it to the mundane, technical, and residual aspects of paperwork. Whereas legal work is often portrayed as a key dimension of the speed of financial market turnover (Peterson, 2006), and legal processes involving banks are seen as having their own unique pacing and discourse (de Goede, 2015), there is a paucity of work examining *how* the law has worked as part of financial crisis governance – both the way in which it grounds financial market practices as authoritative (its force or essence (Bourdieu, 1987; Latour, 2003)), as well as the socially formative work performed by that force (its effects).

This chapter seeks to take up this challenge, and it does so by examining two main questions. First, in what ways were subprime lender practices authorized – how did subprime lending "come into law," and how did the economic relations they embody become "[attached] to a legal or political order" (Kaushal, 2013: 21)? I focus on one set of legal processes set in motion since 2008: class-action litigation by U.S. borrowers (homeowners) against large subprime lenders. In examples such as the fraud cases against Countrywide Financial, which I will take up in this chapter, these have focused on a primary substantive concern: whether lenders can profit by selling their products through fraudulent means. Claims of fraudulent (criminal) practices have been key planks along which recent court cases and regulatory actions against banks have proceeded, not only related to mortgage lending (with both investors and homeowners claiming to have been harmed by fraud), but also in high-profile cases regarding currency trading and the production of benchmark indices such as LIBOR (Ashton and Christophers, 2015). Here, I am concerned with questions of legal authority (Commons, 1924), and with the ways in which "the facts" of problematic transactions are picked up and plotted through legal processes – in particular, within the various forms of legal experimentation that rework public/administrative law by adapting civil procedures (including private rights of action and settlement) to the exigencies of addressing mass claims of lender fraud and discrimination.

Temporality proves to be a key analytic for addressing this question and for understanding the nature of law's regulatory force at the current conjuncture. Analysis of judicial proceedings in the Countrywide case foregrounds the work of legal "technologies of jurisdiction" (Dorsett and McVeigh, 2012: 54), such as writing, categorization, and precedent, that work to secure the past's claim on the present within court adjudication. Faced with private legal claims regarding mortgage contracts in court proceedings over default or foreclosure, these technologies construct a "time-space" (cf. Pryke and Allen, 2000) that mobilizes certain historic legal imaginaries and geographic scales (such as the appropriate "powers" of national banks, or limits to the construction of collective claims regarding financial exploitation) that work to secure the validity of creditors exploitative claims against borrowers' future incomes.

Second, closer theorization of law and its temporality highlights not only questions of how the financial crisis has been governed, but also how we should understand the kinds of social formation set in motion through the crisis and its protracted adjudication (cf. Joseph, 2014). In the phrasing of legal anthropologist Keebet von Benda-Beckman (2014: 1), "temporalities are not just aesthetic qualities of law, they also have important implications for social practices," requiring a move beyond abstracted analyses of law to examine how legal proceedings shape social, economic, and political relations in material ways. Here, attention to how adjudication grounds law's authority by admitting certain socio-spatial facts and denying others – a threshold of admission between law and non-law – helps us understand the social logics of selection at work in the crisis. I argue that the techniques employed by administrative agencies in resolving borrowers' legal claims – including legal settlements and contract modifications – embody certain selectivities that, when applied to concrete experiences of dispossession, transfer uncertainty about the future back to borrowers and structure exploitation as legally unproblematic. The results of this analysis suggest new ways to approach the distributional politics of the financial crisis, pointing to a need for greater attention to the structuring of financial exploitation within the time-spaces of law itself.

Jurisdictional practices: Perpetuity and the time-spaces of adjudication

The question of how law works to write certain economic relations as uncontestable, and thus authoritative across time, has long occupied critical legal scholars. Whereas Marxist accounts of law have postulated the separation of private (civil, contract) and public (administrative) law as essential to the formation of class relations within capitalism, these accounts often work at too high a level of abstraction to be helpful in situating law's historically contingent role in structuring economic relations (Jessop, 1990). A less deterministic approach to this question might focus on the nature of adjudication – that is, how problematic elements of economic relations are picked up and resolved within legal proceedings. The

American institutionalist John R. Commons, in his foundational work on law and industrial capitalism (Commons, 1924), correspondingly looked to private law, and to legal notions of remedy, for an understanding of the contestability of labor and credit relations. Commons cast private law of contract as functioning in a critical temporal register, regularizing an uncertain future by providing remedial powers should a transaction unfold in unexpected and undesirable ways. These remedial powers (such as the right to foreclose on the part of a lender) allow parties to pursue counterparties for lost value or injury should that future not come to pass. This temporal work made private law central to the growth and expansion of capitalism by allowing parties to "anticipate the mediative force of law as operative in the future" (Richland, 2013: 219).

Whether this force *will be* operative, and whether remedies will provide scope to contest exploitative labor and credit relations, were separate questions for Commons, requiring an embrace of legal realism to examine how adjudication adapts to the changing "facticity" of economic relations within capitalism. The powers and exposures mobilized by parties to a transaction – in its fullest meaning as a dynamic, collective entanglement by multiple actors unfolding in historic time – all depend on the exercise of police power by courts and regulatory agencies *at some point in the future* "to compel you to behave as you promised if you do not do so willingly" (Commons, 1924: 22). This opens a distinction between those transactions that are *authorized* through the consent of various parties and those that are *authoritative* by virtue of their recourse to state enforcement of their terms (ibid.: 106–107) – a distinction that marks adjudication as necessarily contingent, varying in availability or force based on changes in legislation, regulatory enforcement capacities, or changing "juridico-political ideologies" (Jessop, 1990).

Questions of legal authority involve more than the availability of a superior entity endowed with adjudicative or enforcement powers; they also hinge on a set of resources *internal* to law that determine how new facts and circumstances become "[attached] to a legal or political order" (Kaushal, 2013: 21). For Foucault (1984; 1996), adjudication's emergence as a form of inquiry and a mechanism of power necessarily involves means of determining truth, which in the modern era fuses law's authority to disciplinary knowledges drawn from psychology, economics, medicine, and the like (cf. Rose and Valverde, 1992). However, Dorsett and McVeigh (2012: 14) describe these internal resources in more pragmatic terms as "technologies of jurisdiction" – "practices, devices, techniques, or organisational [strategies] … designed to, or [capable] of, authorising, changing or altering lawful relations." These might include elements of procedure and writing that produce the *form* necessary for claims to be taken as authoritative. They may also involve modes of *categorization*, central to legal reasoning, that name and order legal knowledges (ibid., 71). Here, *precedent* is a specific temporal form of categorization, one "that works by situating specific instances of social action as parts of broader arcs of social meaning, linking them up, in one way or another to prior moments of social action" (Richland, 2013: 218).

Within quotidian courtroom procedures, categorization and precedent are actively mobilized to establish "type–token relationships" between abstract legal norms or concepts (types) and the objects (tokens) representing "the circumstances of a particular problematic social event that are presented as the facts of a case" (Richland, 2013: 218). As something more than just legal reasoning, this is akin to what Commons (1924: 100) referred to as the "correlating" nature of legal authority, which works to "[bind] the reasoning offered in individual decisions into the institutional arrangements of the administration of justice" (Dorsett and McVeigh, 2012: 68). This situates law's sovereign authority as always inaugural, rooted in the pragmatics of law's attachment to the unfolding present and the way it establishes the "threshold between law and non-law" by "either refusing to reach the matter or extending its authority there" (Kaushal, 2013: 23).

These correlations are at once temporal and spatial. Temporally, they gesture not only to legal events in the past (historicity), but also to events anticipated in the future; precedent "shapes law by stating (instructing) that a like preceding case should be treated as an analogy for, or justification of, subsequent cases" (Dorsett and McVeigh, 2012: 67). By projecting legal principles forwards in transactional time, the type–token relations mobilized within adjudication envision a future that is provisionally settled, and in which sovereign adjudication is operative, even as they point toward "the unfolding horizons of activity and events that are as yet not fully realized" (Richland, 2013: 218–219). Spatially, they mobilize doctrinal concepts and remedies with different degrees of spatial "reach," in the process constituting geographic scales ranging from the micro (the body, the parcel of property) to the macro (the nation, the global). This also references the socially formative work of jurisdictional technologies, notably their ability to draw together or fragment social space. Even as legal technologies link facts and norms across time and space by connecting events to principles, this always involves "rupturing or foreclosing other such connections" (Richland, 2013: 218), in the process structuring economic-juridical relationships, such as credit or wage labor, in spatially intensive or extensive ways.

Thus, we can appreciate how, even within the accelerations of finance capital's circulation, law constructs its own authority within a specific type of time-space and through a jurisdictional threshold – one that works *temporally* to bind together present and future "as simultaneously immanent and transcending the facts and norms it brings together" (Richland, 2013: 219) and *spatially* to "recompose [and] re-rhythm 'real' geographical spaces" (Pryke and Allen, 2000: 279). It is within these time-spaces of adjudication that we find law's (in)capacity to speak to historically and spatially specific configurations of social power.

Time-spaces of adjudication: The subprime mortgage crisis and *In Re* Countrywide Financial

This theorization of jurisdiction and the time-space of adjudication helps us to lay out an analytical framework for approaching the legal issues at stake in the mortgage crisis and their relationship to the contestation of exploitative credit relations. I want to develop these arguments through a focus on recent litigation against US banks, using as a case study a series of interlinked fraud cases involving Countrywide Home Loans (and its parent, Countrywide Financial). The large U.S. subprime lender, along with its various subsidiaries and affiliates, was the object of a class-action lawsuit filed in 2007; while the case was led by a dozen representative plaintiffs, it ultimately covered over 600,000 loans issued between 2004 and 2008 – the height of the U.S. housing boom. Given this scale, the Countrywide litigation represents a signal encounter between the threshold of law and the practices of expropriation that were at the heart of the subprime market. My method here is to proceed, in this section, through a careful reading of the District Court's decisions at various procedural moments in the initial litigation (particularly, the *certiorari* phase of the case), supplementing the decisions with third-party analysis and reporting on the proceedings. In the next section, I will turn to examine the resolution of the claims against Countrywide through a parallel legal proceeding – one involving State Attorneys General that culminated in a 2008 settlement with the lender. Taken together, I will argue that these two adjudicative time-spaces worked in different ways to situate Countrywide's harmful business practices beyond the threshold of law's authority.

Before turning to the litigation, it is worth detouring into the subprime mortgage market for a moment to provide some context. Whereas loans to borrowers with poor credit histories or other "adverse" characteristics (marking them as "subprime" risks) have been a feature of the U.S. credit system for decades, the emergence of a significant market segment focused on those borrowers dates only to the early 1990s (Ashton, 2012). Countrywide was an exemplar of the growth and characteristics of that market. Already a highly successful mortgage lender specializing in refinancing existing home loans, Countrywide found that, the higher probability of default notwithstanding, loans to high-risk borrowers could be tremendously lucrative due the higher interest rates and up-front fees charged. Through the 1990s, Countrywide rapidly expanded its subprime lending operations, purchasing other lenders and turning to a commissioned salesforce to increase lending activity nationwide, often by actively targeting social groups and geographies rich in those borrowers (Bruck, 2009). It also sought to expand the pipeline of borrowers, developing new loan products that tapped homebuyers as well as existing owners, and that further leveraged borrowers' limited incomes or home value to increase loan volumes. By 2004, these strategies had helped Countrywide become the largest home mortgage lender in the United States (ibid.).

There was one loan product that was representative of Countrywide's strategy to gain market share in the hyper-competitive U.S. mortgage market – the "pay option" or "hybrid" adjustable rate mortgage (ARM). The pay option ARM offered borrowers a choice of payment plans, including a "minimal" option that initially included only a portion of the required interest payment for the first 2–3 years of the loan, resulting in a growing principal balance on the loan ("negative amortization"). The low initial payment made it easy for borrowers with lower incomes to qualify, especially if lenders were not underwriting based on whether the borrower could cover the much higher loan payments when the loan recast. By that point, appreciating home prices would (ostensibly) allow the owner to refinance with accrued equity or to sell if the higher payments got them into financial difficulty.[2] Even as Countrywide would later disclose that this loan product was one of the engines of its profitability, Christian Marazzi has usefully described the payment structure of the hybrid ARM as embracing exploitation through a temporal threshold between the *security* of ownership and tenure (during the initial 2–3 years) and the *bare life* of expropriation and foreclosure during the remaining "28 years of exchange-value" (2010: 41).

In 2007, a group of borrowers filed a complaint with the U.S. Federal District Court for Southern California, claiming that Countrywide and its affiliates had orchestrated a systematic scheme to maximize the issuance of subprime loans, using a variety fraudulent means to lure borrowers into hybrid ARMs. This seemed to represent a new take on classic forms of usury and financial fraud. In the plaintiffs' complaint, they described Countrywide's scheme as including failing to adequately disclose or misrepresenting future interest rate increases, "making false representations to borrowers, as set forth in standardized sales scripts, that they were offering the best loans available to the borrowers," and using "an automated, computerized underwriting program that was designed to maximize the number of subprime loans" (U.S. District Court for Southern California, 2011: 4)

The evidence eventually amassed in support of the plaintiffs' claims was compelling. Based on a review of nearly 111,000 pages of Countrywide documents in a later phase in the case, the Illinois Attorney General's office determined that 60% of the lender's hybrid ARM borrowers "would not have qualified at the full payment rate" and that "almost 25 percent of the borrowers would not have qualified for any other mortgage product that it sold" (Morgenson, 2008). It was on this basis that the plaintiffs sought to ground their complaint in California business code violations (based on Countrywide's headquarters in that state), as well as in federal racketeering statutes (RICO), arguing that it was not only problematic lender practices that were at issue in the case but a coordinated criminal enterprise based on financial predation.

In civil proceedings, the plaintiffs' claims survived an early procedural hurdle (the motion to dismiss phase) but failed at the *certiorari* (class certification) stage – that is, the judge determined there was not sufficient merit to the claims as presented to authorize a collective remedial claim against Countrywide. Even as different doctrinal authorizations enabled legal agency for plaintiffs by granting standing to contest Countrywide's practices and behavior, we can see through closer examination how the judicial proceedings constructed a time-space that provided very selective grounds for that contestation.

First, jurisdiction was based on the selective mobilization of certain historic legal imaginaries that worked to deny plaintiffs' complaints and instead secure the validity of creditors' claims against borrowers' future incomes (or their properties, in instances of foreclosure). The various District Court opinions and decisions rendered throughout the case evidence an emergent process whereby the presiding judges sought to establish "type–token" relations between historic precedent and the facticity of claims regarding Countrywide's practices. For instance, one of the primary legal grounds for contesting Countrywide's onerous loan pricing practices, combined with its supposedly fraudulent means for marketing those loans, was the doctrine of *unjust enrichment*. This doctrine establishes an equitable claim for restitution in instances where one party to a transaction received a benefit, but where that benefit was unjustly retained at the expense of another party (ibid.: 90).[3] To determine whether this concept anchored plaintiffs' claims in this case, the Court had to reason through the legal threshold of unjust enrichment relative to historical legal imaginaries of the "transaction" – borrowing from classical liberal notions of a contract between two parties. Based on historical legal-economic presumptions that parties freely choose to enter transactions, *but for* situations of fraud, is a claim for unjust enrichment legally valid when there is a contract between the parties? Whereas precedent dictated that "unjust enrichment [claims failed] as a matter of law [where] there was an express contract between the parties governing the subject matter of the claim" (ibid.: 55), ambiguities in the notion of *contract* in the Countrywide case led the Court, during an interim hearing, to "[decline] to conclude that this claim is legally incognizable" (ibid.: 56).

Similar forms of legal reasoning were evident relative to another fundamental claim of the plaintiffs, namely that Countrywide's systematic employment of fraud constituted the firm and its affiliates as a "criminal enterprise" under the federal Racketeer Influenced and Corrupt Organizations Act ("RICO") of 1970. The RICO claims reinterpreted legal relations within the lender itself, joining together Countrywide, its subsidiaries, and its spatially variegated business relationships with brokers and affiliates into "something more" that could be the object of criminal claims. Were plaintiffs able to successfully draw Countrywide into this time-space of criminality (originally created to provide powerful tools for prosecutors pursuing organized crime syndicates across state lines), they would have much stronger grounds for penalizing the firm's extractive practices.

However, both the unjust enrichment and criminal enterprise tests hinged on a particular form of jurisprudence focusing on the legal constitution of the *class*, a doctrine far removed from the mortgage or contract law that was operative in other parts of the adjudication process. Nagareda (2008) notes the increasing centrality of class-action proceedings to the governance of large, complex corporate entities, with the law joining plaintiffs' claims into a mass legal subject with sufficient authority – far greater than in individualized litigation – to counterbalance the economic power of a large conglomerate like Countrywide. As joint legal actions involving multiple plaintiffs (often numbering in the thousands), class-action proceedings require certification (*certiorari*) under federal rules of civil procedure, which mandate that courts apply tests of whether borrowers in disparate locales have sufficient interests in common to function as a cohesive set of legal claims (*commonality*). In the Countrywide case, certification of a class of plaintiffs hung not on the question of whether Countrywide had designed and marketed a toxic loan product; the Court was clear that ample evidence existed to confirm that

Countrywide was engaged in a "scheme" to maximize originations of pay-option and subprime loans, often to borrowers for whom those loans were unsuitable. Rather, the certification of the class as a legal subject was contingent on demonstration that borrowers had been exposed to harm in a common manner or experienced a common injury through Countrywide's alleged exercise of fraud.

This procedural requirement posed numerous doctrinal challenges related to historical understandings of legal subjectivity. The sheer complexity of Countrywide's business model – which involved two different types of loan issued both directly (by at least four different divisions of the bank, each employing different marketing strategies) and indirectly (through affiliate relationships with hundreds of independent brokers) – divided the putative class into groups with very different experiences of harm.[4] Similarly, claims of unjust enrichment foundered on the different motivations of borrowers, some clearly acquisitive and looking to profit through purchase of investment properties. This complicated the notion that the bank had commonly injured unsuspecting homeowners, individualizing the question of injury for the District Court and causing it to deny class certification. In the Court's analysis, the racketeering claim "involves significant individualized inquiries, and these inquiries are of such a nature and number that they predominate over the common issues ... Plaintiffs have failed to demonstrate the alleged scheme was implemented through a common (or uniform) course of conduct likely to mislead the entire class" (U.S. District Court for Southern California, 2011: 63).

Here, the existence of a business structure organized around churning out high-cost loans fades into the background, as the time-space constructed within judicial proceedings could not wield Countrywide's shifting business practices, and its geographically variegated relationships with brokers and affiliates, into a temporally and spatially coherent whole cognizable to the Court. Despite common experiences of harm, which were recognized by the Court, these diffuse practices produced historically variegated circumstances for each transaction that did not match the historical legal norms for identifying a unified legal subject that can be the basis for claims. Law's very authority to "speak" to the terms and practices of subprime debt hinged on a jurisdictional threshold between law and non-law that retroactively authorized Countrywide's exploitative practices.

Parens patriae: ***Sovereign adjudication and the temporality of the mass settlement***

This account has thus far only focused on the adjudication of private claims against Countrywide – that is, the ways in which the time-space constructed within civil law situated plaintiffs' claims as beyond the threshold of law's authority. This helps us appreciate a form of *general* temporality for law, one that is evident across both private (civil, contract) and public (administrative/regulatory) law. However, this needs to be updated through a more situated argument regarding the futurity of public law, and the particular forms of temporality that come with a focus on the state. These accounts foreground different dimensions to law's futurity, highlighting other aspects to how, within "the institutional version of lawful relations ... the figuration work of [jurisdictional] technologies" binds "persons, places and events ... to the body of law" (Dorsett and McVeigh, 2012: 56). The economic orders that public law seeks to secure through its jurisdictional practices are thus found not only in quotidian courtroom dramas, then, but more fundamentally in the multiple regulatory venues and plural legal spaces grappling with the conjunctures of financial capitalism.

In the Countrywide fraud cases, this involves probing how jurisdiction was entangled within a broader set of legal-regulatory projects aiming to build a more resilient national banking market out of the financial volatility of the 1990s and 2000s. It also involves examining how the Countrywide case was ultimately resolved – which was not through private law proceedings, but through state-led legal action involving multiple state Attorneys General (AGs) resulting in a quick mass settlement with the lender. Closer attention to the latter foregrounds the embrace of *ad hoc* legal norms within emerging financial enforcement techniques, and highlights how those techniques close out legal uncertainty for lenders by transferring it back onto borrowers.

As a first entry point into the temporality of public law in this case, we can examine how the active agency of federal regulators constrained the jurisdictional basis for the Countrywide plaintiffs' claims, most notably by preempting state consumer protection law to reduce regulatory burdens on banks (Immergluck, 2009). In the original civil proceedings against Countrywide, several lead plaintiffs were denied standing to challenge Countrywide's practices under relevant state laws, as it was determined that those laws' more aggressive treatment of subprime lenders conflicted with federal banking regulations, issued in the late 1990s, that aimed to create a uniform legal playing field nationwide (U.S. District Court for Southern California, 2009). These regulations reserved the authority to regulate nationally chartered savings banks (of which Countrywide was one) for the federal Office of Thrift Supervision, overriding any state authority over the exercise of specific bank powers such as the setting of interest rates or the terms of credit. Similarly, "most-favored lender" rules, designed to create a competitive national marketplace for banking, allowed certain bank activities to be governed by the laws of their "home" state instead of the state where they were doing business, thus facilitating the extraterritorial application of particular state laws or removing the authority of state law altogether for particular agents.

Here, the adjudicative time-space for the Countrywide litigation was constructed within legislative and regulatory projects attempting to rationalize or "modernize" the U.S. banking system out of the crises of the late 1980s (Ashton, 2012). The notion of the national banking market – which was embedded in the National Bank Act of 1864 – was not an immutable legal framework in this regard, but took on new meaning as part of a set of market-oriented responses (enacted both through legislation and administrative rulemaking) to the chronic banking crises stretching from the late 1970s onwards. The "national bank" took on a special role within these evolving projects. Unencumbered by a patchwork quilt of state laws, and empowered to issue and price credit following a rapidly shifting market, the national bank could become an agent capable of producing a more resilient and efficient (future) banking system. In the analysis of the federal Office of the Comptroller of the Currency (the primary regulator of national commercial banks) during its preemption rulemaking in 2003, state consumer protection laws produced the opposite – an *undesirable* future, marked by weak and overburdened banks incapable of delivering critical social and economic resources:

> These laws introduce new standards for subprime lending that are untested, sometimes vague, often complex, and, in many cases, *different from established and well-understood Federal requirements.* They also *create new potential liabilities and penalties* for any lender that missteps in its efforts to comply with those new standards and restrictions. Thus, these laws materially increase a bank's costs and compliance risks in connection with subprime lending. Given the already generally higher credit risk of lending to subprime borrowers, *bank lenders will conclude* – and have concluded – that they simply are unable to effectively cover these increased costs and risks ... The practical result of these laws, therefore, is to obstruct, or for practical purposes, prevent, national banks from making certain types of real estate loans, causing an overall reduction in credit available to subprime borrowers. This means that *non-predatory, risk-priced credit will become more limited, or unavailable, to creditworthy subprime borrowers*
>
> (OCC, 2003: 46270, emphasis added).

This analysis is striking for its invocation of events that have not yet come to pass, but that nevertheless pose serious problems for government and populations highly interconnected with fast-paced financial markets. The most important of these future problems is *illiquidity* – the potential reduction in credit that will "inevitably" result from enhanced legal liabilities for banks' exploitative practices. The answer to these problems, in this case produced through federal preemption of state consumer protections, is to deliberately reorganize the threshold of law and non-law to increase the expropriative powers of banks. Mobilized within these legislative initiatives, jurisdiction thus functions as a future-oriented *technology of governance* – a way of constructing "lawful relations" (Dorsett and McVeigh, 2012) capable of governing complex economic and social realities and producing desired futures. It joins with other forms of legal speech "seeking to influence future sensibilities – not merely sensibilities about the future but also sensibilities in the future – to shape the expectations that impel the most fundamental dynamic of market economies" (Holmes, 2014: 10).

As a second entry point to the temporality of public law, we can turn to how federal preemption in turn spurred legal activism by state Attorneys General ("AGs"). As noted earlier, the case against Countrywide's hybrid ARM lending operations did not end with the denial of *certiorari.* Indeed, it was settled through a special, parallel legal proceeding involving litigation by 10 state AGs, led by Illinois Attorney General Lisa Madigan (Illinois Attorney General, 2008). This AG lawsuit, focused as before on Countrywide's scheme to produce and market hybrid ARM loans, originally called for the rescission of all contracts entered between Countrywide and Illinois consumers through unlawful methods from 2004 through 2008. It also asked that the lender pay damages to borrowers as well as civil penalties. Unlike the class-action proceedings detailed earlier, the AG lawsuit was quickly settled by Bank of America, which had acquired Countrywide Home Loans only a month after the Illinois complaint was filed in 2008. The terms of the settlement appeared quite punitive: Bank of America agreed to up to 400,000 mandatory loan modifications nationwide that would write down the principal value of the loans by a cumulative $8.4 billion (Morgenson, 2008). In addition, the lender agreed to direct payments of $8.5 million to borrowers who had lost their homes due to default on specific loan products, as well as $1 million in relocation assistance for homeowners unable to qualify for a loan modification.

This suit was not unique. State AGs had begun filing lawsuits against predatory lenders in the 1980s, employing the longstanding common law doctrine of *parens patriae* to give them standing to pursue corporations whose behavior threatened the health and welfare of the state's citizens. As a legal doctrine, *parens patriae* (literally "parent of the country") "permits states to sue to vindicate sovereign or quasi-sovereign interests," elevating "private interests … to the level of a quasi-sovereign state interest when … the injury in question affects a 'sufficiently substantial segment of [the state's] population'" (Lemos, 2012: 493–95). *Parens patriae* suits had gained traction through the 1980s and 1990s as tools appropriate to new problems of economic governance – in areas such as anti-trust enforcement or environmental protection – and to the disciplining of "groups seemingly beyond the reach of traditional state regulation … and too powerful to be subject to federal regulation" (Ieyoub and Eisenberg, 1999: 1879). Indeed, the irony of jurisdiction in the Countrywide case is that after federal preemption of state predatory lending laws stripped state *legislative* authority to pass laws governing the terms of credit issued by national banks, entrepreneurial AGs began to resort to *parens patriae* doctrine to bring harmful behavior against consumers within the scope of law (Lemos, 2012). The 2008 Illinois AG suit against Countrywide, which grew into a coordinated multi-state action, was the first of many that have emerged since the onset of the foreclosure crisis, using *parens patriae*'s combination of civil procedure (including private rights of action and settlement) and public enforcement powers to address egregious lender behavior.

In both these jurisdictional moves (preemption and *parens patriae*), then, the threshold of law becomes situated within forms of legal agency that fuse historical legal concepts (*national banking* and *quasi-sovereign interests*) to new governance imperatives. These invoke a range of legal authorizations working at different spatial scales, aiming to produce different kinds of future out of complex economic and social realities. For *parens patriae* suits, the results are oriented as much to the future as they are to remedying historical injuries suffered by borrowers, with "provisions for nonmonetary relief, focused on reforming how the defendant does business ... common in state settlements, even when the state is also seeking damages or restitution for injured individuals" (ibid.: 527). As Scheuerman (2004: 174 –175) elaborates, "litigation concerned first and foremost with assigning guilt to one party in reference to a past act may be less useful economically than a relatively quick compromise emphasizing positive lessons to be learned for both sides for the sake of maintaining cordial ties in the future."

This latter point is especially evident on examination of the various legal techniques that were employed within the Countrywide settlement to resolve borrowers' claims of expropriation – a final point where the futurity of public law is evident. Several points emerge from closer examination of the agreement. First, the significant size of the settlement pales when compared to the scale of expropriation it was meant to remedy: $8.4 billion spread among 400,000 borrowers amounts to an average of $21,000 per loan in principal write-downs or reduced interest payments. Given that a typical $150,000 hybrid ARM loan could generate over $200,000 in cumulative interest income over its lifespan, this represents only a marginal tax on the lender's profits.[5]

Second, the techniques employed to resolve borrowers' legal claims within the Countrywide settlement – notably, mandated modifications of the underlying mortgage – actually function to transfer uncertainty about the future back to borrowers. Rather than rescind the original mortgage contracts on Countrywide's hybrid ARM loans (as originally demanded), the 2008 settlement required that Bank of America modify those mortgages to increase the likelihood that owners could afford to stay in their homes. This represents a curious intermixing of borrower remedies with financial stability policy. The hybrid ARMs had been defaulting at an extraordinarily high rate, and modification represented a pragmatic strategy to retain the long-term value of those loans on lenders' balance sheet – a critical consideration given the weakness of U.S. banks in the aftermath of the financial crisis.

Indeed, the modification practices employed in the settlement reveal a specific orientation towards the future. Bank of America would produce an affordable loan by, first, temporarily reducing interest rates to as low as 2%, then by re-amortizing the outstanding principal balance to as long as 40 years, and forbearing any extra principle (payable as a lump sum at the end of the loan period) as necessary. Together, these steps are meant to reduce the overall loan payment to no more than 31% of the borrowers' income. However, this produces owner stability in the short-run (interest rates would begin rising again after 5 years) while securing the lenders' claim for as much of the value of the original loan as possible (Langley, 2009). This effectively restructures the original practices of financial exploitation to make them legally unproblematic.

These problematic framings of consumer injury within damage calculations have been a focus for critics of *parens patriae* actions, who see them as but one example of how the doctrine increases the scope for states to introduce multiple strategic imperatives and tradeoffs into the structuring of settlements. These imperatives can range from the nakedly political – the need to secure political capital in the run-up to elections – to those deriving from broader state determinations of the "public interest." In Jessop's (1990: 67) formulation, jurisprudence's past–future orientation is subsumed to more directly strategic, political, or *ad hoc* calculations as "legal norms are subject to even more elaborate specification by the administration in respect of particular conjunctures, situations, and interests." Drawing on Poulantzas (1978), he notes that legal orders under capitalism are marked by a growing persistence of exceptional law relative to "normal" law – exceptional in that they actively suspend or reorganize legal norms (cf. Christophers, 2013). Rather than representing a procedural culmination to borrowers' claims for relief from Countrywide's exploitative practices, then, the settlement can be seen as its own form of legal adjudicative time-space, closing off historic claims of injury, securing the futurity of creditors' claims for as much of the value of the original mortgage as possible, and clarifying forward-looking rules for exploitation in the future.

Conclusion

In the era of the growing circulation of property capital within global financial circuits, there is an understandable desire to see financial exploitation as fundamentally tied to acceleration, as the techniques used to produce financial hyper-profits – including securitization and structured finance – all decrease turnover time and allow capital to be reinvested in expropriation with increasing speed. Law's role in this regard recedes into the background; in Riles' (2011) formulation of derivatives contracts, law is simply the mundane and technical work of filling out paperwork for the complex financial instruments that secure creditors' (future) claims against debtors' incomes or assets.

However, the futurity of credit – its basis in the "invisible expectations of beneficial behavior" (Commons, 1924: 24) – is fraught with uncertainties, and attempts to regulate that uncertainty through legal "placeholders" can be problematic or the future unfolds differently from the "legal fiction" (Riles, 2011: 173) anticipated in an initial contract. When contracts break down and adjudicative processes are invoked, law ceases to be a passive or technical concern, and becomes a field where relations between borrower and creditor are actively organized (and reorganized) in relation to a threshold of "generality, publicity, clarity, prospectiveness, and stability" (Scheuerman, 2004). It is in this regard that the time-spaces of adjudication need to be approached as more than just secondary or incidental venues, and rather as central spaces wherein the character of financial exploitation is worked out. This perspective foregrounds the work of technologies of jurisdiction, such as precedent/jurisprudence, within judicial proceedings. Faced with private legal claims regarding mortgage contracts in court proceedings over fraud or unjust enrichment, these technologies have mobilized certain historic legal imaginaries (such as the appropriate "powers" of national banks, or limits to the construction of collective claims regarding financial exploitation) that work to secure the validity of creditors' claims against borrowers' future incomes.

A focus on law's temporality also necessarily grapples with jurisdiction as a sovereign technology of government, one actively wielded within state strategic projects seeking to secure a desired future out of a complex and tumultuous present. In relation to subprime lending, the status of consumer contracts was a field of legal experimentation through the late 1990s and early 2000s, as federal regulators sought to create idealized economic agents in the form of national banks unencumbered by inefficient state consumer protection laws. Through their exercise of sovereign powers of legal preemption, regulators placed lenders' ability to produce and market credit within a threshold of legal authorization, restructuring lawful relations between lender and borrower to project an historical imagination of the economic and social benefits of frictionless competition (and the dangers of illiquidity).

However, mortgage lending exists in plural legal spaces, and the practices of large subprime lenders such as Countrywide have also increasingly been organized under the scope of *parens patriae* doctrine by activist attorneys general seeking to protect consumers from the excesses of large corporations and too-big-to-fail banks. Whereas in the Countrywide case this resulted in a quick settlement where private legal proceedings foundered on a series of jurisprudential tests, the use of *parens patriae* doctrine significantly widened the scope for state strategic interests within the adjudication of borrowers' claims regarding expropriation. This is particularly evident in the *ad hoc* nature of the settlement itself and the legal techniques employed to close off Countrywide's (now Bank of America) legal liabilities. Not only were borrowers' claims of expropriation and unjust enrichment sold for cents on the dollar, but the wider forms of remedy were shifted from contract rescission (which would have effectively terminated Countrywide's mortgage claims and forced Bank of America to wipe out hundreds of thousands of loans on its books) to mortgage modifications. Whereas the latter restructure the credit relationship to make payments affordable to a household income (often by temporarily dropping interest rates as low as 2%), they also secured the futurity of Countrywide's claim against each borrower by extending loan amortizations and defeasing principle to a balloon payment at the loan's maturity. These resolution techniques thereby transfer uncertainty about the future back to borrowers and structure financial exploitation as legally unproblematic. The resulting construction of "consumer relief," then, has the effect of erasing high cost mortgages and onerous loan terms from the legal landscape, normalizing precarity by focusing reforms on how distressed borrowers can productively return to the perpetuity that is credit.

Notes

1 I am grateful to Mark Pendras, Sian Beynon-Jones, Emily Grabham, and three anonymous reviewers for insightful comments on earlier drafts of this chapter.

2 However, Countrywide's hybrid ARM loans carried prepayment penalties that protected yields to investors by requiring that borrowers pay as much as six months' worth of interest as a fee to exit the loan.

3 According to Delaney (1993: 55), "'Equity' in the Anglo-American legal tradition is supplemental to 'law,' strictly speaking. It is 'justice administered according to fairness' (Black's Law Dictionary). As such, the application of an equitable doctrine is case-specific and necessarily context-dependent. Unlike, for example, constitutional or statutory interpretation, a ruling in one case is considered to have no bearing on other cases."

4 For instance, "several hundreds of thousands of borrowers whose loans were originated by brokers had no contact with Countrywide at all (other than receiving federally-mandated loan disclosures)," challenging the claim that those borrowers has been harmed through contact with a criminal enterprise (ibid.: 58).

5 Lemos (2012: 526–527) has made a similar argument regarding other large bank settlements, referring to them as "a 'wrist slap' and a 'sweet deal' for the banks, given the vast economic damage [they] wrought."

Bibliography

Anderson, B. (2016). Governing emergencies: The politics of delay and the logic of response. *Transactions of the Institute of British Geographers* 41(1), pp.14–26.

Ashton P. (2012). 'Troubled assets': The financial emergency and racialized risk. *International Journal of Urban and Regional Research* 36(4), pp.773–790.

Ashton, P. and Christophers, B. (2016). Remaking mortgage markets by remaking mortgages: U.S. housing finance after the crisis. *Economic Geography* 94(3), pp.238–258.

Ashton, P. and Christophers, B. (2015). On arbitration, arbitrage and arbitrariness in financial markets and their governance: Unpacking LIBOR and the LIBOR scandal. *Economy and Society* 44(2), pp.188–217.

Barkan, J. (2013). *Corporate Sovereignty: Law and Government Under Capitalism*. Minneapolis, MN: University of Minnesota Press.

Bourdieu, P. (1987). Force of law: Toward a sociology of the juridical field. *Hastings Law Journal* 38(5), pp. 805–853.

Bruck, C. (2009). Angelo's ashes. *The New Yorker*, June 29. Available online at http://www.newyorker.com/magazine/2009/06/29/angelos-ashes [accessed March 23, 2017].

Christophers, B. (2013). Banking and competition in exceptional times. *Seattle University Law Review* 36, pp. 563–576.

Davies, W. (2016). Elite power under advanced neoliberalism. *Theory, Culture, and Society* 34(5–6), pp. 227–250.

De Goede, M. (2015). Speculative values and courtroom contestations. *South Atlantic Quarterly* 114(2), pp. 355–375.

Delaney, D. (1993). Geographies of judgment: The doctrine of changed conditions and the geopolitics of race. *Annals of the Association of American Geographers* 83(1), pp. 48–65.

Dorn, N. (2011). Regulatory sloth and activism in the effervescence of financial crisis. *Law & Policy* 33(3), pp. 428–448.

Dorsett, S. and McVeigh, S. (2012). *Jurisdiction*. New York: Routledge.

Foucault, M. (1996). Truth and juridical forms. *Social Identities* 2(3), pp. 327–342.

———. (1984). The juridical apparatus. In *Legitimacy and the State*, W. Connolly (ed.). New York: NYU Press.

French, S., Leyshon, A., and Thrift, N. (2009). A very geographical crisis: The making and breaking of the 2007–2008 financial crisis. *Cambridge Journal of Regions, Economy and Society* 2(2), pp. 287–302.

Holmes, D. (2014). *Economy of Words: Communicative Imperatives in Central Banks.* Chicago: University of Chicago Press.

Ieyoub, R. P. and Eisenberg, T. (1999). State Attorney General actions, the tobacco litigation, and the doctrine of parens patriae. *Tulane Law Review* 74, pp. 1859–1883.

Illinois Attorney General. (2008). Illinois Attorney General Madigan Leads $8.7 Billion Groundbreaking Settlement of Lawsuit against Mortgage Giant Countrywide. Available online at http://www.illinoisattorneygeneral.gov/pressroom/2008_10/20081006.html [downloaded December 12, 2011].

Immergluck, D. (2009). *Foreclosed: High-Risk Lending, Deregulation, and the Undermining of America's Mortgage Market.* Ithaca, NY: Cornell University Press.

Jessop, B. (1990). *State Theory: Putting Capitalist States in Their Place.* Cambridge: Polity Press.

Joseph, M. (2014). *Debt to Society: Accounting for Life under Capitalism.* Minneapolis: University of Minnesota Press, 2014.

Kaushal, A. P. (2013). *The Jurisdiction of Difference: Groups and Law.* PhD Dissertation, School of Law, University of British Columbia, Vancouver, BC.

Langley, P. (2014). *Liquidity Lost: The Governance of the Global Financial Crisis.* Oxford: Oxford University Press.

———. (2009). Debt, discipline, and government: Foreclosure and forbearance in the subprime mortgage crisis. *Environment and Planning A* 41(6), pp.1404–1419.

Latour, B. (2003). *The Making of Law: An Ethnography of the Conseil d'État.* Cambridge: Polity Press.

Lemos, M. H. (2012). Aggregate litigation goes public: Representative suits by state attorneys general. *Harvard Law Review* 126 (2), pp. 486–549.

Marazzi, C. (2010). *The Violence of Financial Capitalism.* Los Angeles: Semiotext(e).

Morgenson, G. (2008). Illinois to sue Countrywide. *The New York Times,* June 25. Available online at http://www.nytimes.com/2008/06/25/business/25mortgage.html [downloaded December 12, 2011].

Nagareda, R. (2008). *Mass Torts in a World of Settlement.* Chicago: University of Chicago Press.

Office of the Comptroller of the Currency (OCC). (2003). Preemption Determination and Order, Docket No. 03-17, August 5. *68 Federal Register 150*: 46264–46281.

Peterson, C. (2006). Predatory structured finance. *Cardozo Law Review* 28(5), pp. 2185–2284.

Poulantzas, N. (1978). *State, Power, Socialism.* London: Verso.

Pryke, M. and Allen, J. (2000). Monetized time-space: derivatives – money's "new imaginary"?. *Economy and Society,* 29(2), 264–284

Richland, J. (2013). Jurisdiction: Grounding law in language. *Annual Review of Anthropology* 42, pp. 209–226.

Riles, A. (2011). *Collateral Knowledge: Legal Reasoning in the Global Financial Markets.* Chicago: University of Chicago Press.

Ramirez, S. A. (2014). *Lawless Capitalism: The Subprime Crisis and the Case for an Economic Rule of Law.* New York: NYU Press.

Rose, N. and Valverde, M. (1998). Governed by law? *Social and Legal Studies* 7(4), pp. 541–551

Scheuerman, W. (2004). *Liberal Democracy and the Social Acceleration of Time.* Baltimore, MD: Johns Hopkins University Press.

U.S. District Court for the Southern District of California. (2011). *In re Countrywide Financial Corporation Mortgage Marketing and Sales Practices Litigation*, 277 F.R.D. 586, U.S. Dist. LEXIS 118034.

U.S. District Court for the Southern District of California. (2009). *In re Countrywide Fin. Corp. Mortg. Mktg. & Sales Practices Litigation*. 601 F. Supp. 2d 1201, U.S. Dist. LEXIS 18227.

von Benda-Beckmann, K. (2014). Trust and the temporalities of law. *Journal of Legal Pluralism and Unofficial Law 46*(1), pp. 1–17.

4 On delay and duration

Law's temporal orders in historical child sexual abuse cases

Sinéad Ring, Kent Law School

Introduction

Over the course of the past century, law has been called on to perform an important function in relation to historical violence perpetrated by political or religious groups or by States against minorities. In the military tribunals established in Nuremberg and Tokyo, the trial of Adolf Eichmann and the trials of leaders in Rwanda, and the former Yugoslavia, law and legal processes have been called on to decide what happened and to judge those responsible. This dual fact-finding and normative function of law has also been called on in the trials of Holocaust deniers and in quasi-judicial bodies such as the Bloody Sunday Inquiry and the Hillsborough Independent Panel in the UK and the South African Truth and Reconciliation Commission. Commissions of Inquiry have been employed to explore widespread violence against women and children in Canada (the National Inquiry into Missing and Murdered Indigenous Women and Girls) and against children in Australia (the Royal Commission into Institutional Responses to Child Sexual Abuse). In Ireland, commissions of investigation/inquiry have been established to address the revelations of historical wrongs, such as, for example, in relation to the Mother and Baby Homes (Commission of Investigation into Mother and Baby Homes) and the women and girls who were incarcerated in Magdalene Laundries (McAleese, 2013).

One of the primary uses of inquiries in the Irish context has been in relation to the historical, sexual, physical and emotional abuse of children in industrial schools and in residential schools run by the Catholic Church on behalf of the Irish State (Commission to Inquire into Child Abuse, 2009) and various archdioceses (Commission of Investigation, 2009; 2010).

Legal scholars have long been sceptical of the ability of legal proceedings, including transitional justice mechanisms, to establish a historical record or to hold those responsible for historical wrongdoing accountable (e.g. Arendt, 1994; Agamben, 1999; Douzinas, 2000; Douglas, 2001). These critiques have examined the foundational moments of law as they contribute to the epic of a nation (Douzinas, 2000); on the trials of leaders in the context of mass atrocities (Elberling, 2012); on the ability of transitional justice mechanisms to deliver accountability in situations of historical conflict (Turner, 2017) or on the capacity of international courts to ensure victims' participation and to 'provide some measure of restorative justice through the courts' (Kendall, 2015). This chapter seeks to expand on that literature in two ways: by exploring the role of the formal criminal law in determining the contours of the past and, in keeping with the philosophical orientations of this collection, by focusing on time as a tool of legal regulation. The chapter takes as a case study the 'delay' jurisprudence developed by the Irish Superior Courts in the period 1999–2006. It begins with an explanation of the jurisprudence and highlights the courts' use of two key concepts: 'delay' and 'dominion'. Part II argues that these represent a form of temporal ordering imposed by law that sought to create a linear notion of time in historical child sexual abuse prosecutions. For victims,[1] this linear conception of time narrowed the limits of what could be deemed a 'legitimate' experience; and, in so doing, law narrowed the limits of history. Furthermore, closer examination of the roots of delay and dominion in law's past (in outdated myths about criminal law and rape victims) shows that the time of these cases is not linear.

Part III argues that the temporal ordering imposed in the delay cases may be better understood not as linear time but rather as the Bergsonian notion of duration (durée). Duration is time as flow. It challenges linear notions of time as a series of discrete and divisible moments. Instead, thinking law's time through the notion of duration opens up the possibility of thinking of connections, adaptations and change as being part of law's ontology. This allows us to highlight the continuities and recursive modes at work in law's engagement in these cases. Therefore, while law may be holding itself out as reaching towards a necessarily improved future, understanding law's time in these cases as duration allows an understanding of the complex nonlinear relationship law has with its own past, as well as the unpredictability of the future response of law to (historical) violence. This insight may inform progressive scholars' endeavours to understand law's engagement with historical child sexual abuse. The chapter concludes with some observations on what all of this may mean for society's commitment to using law as the state's primary response to addressing historical wrongdoing.

The Irish 'delay' cases

In the early-to-mid-1990s Ireland experienced an unprecedented surge in the number of people talking about and reporting abuse that happened years, often decades, earlier. This was a result of heightened public awareness around the harms and extent of child sexual abuse that flowed out of a number of scandals involving familial, clerical sexual abuse and abuse in residential institutions (e.g. McGuinness, 1993; Moore, 1995; Department of Health, 1996), as well as the courage of individual survivors including Marie Collins, Colm O'Gorman, Christine Buckley, Andrew Madden and Paddy Doyle,[2] coupled with the work of investigative journalists (e.g. Lentin, 1996; Raftery and O'Sullivan, 1999).

In these cases, the lapse of time between the alleged abuse and the eventual prosecution is usually in the order of decades (Ring, 2009). Until large numbers of adults began reporting sexual violence in childhood, the Irish criminal courts generally did not hear cases involving significant lapses of time between the offence and the trial (O'Malley, 2009; Ring, 2013). For example, in *State (O'Connell) v Fawsitt* (1986),[3] a delay of 5 years by the prosecution was described as 'extreme'. In *Fitzpatrick* (1989),[4] a delay of 4 years in prosecuting two charges of larceny was held to justify an order of prohibition. The courts made no exceptions for abused children who did not report 'on time'; as late as 1992 a 1-year delay in reporting rendered a child's complaint of abuse inadmissible.[5] If this legal position had endured, no historical child sexual abuse offences would ever have been tried by a jury, in spite of the changed societal climate of the mid- to late 1990s. In response to the demand for justice presented by the numbers of people coming forward, the Irish Superior Courts (the High Court and the Supreme Court) adopted a more flexible approach to the issue of delayed reporting of historical sexual abuse. They developed a new kind of 'delay' jurisprudence in the context of hearing applications to prohibit the prospective trial brought by defendants charged with historical sexual abuse offences.[6] In these 'prohibition cases' the Superior Courts had to decide whether, due to the lapse of time, the risk of the defendant getting an unfair trial was so great that the prosecution should be halted. Defendants pointed to the effects of the passage of time on their ability to effectively contest the charges; lack of clarity on the details of the date(s) and location of the alleged abuse; missing (potential) witnesses; faded memories; missing real evidence (see Ring, 2009). In response to the large numbers of defendants seeking to have their trial prohibited on the grounds of 'delay', the Irish Supreme Court developed a legal test to be applied in all such prohibition applications. This test, set down in the case of *PC v DPP*,[7] established the approach to be taken in defence applications to prohibit the prosecution of historical child sexual abuse charges and was applied in all such cases from 1999 until 2006.[8] The *PC* test placed central importance on the notion of 'delay', *specifically* the reasons for the delayed reporting. The key question courts hearing prohibition applications were to ask was: what the reasons for the delay were and whether, assuming the complaint to be true, the delay in making it was referable to the accused's conduct.[9] If the answer was positive, the court would prohibit the prospective trial. The focus on the reasons for the delay was surprising because this necessarily entailed a pre-judgement of the question of whether the offence(s) had indeed been committed[10] and, more importantly, the reasons for the delay had no bearing whatsoever on the primary question, which was whether the defendant could have a fair trial.[11] Temporality was key to the law's construction of due process (on which, see further Ring, 2009 and 2013).

The temporalising force of law as expressed through the trope of delay had particular implications for victims. In determining whether the delay was referable to the defendant (and hence fatal to any prohibition request) or not, the courts were required to inquire into the issues of whether the delay was 'reasonable'.

The reasonableness of the delay centred on an evolving psycho-legal concept of 'dominion': the relationship of domination between the abuser and the victim that prevented the victim from reporting the offences at the time.[12] If dominion was found to have existed (following extensive psychological assessments and the reception into evidence of victims' affidavits explaining why they could not report sooner), the delay was reasonable and excusable and the trial would be allowed to take place. In this way, law created and employed a notion of delay that was directly bound up with the question of whether a trial could go ahead. Dominion was found in the majority of cases (Hogan and Whyte, 2003, para 6.5.246; O'Malley, 2009: 661).

In these historic child abuse prosecutions from 1999–2006, the tropes of 'dominion' and 'delay' may be understood as very positive examples of the law's temporalising force; the courts used 'delay' and 'dominion' to circumvent the law's established approach to historic crimes and ensured instead that sexual violence committed against children in the past did not go unprosecuted.[13] Thus the judicial development of the tropes of 'delay' and 'dominion' was a significant and progressive moment for Irish law's engagement with the problem of historical violence against children.

However, despite its laudable aims, the delay jurisprudence remains problematic because of its basis in notions of linear time.

Delay and linear time

Close examination of the decisions of the courts applying the *PC* test reveals that the focus on the reasons for the delay facilitated the creation of a narrative of progress in linear time, which said that law would now address a serious crime that had gone undetected and unpunished for so long. This fitted with a linear conception of law's time, as an irreversible and inevitable progression of moments from past through the present and towards the (better) future. Importantly, this interpretative move allowed the period before the eventual reporting (the 'delay') to be divided into segments, which could be evaluated for their reasonableness, as described above. Unfortunately, however, not all segments of delay were given the same importance. If a total period of delay (e.g. 30 years) was shown to include a period of 'unreasonable delay', the overall delay would be found to be incompatible with a relationship of dominion between the defendant and the victim, and so the trial would be halted. In one case where the victim had been in a supportive relationship for 7 years, the total delay was held to be unreasonable.[14] In another, a period during which reporting did not take place because the victim was concerned disclosure would affect her career in the gardaí (police) precluded a finding of dominion. [15] In one incest case, the victim's fear of causing problems in her family was not enough to 'excuse' the delay in reporting.[16] Indications of psychological health and coping mechanisms in adulthood were also found to be inconsistent with dominion.[17] Therefore, 'delay' and 'dominion', which were based on a notion of law's time being linear, could not comprehend or account for a victim's nonlinear experiences.

However, some victims' experiences had the potential to disrupt law's putative linear time. In interrogating victims' life histories, the courts were confronted with accounts that ran counter to the neat narrative of the victim having remained silent for decades because of the abuser's dominion over him/her. A close reading of the prohibition cases from 1999–2006 indicates that a significant minority of victims did attempt to report at the time of the abuse or closer to that time, but they were frustrated in their efforts by the adults to whom they disclosed (Ring, 2017). The adults to whom these victims disclosed were family members;[18] teachers, [19] doctors;[20] social workers;[21] and even gardaí.[22] These stories were not ones of dominion, but of victims' agency and action and the indifference of adults who should have acted to help children who reported. However, rather than explicitly recognise the complexity of these narratives, the courts brought them within the dominion trope, which located the reason for the delay solely in the victim's response to the abuse. For example, in the *PC* case itself, the defendant, a bus driver, was charged with five counts of indecent assault and three counts of unlawful carnal knowledge dating back to the early 1980s. The victim disclosed the abuse within a few years of its ending, in 1986 or 1987, when she was in her final year of school. She told her classmates, her parents, a teacher and the head teacher. Her motivation for telling the head teacher was to protect other potential victims. She also told a garda sergeant. Unfortunately, instead of pursuing the matter, he told the victim to inform her parents if she had any further problems. The victim finally made a formal complaint in 1995. In the Supreme Court, Denham J held that because of his status as an adult and his position of authority, the defendant had been in a dominant position over the victim while she was in school. The victim's decision not to make a formal complaint in 1988 was 'entirely comprehensible in light of the reaction she got to her initial disclosure of the abuse. She was not supported. She was not brought to a counsellor. She was not brought to a garda station' (p. 63 per Denham J). Thus, the fact that the authority figures in her life did not take appropriate action in 1988 was part of the circumstances. However, Denham J quickly moved on from this insight to say that the delay was, in fact, caused by the defendant: 'The delay was caused by the [victim's] inability to make a formal complaint until 1995. This was a consequence of the alleged sexual abuse, the alleged criminal actions. Thus, fault lies with the alleged perpetrator of the actions – the [defendant]' (63, per Denham J). The only comment she made regarding the inaction by adults was that their failure to act 'probably prolong[ed] the psychological dominance and inhibition'(63, per Denham J). She then went on to inquire as to whether the defendant would risk an unfair trial and held that he would not.

Keane CJ also relied on the psychologist's evidence to say that the delay was explicable in light of all the circumstances, including the lack of action by adults in 1988. However, the delay was ultimately the result of the defendant's actions. These judgments show that the Court placed most emphasis on the negative psychological effects of the abuse on the victim and thus underemphasised her agency in reporting to protect other children. Furthermore, the failures of a number of adults to take the problem seriously became merely a minor detail in the story told by the Court. This theme of minimisation of stories of victims' agency and inaction by responsible adults is also clear in other cases decided under the *PC* test (Ring, 2017). Even in the rare cases in which the court did acknowledge the 'climate of disbelief'[23] in Irish society around sexual abuse of children, the focus remained on the defendant's actions, the victim's 'inadequacy' and not on the inaction of society and the authorities. In this way, the potential for these more 'complex' victims' stories to disrupt law's linear time as expressed through the dominion narrative was defused. Unfortunately, however, this was achieved at the expense of a more honest reckoning with the complex experiences of some victims. The imposition of a linear conception of time onto victims' experiences meant that law failed to reflect the diversity of experiences presented to the courts by victims.

Furthermore, the notion that law's time in these cases was linear was belied by the deeply rooted connections between the delay jurisprudence and older myths about the law and about victims, namely: the myth of criminal justice; and the myth of the untrustworthy rape victim. These are explored in the next section.

The role of myths

The twin notions of delay and dominion in the delay jurisprudence from 1999–2006 were structured around two founding myths: the myth of effective criminal law and the myth of the untrustworthy rape victim.

The myth of effective criminal law

This is the notion that the criminal law is effective at punishing wrongdoers and protecting potential future victims from harm. It is closely linked to the foundational myth of the sovereign State; that the State has control over security and crime within its territory (Garland, 1996). The decisions in the delay cases were based on the implicit notion that sexual violence against children has been criminalised since before the foundation of the State[24] and that if victims had only reported 'in time', the criminal process would have prosecuted and punished abusers. Of course, this claim of law's jurisdiction as timeless was clearly untrue; the surge in numbers of adults coming forward in the mid-1990s to complain was evidence in itself of the historical failure by law to protect children. Indeed, the evidence received by the prohibition courts from victims and psychologists on the reasons why victims delayed reveals that it makes no sense to speak of children in the past having rights to bodily integrity and dignity protected by the criminal law. Furthermore, the evidence of those victims who reported that they disclosed to adults contemporaneously but were ignored, exposes law as contingent and provisional and dependent on the cooperation of society for its effectiveness.

The myth of the untrustworthy rape victim

The constructs of delay and dominion were also structured along the lines of the myth of the untrustworthy rape victim. First, 'delayed reporting' is taken as indicative of unreliability. This myth explains why the interval between the abuse and the report was viewed by the courts applying the *PC* test as inherently suspicious and in need of explanation. It is partly based on the discredited notion that 'real' victims of sexual violence always complain immediately. Thus, a common defence lawyer's tactic was to argue that a jury could only trust a rape victim's word if she had reported the attack promptly (Brereton, 1997; Raitt, 2004). Although this requirement of prompt complaint has been excised from modern law, the core idea that 'real' victims report soon after the assault forms the basis of the contemporary evidential doctrine of recent complaint.

If the witness' credibility is enhanced by an immediate complaint because, in the circumstances there was not time to concoct a false accusation, '*our doubts about the victim's veracity will have been removed*' (Williams, 1982: 664; emphasis added).[25]

According to this doctrine, a consistent prior statement of a fresh complaint may be admitted as part of the prosecution case.[26] The statement, although not corroborative, may be evidence of consistency.[27] This approach, which on first glance may seem to be pro-victim, stands in marked contrast to the law's approach to victims in non-sexual cases, which assumes that the veracity of the victim's account is simply a matter for the jury following examination and cross-examination by counsel. As an exception to the rule against narrative the doctrine of recent complaint seems at first glance to favour victims of sexual offences. However, closer inspection reveals its discriminatory foundations. It has its roots in outdated assumptions; it was useful to rebut the 'adverse inference that might otherwise be drawn from the victim's failure to complain of the attack upon her'.[28] It also went towards rebutting a 'presumption' of consent; Cross (1979: 242) noted that a complaint might be used to rebut the 'factual presumption of consent which might otherwise arise' (Cross: 242). Therefore, the doctrine of recent complaint is, in fact, a rule against the victim, rather than in her favour (Charleton and Byrne, 2010, 13–14; Stanchi, 1976). Similarly, the notions of blameworthy delay and of unreasonable and reasonable periods of delay in the prohibition cases were based on the same discriminatory assumptions about the behaviour of victims of sexual violence.

Second, the myth of the untrustworthy rape victim is also constructed on the myth that law should not trust the word of the victim of sexual violence. The requirement in the delay cases that the prosecution show (using affidavits and testimony from victims and expert psychologists' reports) that the victim was under the dominion of the abuser for the period of the delay demonstrates law's recourse to outdated myths about the need for corroboration in sexual offences cases. Unfounded stereotypical notions about women and children informed the old rule that, in rape cases, the judge had to explain to the jury that it was dangerous to convict on the basis of the victim's evidence unless there was corroborative evidence.[29] The requirement of corroboration was based on the myth that victims of sexual offences were highly unreliable and should therefore be treated with extreme scepticism (Ellison and Munro, 2009).

Although the requirement of corroboration warning in sexual cases has been abolished,[30] trial judges retain a discretion to administer a warning where appropriate on the facts.[31] Corroboration continues to play an important role in decisions to grant appeals against convictions for sexual offences (Fennell, 2009: Ch 6).

In the prohibition cases, the focus on the psychological injury to the victim and the requirement that psychologists provided reports to the courts on the reasonableness or otherwise of the delay has very clear resonance with the notion of corroboration. Thus, the temporal notion of delay and dominion, both of which were associated with it, were forms of ordering based on rape myths.

In 2006 the Supreme Court replaced the *PC* test with a test that simply asks whether the defendant runs the real and serious risk of an unfair trial.[32] There is also a residual discretion to prohibit the trial in exceptional circumstances. Victims are no longer required to explain their reasons for delayed reporting. Instead, the courts have effectively taken judicial notice of the reasons why victims delayed in historical abuse cases.[33] Therefore, the courts now recognise as *prima facie* valid the reasons why victims delay. The fact that the courts had to have 7 years of receiving evidence of what those reasons could be, before reaching this conclusion, betrays the law's attraction to outdated myths about the power of the criminal law and the unreliability of testimony from victims of sexual violence.

The various features of delay and dominion sketched here reveal that in the delay cases examined from 1999–2006, the courts were ultimately most concerned with imposing a linear notion of law's time in historical child sexual abuse prosecutions, and that these forms of temporal ordering had their roots in outdated stereotypes about law and about rape victims. However, the tropes of dominion and delay may be better understood from the perspective not of linear time, but rather through the paradigm of 'duration' as developed by Henri Bergson. This argument is developed in the next section.

Delay, dominion and duration

Henri Bergson (1859–1941) was a philosopher of time, movement and change. Bergson offers a philosophy of movement (Grosz, 2005: 94), i.e. a life based movement that transcends the dualism of ideas/discourses vs. materiality, culture and nature (96). For Bergson, 'time' is objective and mechanical, but 'duration' is always embodied. Indeed, duration is not just lived experience; it is also the condition of experience. The self (consciousness) consists of a continuous flow of duration. The self is not a succession of discontinuous states; number cannot account for the continuously evolving quality of the self's duration. Instead, Bergson presents the duration of consciousness as the hyphen or connecting link that brings the past into the future (Hill, 2013: 302). In *Creative Evolution* (1944), he extends his thinking about duration to life. He argues that the whole universe has a particular, irreducible rhythm of duration that is something like a consciousness (1944: 10). Life is inventive and unforeseeable thanks to the preservation of memory, which he identifies with the vital impetus animating the evolutionary process (Bergson, 1944: 4–5, 23). For a living being, each moment is new insofar as it includes the memory, conscious or unconscious, of all the moments preceding it. For Bergson, duration is 'the indivisible continuity of change' (1946; 2007: 124, cited by Mawani at 257).

Although Bergson never wrote specifically about law, his work allows us to engage with questions about law's ontology and about how law's ontology may relate to ideas of change and multiplicity. Renisa Mawani (2015) has employed Bergson's notion of duration to argue that time is not exterior to or beyond law, rather that its temporal movements forge the basis of its authority and, furthermore, law's internal dynamics influence the conceptions of time it imposes on the world (256).

Mawani (2015) has employed insights from Bergson to re-visit questions of historicity as they relate to the doctrine of precedent in common law (discussing Parker, 2011). Precedent is what gives legal decisions their authority and symbolic force within a community. Importantly, however, the doctrine of precedent is not simply about repeating the past. Rather, law must reach to the past for its authority while responding to the pressures of the present and anticipating the unforeseeable future (Mawani, 2015: 258).

Mawani's reading of Bergson highlights that duration is always becoming and it is part of law's ontology. Adapting to the pressures of the present is not simply a response to things that are exterior to law, such as the claims of victims, but it is also bound up with law's being-becoming. It is interior to law. Thinking of law as duration 'centers the ubiquity of movement, mobility, and change as law's ontology, a shift that holds implications for legal history and legal scholarship. Briefly, duration invites a different conception of legal change' (Mawani, 2015: 262). She notes that, in legal scholarship, there is a tendency to view change as adaptation and response to circumstances exterior or other to law, but law as duration emphasises law's internal temporalities while opening the future as a site of novelty, a recognition that law will always be other than it is, that change is always already happening. (262). Therefore, contingency is not a product of history, but rather it is the ontology of life and law (ibid).

As Part I explained, the Irish courts faced with the advent of huge numbers of historical abuse prosecutions were forced to reckon with an existing precedent and established practice that decreed that delay was fatal to a prosecution. The solution they offered was one of inquiring into the reasons for the delayed reporting. The common law's creative power as a temporalising force that constitutes new responses to present legal problems is clear. However, in seeking to overcome precedent, the courts imposed a linear notion of time on victims' experiences. As noted earlier, this was a useful tool for evaluating experience, however, it has rendered some periods of delay – and hence some victims' experiences – incompatible with dominion.

Therefore, the twin concepts of delay and dominion were also temporalising forces that constituted new subjectivities, by imposing a supposedly linear conception of time onto victims' experiences. Mawani notes that '[i]t is only through duration that we can conceive of time and life as flux and flow rather than as discrete and divisible moments' (2015: 257). Duration allows us to contest the claims made by law, through the tropes of delay and dominion, that victims' experiences are divisible into different moments that can be evaluated and judged by law, and to point up instead the nonlinear and recursive features of law.

Of course, law did not break totally with the past. Instead, the focus on the reasonableness of the victim's delay was bound up with myths about the effectiveness of the criminal law and the reliability of a rape victims' testimony. In this way, law was responding to present pressures by changing its perspective on the past and by doing so it was reaching into the past for different authorities – rape myths and the sovereign power of law – by which it could take law in a new future direction. This is in keeping with duration: as Mawani explains, in Bergson's view of evolution, life does not follow a linear teleology but it manifests competing and even opposing tendencies, 'leaning to the past while reaching to the future, revealing a back and forth that produces indeterminacy, unpredictability, and novelty while retaining continuity' (257). Life unfolds by continually emerging anew, exceeding language, measurement, representation and even law (Mawani, 2014; 2015: 257). Therefore, law was not simply responding to the pressures of the claims for justice from victims, but rather was reaching for the familiar – however outdated – past in order to adapt to the needs of the present in terms of justice for victims and also in order to retain continuity with its own past.

These insights are potentially very important to understanding the law's engagement with historical child sexual abuse in the delay cases examined in this chapter. They open up the perspective that progressive legal change is not simply an outcome of the influence of history and the demands of the present on law. Rather, it is an example of law seizing an opportunity to deliver justice to (some) victims. Furthermore, duration helps us to see that the change involved an exclusion of some victims through the imposition of linear time, as well as a recourse to the past, by reviving outdated stereotypes about law and victims of historical abuse.

Furthermore, viewing law's time as duration allows us to see how law's temporalising force may shape the future in unpredictable ways. Law as duration invites us to think about the 'inventiveness of law is full of possibilities that are positive/negative, desirable/undesirable, not necessarily just and always unforeseeable.' This insight is particularly important when we think about law's role in shaping history; in judging the past, law is also judging and creating the present and the future, a future that is always already contingent and undetermined. In historical sexual abuse cases, law may be creating a future in which wilful ignorance is forgiven, and in which some victims are forgotten.

Conclusion

In law's move towards judgement, it constructs authoritative stories about the past. These stories may or may not correlate with ideas of truth or justice (Agamben, 1999: 18). They certainly may not fit with the stories presented to the court by witnesses, including victims. Nevertheless, the judgments produced by courts become the stories we tell ourselves about our past (Sarat and Kearns, 2002). In this way, law creates subjectivities and histories that are important both for individuals' sense of themselves and for the wider community's memory of its past. This is particularly true of the criminal law, because the formal criminal justice system remains the recognised way of demonstrating that society takes an issue seriously (Hudson, 2002: 629).

Adults who come to the courts claiming to have been sexually abused as children represent a potent challenge to law's authority to determine and judge the past. Historical abuse cases expose law's limited knowledge; law/justice is not eternal and therefore all-knowing, but rather it is contingent and contestable. In order to address the gap between law's precedent and the justified demands on justice from victims, the Irish courts developed a juridical test that introduced the temporalising forces of delay and dominion. Law's use of these temporalities is anticipated by Greenhouse: 'temporality appears to be most useful as a matrix of political improvisation in precisely those contexts where the challenge to legitimacy comes in the form of diversity, as perceived by those challenged' (Greenhouse, 1996: 175). Delay and dominion were positive innovations because they allowed historical child sexual abuse complaints to be heard by the courts. However, they were problematic because they constructed some victims as unreasonable and they erased the societal context in which non-reporting took place. Furthermore, they reinvigorated unfounded stereotypes about victims of sexual violence. Thinking of law's time as duration opens up a space for understanding the dynamics at play in these cases, particularly how legal interpretive tools such as delay and dominion are always contingent and how they can seek to regulate the present and the future.

The argument that law's time in these cases is one of duration also gives rise to further important questions. If time is a form of relationality or ethical encounter (Bastian, 2013; van Rijswijk, 2013), then the courts' construction of delay in the Irish prohibition cases between 1999 and 2006 indicates a failure to witness the complexity of narratives and experiences presented to the courts in prohibition cases. This ethical failure of law reminds us of the need to pay attention to law's power to create history in the sense of a collective memory. As Steffi Hobuss (2011) has argued, following Derrida (1988) and Butler (1997), because memory – in this case, society's collective memory of our history of abuse – is based on performative social practice, an individual or group needs the social authority and must be in the right position, to claim that certain memory acts should be done or what should (not) be remembered. The memory acts that are in play here are those of re-iterating and re-framing reasons for not reporting 'on time'. Serious question marks must arise over the law's ability to declare what should and should not be remembered and how experience should be remembered. Indeed, the problematic ways the Irish courts have employed notions of time and temporality in the cases examined here indicate an urgent need for a reconsideration of law's role in determining the contours of Ireland's history of child sexual abuse.

Notes

1 The term 'victim' rather than 'survivor' or 'complainant' is used in order to give expression to the position of the person who reported the abuse in the cases discussed. It is also appropriate because it is the term that law recognises and requires in order to intervene in people's lives (Mulla, 2011).
2 For an early autobiographical account, see Doyle, 1989. See also Madden, 2004; O'Gorman, 2009.
3 [1986] IR 362. It was 3 years from the return for trial to the institution of the prohibition proceedings. The defendant was charged with two counts of assault causing actual bodily harm.
4 *Fitzpatrick v District Justice Shields and the DPP* [1989] ILRM 243 *per* Carroll J, High Court (*ex tempore*). A delay of 10 months between an abortive trial and the date of the retrial, coupled with a delay of 4 months in serving additional evidence was held along with other factors to justify prohibition: *O'Connor v DPP* [1987] ILRM 723.
5 *People (DPP) v Synott* (29 May 1992, unreported), Court of Criminal Appeal.
6 Judicial review is provided for by Article 34.3.1 of the Constitution. The procedure for judicial review is governed by Ord. 84 of the Rules of the Superior Courts 1986.
7 [1999] 2 IR 25.
8 Defence applications seeking to prohibit their forthcoming trial remain a constant feature of the courts workload. The current test was established in *SH v DPP* [2006] 3 IR 575. The Supreme Court held that its judicial knowledge of issues relating to dominion, as well as inhibition, disparity between the ages of the accused and the complainants and other issues relating to reasons why a complainant might delay, were now well established. It is no longer necessary for a court hearing a prohibition application to inquire into the reasons for the delay, or whether the accused had exercised dominion over the complainant or to make assumptions as to the truth of the complaints. The test is now: has the delay resulted in prejudice to an accused so as to give rise to a real and serious risk of an unfair trial? The Court also held that in exceptional circumstances, where it would be unfair or unjust to put an accused on trial, prohibition could be granted, regardless of whether the accused had established a risk of an unfair trial.
9 There were two other limbs to the test: Whether, depending on the nature of the charges, the delay was such that, despite the absence of actual prejudice, the trial should be prohibited, and Whether the accused had suffered actual prejudice such that the trial should not be allowed to proceed. At this stage, the presumption of innocence would apply [1999] 2 IR 25, 68 *per* Keane J.
10 While the presumption of innocence was temporarily suspended.
11 See Ring 2009 for development of this argument.
12 [1994] 3 IR 140, 197 *per* Denham J.
13 This was echoed in the extension of time limits for civil suits for child sexual abuse: The *Statute of Limitations (Amendment) Act 2000.*
14 *PC v DPP* [2005] IEHC 103.
15 *DPP v JO'C*, unreported High Court, 27 July, 2001.
16 *PC v Malone* [2002] 2 IR 560. This court in this case employed the concept of inhibition, which was closely related to the idea of dominion.
17 *TS v DPP* [2005] 2 IR 595.
18 *NC v DPP and Judge Sheridan* [1991] 1 IR 471. *SF v DPP* [1999] 3 IR 235; PO'C v DPP [2005] IEHC 103; *JO'C v DPP* [2000] 3 IR 478; *DPP v JO'C* (27 July, 2001, unreported) Central Criminal Court *per* Carney J.; TS v DPP [2005] 2 IR 595.
19 DO'R v DPP [1997] 2 IR 274; *PC v DPP* [1999] 2 IR 25; SA v DPP [2005] IEHC 262.
20 PJC v DPP [2005] IEHC 98.
21 RC v DPP [2005]

22 RC v DPP.
23 *S v DPP* 19 February 1999, unreported High Court *per* Geoghegan J.
24 Indecent assault, incest and unlawful carnal knowledge have all featured on the Irish criminal calendar since before the foundation of the State. Ss 58, 61 *Offences Against the Person Act 1861*; ss1, 2 *Criminal Law Amendment Act 1935; Punishment of Incest Act 1908.*
25 *R v Osborne* [1905] 1 KB 551. See Stanchi, 1996.
26 *R v Lillyman* [1896] 2 QB 167. In England and Wales, the rule is expressed in ss120(4) and 120(7) of the *Criminal Justice Act 2003*, which does not require that the prior complaint be made at the first reasonable opportunity.
27 *People (DPP) v Brophy* [1972] ILRM 709; *People (DPP) v MA* [2002] 2 IR 601. Contrast with England and Wales and Northern Ireland, where s120 (4) and (7) of the *Criminal Justice Act 2003* allows for such statements to become evidence of truth.
28 Tapper, 1990, at 283. If the witness' credibility is enhanced by an immediate complaint because, in the circumstances there was not time to concoct a false accusation, '*our doubts about the victim's veracity will have been removed*' (Williams, 1982: 664; emphasis added).
29 *R v Baskerville* [1916] 2 KB 658. Although the requirement of a corroboration warning in sexual cases has been abolished, trial judges retain a discretion to administer a warning where appropriate on the facts. *Criminal Law (Rape) (Amendment) Act 1990*, s7; *People (DPP) v GK* [2007] 2 IR 92, following *R v Makanjuoula* [1995] 3 All ER 730. Corroboration continues to play an important role in decisions to grant appeals against convictions for sexual offences (Fennell, 2009: Ch 6).
30 *Criminal Law (Rape) (Amendment) Act 1990*, s7.
31 *People (DPP) v GK* [2007] 2 IR 92, following *R v Makanjuoula* [1995] 3 All ER 730.
32 *SH v DPP* [2006] 3 IR 575. See Ring 2009 and 2013.
33 Ibid. [2006] IR 575. The new test is also indicative of a renewed emphasis on the importance of the right to a fair trial; the presumption of innocence is no longer suspended and courts will inquire as to whether any actual prejudice has been demonstrated by the defendant.

Bibliography

Agamben, G. (1999). *Remnants of Auschwitz. The Witness and the Archive.* New York: Zone Books.

Arendt, H. (1994). *Eichmann in Jerusalem: A Report on the Banality of Evil.* Harmondsworth: Penguin.

Bastian, M. (2013). Political Apologies and the Question of a 'Shared Time' in the Australian Context. 30 (5) *Theory, Culture and Society*: 94–121.

Bergson, H. (1944). *Creative Evolution*, trans Mitchell, A. New York: New York Modern Library.

Brereton, D. (1997). How Different Are Rape Trials? A Comparison of the Cross-Examination of Complainants in Rape and Assault Trials. *British Journal of Criminology.* 37: 242–61.

Butler, J. (1997). *Excitable Speech. A Politics of the Performative.* London and New York: Routledge.

Charleton, P. and Byrne, S. (2010). Sexual Violence Witnesses and Suspects: A Debating Document. 1, *Irish Journal of Legal Studies*: 1.

Cohen, S. (2001). *States of Denial, Knowing about Atrocities and Suffering.* Cambridge: Polity Press.

Commission to Inquire into Child Abuse. (2009). *Final Report.* Dublin: Stationery Office.

Commission of Investigation. (2009). *Report in the Catholic Archdiocese of Dublin*. Dublin: Stationery Office.

Commission of Investigation. (2010). *Report into Cloyne Archdiocese*. Dublin: Stationery Office.

Cross, R. (1979). *Cross on Evidence*. 5th ed. Oxford: Oxford University Press.

Department of Health and Children (1996). *Report on the Inquiry into the Operation of Madonna House. Dublin. Department of Health and Children*. Available at http://lenus.ie/hse/bitstream/10147/46317/4/MadonnaHouse.pdf. Accessed 30 May 2018.

Derrida, J. (1988). 'Signature Event Context' in *Limited Inc*. Evanston, IL: Northwestern University Press, 124.

Douglas, L. (2001). *The Memory of Judgment*. New Haven, CT: Yale University Press

Douzinas, C. (2000) *The End of Human Rights: Critical Theory at the Turn of the Century*. Oxford: Hart.

Doyle, P. (1989). *The God Squad*. London: Corgi Books.

Elberling, B. (2012). *The Defendant in International Criminal Proceedings*. Oxford: Hart Publishing.

Ellison, L. and Munro, V.E. (2009). Reacting to Rape: Exploring Mock Jurors' Assessments of Complainant Credibility. 49 (2) *British Journal of Criminology*: pp.202-219.

Fennell, C. (2009). *The Law of Evidence in Ireland*. 3rd ed. Dublin: Bloomsbury Professional.

Garland, D. 1996. *The Limits of the Sovereign State*. 36 (4) *British Journal of Criminology*: 445–71.

Greenhouse, C. (1996). *A Moment's Notice: Time Politics Across Cultures*. Ithaca, NY: Cornell University Press.

Grosz, E. (2005). *Time Travels. Feminism, Nature, Power*. Crows Nest: Allen &Unwin.

Hill, R. (2013). 'Bergson on Durée' in Ardoin, P., Gontarski, S.E. and Mattison, L. (Eds.), *Understanding Modernism, Understanding Bergson*. London: Bloomsbury, 301–302.

Hobuss, S. (2011). Aspects of Memory Acts: Transnational Cultural Memory and Ethics. 3 *Journal of Aesthetics and Culture*: 10–34.

Hogan, G., and Whyte, G. (2003). *J.M. Kelly: The Irish Constitution*. 4th ed. Dublin: Butterworths.

Hudson, B. (2002). Restorative Justice and Gendered Violence – Diversion or Effective Justice. 42 *British Journal of Criminology*: 616–34.

Kendall, S. (2015). 'Beyond the Restorative Turn: The Limits of Legal Humanitarianism' in De Vos, C., Kendall, S. and Stahn, C. (Eds.) *Contested Justice: The Politics and Practice of International Criminal Court Interventions*. Cambridge: Cambridge University Press, 352–76.

Lentin, L. 1996. *Dear Daughter*. (Film.) Crescendo Concepts.

Madden, A. (2004). *Altar Boy: A Story of Life After Abuse*. London: Penguin.

Mawani, R. (2014). Law as Temporality: Colonial Politics and Indian Settlers. 4 (1) *UC Irvine Law Review*: 65–95.

Mawani, R. (2015). The Times of Law. 40 (1) *Law and Social Inquiry*: 253–63.

McAleese, M. (2013). *Report of the Inter-Departmental Committee to Establish the Facts of State Involvement with the Magdalen Laundries*. Dublin; Stationery Office.

McGuinness, C. (1993). *Kilkenny Incest Investigation. A Report presented to Mr. Brendan Howlin T.D. by South Eastern Health Board*. Dublin: Stationery Office.

Mee, M. (1994). *Similar Fact Evidence: Still Hazy After All these Years*. 1(1) DULJ 83.

Moore, C. (1995). *Betrayal of Trust: The Father Brendan Smyth Affair and the Catholic Church*. Dublin: Irish American Book Co.

Mulla, S. (2011). Facing Victims: Forensics, Visual Technologies, and Sexual Assault Examination. 30 (3) *Medical Anthropology: Cross-Cultural Studies in Health and Illness*: 271–94.

O'Gorman, C. (2009). *Beyond Belief*. London: Hodder & Stoughton.

O'Malley, T. (2009). *The Criminal Process*. Dublin: Round Hall.

Parker, K. (2011.) *Common Law, History, and Democracy in America, 1790–1900: Legal Thought Before Modernism*. Cambridge: Cambridge University Press.

Raftery, M. and O'Sullivan, E. (1999). *Suffer the Little Children: The Inside Story of Ireland's Industrial Schools*. Dublin: New Island.

Raitt, F. (2004). Expert Evidence As Context: Historical Patterns and Contemporary Attitudes in the Prosecution of Sexual Offences. 12 (2) *Feminist Legal Studies*: 233–44.

Ring, S. (2009). Beyond the Reach of Justice? Complainant Delay Historic Child Sexual Abuse Cases and the Right to a Fair Trial. 2 *Judicial Studies Institute Journal*: 162.

Ring, S. (2012). Due Process and the Admission of Expert Evidence on Recovered Memory in Historic Child Sexual Abuse Cases: Lessons for Ireland. 16 (1) *International Journal of Evidence and Proof*: 66.

Ring, S. (2013). Analysing 'Fairness in Context' in Historic Child Sexual Abuse Prosecutions. 23 (4) *Irish Criminal Law Journal*, 132.

Ring, S. (2017). The Victim of Historical Child Sexual Abuse in the Irish Courts 1999–2006. 26 (5) *Social & Legal Studies*, 562–580.

Sarat, A. and Kearns, T.R. (2002). *History, Memory and Law*. Ann Arbor: University of Michigan Press.

Smart, C. (1990). Law's Power, the Sexed Body and Feminist Discourse. 17 *Journal of Law and Society*: 194–210.

Stanchi, K. (1996). The Paradox of the Fresh Complaint Rule 36. *Boston College Law Review*: 441–78.

Turner, C. (2017). *Violence, Law and the Impossibility of Transitional Justice*. London: Routledge.

van Rijswijk, H. (2013). Stolen Generations: Online Testimonies as Sources of Social Justice: Towards an Ethics of Encounter. 10 *Australia and New Zealand Law and History E-Journal*: 1.

Williams, G. (1982). Corroboration: Sexual Cases. *Criminal Law Review*: 662–71.

5 'Give us his name'

Time, law and language in a settler colony

Genevieve Renard Painter,[1] Concordia University

Introduction

"The land was given to our forefathers by the great God above ... and our forefathers handed it down to us, and we have not given it to anyone. It is still ours, and will be ours till we sign a strong paper to give part of it to the Queen."[2] So wrote Nisga'a chief David Mackay, in reply to British Columbia's premier, William Smithe, who said, "It is the Queen's land ... but the Queen gives it to her Indian children because they do not know so well how to make their own living, the same as a white man."[3]

Law sits at the intersection of time, language, and colonialism, but legal scholarship has only recently turned attention to this intersection. In seeking to understand the relationship between the word of the law and the violence that it promises if brooked, legal scholars can explore the law's role in the colonial encounter through an analysis of temporality (Cover, 1986). By studying the grammar at play in meetings between Indigenous leaders and government officials in 19th century Canada, I suggest that paying attention to language offers a way of understanding how temporality and state law are enmeshed in the project of dispossession.[4]

Scholarship on the law's relation to time considers how time shapes law, how law shapes time, and how law can be thought of as time.[5] Asking how time acts on the law includes activities ranging from understanding how technicalities like statutes of limitations require conceptions of linear time to exploring how law evolves in response to changing political, social, and cultural contexts (Gordon, 1984). In contrast to this model of time existing as external to law, another line of scholarship considers how law acts on time, through "the production and organization of time as past, present, and future [and] ... law's imposition of time on colonial-legal subjects" (Mawani, 2014: 64). Such a turn opens room for thinking about the temporalities internal to law (Parker, 2011; Fitzpatrick, 2001; Borrows, 1997). Time is "integral to the ontology and epistemology of law [and to] ... law's organization of social and political life" (Mawani, 2014: 71).

Noticing how law acts on time and how time acts on law blurs the line between the two. In fact, what looks like "time" is often state elites using ideas about time to consolidate power (Greenhouse, 1996). The Western state has adopted and naturalized linear time, both through Christian narratives of redemption and Messianic time and through Enlightenment narratives of civilizational progress across an expanse of homogeneous empty time (ibid.; Benjamin, 2004; Koselleck, 2004). Colonialism is fundamental to the relationship between time and the Western state because it is through narrating the distance from a colonial Other that the West figures itself as "ahead" in the linear time of "one human history uniting humanity" (Said, 1985: 101). Settler colonialism has an intrinsic temporality in that its *telos* is the point where there are only settlers, as the Indigenous have been drawn out of the anachronistic space of a "permanently anterior time" through assimilation (Mawani, 2012a; Veracini, 2010; McClintock, 1995). The modern state's debts to time predate the era of empire. Yet it was post-colonial studies that highlighted the ongoing plurality of dense, uneven temporalities under colonialism and the extent of resistance to the state law's reliance on time and time's reliance on state law (Esmeir, 2012; Chakrabarty, 2000; Bhabha, 1990).

Law works through language; many scholars study how so (Freeman and Smith, 2013; Constable, 2011; Winter, 2001; Mertz, 1994; Cover, 1984). Recent work knitting together theory about how legal speech acts with theory about jurisdiction suggests that by analyzing legal technicalities as linguistic practices, it becomes possible to see how language and narration are the threads that weave the law's claimed legitimacy (Richland, 2013: 217; Dorsett and McVeigh, 2012: 54–62). In speaking legal language, social actors speak the law into existence and bring the law's authority into the present and the future through their speech acts (Constable, 2014: 13–14). Declarations about what the law is contain a synchronous assertion of the jurisdiction to declare the law, but the latter is concealed (Rush, 1997: 150).

Language and narrative are integral to the law's temporalities. The law creates and upholds a specifically legal narrative time-space of perpetuity, where the current manifestation of legal speech is figured as the latest instance of an ongoing, seamless, and coherent language backed by sovereign authority (Richland, 2013: 289). This legal time of perpetuity is asserted in the face of constant rejoinders by "outsider" jurisprudences and temporalities. The law's temporal techniques are a response to "the multiple and unforeseeable temporalities of specific subjects, objects, and events that continually exceed and escape legal order and arrangement" (Mawani, 2014: 72).

Language offers an interesting means of asking about time. Tense is often presumed to be how language expresses time, but linguists understand it to be only one of the six devices used to encode time in language.[6] That language expresses time has been offered as evidence of an anti-relativist, universal understanding of time: "If other people really had different concepts of time we could not do what we patently do, that is communicate with them … if all syntax is based on the same logic, all speakers must at a fundamental level apprehend time in the same way" (Bloch, 1977: 283). Although such views are highly debatable, this assertion epitomizes how time and language are entangled with the idea of "the human" (see, e.g., Greenhouse, 1996; Fabian, 1983). Linguist Emile Benveniste argued that language has an intrinsic temporality because "there is no other criterion and no other expression by which to indicate 'the time at which one *is*' except to take it as 'the time at which one is *speaking*'" (Benveniste, 1999: 227). As verb tenses can define time relative to the speaker, language contains a specific temporality distinct from calendar time. If, as some jurists think, legal declarations of jurisdiction are speech acts, what temporalities are invoked and produced by their language?

This chapter explores this question through close reading of the partial records of meetings between Nisga'a and Tsimshian leaders and government officials about the Naas River (present-day Nass River) valley region. After setting the scene of these meetings, I analyze, first, how the theme of time runs throughout their conversations, and, subsequently, how temporality shapes Indigenous and settler understandings of the land and the reserve. I then invite the reader to consider the temporalities generated by the legal speech acts recorded in these documents.

Meetings on the Naas River

Mid-winter made for a cold, wet trip from the Naas River valley to the southern tip of Vancouver Island. The situation along the river had become untenable, compelling Nisga'a and Tsimshian chiefs to travel to Victoria to demand a remedy. They came via steamer from Alaska, after trekking and canoeing from Kincolith, located at the river's mouth, and from Fort Simpson, down the coastline of the strait that separated Tsimshian territory from the Haida islands (Harris, 2002: 205). John Ryan, Richard Wilson, John Wesley, Matthew Naas, and Arthur Gurney had been nominated to this delegation. Resolving the situation on the Naas River was urgent because spring was around the corner. The river would again teem with oolachan, the tiny fish that, when rendered to an oil, was vital to life along the river basin. The Gitxsan, among others, traveled down from the river's head every spring to trade furs for the oil. Although the oolachan run brought trade and renewal of relations, it sometimes came with conflicts among the Gitxsan, Nisga'a, Tsimshian, and Haida drawn to one of the coast's largest fisheries.

Spring on the river had long been a time of potential conflict, but, once Europeans arrived to set up fishing and canning industries, the number of conflicts had multiplied. This steamer bound for Victoria was not the first effort by leaders to demand a remedy from the White man's government for the problems they had catalyzed along the river. Earlier, the Tsimshian chiefs, John Tait, Edward Mathers, and Herbert Wallace, had gone to Ottawa to meet with Canada's Prime Minister, John MacDonald. They returned bearing promises that yielded no action. Nisga'a and Tsimshian chiefs met to discuss these broken promises, and, in spite of the absence of leaders from the Nisga'a from Kincolith, decided to demand a meeting (Tennant, 1990: 55). Thus did they find themselves sailing to Victoria in terrible weather.

Their complaint concerned the White men with sketchbooks, maps, chains, and expedition tents who arrived on their territories intent on drawing lines on the land and giving land and fishing sites to specific groups. This was nonsense since the land and water was not the White men's to give. The last such official was Peter

O'Reilly. He had come before the bad weather set in and spent only 13 days touring the Naas River valley. Villages were deserted as it was the peak fishing season. Careening from one village to the next, he asked whoever was there to point out which land they wanted "reserved."[7] He left an uproar in his wake that did not ebb. When a surveyor came after O'Reilly had completed his initial sketches, the Tsimshian in Metlakatla and the Nisga'a in Gitlakdamix had refused to let him measure their land (Raunet, 1984: 81).

O'Reilly's maps had almost no relation to the complex system of seasonal sharing that had been developed over time to preserve a fragile peace in the watershed (Sterritt, 1998). His reserves fueled existing conflicts and sparked new ones in a context that had been reshaped by the missionaries. O'Reilly had awarded a once shared, prime fishing site to a break-way community of Nisga'a living in Kincolith, a settlement founded about 20 years earlier by Anglican missionaries, Robert Doolan and Robert Tomlinson, who had set out to establish a model Christian village for their Nisga'a converts (Patterson, 1992). Doolan and Tomlinson were following the example set by another Anglican missionary, William Duncan, who evangelized among the Tsimshian at Fort Simpson. The missionaries found the work hard going and the converts few, as they encountered a strong political system of chiefs, clans, and houses. In response, Duncan had founded a new settlement, Metlakatlah, where the converted would be shielded from contact with Europeans and the allure of old "heathen" ways (Fisher, 1977: 130). The Methodist missionaries, Thomas Crosby and Alfred Green, sought to save Indian souls in Port Simpson and Greenville.[8]

Thomas Crosby was aboard the steamer bound for Victoria – he was to be the interpreter.

* * *

On Thursday, February 3, 1887, at 11 o'clock, Premier William Smithe welcomed a delegation from Fort Simpson and the Naas River to his home. He blocked the entry of the missionary, Thomas Crosby, forcing the delegation to appoint one of their party, Charles Barton, as their interpreter.[9] In Victoria circles, the missionaries were seen as troublemakers responsible for giving Indians ideas about justice. Premier Smithe had gathered four government officials to meet the delegation: the provincial Attorney General, Alex Davie, the Provincial Secretary, JNO Robson, the federal Superintendent of Indian affairs, Israel Wood Powell, and the Indian Reserve Commissioner, Peter O'Reilly. Together, they represented the political and legal regime for the settlement of British Columbia.

Smithe, like the others in the living room, had some settled views on a topic that had dogged the province since its founding. He had been up to his neck in the land question since his election to the assembly in 1871 and his rise to premier in 1883. The experience had left him favorably disposed to the approach being zealously implemented by his colleague, Peter O'Reilly. Smithe appreciated the speed and economy with which O'Reilly laid out reserves, as he hated to see land in a "wild, waste condition" when it could be farmed by settlers (Harris, 2002: 189). Smithe thought that Indigenous people should be granted small reserves and that, in the long run, once Indigenous people had "become more advanced", they would "take the land in the same way ... as other citizens do" (ibid.). The provincial government had quickly approved the reserves laid out by O'Reilly in 1881, thus provoking the disputes that brought this delegation to Smithe's living room.

Smithe heralded O'Reilly's work because it sharply diverged from the approach of the former Indian Reserve Commissioner, Gilbert Sproat. O'Reilly did not mince words in denouncing Sproat for having laid out reserves that were "out of all proportion to the actual or prospective requirements of the Indians" (Fisher, 1977: 199). O'Reilly did not mince his deeds, either. Whereas Sproat had worked with meticulous deliberation, often spending weeks at a time in a place, O'Reilly conducted the work of Indian Reserve Commissioner as a whistlestop tour, spending no more than a few days in a location before making his decisions (ibid.: 201).

In taking a red pen to Sproat's reserves, O'Reilly was heeding the wishes of many of British Columbia's settlers. Settlers had thought Sproat was prodigal towards the Indians and responsible for stirring up trouble by talk of land rights, leading to Sproat's ouster in 1880 (Harris, 2002: 161–166). Sproat sought consultation with the chiefs and some measure of reconciliation between Indians and settlers (ibid.: 136–138). The province would have none of it and delayed or denied Sproat's carefully laid out reserves (Fisher, 1977: 197).

The land problem had crystallized during British Columbia's entry into Confederation in 1871. Under the Terms of Union, the Dominion was responsible for the "charge of the Indians, and the trusteeship and management of the lands reserved for their use and benefit," and the province was obligated to convey tracts "to the Dominion Government for the use and benefit of the Indians".[10] Provincial officials denied the existence of Indian title and hence any obligation to sign treaties to acquire land. The Dominion argued that "from the earliest times, England has always felt it imperative to meet the Indians in council, and to obtain surrender of tracts of Canada" (Raunet, 1984: 77). The federal government wanted policy in British Columbia to cohere with its policy in the Prairies, where the Dominion was in the process of signing treaties, the first of which was signed in 1871, providing for minimum acreage per family (Tennant, 1990: 38). The Terms of Union had the Dominion and the Province locked in embrace, as the province felt it had the land and the Dominion felt it had the charge of the Indians. It was in response to this impasse that an Indian Reserve Commission had been struck (Fisher, 1977: 83).

The impasse was due to diverging interpretations of the Terms of Union's provision that tracts were to be "of such extent as it has hitherto been the practice of the British Columbia Government to appropriate for that purpose" (Fisher, 1977: 183). The province's land policy had been pendular, if not erratic. In a view shared by Premier Smithe, the province claimed that practice in BC had been pro-settler and hence

Indian reserves were justifiably small. As proof, the province cited the practices of Joseph William Trutch, director of Indian land policy from 1864 to 1871. Indigenous people were "uncivilized savages" so far as Trutch was concerned, "bestial rather than human" (Tennant, 1990: 39). He denied that Indigenous people had ever owned the land and sought to transfer as much land as possible to Europeans for cultivation.

Trutch's policies had been a response to those of the former governor, James Douglas.[11] Trutch either annulled or shrank the reserves that Douglas had set out (Fisher, 1977: 163). Douglas' policy, too, had been meandering, rather than linear (Harris, 2002: 17–45). Until the late 1860s, James Douglas had governed some of the most remote outposts of Britain's empire as the head of the Hudson's Bay Company. Settlement had never been a principal objective of either Crown or Company; indeed, it was not until gold was discovered in 1857 that the British Crown saw fit to establish direct rule over the Colony of Vancouver Island and the mainland Colony of British Columbia. But, in the vicinity surrounding the Company's forts, Douglas sought legal title to the land through agreements that "recognize[d] each Indian community as initially owning the 'whole of the lands' it traditionally occupied," compensating them for the surrender of land, and providing for reserve sites (Tennant, 1990: 20). One of the agreements concerned the lands surrounding Fort Victoria. Premier White met this delegation on lands that Douglas believed he had "bought" from the Songhees.

In 1854, Douglas abruptly ceased signing these agreements and grew more tight-fisted in his reserve allocations.[12] With the first gold rush, miners and settlers clamored for secure title to land. Settlers wanted the imperial government, not the province, to purchase lands from the Indians. The Treasury rebuffed the request: the British taxpayer would not be made to underwrite this purely colonial problem (Fisher, 1977: 152). Neither government would pay, and the Colonial Office did not pressure Douglas to clarify the issue of title (Harris, 2002: 32). Reserves continued to be made, without compensation to Indigenous people or cession of title. Now, 30 years later, Premier Smithe found himself face to face with this Nisga'a and Tsimshian delegation.

* * *

The Nisga'a and Tsimshian chiefs returned home from Victoria with two promises. The government would prepare a report of their conversation and deliver it to them. The government would also send a commission to the Naas River valley to investigate their complaint.

* * *

On October 14, 1887, a steamer made landfall at Metlakatlah. Aboard were two commissioners, Joseph Planta for the province and Clement F. Cornwall for the Dominion, and a secretary, Alex Lindsay. The commissioners were tasked with "making enquiry into the state and condition of the Indians of the Northwest coast of British Columbia" (ER 1). They left for the Naas River the following day. The inquiry opened on October 17 at Kincolith and continued to Naas Harbour on October 18, Port Simpson on October 21, and Metlakatlah on October 25. On their return to Victoria, the commissioners wrote their report.

The secretary prepared "Minutes and Proceedings" of the meetings between Indigenous leaders and the commissioners.

* * *

Two documents are on my desk. The first document is a 19-page transcript of the meetings at Premier Smithe's home.[13] The second document includes the Commissioners' report and a verbatim transcript of their meetings along the Naas River.[14]

Both reports are written in English. Most Indigenous delegates spoke in Nisga'a or Tsimshian, and, undoubtedly, much was lost in interpretation into English and transcription. These documents cannot be read as a complete, unmediated account; furthermore, the Nisga'a and Tsimshian have their own records of these meetings.[15] These documents, like the archives that house them, helped to produce the world they narrate, rather than offering a window into it (Stoler, 2009). In what follows, I consider how language works in a partial, English-language representation of these meetings.

Times in the documents

As reports of legal encounters, these documents exemplify how state law relies on and produces temporalities. On the one hand, the legal process of a commission of inquiry produces certain times, but, on the other hand, the law is buffeted by times that exceed its control.

The documents vibrate with a tremendous shortage of time. Indigenous speakers are reminded to "Come right to business now" as the officials have little time (VR 254). Paul Kledah opened his remarks by stating: "[M]y canoe capsized and I was nearly drowned. I was in a hurry to get here; I was afraid I would not be in time to see you" (ER 26). O'Reilly attributed his hasty survey of the area in 1881 to the urgency of laying out the reserves before the land was taken by the canneries (ER 44).

Running counter to this urgency is a bureaucratic time that grinds on. When explaining what might happen as a result of the Commission's work, Cornwall summarized that "[A]ll this ... will take considerable time. ... you can hardly expect an answer before next spring or early summer" (ER 29). Indigenous speakers, too, evoked listless, bureaucratic time in speaking of their letters that had met with no response: "We want to know if any answer is coming, when it will come" (ER 29).

But whether time is rushing or stagnant, its pace is determined by the settlers. The shortness of time available before the commissioners, the urgency to set out reserves before land is occupied by Whites, and the delays of bureaucratic time were all rooted in the settlers' legal processes.

Demarcations of time, like pace, reflect European temporality. Days of the week, months, and years march through the documents like ants. Facts about time mark the progress of the Commission through space and the progress of the reader through the report. Changes in seasons are transposed to dates, as when Nisga'a leader Barton invites the Commission to visit in the "oolachan fishing season, which is from the 22nd March til about the 1st May" (VR 264). David Mackay says that the Whites "saw the land for 20 years" (ER 22). This calendar time is proved by reference to books. When commissioners ask Indigenous people to provide specific dates, the commissioners fall back with relief on a "published account of what happened" (ER 32). Frederick Allen proves how long his people had been in Kincolith by opening the Bible and reading out the date on which the settlement was founded (ER 14).

That the time being demarcated is a European time appears most vividly in the way that Indigenous people are woven into the report's temporality through civilizational discourses. Premier Smithe said that "Indians ... in the past ... were little better than wild animals that rove over the hills" (VR 256). Their condition had since changed, having "been taught other and better ways" (VR 256). Premier Smithe explained to the delegation that, "being still Indians, or ... in the position of children, you are not permitted, so far, to exercise the franchise" (VR 255). The statement casts the "Indians" as having only temporary incapacities. Settlers remained "ahead" of Indigenous people because "the white man knows and has been taught more" (VR 256). In the colonialists' mentality, colonization allowed Indigenous people to escape the past and enter the present. By entering this racially ordered civilization marathon, they entered the same time as the Whites – just always behind them.

Yet for all this talk by the Premier about education paving the road to civilizational advancement, for the commissioners, the indicators of progress were neither wisdom nor English literacy, but street lamps, sidewalks, comfortable rooms, fire brigades, strings of bunting, brass bands, and cannon salutes (ER 3, 5). Knowledge was hindering, rather than furthering, their advancement, as it was implied that the missionaries had filled their heads with nonsense about their land rights. It was not missionaries but the firm guidance of an Indian agent, empowered under the Indian Act, who would "advance" them along the civilizational path (ER 40). When Indigenous leaders were half an hour late, Commissioner Cornwall castigated them, stating that "punctuality in business is one of the most important things in civilized life" (ER 35). Indeed, some of the indicia of "civilization" applauded by the Commissioners mark out and manage time. The street lamps extended the day past nightfall; the brass bands brought Indigenous musicians into playing structured, metered, and partitioned music (Neylan and Meyer, 2006).

But European calendar time is not hegemonic. Rival temporalities interrupt. Time is indexed through human lifetimes, family lineages, and memory. Sabousash speaks of "taking care of the land which belonged to my forefathers" (ER 23). The future is referenced by speaking of the consequences of a treaty between the Nisga'a and the Queen for our "children and children's children" (ER 22).

Time is identified and measured through the experience of movement, and space is measured with time. For example, when Mountain explains why they did not go with O'Reilly, he said, "O'Reilly was going so far up the river that we did not go with him – he was gone for a week or more" (ER 16). When asked how far away a place was, Allen replied, "it is as far as we can go by noon if we set out early" (ER 13).

The land and the river are not only measured with time, but the land itself measures time. The river brings seasonal time when, for example, it teems with fish in the spring. The land offers evidence of past time and past occupation. When they dig up their gardens, Hawillah says, they find the "stone implements, crests, and other things" that their forefathers once used but are no longer used (ER 24).

The documents pulse with a European time, slow or harried, ordered, divided into hours and days, in which the European is always ahead of the Indigenous. Yet, this temporality is not hegemonic. Indigenous speakers invoked rival temporalities, defined by human genealogies and the land.

Time and the land

The dialogue captured in these documents shows that land and time are knit thickly together. This can be seen by attending to grammatical tense and aspect in how Indigenous and White speakers described relationships to the land.

Indigenous speakers made declarative statements about their relationship to the land, as in the following extracts:

> RUSS: "What we want is to speak about our property – our land." (ER 18)
> ABBOTT: "The whole place *is* the Indians' land." (ER 37)
> RUSS: "If you ask the Hydahs, Alaskas, Stickeens, Bella Bellas, and Fort Ruperts, they *will tell* you that all this country is the Naas People's land." (ER 18)
> BARTON: "We have come for nothing but to see about the land *which we know is ours.*" (VR 257)

These declarations are made in an active voice in direct sentence structures. Russ spoke of the knowledge of Nisga'a ownership held by other Indigenous nations, while Barton spoke of the Nisga'a's own knowledge of ownership. "We know" connotes a time in the past from which this knowledge was carried, while "they will tell you" asserts continuity of this ownership.

Continuity across time in the relationship to the land and the water is also evoked by Indigenous speakers' use of activity to describe the land, as follows:

> ALLEN: "Each chief *has always had* certain places where he and his tribes always *hunted and caught* salmon." (ER 13)
> SABASSAH: "I have been *taking care* of the land which belonged to my forefathers for generations." (ER 23)
> NAAS: "I asked for a piece of land to be reserved on Observatory Inlet, which my *forefathers and uncles and I have used* for drying salmon." (ER 18)

These activities took place in the past, as signaled by the past tense "hunted" and "caught." But, more significantly, these actions bring out the enduring relationship to the land. "Hunting," "fishing," "drying," or "looking after" take place over time. Such action depicts people in an ongoing relationship with land or water, in a way that verbs like "own" or "belong" do not.

Naming specific people located relationship to the land in the past. For example:

> ALLEN: "The big chiefs who owned that part of the Naas River are now alive. They are George Kinsada, of Kincolith, who was the head chief, and Mountain, Tat-qua-kaas, and Kledach." (ER 13)

Furthermore, speakers anchored relationships to the land in genealogies, as follows:

> DAVID MACKAY: "These chiefs . . . know the land is their own; our forefathers for *generations and generations* past had their land here all around us . . . it has always been so. It is not only during the last four or five years that we have seen the land; we have always seen and owned it, it is no new thing, it has been ours for generations." (ER 22)
>
> TAL-A-HAAT: "It belonged to my forefathers and my *people bearing my name* have always had charge of it." (ER 21)

When Tal-a-haat said that the land belonged to "people bearing my name," he spoke of law that attaches people to places across time.[16] Such Nisga'a law resembles the Tsimshian system, in which relationship to the land resides in names, not their wearers. Names "link members of a Tsimshian lineage to the past and to the territory on which that past unfolded" (Roth, 2008: 30). Hereditary name-titles are "not so much an appellation . . . as . . . a mandate to authority and a deed of sovereign land title" (ibid.: 30). Geography is composed of oral histories of lineage.

This stands in marked contrast to how White officials talked about Indigenous people's relationship to the land and the water:

> O'REILLY: "They each have a little spot which they *are in the habit of calling their own*. Every inlet *is claimed* by some one." (VR 257)
>
> REPORT: "Doubtless most of the hunting and fishing places asked for *are regularly used* by the Indians demanding them." (ER 9)
>
> REPORT: "All evidence goes to show that these hunting grounds *have been held in the past* by different chiefs and families for the use of their people." (ER 9)

Whereas Indigenous speakers used active voice in the past and present tense, White officials spoke and wrote about Indigenous relationship to the land and water in the passive voice and present tense (*is claimed, are used*). That the verb is never active, as in "These Indians hunt in those grounds," means that the "Indian" is never the active subject in relationship to the land. The phrase, "in the habit of," connotes a past time that continues into the present. But the temporality of "habit" is about the frequency or the consistency of a disposition or usage, not about the past-ness of a habit itself. "[T]hose who have been in the habit of fishing" means something different from "those who have been fishing." Only in the passive voice phrase, "have been held in the past," do Indigenous people have a past relationship to the land. For White speakers, the Indigenous relationship to the land and water is through ongoing, present-day habits of a passive subject.[17]

Whereas the sentences about Indigenous relationship to the land abound in passive voice muddles, sentences about the Queen's relationship to the land are as clear as gin, as in Smithe's statements to the delegation in Victoria:

> "The land all belongs to the Queen." (VR 256)
> "It is the Queen's land … but the Queen gives it to her Indian children." (VR 256)
> "[G]old and silver … belong particularly and specially to the Queen." (VR 261)

All these sentences situate the Queen's relationship to the land in the present tense. There is no past to the Queen's relationship to the land; neither is there any explanation of when or how this present-day condition of "belonging" arose.

In sum, Indigenous speech about the land is syntactically direct and active. The idea that Indigenous relationship to the land spans past, present, and future is evoked by referring to genealogies, Nisga'a and Tsimshian law, and ongoing activities. In contrast, White speech about the Indigenous relationship to the land locates it in the present, and reference to the past happens as an incident of description of ongoing usage. For White speakers, the Queen's relationship to the land is declared directly, actively, in the present tense.

The time of a reserve

You may well be wondering now why verb tense and aspect matter. Let us return to a core complaint brought before the Commission: the reserves. How did these reserves come to be? By attending closely to the grammar of "setting aside" the land, we gain insight into the mechanisms of Indigenous dispossession.

Commissioner O'Reilly described the process thus:

> All the way coming down the river I was accompanied by half a dozen canoes with Indians; and if the Indians said 'Stop there' or 'Go there,' we did so; and went to every place; and every one they pointed out was reserved. (VR 271)

Let us take his word that this is what happened. If so, a reserve started through travel and the arrival of an official carrying a law. He talked with Indigenous people. They set out together, and Indigenous leaders pointed and talked, while the official looked and wrote notes. The official made a decision and recorded it. The whole process of identifying and measuring the land and water happened through language. The surveyor's instruments came only months or years later.

Words bring the Indian reserve into being. Which words? Here are the words that set out "Reserve No. 14":

> A Reserve of 1250 acres, situated at the mouth of the Nass River on its right bank, and known as "Kin-co-lith":
>
> *Commencing* at a dead fir tree ¼ mile West of the mouth of "Trout Stream," and running North 10 chains; thence East 200 chains; thence South to the Nass River; and thence down the right of bank of the said river to the place of commencement.[18]

The vast majority of the reserves set out by O'Reilly follow this structure: a numerical measure of a territory, a geographic location, a name, and a description.

The description comes from O'Reilly's physical movement over the land and the water. They are movement words – "running North ... East ... South ... down." The land is measured through an experience of moving across space that takes time. But this movement has one important feature: It goes nowhere. Because a reserve is an enclosure, the line of its starting point must by definition meet itself as its ending point. Every reserve's "commencing" ends at its "point of commencement." The line drawn must return onto itself, back to the beginning.

The descriptions all begin with the point of commencement, often a naturally occurring place, like a fir tree or the mouth of a river. Natural demarcations are (presumably) legible by any reader, but, in other cases, the point of commencement takes local knowledge: as in Reserve No. 13, which commences "due North of a rock known as 'The Heart of the Nass'" (ibid.: 37). In still other cases, as in Reserve No. 10, the point of commencement is "a cottonwood tree, marked 'Indian Reserve'," implying that O'Reilly left behind him a landscape of labeled trees and rocks (ibid.: 35).

The difficulty in naming the point of commencement is significant because something incredible and awful is happening through and after this word "commencing." Consider again the stock phrase, "A reserve ... *commencing* ... running ... to the place of commencement." What if, as an alternative, these descriptions read, "A reserve ... TO commence ... and TO run ... to the place of commencement"? The infinitive tense is consistently future-oriented as "the time frame of the infinitival clause is unrealized" (Duffley and Joubert, 1999: 252). If the reserve were described with an infinitive, we would hear it as coming into being in the future – say, after Indian title was extinguished or the reserve was approved by the province. Instead, the present participle "commencing" creates the sense that the reserve already exists and that its starting point is already identifiable.

Yet if the reserve is already there when it is being described by this phrase, when did it come into being? The reserve does not exist when people are pointing out places to O'Reilly. It does not exist when O'Reilly weighs up everything he was told, or when he decides where to draw the line. Rather, it comes into being precisely through the words that follow the word "commencing" in each "Minute of Decisions." The writing of these words draws the line that encloses and reserves a space. As a legal speech act, the sentence beginning with the word "commencing" carries the "peculiar temporality" of an "utterance [which] cannot be (said to be) the act it is until it is or has been completed" (Constable, 2014: 73). The reserve cannot be until the sentence is completed. The reserve both requires the future completion of the utterance, while also having "been" before the utterance.

This slippery, faceless origin moment is a sign of the ticking of state law's internal temporality. When a common law judge reaches into the past and turns a case into precedent for a present-day legal problem, a legal utterance turns some un-marked fir tree of a judgment into the "beginning" of a line of cases that lead teleologically to the present (Mawani, 2012b: 354). The common law's conceit is that this line of precedent was already there, in waiting, poised for commencing. The line on the land and the line of precedent work on time in the same way.

This "commencing" phrase is, paradoxically, how the origin moment of the reserve disappears. Just as the line that runs through the land must, axiomatically, return to its starting point, the phrase must, axiomatically, locate the reserve in the past, as having already happened. That there was a moment of origin – and a time before the reserve, a time before Indigenous dispossession – seems to fall away just as the reserve comes into being.

Speaking the law

How did the verbs that made the reserves acquire such a power? Who was their subject? The phrases setting out the reserves begin self-referentially. "The reserve" is the subject of the "commencing" phrase that creates a reserve, not the Indian Reserve Commissioner, the Province, or the Queen. That the phrase setting out the reserves effaces the subjects who cause dispossession exposes the jurisdictional declaration in making reserves and the specifically colonial character of this legal speech act that does what it says in its saying.

Scrutinizing the language of White officials as an instance of jurisdictional speech shows how verbs, through tense and aspect, help to conjure a juridical world that connects past, present, and future. Consider the following excerpts:

> ATTORNEY GENERAL DAVIE: "Some 16 years ago, when British Columbia *became* part of Canada, the agreement between British Columbia and Canada *was* that reserves should be made for the Indians, and the Dominion Government *were to take charge* of the Indians and look after them." (VR 269, my emphasis)
> COMMISSIONER PLANTA: "The whole question of the Indian lands in British Columbia *was settled* long ago by law, and the Government cannot go

> beyond the law. Once the Provincial Government *had* the sole charge of the Indians, but about twenty years ago, the Imperial Parliament *passed* a statute called the 'British North America Act', and under its powers the Queen made an Order in Council, which admitted British Columbia into the Dominion under certain conditions. These conditions, which are known as the 'Terms of Union', *have* the full force of law … Under this law (reading from 'Terms of Union'), 'The charge of the Indians, and the trusteeship and management of the lands reserved for their use and benefit,' *belongs* entirely to the Dominion Government, and all the Provincial Government has to do in the matter is *to reserve* enough lands for the Indians' use." (ER 19, my emphasis)

In these passages, the past is almost entirely empty, save for one important word – the law. The law, in the form of the Terms of Union, is what came before. The land does not appear in the past or present. Rather, the land appears through the anticipated legal creation of "reserves": "reserves *should* be made" and "the Provincial Government has … *to* reserve enough lands." "[T]he whole question of the Indian lands" is propelled into a future time, in the same breath as it is declared to be settled "long ago" through an agreement between the Queen, the Dominion, and the province. The "Indians" are under the future charge of the Dominion Government (*to take charge of*). Synoptically, the words about the land suggest that the past is the law, the present is the Queen and her land, and the future is the Indians on well-tilled reserves.

In contrast, Indigenous speakers articulated a very different relationship between time and the White man's law. This law, they said, held the promise for future co-existence on the land. David Mackay wanted leaders from both sides to "write their names down" and "this paper would be handed down to our children and children's children" (ER 22). Charles Russ wanted "the words and hands of the chiefs on both sides, Indian and Government, to make a promise on paper – a strong promise – that will be not only for us but for our children and forever" (ER 18). In contrast to Planta's vision of a past empty but for the White man's law, these speakers locate the White man's law only in the future. If this is a meeting between jurisdictions, it is one in which the legal jurisdictions being declared fail to meet in time.

The missed connection happens not only in time, but in space. Indigenous leaders repeatedly demand that "it be acknowledged the land is ours" (ER 38). Commissioners assure them that their reserves are protected from seizure. Mutual incomprehension reigns until David Mackay unearths the root of the problem:

> What we don't like about the Government is their saying this: 'We will give you this much of land.' How can they give it when it is our own? We cannot understand it. They have never bought it from us or our forefathers. They have never fought and conquered our people and taken their land in

> that way, and yet they say now that they will give us so much land – our own land. (ER 22)

The Nisga'a and the Tsimshian demand reserves of the correct size and location and, "[w]hen we get that land . . ., we wish the Government to pay us for the land *outside*" (ER 22). They are there to talk about *all* the land. Charles Russ elaborates:

> We have no word in our language for 'reserve'. We have the word 'land', 'our land', 'our property'. Your name for our land is 'reserve', but every mountain, every stream, and all we see, we call our forefathers' land and streams. It is just lately the white people are changing the name. Now it is called the Indian reserve, instead of the Naas people's land. . . . But now it is called 'reserve' we want the word 'treaty' with it. The change that was made from 'our land' to 'reserve' was made by the white people, and 'treaty' is to come from them too. (ER 18)

It is so self-evident that *all* the land is theirs that the only possible explanation for the commissioners' remarks is that the Whites had changed the name of their land to "Indian reserve." The commissioners, by way of contrast, think they are there to discuss whether the reserves' boundaries are in the right place. When Richard Wilson says "our land," Commissioner Planta asks, "you mean the land forming your reserves?", leading Wilson to reply, "[w]e don't wish for reserves . . . the land is our own" (ER 33). These meetings are not about the reserves but about what the reserves are being "set apart" from: to wit, whether they are being set apart from an un-mapped, un-named, un-known, and un-signified space – "the Queen's land" – or a generationally inhabited, law-filled, used, and known space – "our land." What is misunderstood is the signifier, not the signified.

This confusion makes this encounter painfully audible as an encounter of mishearing of jurisdictional speech. Charles Russ and David Mackay demand adequate reserves and a treaty to recognize their ownership of all the land outside the reserves, for which they will be paid. The Commissioners reply not by clarifying the match between words and areas of geographic space ("reserve" and "our land") but by clarifying the law and describing its future effects. The Commissioners literally read the law out loud. Planta recites from the Terms of Union (ER 20). Cornwall reels off articles from the Indian Act (ER 22). It is as though reading out loud the word of the law will bring forth the world declared by the law.

This is merely a brazen example of the ways in which legal speech acts are performative utterances that make deeds out of words. But, here, the total speech situation is a colonial one. And legal speech acts, like all speech, do not always take. One reason that speech acts are infelicitous is due to how they are heard (Constable, 2014: 33–39). After Planta's recital of the Terms of Union, Charles Russ did not dispute Planta's conclusion on the contents of the law. Rather, Russ said he did not hear what was said *as* law:

> We hear your words and you have heard the words of our chiefs, but the words you have to read to us we never heard before in our lives. When they made the laws that you speak about they had never been to see us; they did not know what we used or what we wanted. I would like to ask, sirs, if there was one chief of the Naas present when that law was made, and whether they asked him to speak for the Naas people? Or did they write a letter asking them about it? Why, they never even sent us a letter to tell us it was done. You see these chiefs present laugh. We cannot believe the words we have heard, that the land was not acknowledged to be ours. (ER 19)

Russ denies that Planta's words were law because the Nisga'a were not there when these words were first uttered neither had they been informed about them. Planta's speech fails to be heard *as law* because it is a speech act taking place without "speakers' and hearers' shared background knowledge of speaking and living, over time" (Constable, 2014: 91). They are words without the bonds, the "we," that make them legal speech.

Absent subjects are precisely the problem in this encounter between jurisdictions. Planta bellows on with more law:

> The Provincial Government will always perform the duty cast upon them by clause 13 of the Terms of Union, by setting apart and handing over to the Dominion Government such tracts of land as may be deemed reasonably sufficient for all the purposes of the Indians. (ER 20)

Russ counters Planta's abstract, juridical subjects with specific, embodied subjects:

> Set it apart; how did the Queen get the land from our forefathers to set it apart for us? It is ours to give to the Queen, and we don't understand how she could have it to give to us. (ER 20)
>
> (ER 20)

Planta's recital of the law is an instance of a speech act that, as an attempted performative, seems to have a temporality of the present tense. In contrast to constative utterances, in which temporality is ordinarily relative to the present of the speaker, the time of the performative utterance and the time of the act are identical, and the temporality of the utterance is relative to itself (Benveniste, 1999: 230). But performative speech acts work only if they comply with the Austinian "condition of validity, related to the person making the utterance and to the circumstances of the utterance" (ibid.: 236). Because these conditions of validity must precede the utterance, a performative act needs the past, just as Russ insisted. Speech acts that are legal also need the future, because their felicity depends on how they are heard or apprehended (Constable, 2014: 84). Such legal speech acts have the linguistic temporality of the future perfect, as they are "completed over time or 'perfected' in a future" (ibid.: 74).

As a legal speech act, this declaration of jurisdiction by the Dominion and the province tried not only to bring off something with words, as all performative speech acts do. It also tried to create the prior existence of its conditions of validity – hence, why the Queen was always present and the past already held the law. This is what is particular to the temporality of a colonial legal speech act. It explains why the ground for resisting Indigenous dispossession *is* the past and the ways the past is held through words, because jurisdictional speech acts, tensed in the present and future perfect, need a past, both in word and world. The absence of the subject causing dispossession suggests that, as Greenhouse argues, states use time to consolidate agency and paper over absences of legitimacy.

Meanwhile, the chiefs present laugh. As Am-Clamman explains the next day, "[Y]ou opened the book and told us the land was the Queen's and not the Indians'. That is what we laughed at. No one ever does that, claiming property that belongs to other people" (ER 24). I hear the laughter at the commissioners' absurd speech. The laughter subsides when "Neis Puck jumps up" and cries:

> I am the oldest man here and can't sit still any longer and hear that it is not our fathers' land. Who is the chief that gave this land to the Queen? Give us his name, we have never heard it. (ER 20)

Neis Puck names the place where the ground falls away and where jurisdiction, the authority to speak the law, rests on fiat. For there is no chief who gave away the land, in the same way that there was no "we" prior to the Declaration of Independence, in the same way that there is no origin that gives jurisdiction to the law, tout court (Derrida, 1986: 10; Douzinas, 2007: 26). The law's jurisdiction wells up as it speaks. And sometimes it is laughable.

Notes

1 PhD, Assistant Professor, Concordia University. genevieve.painter@concordia.ca Thank you to Liam McHugh-Russell, Tobias Smith, Christopher Tomlins, Kirsten Anker, Justin Richland, Ritu Birla, and participants of The New Legal Temporalities Conference (2016) and American Society for Legal History conference (2016). All errors are my own.

2 Letter from David Mackay et al to Planta and Cornwall, Papers relating to the Commission Appointed to Enquire into the Condition of the Indians of the Northwest Coast, British Columbia, *Legislative Assembly Sessional Papers*, 1888, Appendix C, 47–48.

3 Hon Mr. Smithe, Report of Conferences between the Provincial Government and Indian Delegates from Fort Simpson and Naas River, 3, 8 February 1887, British Columbia, *Legislative Assembly Sessional Papers*, 1887, 256.

4 I use the term "Indian" when quoting or paraphrasing from 19th century settler terminology. I use "Indigenous" as a collective term for those polities living prior to European settlement in the territory now known as British Columbia, while cognizant of the differences among Indigenous nations. I use settler, White, and European to refer to those newly arrived to British Columbia. I use "law" and "state law" to refer to Canadian law, without prejudice to the fact that Nisga'a and Tsimshian law is law.

5 For a review of this literature, see Mawani, 2014.

6 The six devices are: tense, aspect, *Aktionsart*, temporal adverbials, temporal particles, and discourse principles: see Klein, 2008.
7 O'Reilly's lightning speed tour remains legendary in Nisga'a history: see Raunet, 1984: 80.
8 Reverend Green founded the region's first brass band: see Raunet, 1984: 60.
9 Charles Barton was a Nisga'a leader from Kincolith. His name was misspelled in the Report as 'Burton'. I have used the corrected spelling throughout. See Tennant, 1990: 86.
10 Terms of Union 1871 and Order of Her Majesty in Council Admitting British Columbia into the Union, 16 May 1871, reprinted in R.S.B.C. 1979, volume 7 (App.), 83–86.
11 See, further, Perry, 2015.
12 The explanation for Douglas' policy change regarding treaties remains a subject of controversy among historians. Compare, e.g., Tennant, 1990: 26–38 with Fisher, 1977.
13 Report of Conferences between the Provincial Government and Indian Delegates from Fort Simpson and Naas River, 3, 8 February 1887, British *Columbia, Legislative Assembly Sessional Papers*, 1887, 253 [henceforth 'VR'].
14 Papers relating to the Commission Appointed to Enquire into the Condition of the Indians of the Northwest Coast, British Columbia, *Legislative Assembly Sessional Papers*, 1888 [henceforth 'ER'].
15 The Nisga'a and Tsimshian have their own archival practices, to which I do not have access, neither do I feel it appropriate to press for access. I acknowledge the existence of this archive and the likelihood that it would tell different stories of the events and issue I analyze in this chapter.
16 Knowledge about names and crests might not be my business. Significant nuances were likely lost in translation, as Nisga'a and Tsimshian terminology describing clan and crest do not match English words for familial relations.
17 Of further relevance here is Mawani's (2015) study of law and temporality as duration.
18 Indian Reserve Commission, Provincial Collection, Minutes of Decision, Correspondence, and Sketches, May 1882–November 1882, Volume 7 (Box 3) (Typography as in original).

Bibliography

Benjamin, W. (2004). On the Concept of History. In Jennings, W. M. and Eiland, H. (Eds.), *Walter Benjamin: Selected Writings*. Cambridge: Belknap Press.

Benveniste, E. (1999). *Problems in General Linguistics*. Coral Gables: University of Miami Press.

Bhabha, H. K. (1990). DissemiNation: Time, Narrative, and the Margins of the Modern Nation. In Bhabha, H. K. (Ed.), *Nation and Narration*. London: Routledge.

Bloch, M. (1977). The Past and the Present in the Present. 12:2 *Man*, 278.

Borrows, J. (1997). Frozen Rights in Canada: Constitutional Interpretation and the Trickster. *American Indian Law Review*, 37.

Chakrabarty, D. (2000). *Provincializing Europe: Postcolonial Thought and Historical Difference*. Princeton: Princeton University Press.

Constable, M. (2011). Law as Claim to Justice: Legal History and Legal Speech Acts. 1 UC *Irvine Law Review*, 631.

Constable, M. (2014). *Our Word Is Our Bond: How Legal Speech Acts*. Stanford: Stanford University Press.

Cover, R. M. (1984). The Folktales of Justice: Tales of Jurisdiction. 14 *Capital University Law Review*, 179.

Cover, R. M. (1986). Violence and the Word. 95:8 *Yale Law Journal*, 1601.

Derrida, J. (1986). Declarations of Independence. 7:1 *New Political Science*, 7.

Dorsett, S. and McVeigh, S. (2012). *Jurisdiction*. New York: Routledge.

Douzinas, C. (2007). The Metaphysics of Jurisdiction. In Shaun McVeigh (Ed.), *Jurisprudence of Jurisdiction*. New York: Routledge-Cavendish, 21.

Duffley, P. J. and Joubert, J. F. (1999). The Gerund and the Infinitive with the Verbs intend, mean, propose and their Close Synonyms. 44:3 *Canadian Journal of Linguistics*, 251.

Esmeir, S. (2012). *Juridical Humanity: a Colonial History*. Stanford: Stanford University Press.

Fabian, J. (1983). *Time and the Other: How Anthropology Makes Its Object*. New York: Columbia University Press.

Fisher, R. (1977). *Contact and Conflict: Indian-European Relations in British Columbia, 1774–1890*. Vancouver: University of British Columbia Press.

Fitzpatrick, P. (2001). *Modernism and the Grounds of Law*. Cambridge: Cambridge University Press.

Freeman, M. D. A and Smith, F. (2013). *Law and Language*. Oxford: Oxford University Press.

Gordon, R. W. (1984). Critical Legal Histories. 36 *Stanford Law Review*, 57.

Greenhouse, C. J. (1996). *A Moment's Notice: Time Politics Across Cultures*. Ithaca: Cornell University Press.

Harris, C. (2002). *Making Native Space: Colonialism, Resistance, and Reserves in British Columbia*. Vancouver: University of British Columbia Press.

Klein, W. (2008). Time in Language, Language in Time. 58 *Language Learning*, 1.

Koselleck, R. (2004). *Futures Past: On the Semantics of Historical Time*. New York: Columbia University Press.

Mawani, R. (2012a). Specters of Indigeneity in British-Indian Migration, 1914. 46:2 *Law & Society Review*, 369.

Mawani, R. (2012b). Law's Archive. 8:1 *Annual Review of Law and Social Science*, 337.

Mawani, R. (2014). Law As Temporality: Colonial Politics and Indian Settlers. 4:1 *UC Irvine Law Review*, 65.

Mawani, R. (2015). The Times of Law. 40:1 *Law and Social Inquiry*, 253.

McClintock, A. (1995). *Imperial Leather: Race, Gender, and Sexuality in the Colonial Contest*. New York: Routledge.

Mertz, E. (1994). Legal Language: Pragmatics, Poetics, and Social Power. 23:1 *Annual Review of Anthropology*, 435.

Neylan, S. and Meyer, M. (2006). "Here Comes the Band!": Cultural Collaboration, Connective Traditions, and Aboriginal Brass Bands on British Columbia's North Coast, 1875–1964. 152 *BC Studies*, 35.

Parker, K. M. (2011). *Common Law, History, and Democracy in America, 1790–1900: Legal Thought Before Modernism*. Cambridge: Cambridge University Press.

Patterson, E. P. (1992). Kincolith's First Decade: A Nisga'a Village (1867–1878). 12:2 *Canadian Journal of Native Studies*, 229.

Perry, A. (2015). *Colonial Relations: The Douglas-Connolly Family and the Nineteenth-Century Imperial World*. Cambridge: Cambridge University Press.

Raunet, D. (1984). *Without Surrender, Without Consent: A History of the Nishga Land Claims*. Vancouver: Douglas & McIntyre.

Richland, J. B. (2013). Jurisdiction: Grounding Law in Language. 42:1 *Annual Review of Anthropology*, 209.

Roth, C. F. (2008). *Becoming Tsimshian: The Social Life of Names*. Seattle: University of Washington Press.

Rush, P. (1997). An Altered Jurisdiction – Corporeal Traces of Law. 6 *Griffith Law Review*, 144.

Said, E. W. (1985). Orientalism Reconsidered. 1 *Cultural Critique*, 89.

Sterritt, N. J. (1998). *Tribal Boundaries in the Nass Watershed*. Vancouver: University of British Columbia Press.

Stoler, A. L. (2009) *Along the Archival Grain: Epistemic Anxieties and Colonial Common Sense*. Princeton: Princeton University Press.

Tennant, P. (1990). *Aboriginal Peoples and Politics: the Indian Land Question in British Columbia, 1849–1989*. Vancouver: University of British Columbia Press.

Veracini, L. (2010). *Settler Colonialism: A Theoretical Overview*. New York: Palgrave Macmillan.

Winter, S. L. (2001). *A Clearing in the Forest: Law, Life, and Mind*. Chicago: University of Chicago Press.

6 Traditional medicines, law and the (dis)ordering of temporalities

Emilie Cloatre[1], *Kent Law School*

Introduction

In this chapter, I explore the regulation of alternative and traditional medicine, in order to reflect on how particular temporalities shape, and are shaped by, the interface between law and medicine. This chapter makes two key points: first, it argues that both biomedicine and law have relied on a particular sense of 'modernity' as a linear temporal process; in turn, this has been key in developing both crude, and more subtle, social patterns of power, dominance, and exclusion that continue to impact on contemporary societies. Second, it argues that as law increasingly engages in the regulation of other types of medicine, it continues to emulate biomedical models and assumptions as to what 'modern medicine' should look like, including its temporal features. This chapter is written as I am starting a large investigation of the multiple ways in which traditional and alternative medicines apprehend and are apprehended by law in several states in Europe and Africa.[2] Although the project has several aims, my interest in the field came, in part, from the ambivalent and complex ways in which the idea of 'modernity' seemed to be shaping the field and, in turn, how law and medicine as institutions were involved in this ambivalence. It is useful, to 'set the scene' of this chapter, to return to this briefly.

In 2012, as I was carrying out fieldwork in Ghana on a different project, I learnt of the relatively recent and ongoing efforts made by the Ghanaian government to 'regulate better' the field of traditional medicine and, indeed, as some of my informants were putting it at the time, to 'modernise' some of its features. In those conversations, constant push and pulls appeared between a variety of understandings of what modernity meant in the postcolonial context of Ghana, where vast sections of the population navigate between a poorly resourced biomedical system and more accessible traditional healers (a mixed category in itself, as I return to later). But I was also intrigued by the turn to law and regulation (broadly understood) that was being operated through governmental responses. This was particularly interesting because one finding from the project I was undertaking was that, in the field of pharmaceutical distribution where laws and regulatory systems where numerous, my informants all underlined the lack of practical effectiveness of the law and their powerlessness in implementing much of it (Cloatre, 2013). In this context, the idea of setting out to regulate the even messier, even more complex field of traditional healing through a new set of centralised regulatory tools, was for me very interesting. I became curious to understand better what it meant for the state then, and for its individual actors, to reach out to law in order to rearrange such a previously unregulated field. A multiplicity of narratives was clearly at play there, carrying expectations that were about law, and about medicine, and about what each of them should look like and do in contemporary times.

A couple of years later, as the Ebola crisis broke out in West Africa, some of this ambivalence around traditional medicine and what it meant in present days reappeared: while in the early days of the Ebola crisis, traditional practices (of healing and burial) were pointed at as being responsible for the fast spread of the epidemic, the success of public health interventions to tackle it were later thought to have been possible only because of the ultimately effective enrolment of traditional healers by public health officials (Buseh et al, 2015). There, tensions were again at play in relation to what past ('tradition'), present and future were made of: for initial commentators, the line between the ancestral and what was 'adequate' to contemporary healthcare appeared relatively clear. But as it became obvious that 'modern' public health systems may need 'traditional' healers and that they constituted important actors of contemporary public health, those narratives were, again, challenged.

Of course, those events are part of broader patterns: the WHO has developed strategies and plans for traditional medicine (or at least some sections of it) to be revalued in public health systems (WHO, 2005). All over the western world, patients are being drawn towards a range of alternative or traditional medicines (and sometimes, although not always, away from biomedicine) (House of Lords, 2000; Academie de Medecine, 2013). At stake in those stories and movements, are conflicting understandings of 'modernity': clearly, for a very vast set of people around the world, the future was not only or purely biomedical and clearly traditional medicines were neither settled in the past nor fixed. For them, modernity is arguably multidirectional rather than linear – it is about twists and turns and borrowings across time and space and about redefining futures as we experience them. For sociolegal scholars, this raises another series of questions that link to the core of legal temporalities: if looking more closely at those debates, they are all deeply entangled with claims about what law should do, and what law is for, in contemporary societies and their relation to medicine. This raises important questions: What do efforts to 'modernise' traditional medicine through law (as was the case in Ghana, or as the WHO suggests) *mean*, where both tradition and modernity in medicine are so layered and unsettled? And what do such efforts *do* to medical practices? These questions are particularly interesting because law has, for a long time, arguably embraced biomedicine as the true face of modernity, as I illustrate later. Contemporary movements therefore need to be understood against a particular background in which law has reinforced biomedicine's reliance on its own sense of uniqueness as modern knowledge system.

Conceptually, this chapter rests on preexisting engagements with the temporal dimensions of medical practice, in medical anthropology and Science and Technology Studies (STS) (Adams, Burke and Whitmarsh, 2014). Medicine is envisaged as a field in which time 'matters': knowledge practices are inherently shaped by particular, often divergent, senses of temporality; at the same time, they become conditioned by series of temporal assumptions predominant in the practice of medicine. The chapter seeks to put these questions of medical temporalities in conversation with reflections on legal temporalities: interrogations of the temporal movements that animate law and that, in turn, come to condition its creation, its practice and its effects on social relations. On both counts, my analysis is influenced heavily by ideas derived from STS, most notably those derived from Actor-Network Theory (ANT), that emphasise the fluidity, fragility and multiplicity of social relations (Latour, 1991; 2005). When thinking about time, at the nexus between law and medicine, the chapter makes two sets of contributions to the study of legal temporalities: first, it uses the law/medicine nexus as a site to demonstrate that time is folded, rather than linear. Its movements are not fixed or predefined and are, therefore, always open to renegotiations. While the folding of time in medicine per se has been carefully explored by others, the significance of this in relation to law have been given less attention. Second, it looks at events at the crossroad of law and alternative/traditional medicine in order to demonstrate that legal temporalities are performative: more than embedding time as social reality, law participates in creating new states of being and new relations. The temporalities at play in medical practices, and in the law surrounding it, are never fixed or fully determined, but revisited as practices themselves come to be reshaped or experienced. Throughout, the chapter argues that the close relationship between law and biomedicine, and their shared assumptions about the nature of modernity in medicine, renders some of these movements, and some of the politics they entail, less visible than they maybe should be.

The structure of this chapter reflects those two sets of concerns: first, it explores the question of 'modernity' in medicine and how it has been embraced by law. Second, it reflects on how efforts to regulate traditional medicines impact on the very temporalities of the practices they seek to regulate (and, in turn, on the broader socialities of these practices).

Modernities, law and medicine

In this section, I argue that law and medicine, as institutions, have relied on a shared idea of modernity in medicine as a linear process that does not reflect the lived realities of temporalities in medicine and rests on a fixed understanding of time itself as unidirectional. This shared understanding of what constitutes 'modern medicine' has had deep political ramifications. In addition, as patient demands and some public discourses with regards to alternative and traditional medicines evolve, the inadequacy of the straightforward 'modernity' narrative at the interface between law and medicine is made increasingly visible.

Modernity in the law and medicine nexus – challenging linearity as dominant narrative

The idea of scientific rationality as a cornerstone of modernity has long been essential to the constitution of biomedicine as institution. If looking back at the history of the progressive establishment of biomedicine as the main system of healthcare in Western Europe, a few features can be highlighted. First, and as a somehow simplistic summary, biomedicine has rested on the joint ideas of rupture and linearity in its institutional development. It has increasingly sought, on the one hand, to position itself as 'radically different' from the other preexisting (and often coexisting) systems of therapeutic practices and, on the other hand, to position itself as a field defined by a linear process of experiment, discovery and advancement. For biomedicine, as for science more generally, the process of scientific progress is one of a linear move from error to truth or from uncertainty to established knowledge. Biomedicine has grown institutionally, in part, by portraying itself as located along a linear timeline that starts with ancestral practices, to become something radically different as it becomes 'scientific' and has followed since then a progressive evolution towards ever increasing knowledge. This idea persists, if under increasing pressure, in the deployment of ideas of tradition and modernity in relation to therapeutic practices today. Importantly for our purpose, the possibility for biomedicine to continue to position itself as radically different, and undeniably 'modern', has been facilitated by law. Indeed, the history of biomedicine is also a history of entanglement between a powerful medical institution and a state recognition that has, largely through law and regulation, enabled it to occupy a unique and protected place, for reasons that were almost never purely scientific. This raises at least two issues: one is analytical, in that the reality of time in medicine and of medicine over time is more complicated than dominant narratives suggest. The other is political: these dominant narratives have enabled law and medicine to work jointly as institutions of state power, in turn generating deep patterns of exclusion, appropriation and violence. I turn to these now, before reflecting on some implications of the notion of modernity at the nexus between law and biomedicine for contemporary regulatory practices.

Detailed histories of the long coexistence of a multiplicity of healers with biomedicine in Europe and North America have illustrated how their relationships were always about more than knowledge making, certainty or new discoveries. Of course, this feeds into a broader challenge that STS scholars have brought to the idea of modernity, and of linearity, in scientific development: the production of science, and in turn the evolution of available knowledge, is always subject to deep socio-political patterns and far from the often assumed idea that knowledge becomes settled when it has achieved a higher form of 'truth' (Hess, 2003; Pinch and Bijker, 2012). In the context of medicine, as elsewhere, the relationships between different knowledge systems have been deeply shaped by professional interests and strategies, by the relative positioning of different groups in society, and in relation to state powers, and by other political stakes (such as, as one example, the relations between Church and State in revolutionary France) (Ramsay, 1999; Bivins 2007). Crucially, historians have demonstrated that the organisation of biomedicine as a dominant field of knowledge long preceded the medical discoveries that now constitute its key knowledge base: biomedicine as an institution started establishing itself, and claiming its superiority over other systems, before it had made the breakthrough discoveries that would lead to its biggest therapeutic successes. It is important to keep in mind, therefore, that the processes of exclusion that I describe below simply cannot be read as only the effects of the successful advancement of particular forms of knowledge over others (Saks, 2015; Wahlberg, 2007).

Importantly, too, the uniqueness of biomedicine as symbolic of modernity has also been built on the assumption that could be opposed to a set of practices that are 'traditional'. This idea of what Bruno Latour (1991) has named for other purposes 'the Great Divide', between the moderns and their Others, has been extensively discredited: this imaginary of a fixed traditional sphere, opposed to a determinately modern biomedicine, and separated by a clear line dependent on an evolutionary vision of time, simply cannot be sustained in light of the lived practices of medicine. Far from being static, stuck in time or untouched, most 'traditional' medicines have changed over time and continue to be frequently revisited. They have also, and have been since their early encounters, been complicated by exchanges with biomedicine itself, other imported therapies and with global and governmental interventions (Adams, 2002; Hampshire and Owusu, 2013). The sense that 'traditional' medicine is such is itself the product of particular historical and political movements. Indeed, the use of the term 'traditional' remains politically loaded in a number of ways (sometimes also being reappropriated by its users) and grounded in heavy assumptions about the relationship between medicines and modernity.

'Progress' as a tool of dominance in the history of medicine

The self-projection of biomedicine as an undeniable example of modernity is important to reflect on because of its political implications. This narrative participated, historically, in sustaining multiple processes of (dis)empowerment, in which particular forms of knowledge, and particular social groups, came to thrive or be dismissed. In those processes, law played an influential role. If taking apart the idea that biomedicine is an objective pillar of social advancement and that it is a unique form of knowledge that others cannot and should not challenge, it becomes easier to see some of the social processes at play in the expansion of biomedicine as tool of social control (English and Ehrenreich, 2010). With this in mind, challenging linear visions of time and modernity in medicine and their taking up by law *matters*: where law and medicine have embraced linear understandings of modernity as (scientific) progress, the outcome has always been more than 'just improving' the delivery of healthcare. Rather than seeing biomedicine as purely the outcome of a rational model of scientific development, it may be more analytically and politically telling to view it also as an institutional site of political power, enhanced and facilitated by its embracing by law as exemplary site of modern knowledge.

There is no space here to do justice to the complexity of histories of exclusion that surround biomedicine, but a few points of example are worth focusing on. In Europe, while multiple practices of healthcare coexisted for centuries without a clear sense of hierarchy, or clear interventionism from the state (Bivins, 2007, 2015; Wahlberg, 2007; Cooter, 2008; Saks, 2015), the emergence of biomedicine as the primary source of healthcare was associated with the progressive dismissal of, and restrictions to, other types of medicine. In this process, it is no coincidence that those who emerged as holding a dominant role in therapeutic practices were, mostly, educated white men; those who became framed as lesser therapists were also those who could not access the professional circles that constituted biomedicine because of class, resources and gender. As what is today biomedicine grew as an institution, the social constitution of particular fields shifted, and professional boundaries and hierarchies became constituted: childbirth shifted from the domain of midwives to that of (mostly male) obstetricians; nursing and medical practice became divided along gendered line; the knowledge of (mostly female) herbalists became devalued. In those processes, legal, as well as professional regulation was always crucial. It determined who could practise what and what labels they could use; it mediated relationships, entitlements and responsibilities; it enabled decision making to shift across professional and, in turn, social groups (English and Ehrenreich, 2010). Regulatory interventions contributed to shaping the way in which particular practices could be maintained, promoted and defined and, in turn, contributed to reimagining the temporal development of medicine as a story of evolution. For a long time, an effect was to reinforce the power of a class of predominantly white men in defining not only the boundaries of legitimate and illegitimate knowledge and practice in healing, but also the very nature of temporal evolution in medicine (with some of these patterns still influencing practices today).

If Europe is a useful terrain to observe power shifts around gender and class in medicine, the dangers of adequating biomedicine with a sense of linear modernity and its embracing by law, are most visible in the context of colonial expansion. European states actively and through both legal and practical interventions rewrote what they saw as 'forward-thinking' or 'modern' medicine (Ciekawy, 1998; Hess, 2003; Bigon, 2012). Indeed, biomedicine became one of the key tools used by colonisers to promote the narrative of modernisation that they relied upon in establishing their power over local populations in colonised territories (Vaughan, 2001; Echenberg, 2002; Langwick, 2011). It also became one of the key tools of dominance used to reshape communities and populations and to acquire power over individual bodies: colonial states, relying both on new (if still uncertain) forms of medical knowledge, and on purpose-built regulatory apparatus, used medical interventions as highly problematic, yet powerful, tools of population management (Bado, 2006). Violent practices were justified on the basis of newly developed medical theories, and newly acquired knowledge, that were dependent on an idea of biomedicine as the only valid, modern way of handling public health. In this context, health systems and practices that preexisted colonialism were often actively denounced, sidelined or attacked as relics of pre-modernity (Bruchhausen and Roeckle, 2002). Importantly, this narrative was not aligned with the state of knowledges: biomedical knowledge at the time was still very fragile and uncertain and, indeed, many theories relied upon were later disproved.

At the same time, as they were pushing away particular sets of practices as belonging to another, more backward, era, colonisers would find some inspiration in these practices or in the substances used that generated the first cases of what became known as bioprospecting. Here, the construction of modernity and 'tradition', or 'tradition-as-backwardness', are co-productive stories of power; they are also stories of mutual, if deeply unbalanced, exchange. On the side of colonial states and biomedicine, this exchange was in the form of appropriation. At the same time, local medicines, while resisting and often rejecting biomedicine as violent expression of imperial power, were also often influenced by it, integrating some of its elements in their own practices (Baronov, 2010). As Vincanne Adams (2002, p. 665) reminds us for example of 'Indian and Chinese medical scholars of earlier generations who sat on the edges of, or in the full throes of, Euro-American colonialism, and who responded by proposing alternative sciences based on their own traditions, all the while internalizing biomedical professional forms and epistemology.'

An important feature of those movements, for the purpose of this chapter, is the interlocking of a particular type of medical and legal temporalities in the idea of 'modern' medicine. Effectively, although contexts vary at closer scrutiny, law and medicine as institutions have worked to co-produce a particular sense of modernity as linear and unidirectional, paved essentially by the discoveries of modern medicine. Legal systems could support this by preserving the professional spaces of medical practitioners, shaping them and the spaces of the Others, but also protecting and rewarding certain types of knowledge-products over others, through intellectual property (Coombe, 2005). I return below to how this interlocking of law and medicine impacts on contemporary attempts to regulate alternative and traditional medicines, especially where they have not been recognised or engaged by the law before.

Contemporary challenges to 'modernity' narratives

If looking at movements around alternative and traditional medicines worldwide at the moment, the past, present and future of medicine is being challenged and indeed the idea of biomedicine as the main form of modern healing is harder to sustain. As more patients are driven away from biomedicine and towards alternative sources of care, the dominant narratives put forward in law and biomedicine about what constitutes modernity are increasingly revisited: the resurgence of alternative and traditional medicines since the 1970s in Europe and North America and arguably in a more generalised way in the last 15 years or so, suggest that at least some groups of patients want to redefine imaginaries of modern medicine as being more than enhanced visions of biomedicine – to them, the future needs to somehow drive away from medicine as a top-down, science-based and mostly industrialised enterprise (Fadlon, 2012; MacArtney and Wahlberg, 2014). Discourses suggesting a return to a more 'natural' way of healing have been frequent. While the response of states has varied – from the liberal UK system to the much more restrictive French system, for example – the idea that 'modern humans' may not be tending towards only one type of (western science-based) medicine has progressively become common place (Wahlberg, 2007). The WHO, in setting up the need for traditional healing systems to be reengaged and better valued in designing public health strategies, is similarly challenging the assumption that healthcare systems should be moving towards biomedicine and its imaginaries, leaving behind 'ancestral' practices, in the way colonial states were arguing not so long ago. Overall, for many patients, and at least some regulators, modern times call for a return to practices that biomedicine had seemingly pushed aside.

This has created visible pressure on regulators, as predominant ideas of 'modernity' are being challenged. In turn, looking at some of the contemporary debates surrounding how law should approach systems other than biomedicine provides some fascinating examples of how this narrative continues to play in unchanged terms in some public debates.

Transcripts from a 2013 special commission in the French Senate offers such examples. As brief background, France has a particularly restrictive (if not uniquely so) approach to alternative or traditional medicines. To summarise it briefly, criminal law does not allow anyone who is not a qualified medical practitioner (or, for certain acts, belongs to associated professions, such as nursing, midwifery or dentistry) to 'diagnose' or 'treat' patients. Anyone else who engages in such activities can be charged with 'exercice illegal de la medecine', which carries a fine and prison sentence. Alternative medicines, such as acupuncture or homeopathy, may be legally practised, but only by those who are also medical practitioners (and have followed further specialised training in those practices) (Cloatre, 2018). Therapists such as Traditional Chinese Medicine practitioners, naturopaths and ayurvedic healers may only operate within the strict limits set by the law, for example by providing well-being advice rather than diagnosis, energy boosters rather than treatment. They are also under the surveillance of Miviludes, a peculiar French agency whose main purpose is to monitor sects (the understanding being that alternative medicines are seen by the French authorities as a common entry point into sects). This has led to two sets of debates in France. First, some challenges by alternative practitioners to try to have their professions or practices recognised by the state. And second, attempts by sections of state institutions to reinforce yet further the protection of vulnerable patients against 'les derives sectaires dans la santé' (which could be translated as 'sectarian excesses/abuses in the health sector'). In 2013, a Senate commission was constituted with the latter aim and proceeded to a series of interviews with representatives of health communities and public institutions in charge of both health and/or sectarian matters. The transcript of those debates is a rich illustration of the strong narratives that frame medicine as both radically different from other therapeutic practices and the result of a progressive and linear evolution that it would be dangerous to challenge. As one example, a quote from one of the participants reads (Sénat 2013, p. 75): 'The XVIIIth and XIXth centuries have seen the transition from l'Hotel Dieu to the public hospital. The legacy of the Enlightenment has enabled the development of Western, scientific, medicine. The XXst century may see a descent from the Public Hospital to the altar of gurus. The Lights would then be extinguished by the sectarian obscurantism that imaginary therapeutic methods participate in disseminating to an eager, suggestible, public!.'

Postcolonial contexts add a further layer of complexity to these temporal entanglements and to the various tensions at stake in determining what it means to be modern. Against the background of violence through law and biomedicine, in the name of modernity introduced earlier, postcolonial states have had to rethink how local medicines may fit in the institutional settings of contemporary public health (Fassin and Fassin, 1988). Those negotiations are, fundamentally, about rethinking the relationship between the imagined spheres of tradition and modernity, while negotiating with the messiness of diverse everyday practices. This is done in a context of the complex historical relationships introduced earlier, but the broader political stakes of locating state regulatory strategies within global health governance. This has produced a range of responses. For some states, traditional medicine has been re-embraced as a key component of an alternative modernity and a shared national identity (Wahlberg, 2006); for others, it remains seen as a problematic and less worthy set of practices that need to be pushed aside. Often, however, it sits somewhere in between, as potentially valuable but only when meeting certain conditions that the legal system is expected to determine. As I argue below, those conditions are often so closely inspired by biomedicine and its modes of making that the outcome is far from genuine alternative futures and knowledge making.

To sum up, current multidirectional moves towards a fluid modernity in therapeutic practices and the expectation that law should continue to intervene in setting boundaries between legitimate and illegitimate healing systems creates genuine challenges for the law. One aim of my project is to reflect on these pressures: how do legal systems reconcile supporting 'biomedicine in its modernist projection' with other forms of therapeutic practices? Here, the challenges are both about the present – what do we imagine valuable medical knowledge to look like in contemporary societies? – and the future – where do we see trends in healing moving in the times to come? In doing so, however, law continues to operate on a series of assumptions about what modernity within the challenge should look like – and here it is still 'more like biomedicine'.

Regulating medical temporalities: Legal temporalities as productive of new realities?

The particular relationship between law and biomedicine, and its rationalisation through the notion of modernity, have had an impact on what law imagines 'modern' medicine to look like: often, for law, 'modern medicine' can be proven in the particular scientific ways that biomedicine relies on; emerges from a particular process of research and development; rests on particular methods of learning and transmission of knowledge and on particular forms of institutions. In this section, and with this in mind, I would like to focus on the way in which legal interventions constrain the temporalities of medicine, reshaping alternative systems to look more like, and function more as, biomedicine than they may otherwise. The section argues that law's embracing of biomedicine as the model of modernity towards which all systems should tend continues to impact on how it deals with other therapeutic systems – even when it appears to be recognising the possibilities of an alternative in medicine.

A few points of background and clarification are helpful here. First, the relationship of practices other than biomedicine with law varies across jurisdictions: while some states have clearly established systems of recognition and regulation of some medicines other than biomedicine, for others only biomedicine is formally surrounded by state regulation. There, other practices may be prohibited through a strict regulation of substances, processes or professions they rely on (although often, in practice, still used too) (WHO, 2005; McHale, 2015). Often, however, some form of traditional, folk or alternative medicine is left outside of the regulatory sphere and practiced with no clear engagement from the state (Stone, 2010). Even when states regulate certain forms of traditional or alternative medicine, some practices always remain outside the regulatory sphere – for example family and community healing practices carried in the private sphere will often remain outside the control, and interest, of the states (Barimah, 2013). Movements in regulation are therefore complex to map out, but also become complicated choreographies in which the spaces of regulation/non-regulation and forms of regulatory influences are constantly being redefined, both spatially and as legal and medical practices change over time. At the same time, it is fair to say that in a majority of contexts (both in Europe and through colonial expansion), legal systems have, at least since the 19th century and, as developed above, enabled biomedicine to establish itself as the main system of healthcare provided to population. This is important for understanding some of the questions raised in this section.

It is useful to specify as well that in my research, I am interested broadly in practices other than biomedicine (under the broad – and inevitably unsatisfactory – label of 'alternative and traditional' medicines). It may to some make little sense to refer in the same space, to practices as diverse as (for example) acupuncture, herbalism, homeopathy and the more localised forms of African healing that coexist on the continent. It also complicates yet further some attempts to map out the regulatory field. At the same time, this complicating of the field is also what enables its very diversity to be seized: temporalities of law in relation to medicines are complex because the field is plural and many different 'things' are happening at the same time, in very different ways, yet under a common umbrella of 'healing and healthcare'. One of my aims is precisely to disrupt the apparently neat categories or processes on which discourses surrounding medicine often rest and to emphasise messiness and diversity. In addition, much as these different practices appear to differ from one another, they all tend to be in a position of relative subordination towards biomedicine as the predominant, state-recognised form of medical care: they often (albeit with geographical exceptions) share a position of 'subaltern' in both healthcare and law.

Finally, it is also worth noting at the outset of this section that temporality is a key element of differences and divergences between systems of medicines: temporalities of health and treatment practices, of production of medicines, of the relationship between medical practitioner, patient and disease, are a key point of difference between how different therapeutic and knowledge systems operate. For example, these mean that the positioning of medical practitioners within health processes may navigate from a logic of prevention to a logic of intervention once disease has been established – a diseased body may similarly be either where medicine needs to intervene or where medicine has already failed (Ecks, 2013). It also means that the temporal links between disease-diagnosis-treatment that biomedicine tends to rely on are less linear in the context of traditional practices that rely on a circular process of experimental treatment as diagnosis or that understand disease as being a symptom of longer term imbalances (Adams, 2002). Finally, it means that the temporality of treatment and healing itself varies – ayurvedic medicine, like traditional Chinese medicine or Tibetan medicine, for example, will not necessarily be expected to yield immediate short-term results, as it seeks to address the underlying long-term causes of disease as opposed to its visible symptoms (Tsey, 1997; Awah and Philimore, 2008). Consequently, treatment becomes conceived as a slow-process, as opposed to a short course of medicines with a view to immediate change. As I return to below, this will mean that systems of evidence and perceptions of efficacy may also vary – something that law may not easily accommodate. Paying attention to the question of time in legal movements and, in particular the idea that legal temporalities are productive of their own realities, enables us to see that attempts by law to engage with new therapeutic practices also reshape the very nature of those practices and their own alternative temporalities.

A few examples can be used here to open up some of those questions: first, the question of training and registration of health professionals; second, the idea that medicine needs to be 'evidence based' and largely dependent on clinical trials as the central way of proving reliability and safety; third, and underlying all this, that medicine should be able to prove its own effects within particular time frames (Barry, 2006; Iyioha, 2010). When those temporal assumptions are applied to other forms of medicine, they almost inevitably efface the particularities of the medical systems they regulate, reshaping both medical practices and the nature of what becomes the new 'unregulated' spaces of medicines. Effectively, as alternative and traditional medicines become regulated, pluralistic past and presents are turned into shared futures in which all medicines need to conform to shared modes of operation if they are to persevere: in the transmission of knowledge; processes of evidence making; and industrial production. Medicines can operate and travel if they have the power to be replicated over time in ways that can be packaged and traced.

A first example we can use is that of the regulation of the medical profession and its relation to how the temporality of learning and of treatment are envisaged through it. The regulation of professions in medicine typically happens through systems of certification and training – which may be more or less organised by the state itself or by professional associations. For example, schools of ayurvedic medicine are now well-established in India, training for homeopathy is integrated in some medical schools in Europe and some schools of pharmacy in Ghana have created streams for herbal and traditional medicine alongside pharmacy degrees. While the process may provide some guarantee of uniformity in the knowledge acquired by practitioners, it also transforms processes of learning, processes of selection for practice and processes of transmission – the outcome of which is inevitably to produce a new form of medicine or a newly emerged 'modern traditional medicine'. The generational underpinnings of transmission in forms of traditional medicine that have relied on apprenticeship from a young age are also progressively erased in this process – as the links between personal experience and learning experience become reshaped in the context of university training (Adams and Kaufman, 2011). Underlying these changes are significant assumptions about regulation. As states intervene to reshape professional training (and indeed, although this is opening other questions maybe less relevant to my purpose here, as professions themselves seek to self-regulate), regulatory systems return to the formats of transmission that they have become familiar with in the context of biomedicine. Regulatory movements are also illustrations of the powerful yet discreet workings and influence of biomedicine as an institution and of law and biomedicine as engines of a particular sense of shared modernity.

Similar yet possibly more complex movements are also at play in the certification of substances and medical processes. As mentioned earlier, biomedicine is based on particular underpinnings in terms of the temporality of disease, treatment and effects – as Stefan Ecks (2013) documents in his work in India, and as developed earlier in this chapter, it is commonly seen as 'quick' medicine: its drugs are seen to produce immediate effects on symptoms without necessarily seeking to address long-term conditions. As a result, systems of evidence in medicine have become organised around a temporal logic that suits biomedicine, as the dominant health system in terms of its influence on state decisions, if not in terms of its patients' uptake. Clinical trials in which pre-identified symptoms are shown to be alleviated by a particular treatment are therefore the main way by which the effectiveness of medical products is proven – the gold standard of evidence. Vincanne Adams (2002) documents how this may end up being problematic for medical traditions such as Tibetan medicine that do not necessarily put emphasis on short-term effects, as well as for traditions that more heavily seek to associate substances with, for example, spiritual engagement. Similarly, the methods of production of certain forms of drugs used in traditional medicine may not suit those that are predominantly used by biomedicine and therefore the folding of these into mainstream forms of regulation and ordering may again not be immediately suitable – as an example the slow process through which ayurvedic or homeopathic medicine in their most original practice are produced are unlikely partners to the system of testing, verification and certification that most 'mainstream' pharmaceutical products are subject to. Importantly, those features, imported from biomedicine and transmitted through regulatory systems, are not simply about knowledge or 'treatment' making: they are also about creating abilities, or inabilities, to access the industrial markets of the global economy.

Where does this leave non-biomedical forms of medicine in the face of law? For some practitioners and for some substances, meeting such new standards and frameworks set by new regulatory systems may just not be possible: often, this will mean that activities can only remain aside of the law, as a new form of illegal but persistent activities that states are known to let exist – indeed, in the context of medicine, an unregulated sphere always operates, either in discreet public spheres or in the home and through informal and individual exchanges of treatment. For others, legal accreditation will mean inevitable transformation (Davey, 2014). Forms of ayurvedic medicines have become standardised and produced in formats and scales that make them easier to approve, although critiques may say they bear little resemblance to original products. Herbal medicines can be transformed and repackaged, from plants to industry-produced tablets in which lab-manufactured pills based on plants have been developed, that seem to bear only distant relations with traditional practices. One of the characteristics of herbal products may therefore be, as Vincanne Adams (2002) points out, that they become caught between existing in their original state in the fragile sphere of illegality or non-recognition, or becoming accepted only once transformed to the point that they may be unrecognisable. While research has shown how the process of industrialisation transforms medicines, ayurvedic medicine being a case in point, it should therefore be remembered that much of these transformations are dictated by the regulatory demands that are placed on industrialised production and that assume, among other things, that distribution, use and results should respond to particular temporalities (Pordié and Hardon, 2015; Pordié and Gaudillière, 2014).

The implications of those various movements are multiple. First, regulatory systems continue to assume a certain degree of uniformity in 'modern medicine'. That uniformity operates in tension with continuous demands for pluralism in health practices that are both therapeutic and, arguably, political: those demands are also about being able to move away from the idea of modernity as scientific and industrial, that western states have long assumed, but this aspect is commonly effaced as regulations seize new fields. Second, assuming the model of biomedicine is not simply about assuming one way of proving knowledge over another: it also has implications for determining who may move across global markets and how and who is to be included in those or not. Third, this has implications at local levels, in allocating what others have termed biocitizenships: for example, the law is not just about regulating professions, but also about shaping the legitimate healer, the legitimate user and the legitimate interlocutor of the state in making future regulatory decisions. In those movements, the very notion of what traditional medicine may be or what it means are constantly being reshaped as terminologies and practices become relabeled and transformed to fit the needs of various publics, demands or beliefs or, indeed, regulatory pressures.

Conclusion

Overall, in those movements for legitimacy of medical practices, a key feature is the permanent imposition by biomedicine of certain assumptions about how bodies work, how knowledge can be proven and how treatment should be legitimised, that are themselves resting on particular notions of modernity and linear times. While the dichotomies between nature and society, irrational spirituality and rational science have commonly been pointed out as some of the key elements that make it difficult to conciliate biomedicine with other forms of medical knowledge, the assumptions that different practices make about the times of medicine and about bodily temporalities also seem significant in the fostering of these differences. While law as an institution has responded to and helped shape biomedicine since at least the 19th century in Europe, it has also participated in reinforcing particular temporalities in medicine. As the question of the regulation of practices other than biomedicine is seized again by contemporary states, these conflicting temporalities continue to require adjustment and questioning. In these choreographies of legitimacy, recognition and persistent practice, the question of modernity in medicine is also entirely reopened: from postcolonial states' reengagement with pre-colonial practices of medicine, to global pressures for 'adequate' regulation, to the new faces of medical pluralism that have been generated in western states through global movements and multicultural patient communities, definitions of what constitutes both the present, but also the imagined future of medicine continue to shape state strategies and create tensions between understandings of how progress should be imagined in medicine. While biomedical research continues to play a key part in the projected future of most actors of public health (patients, researchers, officials or practitioners), for others the future of medicine may depend on the possibilities for alternative forms of healthcare that are less heavily entangled in neoliberal industrial strategies and temporalities than biomedicine, as it is currently framed and regulated, would suggest. Conflicting visions of modernity in medicine may therefore also be a significant site to explore broader tensions in understandings of both the pace and the political underpinnings of projected social futures.

Throughout this chapter, I aimed to engage with the challenge of thinking about, and thinking with, legal temporalities and I would like to end this chapter by offering a few concluding thoughts about what such approach can offer to thinking about law in the context of medicine (and, maybe, more generally). A particularity of the field is the apparent effacement of legal temporalities behind those of medicines and those of science: as the first part of this chapter aimed to demonstrate, an idea of modernity that is arguably, in many ways, specific to science, although often successfully reified by science as quasi-independent, has been embraced by law in the contexts explored here. This makes the identification of temporalities that are embedded in law difficult, but also necessary: the process of political construction at play in the normative movement is made more visible by unpacking the assumptions about time that law has rested on, seemingly 'neutrally'. Once this idea of neutrality through the assumption that time is linear and given is unpacked, it becomes possible to view some of the unexpected effects of the law, in addition to and aside of what it explicitly sets out to regulate – which, arguably, remains one of the key contributions sociolegal scholars can continue to make. The question of 'what else is the law doing?' becomes informed by a critical perspective on its performative nature in relation to what it often presents, and what we often take as given, including the temporal framing of social relationships. As we continue to unpack the multidirectional workings of law in social processes in general, and in relation to medicine in particular, a focus on legal temporalities can continue to open up new critical routes. Of course, it cannot tell us 'everything' about the complex workings of law in action: but it can at least contribute to understanding better both the complexity of law in its making (always full of politics and always more socially complex than the neutrality it aims to portray) and in its deployment (always multiple, contested, and performative of the very realities it sets out to regulate).

Notes

1 I am grateful to the editors, Siân Beynon-Jones and Emily Grabham for their insightful feedback, and their thorough and supportive work as editors. I am also grateful to the Wellcome Trust for funding the research on which this chapter is based.
2 Wellcome grant 200380/Z/15/Z.

Bibliography

Academie Nationale de Medecine (2013). *Therapies Complementaires – Acunpuncture, Hypnose, Osteopathie, Tai-chi: Leur Place Parmi les Ressources de Soins.* Paris: Academie Nationale de Medecine.

Adams,V. (2002). Randomized Controlled Crime Postcolonial Sciences in Alternative Medicine Research. *Social Studies of Science* 32, 5/6, pp. 659–690.

Adams, V., Burke, N. and Whitmarsh, I. (2014). Slow Research: Thoughts for a Movement in Global Health. *Medical Anthropology* 33, pp. 179–197.

Adams, A. and Kaufman, S. (2011). Ethnography and the Making of Modern Health Professionals. *Culture, Medicine and Psychiatry* 35, p. 333.

Adams,V., Schrempf, M. and Craig, S. R. (2011). *Medicine Between Science and Religion: Explorations on Tibetan Grounds.* New York: Berghahn Books.

Awah, P. and Philimore, P. (2008). Diabetes, Medicine and Modernity in Cameroon. *Africa* 78(4), pp. 475–495.

Barimah, K. B. (2013). Traditional Healers as Service Providers in Ghana's National Health Insurance Scheme: The Wrong Way Forward?. *Global Public Health* 8(2), pp. 202–208.

Baronov, D. (2010). *The African Transformation of Western Medicine and the Dynamics of Global Cultural Exchange.* Philadelphia: Temple University Press.

Bado, J. P. (ed). (2006). *Les Conquetes de la Medecine Modern en Afrique.* Paris: Karthala.

Barry, C. A. (2006). The Role of Evidence in Alternative Medicine: Contrasting Biomedical and Anthropological Approaches. *Social Science & Medicine* 62(11), pp. 2646–2657.

Bigon, L. (2012).A History of Urban Planning and Infectious Diseases: Colonial Senegal in the Early Twentieth Century. *Urban Studies Research* pp.1–12.

Bivins, R. (2007). *Alternative Medicine? A History*. Oxford: Oxford University Press.

Bivins, R. (2015).Limits and Liberties: CAM, Regulation and the Medical Consumer in Historical Perspective'. In Gale, N. and McHale, (Eds.), *Routledge Handbook of Complementary and Alternative Medicines: Perspectives from Law and Social Sciences*, 1st ed. London: Routledge.

Bruchhausen, W. and Roeckle, V. (2002). Categorizing 'African Medicine': the German discourse on East African healing practices, 1885–1918. In Ernst, W. (Ed.), *Plural Medicine, Tradition and Modernity, 1800–2000*, 1st ed. London: Routledge.

Buseh, A., Stevens, P., Bromberg, M. and Kelber, S. (2015). The Ebola Epidemic in West Africa: Challenges, Opportunities, and Policy Priority Areas. *Nursing Outlook* 63(1), pp. 30–40.

Ciekawy, D. (1998). Witchcraft in Statecraft: Five Technologies of Power in Colonial and Postcolonial Coastal Kenya. *African Studies Review* 41(3), pp. 119–141.

Cloatre, E. (2013). *Pills for the Poorest: An Exploration of TRIPS and Access to Medication in Sub-Saharan Africa*. London: Palgrave Macmillan.

Cloatre, E. (2018). Regulating Alternative Healing in France, and the Problem of 'Non-medicine', *Medical Law Review*, (online first).

Coombe, R. (2005). Legal Claims to Culture in and Against the Market: Neoliberalism and the Global Proliferation of Meaningful Difference. *Law, Culture and the Humanities* 1(1), pp. 35–52.

Cooter, R. (2008). *Studies in the History of Alternative Medicine*. London: Macmillan.

Davey, S. (2014). *Unintended Consequences of Regulating Traditional Medicine*. WHO, pp. 131.

Echenberg. M. (2002). *Black Death, White Medicine: Bubonic Plague and the Politics of Public Health in Colonial Senegal, 1914–1945*. Porstmouth, NH: Heinemann.

Ecks, S. (2013). *Eating Drugs: Psychopharmaceutical Pluralism in India*. New York: NYU Press.

English, D. and Ehrenreich, B. (2010). *Midwives, Nurses and Witches*. Feminist Press.

Fadlon, J. (2012). *Negotiating the holistic turn: The domestication of alternative medicine*. New York: SUNY Press.

Fassin, D. and Fassin, E. (1988). De la Quête de Legitimation à la Question de la Légitimité: les Thérapeutiques 'Traditionnelles' au Sénégal. *Cahiers d'Etudes Africaines* 28(110), pp. 207–231.

Gale, N. (2014). The Sociology of Traditional, Complementary and Alternative Medicine. *Sociology Compass* 8(6), pp. 805–822.

Gale, N. and McHale, J. (2015). Introduction. In Gale, N. and McHale (Eds.), *Routledge Handbook of Complementary and Alternative Medicines: Perspectives from Law and Social Sciences*. London: Routledge.

Hampshire, K. R. and Owusu, S. A. (2013). Grandfathers, Google, and Dreams: Medical Pluralism, Globalization, and New Healing Encounters in Ghana. *Medical Anthropology* 32(3), pp. 247–265.

Hess, D. (2003). Technology, Medicine, and Modernity: the Problem of Alternatives. In Misa, T. J., Brey, P. and Feenberg, A. (Eds.), *Modernity and Technology*. London: MIT Press, pp. 279–302.

House of Lord Science and Technology Select Committee Report (2000). *Sixth Report: Complementary and Alternative Medicine*. HL, 123.

Iyioha, I. (2010). Law's Dilemma: Validating Complementary and Alternative Medicine and the Clash of Evidential Paradigms. *Evidence-Based Complementary and Alternative Medicine*, Volume 2011.

Langwick, S. (2011). *Bodies, Politics, and African Healing: The Matter of Maladies in Tanzania*. Bloomington, IN: Indiana University Press.

Latour, B. (1991). *We Have Never Been Modern*. Cambridge, MA: Harvard University Press.

Latour, B. (2005). *Reassembling the Social-an Introduction to Actor-Network-Theory*. Oxford: Oxford University Press.

MacArtney, J. and Wahlberg, A. (2014). The Problem of Complementary and Alternative Medicine Use Today: Eyes Half Closed?. *Qualitative Health Research* 24(1), pp. 114–123.

McHale, J. (2015). Legal Frameworks, Professional Regulation and CAM Practice: Perspectives from the UK. In Gale, N. and McHale (Eds.), *Routledge Handbook of Complementary and Alternative Medicines: Perspectives from Law and Social Sciences*. London: Routledge.

Pinch, T. and Bijker, W. E. (2012). The Social Construction of Facts and Artifacts: or How the Sociology of Science and the Sociology of Technology Might Benefit Each Other. In Bijker, W. E., Hughes, T. P. and Pinch, T. (Eds.), *The Social Construction of Technological Systems: New Directions in the Sociology and History of Technological Systems*. Cambridge, MA: MIT Press.

Pordié, L. and Hardon, A. (2015). Drugs' Stories and Itineraries. On the Making of Asian Industrial Medicines. *Anthropology & Medicine* 22(1), pp. 1–6.

Pordié, L. and Gaudillière, J.-P. (2014). Industrial Ayurveda. Drug Discovery, Reformulation and the Market. *Asian Medicine* 9(1–2), pp. 1–11.

Ramsey, M. (1999). Alternative Medicine in Modern France. *Medical History* 43, pp. 286–322.

Saks, M. (2015). Power and Professionalism in CAM: A Sociological Approach. In Gale, N. and McHale (Eds.), *Routledge Handbook of Complementary and Alternative Medicines: Perspectives from Law and Social Sciences*. London: Routledge.

Sénat (2013). *Rapport Fait au Nom de la Commission d'Enquête sur l'Influence des Mouvements à Caractère Sectaire dans le Domaine de la Santé*. N.480, 2012–2013.

Stone, J. (2010). Beyond Legislation: Why Chicken Soup and Regulation Don't Mix. In Moore, R. and McClean, S. (Eds.), *Folk Healing and Health Care Practices in Britain and Ireland*. Oxford: Berghahn Book.

Tsey, K. (1997). Traditional Medicine in Contemporary Ghana: A Public Policy Analysis. *Social Science & Medicine* 45(7), pp.1065–1074.

Vaughan, M. (2001). *Curing their Ills: Colonial Power and African Illness*. Stanford, MA: Stanford University Press.

Wahlberg, A. (2006). Bio-politics and the Promotion of Traditional Herbal Medicine in Vietnam. *Health* 10(2), pp. 123–147.

Wahlberg, A. (2007). A Quackery with a Difference – New Medical Pluralism and the Problem of 'Dangerous Practitioners' in the United Kingdom. *Social Science & Medicine* 65(11), pp. 2307–2316.

World Heath Organization. (2001). Legal status of traditional medicine and complementary, available at http://apps.who.int/medicinedocs/pdf/h2943e/h2943e.pdf.

World Health Organization. (2005). National policy on traditional medicine and regulation of herbal medicines: Report of a WHO global survey, available at http://apps.who.int/medicinedocs/pdf/s7916e/s7916e.pdf.

7 Making land liquid

On time and title registration

Sarah Keenan, Birkbeck College, University of London

Around the world, title registration systems are being adopted by states as the most efficient means of facilitating a legal market in land (Raff, 2003: 8). Title registration systems were designed with the explicit purpose of making land a more liquid asset – one that is easily tradable and convertible into cash. However, land is not liquid – it is mainly solid and immovable and thus historically difficult to trade in. The creation of a market in land has only been possible with the assistance of the legal architecture of property law. In the common law world, title – that is, the entitlement to exclusively possess land – is an essential part of that architecture. Prior to the development of registration systems, title to land was constituted through the 'raw fact' of physical possessions evidenced through local testimony and paper documents (Gray and Gray, 2009: 180–182). Prior to registration systems, conveying land was a laborious and slow process requiring careful compilation of title deeds reflecting years of possession, along with physical inspections of the land and discussions with locals. In contrast, under registration systems, title is constituted through the singular act of registration and conveyances of land happen far more simply and swiftly, through a central registry. Title registration systems make title an almost liquid asset and create the illusion that land is also liquid.

The liquidity afforded to title through registration not only changes the administration of land ownership, but also its legal form. The estate or 'slice of time' in land that was a feature of the ownership scheme under title deed systems no longer exists as an independent legal entity. This 'slice of time' or 'fourth dimension' of land is made effectively redundant in the temporal order produced by title registration systems. Title registration systems regulate the temporality of title according to the registry's 'mirror', 'curtain' and insurance principles. Operating together, these principles produce a centralised, authoritative temporality for land that is disconnected from the land's local history and present physical use. Whereas deed systems operate on the basis that the title to be transferred already exists, being based on a history of physical possession of the land, registration systems operate on the basis that title is produced anew on every conveyance. Title registration systems empower the registry to create title in a process that some commentators have described as akin to magic: new, perfect title is conjured up each time land is transferred.

In this chapter, I discuss title registration systems in four different contexts: first, the English and Welsh Land Registration Act 2002; second, the Torrens title registration system in Australia; third, title registration systems introduced in the Global South at the behest of international financial and development institutions; and finally, the Mortgage Electronic Registration Systems (MERS) in the USA. While each context is historically and geographically distinct, the systems examined in each context share the 'magical' quality of creating new title rather than recording pre-existing title, thus imposing a distinct temporal order and producing a number of similar effects. Analysed together, these discussions show that there is a disjuncture between the temporality of registered titles and the temporality of the land to which those titles pertain: registered title and land are out of sync. Titles take on a life and pace of their own through the registry, while unregistered and/or unregisterable connections to land that have been constituted through years of local use are wiped from legal memory. Registries produce a temporal order that facilitates the coordination of an increasingly complex and rapid trade in titles by parties who need not have anything but a purely financial connection to the land. For these parties, the local history of the land is not only irrelevant, but is preferably ignored lest a historical event threaten their investment in it.

Title deeds: Keeping and transferring slices of time

In the common law world, title to land has traditionally been based on physical possession proven through paper deeds. There was no centralised conveyancing system. Rather, conveyancing was done privately and law would intervene in ad hoc disputes only when parties approached the courts. True to its feudal origins, English land law does not have any overarching notion of individual ownership. Individual landholders do not directly own land, but instead own an 'estate' or 'slice of time' in land, which is ultimately owned by the Crown (Gray and Gray, 2009: 58). An estate is a legal concept that combines land with time; estates are 'the fourth dimension' of land (Gray and Gray, 2009: 56). Common law 'title' is the entitlement to assert rights over the estate; it is ultimately based on possession and is relative rather than absolute. The relativity of title means that more than one person can hold title to the same estate and that title might be lost if the estate owner fails to possess the land for an extended period of time (this period differs according to jurisdiction; it is currently 12 years in England and Wales).[1] If, during that period, a squatter takes continuous possession of the land, the 'paper owner' will be prevented from bringing an action for possession, leaving the squatter with the better title to the estate. This loss of title by adverse possession occurs only rarely, but demonstrates the separability of title and estate in this system – the 'slice of time' in the land exists as a legal form independent of its owner. The estate, to draw on Mariana Valverde is an example of a legal conceptualisation of time 'thickening' and 'taking on flesh': it becomes spatialised in distinct ways and responsive to events that occur on the land's other three dimensions (i.e. its width, length and depth) (Valverde, 2015: 10). The estate is a temporal concept with legal flesh, its responsiveness to possession tying title to land (the two must not fall more than 12 years out of sync).

Retaining common law title to land thus requires an ongoing performance of estate ownership: ownership of one's slice of time must be performed through possession. Such ownership was difficult to securely convey. In medieval times, the transfer of land ownership involved the local community at large – public ceremonies around estate transfer were designed to embed the event in local memory (Pottage, 1994: 361). These public ceremonies were eventually replaced with title deeds, which still require a level of ceremonial formality, but which prove in document form the titleholder's right to possession based on the genealogy of the estate. The details of the estate recorded in the deeds are checked as against facts on the ground, meaning deeds are connected to and conditional on local memories of physical realities external and prior to the deeds themselves, memories carved out through years of local land use and custom. The temporality of land title under this system is thus produced by the local history and present of land use, via the legal concepts of estates and possession.

The conveyancing rule of *nemo dat quod non habet* (you cannot give what you do not have) further orients the title deeds system towards the past. The *nemo dat* rule means that all conveyed title is dependent on its predecessors: during a conveyance of land, the titleholder must be able to prove that the title has 'a good root' (Burns, 2011: 791). As such, title deeds orient their users toward the local history of the land. Pottage writes that title documents 'stored up the past and projected it into the future' (1998: 135), with the purpose of keeping estates in the family for future generations. This system of conveying title is productive of a linear temporality: every title is dependent on its predecessors and the slices of time are extended out as far into the future as was possible through documentary techniques. Linear time strongly links the past, present and future and tends to naturalise events and structures by rendering them part of a seemingly irreversible, logical progression from past to present (see Greenhouse, 1996). The linear time of the title deed system orients titleholders toward the history of the land and helped keep an elite class of families closely aligned with English land over multiple centuries.

English title registration

Prior to land registration, conveying land in the heart of the common law world was slow. The English title deed system for conveying land required prospective buyers to satisfy themselves of the seller's legitimate ownership of a slice of time in the land, which was a cumbersome and difficult process. The details contained in paper title deeds would need to be verified by locals, and solicitors would be hired to construct a chain of deeds that stretched as far back in time as possible. During the British industrial revolution, proving that title had 'a good root' came to be regarded as an inefficient and onerous task for purchasers, particularly by those from outside the elite class that had traditionally owned estates in land. Throughout most of the 1800s, English law required that 'a good root' of title be at least 60 years old (Pottage, 1994: 139). This was reduced to 40 years in 1874, as title transactions became more frequent and the process of proving title genealogy became more of an impediment to commercial transactions (it is 15 years for unregistered land in England and Wales today).[2]

Consistent with the push to make land more marketable, throughout the 1800s there were also several attempts in England to introduce a state-backed title registration system in order to make the process for conveying land faster and easier for the growing pool of people keen and financially able to purchase property in land (Anderson, 1998: 116).[3] Proposals were made for a title registry in which 'the entries in the register must constitute the title, the entire and only title' (Hogg, 1830 in Simpson, 1976: 40). Such a system would simplify and speed up conveyancing because law would no longer refer a prospective purchaser 'to a tedious and uncertain list of by-gone transactions and events, in which he has no concern or interest, but to an authentic statement of a present fact, which alone he wishes to know, namely the fact that the person from whom he is buying is entitled to sell' (Wilson, 1850 in Simpson, 1976: 41). That is, conveying title would no longer orient prospective estate owners toward the land's local history, because title would no longer be dependent on its predecessors. The registry would provide conclusive information relevant to the immediate transaction. That conveniently centralised information is all that would matter for the title's legal validity, with registered titles being indefeasible and guaranteed by the state.[4] The rights and interests encompassed in each title would be frozen in time at the point of initial registration, after which any changes to the title could only be made via the registry. The singular act of registration – rather than years of physical possession of the land – would legally constitute title, making the proposed registry a title-making machine for the industrial age.

The push for a title registration system was associated with wider land reform and political enfranchisement and the landed elite was generally opposed to the introduction of title registration (Anderson, 1998: 109). The singular machinery of the registry would replace the old system of relativity, possession and documentary genealogies and would orient its users not toward the local past but to the present as it was captured in the registry. Conveyancing would involve the production of new titles via the registry, rather than the transfer of already existing title to an estate. By maintaining the title registry and acting as statutory insurer of registered titles, the proposed title registry would involve a significantly more active and interventionist role than the state had previously taken in regard to land title, just at the time when the state itself was undergoing democratising reforms.[5] By doing away with title documents that projected the past into the future and instead giving a centralised registry the power to continually dictate the present, title registration threatened to disrupt the linear temporality of the class system.

Despite opposition from the landed class, voluntary title registration was introduced in England and Wales in 1862 (Simpson, 1976: 43) and has been made steadily more compulsory and widespread since then. A number of Acts were passed in 1925 with the purpose of making English and Welsh land 'as easily and securely transferable as possible, as readily exchangeable as any other asset, and to deny the idea that land had any special meaning' (Cowan, Fox O'Mahoney and Cobb, 2012: 49). The Law of Property Act 1925 made title easier to register and the Land Registration Act 1925 for the first time allowed the central government to initiate compulsory registration of title (Simpson, 1976: 46). Since 1990, all land in England and Wales must be registered when it is sold and the Register is open to public inspection.[6] The Land Registration Act 2002 took the final step of transforming the basis of entitlement to land in English law from possession to registration (Law Commission, 1998: 24) and also laid the groundwork for electronic conveyancing. Unregistered land still exists in England and Wales; however, Her Majesty's Land Registry today maintains and guarantees over 24 million titles to a value of over £4 trillion.[7] The practical goals of making conveyancing simpler and faster and making estates in land available to purchasers from outside the established landed class, have been achieved. While the ideal of the good landowner and class alignments still persist,[8] title to English and Welsh land today is an asset available for purchase by anyone who can pay the asking price.[9]

Gray and Gray describe the initial registration of title for previously unregistered land as 'the terminal event' in the estate's lifetime (2009: 195), as the temporal order of the Land Registry takes over. With physical possession no longer legally constitutive of title, the local and the past have lost much of their power to the centralised, increasingly digital Land Registry, as have the principles of relativity, possession and the concept of estates. The titles produced by the registry cannot be conceptually separated from the land to which they relate.[10] The 2002 Act introduces a scheme[11] to replace the rules of adverse possession, which no longer make sense when the basis of title is registration rather than possession. The temporal order of the Land Registry is produced in part by 'the mirror principle' that the entry on the register reflects the full range of interests that affect the land at any moment in time (Gray and Gray, 2009: 190). Like actual mirrors, mirror-principle registers represent the reality they reflect as a continually produced superficial 'now'. Nothing that appears in the mirror leaves a trace on it and nothing behind the surface appears in the mirror at all. The temporality of registered title is thus very different from the linear temporality of the deeds system, which allows past title to define present and future title and which is ultimately dependent on significant physical relationships with land. The 2002 Act preserves the legal validity of particular interests even though they are unregistered, meaning that there are 'cracks in the mirror': relics from the unregistered past that survive into the registered future.[12] However these cracks are exceptions to the mirror rule: unregistered, historical interests should not legally appear in real life if they do not appear on the register. As Gray and Gray point out, title can no longer be detached from the estate to which it relates: the 2002 Act speaks indiscriminately of registration of an 'estate', of 'title' to an 'estate' and of a person as 'proprietor' of an 'estate'... 'the overall effect is to weld concepts of "title", "estate" and "proprietor" into a form of statutory ownership of land' (2009: 183). The 'estate' as a legal form, is subsumed into the registered title and the subject to whom that title is registered.

With the 2002 Act making the 'estate' a redundant concept, what happens to the slice of time in the land it used to represent? Does registration reduce land to three dimensions? The simple answer is no – registered land still has a temporal dimension, as the duration of title is recorded in the registry along with the land's spatial dimensions.[13] The estate is a legal concept that represents time in land for the purposes of private property; it is an abstraction from, rather than a reflection of the temporality of the physical and living matter that constitutes land. As discussed above, the methods used to convey estates – *nemo dat* and paper title deeds – produced a liner temporality that helped maintain the English class system. The redundancy and practical disappearance of the estate on registration does not eliminate the temporal dimension of land, but changes the way it is legally determined. Whereas the grounding of title in possession ensures that the legal 'flesh' taken on by estates is connected to the land's local history, with registration as the basis of title, the register is the sole legal determinant of all four dimensions of land. Whereas paper deeds prove the existence of *already existing* title, registration brings title into being: each registered title is new, manufactured and guaranteed by the registry. The rules of adverse possession that keep title and land within 12 years of each other no longer apply. No ongoing performance of possession is required to retain title, neither are paper title deeds required to convey it. The temporal order of the registry replaces the 'slices of time' strung together over generations to produce the linear temporality of unregistered title. The new temporal order is a series of staccato-like slices of time in the land that are detached from the past and from any unregistered present land use (Keenan, 2016: 12). Land becomes a more marketable asset as it is assumed to be the mirror of title and title can be bought and sold swiftly and easily through the registry. Registration facilitates liquidity by producing new titles on every conveyance and rendering irrelevant the cumbersome realities of land use and local history.

New world, new title: The Torrens system

While the introduction of title registration is relatively new in England, it has a longer history in many former British colonies. Land in British colonies was understood by colonisers as 'new' and thus socially and politically different from English land (Rogers, 2006: 127). English land law was modified in various ways to increase the alienability of land in settler colonies. In 1858 the Torrens system of title registration was introduced in the colony of South Australia (Simpson, 1976: 69). While the introduction of title registration in England was stalled by political opposition from the landed class and the practical barrier of land laden with centuries of convoluted estates, in South Australia there were no such political hurdles. Indeed, with Australian land being treated as *terra nullius* (belonging to no one), it offered notionally blank slate land on which a title registration system that manufactured new titles could operate.

Robert Torrens, the South Australian politician after whom the system is named, successfully argued for the system in part by pointing out that the costs of transacting South Australian land under the old conveyancing system were often greater than the cost of the land itself and suggesting that land could more efficiently be traded by adopting a registration system akin to that already used for ships and shares (Raff, 2003: 27–36; Mawani, 2016). Designed to facilitate a new market in cheap and legally unencumbered land, the Torrens system is based on three key principles: 'the mirror' (mentioned above) – the register will accurately and completely reflect the interests that affect the land within its coverage; 'the curtain' – interests that are not on the register will not bind new titleholders, the register is the sole source of information for prospective purchasers to check; and 'the insurance principle' – the state guarantees the accuracy of the register and will compensate any registered titleholder who suffers a loss due to a defect in the register (Taylor, 2008: 11–14). These principles operate together to produce new titles free of the encumbrances of local land use and custom. The Torrens system makes the sale and resale of land by investors on the other side of the world simpler, cheaper and faster because the register is the basis of title to land – rather than possession and a chain of title back to a 'good root'. South Australia thus made in 1858 this crucial change to the basis of title that would not occur in England until 2002.

In its strict adherence to the mirror, curtain and insurance principles, the Torrens system produces titles that are indefeasible rather than relative.[14] As famously described in *Breskvar v Wall*, Torrens is 'not a system of registration of title but a system of title by registration'.[15] That is, registration in the Torrens system is not merely the recording of pre-existing title, it is what *creates* title – perfect, new, indefeasible title. As I have argued elsewhere, by producing perfect titles, the Torrens register has been understood as having an almost magical quality, the moment of registration starting time anew for the registered land and thus freeing title from the land's local history (Keenan, 2016). Greg Taylor describes the Torrens system as 'a hospital' which 'cures invalidities' and makes people's titles certain 'by taking away the need to show [from the moment of registration] that the registered owner's title originated in the seller's right to sell the land. The Torrens system therefore means the end of the need to look backwards for possible flaws' (2008: 10).

In its production of new titles free of legal encumbrances, the Torrens system favours 'dynamic' over 'static' security – that is, security of title for new owners, at the expense of existing and previous owners (O'Connor, 2005, 2009). As Hickey and Harding have argued, the choice between a system that favours dynamic security and one that favours static security is political, as it will ultimately favour particular human values over others (Hickey and Harding, 2011). Legal commentators have described this choice as being between security of title, on the one hand, and ease of title transfer, on the other (Harris and Au, 2014). Another way to understand the choice between static and dynamic security is as a choice between old and new relationships with land. The Torrens system favours new relationships with land; indeed, it operates on the basis that every title is new. Whereas the English title registration system retains exceptions to the mirror and curtain principles by allowing particular old, unregistered relationships with land to survive into the registered present, the Torrens system's strict operation of its three principles means that if a relationship with land is unregistered it cannot bind a new registered purchaser. The system makes land title a more liquid asset than it has ever been before, but it can only do so via the magical/hospital-like mechanisms of the mirror, the curtain and the insurance principle. These Torrens mechanisms produce the fictional starting point for each registered title – a starting point that is reinvented on each conveyance, allowing land to be swiftly transferred.

The Torrens system thus has its own temporality separate from the land to which it relates. Unlike the title deeds system, its temporally 'thick' estates and its reliance on historical documents and local testimony, Torrens title registration is future focused. The temporality of registered land is determined by the registry, which assists buyers and sellers of land title to efficiently coordinate their trade. Although seemingly objective, the temporality of land produced by the Torrens register involves subjective decisions about which changes are worth noticing and which are to be ignored. As Michelle Bastian writes: '[E]ven the seemingly objective clock requires ongoing decisions about what is of significance to us, and consequently which elements of our world we want to keep to time with and which elements we can afford to drop from our sphere of direct concern' (Bastian, 2012). Torrens registration produces a temporal order that allows for the land's local history to be dropped from the sphere of direct concern of titleholders, who instead direct their attention only to future changes in the land that law will recognise as registrable. In settler colonial contexts such as Australia, this means that the temporality of registered title is noticeably out of sync with the land's local indigenous history. Indeed, indigenous activists have long argued that the Torrens system was invented 'in order to complete the dispossession of the Aboriginal people' (Pearson in Ainger, 1991: 18).[16] While it is difficult to prove Torrens' intentions in regard to colonial dispossession, it is beyond doubt that the dynamic security favoured by this registration system – its magical conjuring of new titles, curtain drawn across the pre-colonial past and the fast-moving and internationally accessible market in land it facilitates– has been of great benefit to the settler colonial project of taking Aboriginal land.

Catching up by selling off? Title registration in the Global South

Title registration systems in which the act of registration is the basis of title, are now increasingly favoured around the world (Raff, 2003: 8). The Torrens system has proved highly influential and was used as a reference point in the design of England and Wales' Land Registration Act 2002 (Law Commission, 1998). The introduction of Torrens-like title registration systems has been supported, promoted and insisted on by the UN, World Bank and IMF as a way for states of the Global South to 'modernise' their relationships with land and bring them into sync with the Global North (Deininger, 2003). A 1975 World Bank land reform report on Africa strongly suggested title registration be introduced to replace unregistered communal customary tenure, which it described as 'static in its technology and relatively insular' (Besteman, 1994: 484–487). Development scholars argue that title registration systems 'contribute toward solving production, credit, poverty, and employment' (Hanstad, 1997: 702) primarily because property owners with registered titles are more likely to invest and to be granted credit than those with informal property rights (World Bank Group, 2014); but also, because title registration can improve local governments' ability to generate resources through taxation (Deininger and Gershon, 2009: 248). Title registration systems are thus framed by international financial institutions and some development scholars as offering states of the Global South 'a new start' and a brighter economic future.

The academic and institutional encouragement of title registration as development policy has been particularly strong since Hernando de Soto's influential call for the formalisation of land title as the answer to poverty in the Global South (2000). De Soto's focus was on formalisation rather than registration specifically, but his vision for secure, marketable and future-oriented land titles that could be easily bought, sold and secured against by anyone with the appropriate funds is clearly consistent with the principles of title registration. The extent to which title registration has been adopted as part of broader land management policies in the Global South indicates that it has become a taken-for-granted element of many such policies (Raff, 2003: 8–9; Deininger and Gershon, 2009: 244). The World Bank Group's 'Doing Business' project which ranks nations on the ease of doing business there includes 'registering property' as a key determinant.[17] The 'Our Land, Our Business' campaign argues that the rankings help facilitate 'land grabs':[18] swift and large-scale acquisition of land in the Global South by corporations of the Global North, resulting in the forced displacement of local farmers.[19] Title registration is an important part of reorienting the land and economies of the Global South toward a future of global capitalism and the growing international market for land.

Like settler colonial contexts such as Australia, states of the Global South were also invaded by European colonisers. However, while in settler colonies land is and was treated as a blank slate on which to build a 'new world', land in the Global South has been treated more as an extractive resource than a home for white people.[20] The land now being subject to title registration in the Global South includes some of the most densely populated urban areas in the world (see Gupta, 2010). As such, the introduction of title registration faces some of the same practical hurdles as the introduction of the system in England – in both England and the Global South, the land is understood by those implementing the system as 'old' rather than 'new' and encumbered by long histories of unregistered interests in land. However, whereas in England title registration has been introduced slowly and carefully over the course of more than a century, with multiple acts of Parliament refining the mechanisms of title registration to best suit the English landscape, in the Global South title registration has been introduced quickly and often with little local support.

The implementation of title registration systems in the Global South has not had the poverty-curing effects its advocates had hoped for. As David Kennedy argues, title registration focuses attention on the current allocation of land rights, reducing attentiveness to past and future possible allocations and oversimplifying the complex political questions involved in relationships with land (2011: 55). Case studies from different areas of the Global South show that local farmers and residents can be reluctant to register their title even when registration is compulsory, as they are wary of this foreign system of land regulation and its potential to deprive them of their land (e.g. Besteman on Somalia and Kenya, 1994: 499; Musembi on sub-Saharan Africa, especially Kenya, 2007). Writing on the recent introduction of the Torrens system in India, Priya Gupta points out that many people in India live on land for which they cannot prove title (2010: 90), and that it is those living in slums and other poor areas who are asked to prove and formalise their rights to land, unlike those in nearby middle-class neighbourhoods who are assumed to already have such rights (2014: 80). Analysing the effects of the recent introduction of the Torrens system in Samoa, Ruining Ye argues that the system not only puts customary land rights at risk, but may, in some instances, even be unconstitutional (2009: 827). With regard to the institution of title registration systems in eastern and central African states, Patrick McAuslan has argued that such systems are mainly concerned with the registration of non-African owned land (2013: 73), thus potentially putting African property rights at risk of being superseded by registered foreign ownership. In each instance, those with relations to land that have been produced through years of local use and custom but that are now unregisterable – who are often very poor and already socially marginalised – become precariously unlawful in their residence and vulnerable to dispossession in favour of newly registered titleholders (see Home and Lim, 2004).

Title registration systems have been implemented in states of the Global South with the assumption that what is recorded on the registry will mirror the interests that in fact exist, but the mirror's superficial representation of land does not fit with the reality of most human relationships with land. The temporal assumption that the constantly produced superficial 'now' of the mirror accurately reflects the reality of interests in land at any moment is an essential part of title registration systems in any context and it is also fictional in any context. In settler colonies, the fiction of the mirror fits with the fiction of *terra nullius*; in England, the fiction of the mirror fits with the speculative market in English land, but has been introduced slowly and with many provisos ('cracks in the mirror') for unregistered historical realities. In the Global South, the fiction of the mirror fits with the growing speculative market in notionally 'under-developed' land, but pre-existing customary tenures – some of which have long histories and others which have come about as a response to colonial and post-colonial land distribution – continue on the land despite their absence on the registry, cracking the mirror and rendering unregistered residents vulnerable to forced removal. In each case, the future-oriented title registration systems facilitate an efficient market in land by producing new titles guaranteed by the state against the vestiges of history; and, in each case, the physical reality of re-existing relationships with land makes clear that the synchronicity promised by the mirror and the curtain is fictional.

The Mortgage Electronic Registration System: Title to mortgaged land in the USA

The final title registration system I will discuss in this chapter is slightly different from those discussed above: the Mortgage Electronic Registration Systems, Inc. (MERS), an American company. MERS is different, first, in that it is a private rather than a state registry;[21] and, second, in that it only registers *mortgage* titles, rather than freehold and leasehold titles. Indeed, the United States federal government does not operate a system of land title registration. MERS is the one title registration system in the US that spans state jurisdictions and it is a private, national electronic register of mortgage titles. I conclude this chapter with a discussion of MERS because, like the title registration systems discussed above, MERS was designed to make land a liquid asset and it operates by manufacturing new titles, albeit with a less clear legal status than Torrens-based systems. While MERS cannot be described as a title by registration system because formally it only records pre-existing title, in practice, it effectively produces new titles and a temporal order appropriate for a land market of unprecedented (and ultimately unsustainable) liquidity. As electronic mortgage registration becomes an increasingly significant part of other title registration systems,[22] the operation and effect of MERS is worth paying cautionary attention to.

As of 2013 MERS had more than 70 million mortgages – more than 60% of all residential mortgages in the country – registered on its database system (Card, 2011: 1634). To understand how MERS operates, it is necessary to briefly set out the legal architecture of American mortgages. American mortgages are securities given over land in exchange for monetary loans. They are created by paper documents and these documents must be produced as proof of the mortgage terms in the event that the borrower defaults on the loan and the lender seeks to take the securitised land through the foreclosure process. Once the mortgage is created, the mortgage documents are recorded at the county clerk office for a fee. Any subsequent assignment of the mortgage (that is, assignment of the security interest over the mortgaged land from the original lender to another investor) will also be recorded at the county clerk office for a fee.[23] Mortgage assignments were traditionally fairly rare, but became significantly more frequent in the 1990s, with the onset of large-scale securitisation, a complex financial practice that involves multiple bulk assignments of mortgages.

MERS was created in 1995 – in the midst of the mortgage securitisation boom – in order to save banks and investors from having to pay the county fee or process the corresponding paperwork each time an assignment of mortgage occurs (Weber, 2011: 102). When mortgages are registered with MERS, MERS is recorded as mortgagee at the county office, instead of the lender who actually owns the mortgage charge: MERS acts as the 'nominee' of the lender. Once MERS is recorded as owner, the actual owner of the mortgage charge can assign that charge multiple times without changing the county office record. When subsequent assignments take place, they are recorded in the MERS system, but not at the county office, where the original recording of MERS as owner remains unchanged (Steven,

2012: 254–255). A mortgage registered with MERS can thus be sold and resold, assigned and reassigned ad infinitum without ever changing the county records or paying the fee. Christopher Peterson argues that MERS works by 'pretend(ing) to own all the mortgages in the country' (2011: 116). True to its trademarked slogan 'process loans not paperwork',[24] MERS affords mortgage titles an unprecedented level of liquidity as they can be sold and resold more quickly than they could if the lenders assigning them filled out the paperwork that traditionally accompanied such assignments.

Like the Torrens system, MERS operates with a seemingly magical quality on the titles in its system – each title (here the title to a mortgage charge) being given a new life on each assignment, a financial life which is likely to be disconnected from the land to which the mortgage relates. Like Torrens and Torrens-inspired systems, MERS attempts to act as a hospital for titles, perfecting mortgage titles and curing them of their defects, even when the documents and processes legally required to transfer them have not been executed (White, 2011; Levitin, 2013). Unlike the Torrens system, MERS does not operate on the principles of the mirror, the curtain and insurance, though it is clear that it does operate a curtain-like principle by keeping borrowers' interests off the register and transfers off the county clerk records. MERS also operates something of a mirror principle, but its mirror is only held up by the lenders and investors, not by the borrowers/residents. As such the only interests it reflects are those of the lenders and investors – the mirror is angled away from those who physically live on the land. David Weber argues that the only way MERS can perform its dual claim to be both the mortgagee (as it is on county clerk records) and the nominee for the mortgagee (as it in fact operates) is through magic (2011: 107). The magic of MERS is its disappearance of the chain of title of mortgagees within its system, only to re-emerge unscathed at the moment a borrower defaults and foreclosure proceedings are instigated.

This kind of magic is needed for financial markets to operate, including the large financial market secured through mortgages on land. Annelise Riles refers to 'the problem of the "meantime"' in financial markets – the gap in time between the pledging of security for a loan and the ending of the loan arrangement (either through repayment or default) in the context of derivatives markets (2011: 168–169). The solution to the problem of the meantime in Riles' study is that the actors involved agree to act *as if* the holder of the security already has clear and complete rights to it (ibid: 169). Mortgage titles registered with MERS are also held for the meantime and MERS members trade mortgage titles *as if* they had clear and complete rights to them even though legally they do not, because the paperwork does not legally support their entitlement to foreclose.[25]

MERS produces a temporal order that facilitates the rapid trade in mortgage titles on international financial markets. As became evident during the foreclosure crisis that began in 2007, that temporal order is out of sync with both the land to which the mortgages are bound and the order of legal events typically required of American mortgages. Lenders and investors are not coordinated with the land – its physicality, its residents or its local day-to-day life – because it is irrelevant to them.

MERS enables lenders to coordinate solely with one another and deal with mortgage title as an abstract financial object.

On the event of foreclosure, homeowners (or their tenants) are informed that their time on the land is up. MERS distributes the proceeds of the subsequent sale to the lender, which, according to its mirror principle, owns the mortgage at that point in time. Given notice to leave, the residents are rendered out of place in their homes, with some banks hiring contractors to preserve foreclosed homes in an empty state, thus turning the mainly Black and Hispanic residents into objects to be cleared from the property.[26] The temporal order of MERS renders their relationship of permanence and belonging with their homes temporary, their futures erased. As Darden and Wyly write, 'while quicksilver capital is back up to speed, time has slowed down in the families and neighborhoods devastated by a kind of violence' (2010: 432). With title registration systems around the world becoming increasingly digitised and mortgages continuing to be the only way many residents can afford to buy land, it is worth taking heed of just how out of sync MERS enabled mortgage title and residential land become, and the consequences of that temporal discord.

Conclusion

> '[Y]ou cannot avoid the past' (Patrick McAuslan, 2013: 77).

This chapter has explored how title registration systems, in particular systems of title *by* registration, make land seem like a liquid asset by rendering title a three-dimensional object with a temporality wholly determined by the register. Title registration systems can be contrasted with title deed systems, pursuant to which title was dependent on local histories of possession as proved through documents and testimony. Title registration systems are future oriented and free of the cumbersome estates that gave land its own temporal dimension and kept land in sync with title through the need for estate owners to perform their rights of possession.

The discussion of various such systems in this chapter – in the contexts of England and Wales, Australia, the Global South and mortgaged land in the USA – suggests that title registries produce a temporal order that is out of sync with the multiple durations of time experienced by those actually living on the land. The fiction of the mirror is that what is on the register now accurately reflects who and what are on the land now. This fiction, which is given a totalling force in Torrens systems, renders historically derived but unregistered and/or unregistrable relationships with land out of place and precarious. While land registries erase all official traces of a time outside of its own overarching time, the living bodies of the dispossessed remain, disoriented and vulnerable, but haunting and unsettling these jurisdictions. The liquidity seemingly afforded to land by title registration cannot wash away the living reality of the land itself.

Notes

1 The length of time has varied according to what is set by the Statute of Limitations. Currently the period is 12 years for unregistered land in England and Wales (Limitation Act 1980 s15). For registered land the doctrine of adverse possession is now governed by the statutory scheme set out in the Land Registration Act 2002.
2 Law of Property Act 1969 s23.
3 In 1846 a select committee of the House of Lords reported that 'the marketable value of real property is seriously diminished by the tedious and expensive process attending its transfer' and proposals were made both for a register of title deeds (i.e. a register of copies of existing documents evidencing title) and a register of title (i.e. 'a registry which should in itself be evidence, not of a deed, but of a title': Fonnereau 1830 in Simpson 1976: 40), in order to make land transfer faster and easier (Simpson 1976: 41–45).
4 The state would indemnify all registered title holders, undertaking to pay compensation if the operation of the register caused a loss: Simpson 1976: 175.
5 The Representation of the People Act 1832 was the first of multiple Acts extending the franchise to eventually make it independent of land ownership.
6 Land Registration Act 1986 s2(1); Land Registration Act 1988 s1.
7 HM Land Registry Business Strategy 2017 to 2022 Corporate Report, published 29 November 2017 https://www.gov.uk/government/publications/hm-land-registry-business-strategy-2017-to-2022/hm-land-registry-business-strategy-2017-to-2022 (Accessed 4 June 2018).
8 The racialised, moralistic language of recent anti-squatter rhetoric echoes Kate Green's argument in her 1998 article "Citizens and Squatters: Under the Surfaces of Land Law": see Manjikian, Mary, *Securitization of Property Squatting in Europe* (Routledge, 2013), chapter 2.
9 Association of Foreign Investors in Real Estate named London as the best city in the world for investment opportunities for foreign investors in 2014.
10 Land Registration Act 2002 s132(1).
11 Land Registration Act 2002, Schedule 6.
12 Schedules 1 and 3.
13 The benefits and burdens of the estate will be recorded in the registry and vested in the titleholder on first registration of the estate: LRA 2002, ss11–12.
14 The Torrens principles do not sit easily with the principle of relativity of title. If the register is the guaranteed authority of all the interests in land, then registered title is indefeasible and it does not make sense for title to be obtainable through adverse possession. Torrens jurisdictions have found different ways of modifying the common law principles of adverse possession to accommodate it within the system of title registration (for example O'Connor 2005), but it is clear that registered title is more absolute than relative.
15 (1971) 126 CLR 376: 381.
16 A similar argument has more recently been made in terms of title registration and creation of racial value in settler colonies: Bhandar, B. "Title by Registration: Instituting Modern Property Law and Creating Racial Value in the Settler Colony." 2015 *Journal of Law and Society* 42(2): 253–282.
17 World Bank Group, "Doing Business: Economy Rankings" http://www.doingbusiness.org/rankings (Accessed 2 June 2015).
18 While local reactions to land grabs are more complex than is often acknowledged (Hall et al, 2015: 467–478), there has been a rapid increase in the volume and geographical spread of foreign acquisition of land in developing countries, particularly in Africa, since 2006 (Sassen, 2014: 80).
19 "Our Land Our Business" http://ourlandourbusiness.org (Accessed 2 June 2015).
20 Land in settler colonies is also treated as an extractive resource, and land in the Global South is also treated as a home for some white people. For a compelling

critique of the academic separation of settler colonies from non-settler colonies, see Mawani, 2016.

21 It is worth noting that the British government has in 2016 proposed (for the second time since 2014) the introduction of a private Land Registry service delivery company.

22 See, for example, Land Registry Blog "Looking Forward to the First Truly Digital Mortgage" (8 August 2016) http://blog.landregistry.gov.uk/looking-forward-first-truly-digital-mortgage/?utm_content= &utm_ medium=email&utm_name=&utm_-source=govdelivery&utm_term= (Accessed 16 January 2017).

23 Typically, around $15–$30 for the first page and $2–$3 for each additional page: Phillips 2009: 263.

24 See MERS Servicer ID https://www.mers-servicerid.org/sis/index.jsp (Accessed 23 June 2015).

25 Specifically, the security instrument is separate from the note.

26 Ben Halman, "Bank Contractors Break Into Occupied Homes, Terrify Residents, Lawsuits Say." *Huffington Post*, 18 July 2012 http://www.huffingtonpost.com/2012/07/18/bank-contractors-break-ins_n_1682672.html (Accessed 2 June 2015); Christopher Odinet, "Banks, Break-ins and Bad Actors in Mortgage Foreclosure." 2015 *University of Cincinatti Law Review* 83: 1155–1214.

Bibliography

Ainger, S. (1991). "Aboriginal Trailblazer Discovers 'Extraordinary Conspiracy'." *Sydney University Gazette*: 18–19.

Anderson, S. (1998). "The 1925 Property Legislation: Setting Contexts." In *Land Law: Themes and Perspectives.* Edited by Susan Bright and John Dewar. Oxford: Oxford University Press.

Bastian, M. (2012). "Fatally Confused: Telling the Time in the Midst of Ecological Crises." *Environmental Philosophy* 9, 1: 23–48.

Besteman, C. (1994). "Individualisation and the Assault on Customary Tenure in Africa: Title Registration Programmes and the Case of Somalia." *Africa* 64, 4: 484–515.

Black, C. F. (2011). *The Land Is the Source of the Law: A Dialogic Encounter with Indigenous Jurisprudence.* Abingdon: Routledge.

Blomley, N. (2003). "Law, Property, and the Geography of Violence: The Frontier, the Survey and the Grid." *Annals of the Association of American Geographers* 93, 1: 121–141.

Burns, F. (2011). "Adverse Possession and Title-by-registration Systems in Australia and England." *Melb. UL Rev.* 35: 773–820.

Card, J. J. (2011). "Homebuyer Beware: MERS and the Law of Subsequent Purchasers." *Brook. L. Rev.* 77: 1633–1664.

Cowan, D., Fox O'Mahony, L. and Cobb, N. (2012). *Great Debates in Property Law.* Basingstoke: Palgrave Macmillan.

Darden, J. T. and Elvin W. (2010). "Cartographic Editorial Mapping the Racial/Ethnic Topography of Subprime Inequality in Urban America.E *Urban Geography* 31, 4: 425–433.

Davis, M. (2006). *Planet of Slums.* London: Verso.

Deininger, K. W. (2003). *Land Policies for Growth and Poverty Reduction: A World Bank Policy Research Report.* Washington, DC: World Bank; New York: Oxford University Press.

Deininger, K. and Gershon F. (2009). "Land Registration, Governance, and Development: Evidence and Implications for Policy." *World Bank Research Observer* 24, 2: 233–266.

De Soto, H. (2000). *The Mystery of Capital: Why Capitalism Triumphs in the West and Fails Everywhere Else.* New York: Basic Books.

Gray, K. J. and Gray, S. F. (2009). *Elements of Land Law.* Oxford: Oxford University Press.

Green, K. (1998). "Citizens and Squatters: Under the Surfaces of Land Law". In *Land Law: Themes and Perspectives.* Edited by Susan Bright and John Dewar. Oxford: Oxford University Press.

Greenhouse, C. J. (1996). *A Moment's Notice: Time Politics Across Cultures.* London: Cornell University Press.

Gupta, P. S. (2010). "Ending Finders, Keepers: The Use of Title Insurance to Alleviate Uncertainty in Land Holdings in India." *UC Davis Journal of International Law and Policy* 17: 63–109.

Gupta, P. S. (2014). "Judicial Constructions: Modernity, Economic Liberalization, and the Urban Poor in India." *Fordham Urb. LJ* 42: 25–90.

Hall, R., Edelman, M., Borras, S. M. Jr., Scoones, I., White, B. and Wolford, W. (2015). "Resistance, Acquiescence or Incorporation? An Introduction to Land Grabbing and Political Reactions from Below." *Journal of Peasant Studies* 42, 3–4:467–488.

Hanstad, T. (1997) "Designing Land Registration Systems for Developing Countries." *Am. U. Int'l L. Rev.* 13: 647–703.

Harris, D. (2010). "Law of the Land: The Advent of the Torrens System in Canada by Greg Taylor." *UBC Law Review* 43, 1: 259–267.

Harris, D. and Au, M. (2014). "Title Registration and the Abolition of Notice in British Columbia." *UBCL Rev.* 47: 535–785.

Harvey, D. (1989). *The Limits to Capital.* Midway Reprint ed. Chicago: University of Chicago Press.

Hickey, R. and Harding, M. (2011). "Bijural Ambiguity and Values in Land Registration Systems." In *Modern Studies in Property Law.* Edited by Susan Bright. Hart Publishing: Oxford.

Home, R. (2013). "Outside de Soto's Bell Jar: Colonial/Postcolonial Land Law and the Exclusion of the Peri-Urban Poor". In Home, R. and Hilary Lim. *Demystifying the Mystery of Capital: Land Tenure & Poverty in Africa and the Caribbean.* Basingstoke: Routledge.

Home, R. and Lim, H. (2013). *Demystifying the Mystery of Capital: Land Tenure & Poverty in Africa and the Caribbean.* Abingdon: Routledge.

Kain, R. J. P. and Baigent, E. (1992). *The Cadastral Map in the Service of the State: A History of Property Mapping.* Chicago: University of Chicago Press.

Keenan, S. (2016). "Smoke, Curtains and Mirrors: The Production of Race Through Time and Title Registration." *Law and Critique* 28, 1: 87–108.

Land Registry, About Us. [online] Available at: https://www.gov.uk/government/organisations/land-registry/about [Accessed 18 May 2015].

Law Commission. (1998). *Land Registration for the Twenty-First Century: A Consultative Document.* London: Law Commission.

Levitin, A. J. (2013). "The Paper Chase: Securitization, Foreclosure, and the Uncertainty of Mortgage Title." *Duke Law Journal* 63: 637–734.

Lim, H. and Green, K. (1995). *Cases and Materials in Land Law.* 2nd ed. London: Pitman Publishing.

Manjikian, M. (2013). *Securitization of Property Squatting in Europe.* Abingdon: Routledge.

Mawani, R. (2016). "Law, Settler Colonialism, and 'the Forgotten Space' of Maritime Worlds." *Annual Review of Law and Social Science* 12, 1: 107–131.

McAuslan, P. (2013). *Bringing the Law Back in: Essays in Land, Law, and Development.* Aldershot: Ashgate.

Musembi, C. N. (2007). "De Soto and Land Relations in Rural Africa: Breathing Life Into Dead Theories About Property Rights." *Third World Quarterly* 28, 8: 1457–1478.

O'Connor, P. (2005). "Registration of Invalid Dispositions: Who Gets the Property?" In *Modern Studies in Property Law*. Edited by Elizabeth Cooke. London: Bloomsbury.

———. (2006). "Private Taking of Land: Adverse Possession, Encroachment by Buildings and Improvement Under a Mistake" *UW Austl. L. Rev.* 33: 31–62.

———. (2009). "Deferred and Immediate Indefeasibility: Bijural Ambiguity in Registered Land Title Systems." *Edinburgh Law Review* 13, 2: 194–223.

Patton, R. G. (1951). "Extension of the Torrens System Into Hawaii, the Philippine Islands and Latin-American Jurisdictions." *Minn. L. Rev.* 36: 213–226.

Peterson, C. L. (2011). "Two Faces: Demystifying the Mortgage Electronic Registration System's Land Title Theory." *Wm. & Mary L. Rev.* 53: 111–161.

Phillips, B. (2009). "MERS: The Mortgage Electronic Registration System." *Consumer Fin. LQ Rep.* 63: 262–274.

Pottage, A. (1994). "The Measure of Land." *Modern Law Review* 57, 3: 361–384.

———. (1998). "Evidencing Ownership." In *Land Law: Themes and Perspectives*. Edited by Susan Bright and John Dewar. Oxford: Oxford University Press.

Raff, M. J. (2003). *Private Property and Environmental Responsibility: A Comparative Study of German Real Property Law*. New York: Kluwer Law International.

Razack, S. H. (2012) "Memorializing Colonial Power: The Death of Frank Paul." *Law & Social Inquiry* 37, 4: 908–932.

Riles, A. (2011). *Collateral Knowledge: Legal Reasoning in the Global Financial Markets*. Chicago: University of Chicago Press.

Rogers, E. (2006). "The Impact of the Australian Torrens System on the Land Transfer Debate in the United Kingdom, 1858–1914." *Australia and New Zealand Law and History E-journal* 4: 125–132.

Sassen, S. (2014). *Expulsions: Brutality and Complexity in the Global Economy*. Cambridge, MA: Harvard University Press.

Simpson, S. R. (1976). *Land Law and Registration*. Cambridge: Cambridge University Press.

Steven, L. A. (2012). "MERS and the Mortgage Crisis: Obfuscating Loan Ownership and the Need for Clarity." *Brooklyn Journal of Corporate, Financial & Commercial Law*: 251–276.

Taylor, G. (2008). *The Law of the Land: The Advent of the Torrens System in Canada*. Toronto: University of Toronto Press.

Valverde, M. (2015). *Chronotopes of Law: Jurisdiction, Scale and Governance*. Abingdon: Routledge.

Weber, D. P. (2011). "The Magic of the Mortgage Electronic Registration System: It Is and It Isn't." *Am. Bankr. LJ* 85: 239–264.

White, A. M. (2011). "Losing the Paper-Mortgage Assignments, Note Transfers and Consumer Protection." *Loy. Consumer L. Rev.* 24: 468–504.

8 Regulating the 'half-timer' in colonial India

Factory legislation, its anomalies and resistance

Maya John, University of Delhi

This chapter discusses the colonial state's regulation of child labour in Indian factories from the late 19th to the early 20th century. In the process of regulation, the category of half-timer was borrowed from English factory law.[1] It was imposed in the colonial context and regulated in such a manner that children remained tied down to the factories for long hours and, in fact, they laboured for more than *half* the workday of adult labour. The discussion briefly highlights the social and economic context that structured the lived experience of child labourers within the new regulative regime enforced in factories.

We will emphasize the challenges faced by working-class families due to the regulation of child labour, as well as highlight the persistent efforts of child labourers and their kin to circumvent the law. Such resistance will be discussed in the light of the inherent hollowness of factory legislation, the neglect of educational needs of labouring children and the failure of the paternalistic middle-class discourse on child labour to engage with the precarity of working-class lives.

The underlying argument of the chapter is that the regime of regulated time under factory legislation came to be based on enhanced exploitation of labouring children. The lack of adult wage regulation by the state, coupled with the denial of education, ultimately ensured the reproduction of these children as part of the same class as that of their parents.

The chapter highlights the disciplining effects and resulting social ordering of working-class life by the new temporality informing factory production. It also provides a critical assessment of the evolving legal framework that shows how much this new temporality was implicated in the project of legal regulation of factory labour.

Colonialism and the emergence of child labour

In early colonial India, the labour market largely comprised of a sizeable proportion of labouring groups that had traditionally been mobilized for manual work through hierarchical systems of production based on family, caste and community (see Anderson, 1993: pp. 87–120). In such a historical setting, children were often put to work as part of household production. Their labour, however, was rarely identified as a *separate, distinct* category of labour. Clearly, the notion of 'child labour' did not emerge.[2] Further, in the pre-industrial context, work was more in sync with 'natural' rhythms of time in that the work performed/ extracted was in tune with the *concrete* conditions in which the worker was situated and laboured.[3] This pre-industrial system of work arrangement thus allowed workers to determine their hours of work, intensity of work, etc. much more in accordance with their needs, prevailing practices of leisure and other calculations, than was the case in industrial work regimes.

The working day was consequently marked by a certain degree of irregularity since personal rhythms of labour and the task orientation of work usually allowed for its lengthening and contracting as the need arose. Not driven by a temporality of *linear, homogenous* time that came to characterize industrial work organization, a pronounced demarcation between time for 'work' and 'life' was less evident in the pre-industrial period. In contrast, the factory system abstracted the measurement of work from the *concrete* conditions of a worker's life and needs. The imposition of *abstract passage of time* over work relations by capitalist enterprises seeking to extract maximum profit over an extensive period of time (dawn to dusk) from a *heterogeneous* labour force meant the imposition of *homogenous* units of time for work calculation and corresponding wage payment. The new temporality came to be measured in clock time, which directly clashed with pre-existing, more flexible, *personal* rhythms of work.

The gradual development of capitalist forces, the resulting emergence of *wage labour* and *individual* property rights within the colonial–capitalist political economy triggered notable transformations in the working lives of labouring groups. By the 19th and early 20th century, we witness labour mobilization in new avenues of employment provided by emerging capitalist enterprises such as tea and coffee plantations, private mining companies, the railways, jute and cotton textile industries and the leather industry, among others. Children emerged as an important component of the labour force that was recruited for these new enterprises.

One of the subsequent transformations in working lives pertained to the entrapment of labour in a less flexible working day structure. As is typical of urban industrial work organization, factory enterprises worked towards steady synchronization of labour. This meant that workers coming from pre-industrial work organization of the Indian countryside were increasingly compelled to give up flexible patterns of working and to coordinate their activities with an *abstract* passage of time. They were disciplined into a clock-timed temporality in which a straightforward notion of time measurement was used to determine wage levels and, at times, this time-rate system was even clubbed with the amount of work performed (piecework) to determine wages.[4] Now it was capitalist employers who decided the hours of work. In most cases, they imposed long hours of work that spread over the whole day, denying adequate recess periods for meals and leave (see Report of the Indian Factory Labour Commission, 1908: pp. 6, 8, 10, 12).

The coordination between the amount of work and per unit of time made work tedious, and more so due to the appended supervision that unfolded in industrial enterprises. For every diversion from the abstract passage of factory work time, labourers paid the price in fines, wage cuts, loss of employment, etc. (see Myers, 1958: pp. 85, 97, 102).

Entering the new sites/regimes of work, both child and adult labour were exposed to a new time discipline. Indeed, factory sirens, clocks, fines, wage commutation based on the units of time that were clocked, denial of holidays for fairs, festivals and weddings, as well as factory schooling together constituted an oppressive work regime.

Child labour in the colonial labour market

The precariousness of rural households, in particular, the declining value of rural artisanship, as well as of agricultural occupations that were usually performed by women and children, pushed child labourers into the country's emerging factories, mines, plantations, etc. where *wage labour* predominated. This is a fact recorded in testimonies of child labourers before the 1890 Factory Labour Commission. A young boy by the name Ramdeen, who worked in the Kanpur Woollen Mills, explained that he joined the mill because 'his fields have been taken by the zamindar since his father's death' and also because 'he did not find the occupation of a herd boy sufficiently remunerative for him' (Report of the Indian Factory Labour Commission, 1890).

The employment of a large number of children in industrial work reflects that many working-class children were reproducing not only their own labour power but that their labour was crucial for the survival and maintenance of their families (RCLI, 1931: pp. 203, 320, 462).[5] This was aptly recognized in the testimony of the social reformer, K.A. Keluskar, before the Indian Factory Commission, 1907:

> Parents and other relatives of children are anxious to see their children begin to support themselves, as they are too poor to feed them. So, it is but natural that they do not look to the health or age of the child whom they put to work.
>
> (Report of the Indian Factory Labour Commission, 1908, Vol. II, Evidence, p. 88)

Once in the city and faced with the rigidities of the segmented labour market that often offered casual over more secure forms of employment, the migrant working-class family pushed more and more of its members to take up waged work in order to make up for the lack of a family wage in the city. The 1890 Factory Labour Commission, for instance, carries testimonies of children who reported the exact reason for coming to join waged work in the city (Report of the Indian Factory Labour Commission, 1890). Of course, most children did not willingly enter waged work in the city, based on a personal rational decision on the benefits of urban occupations. A 25-year-old woman, Kondee's reply to why she became a mill hand at the tender age of 10 is painfully indicative of the physical force with which children were pressed into waged work by their parents due to depressed family incomes. In her reply, Kondee stated that 'her parents beat her and compelled her to go to the mill' (Ibid.).

These accounts of child labourers and their painful journey of joining the ranks of the urban workforce are highly illustrative of the specific significance of child labour for the working-class family that was emerging alongside industrialization. In the same Factory Commission report, we also get some important references to the social background of child labourers. For example, Kashimadoo, a young boy working in the Kashipur Gun Shell Factory in Calcutta claimed that his father was a fruit seller. Baboo, a young Muslim boy working in the Bally Paper Mill, stated that his father was a thatcher. Venkoo Ramaya, an 11-year-old boy, was employed in the Hindustan Mill, Bombay, while his mother earned a little by selling cheroots. Mahabeer, a 9-year-old Dalit boy from the chamar caste, worked in the Cooper, Allen and Company's Boot factory in Kanpur, while his father worked as an independent artisan in the local bazaar.

Child labourers entering the labour market to contribute towards family income were paid abysmally low wages during the late 19th and early 20th century (Report of the Commissioners Appointed by the Governor of Bombay in Council to Inquire into the Condition of the Operatives in the Bombay Factories, and the Necessity or Otherwise for the Passing of a Factory Act, 1875 (henceforth Arbuthnot Commission)).[6] Apart from low wages, the children, like the rest of the factory labour force, were subjected to very long hours of work. Both the 1875 Arbuthnot Commission and the 1890 Factory Labour Commission verified the long hours put in by children. According to their assessments, children's work hours were from sunrise to sunset and, hence, equivalent to the time put in adult factory workers or full-timers. The Factory Labour Commission, 1890, recorded the statement of Tanu Dewkiya, a 12-year-old boy, who stated that he 'begins work at 5 and goes at 7 p.m. Gets up at 4 in the morning and gets home at 8, and takes his food and goes to sleep at 9' (Report of the Indian Factory Labour Commission, 1890, op. cit., p. 43).

Such long hours were, in fact, imposed on the children not always by desperate parents trying to make ends meet, but by the factory overseer. Testimonies dating to the 19th century when 'protective' legislation regulating child labour was just about taking off are insightful in this regard. Bhimi Luckha, a 10-year-old girl, told the Factory Labour Commission, 1890, that 'she is willing to work for half day, but she is afraid the overseer will not allow this; he will beat her' (Ibid., p. 40).

The factory work regime synchronizing labour and linking abstract, linear passage of time with wages is what actually propelled working-class parents' decision to push their children into factory work, as well as the 'willingness' of child labourers to put in long hours of work. For instance, child labourers appearing before the Bombay Factory Commission in 1875 expressed an unwillingness to avail of 2 additional days of holidays in a month if it meant a reduction in salary.[7] Similarly, factory supervision that evolved around overseers also compelled child labourers to work more than what factory legislation stipulated for them. Given their long hours of work, which more often than not matched the hours of work extracted from adult labour, what actually came to distinguish child labourers as 'half-timers' were the wages they drew. The identification of 'child labour' in a distinct legalistic vein and the critique of such labour extraction were, of course, triggered by the defensive interests of metropole capital.

The making of factory legislation

Significantly, although child labour was an important component of many new enterprises, such as plantations, mines, the jute mills etc., it was the competitive advantage of Indian capital in the cotton textile industry of Bombay that triggered the concern of metropole (British) capital and the subsequent lobbying for regulation of child labour.

Notably, the cotton mill industry of western India was heavily concentrated by Indian capital, unlike in the case of the tea plantations, mines, railway companies, the jute industry etc. that were largely financed by metropole capital. From the late 1870s to World War One (WWI) it was the Lancashire and Manchester employer lobbies that vigorously pushed for regulation of Bombay's cotton textile industry. Their purpose for demanding factory legislation in India was to curtail the competitive edge of Indian textile industries and thereby safeguard their share of the Indian textile market. An illustration of where this tension emerged can be seen in Table 8.1.

Rather than the concern for the harshness of work performed by thousands of child labourers across India, it was actually their presence in *industrial work* that triggered criticism from Lancashire and Manchester. Child labour in agriculture or the cruelty of bonded labour agreements in rural India were of little consequence. In fact, the Manchester lobby strategically lobbied for regulatory action by the colonial state on the grounds that the Indian populace was more 'suited' for agrarian work than for industrial employment and that such an arrangement

Table 8.1 Hours of work of people of different ages[1]

			England	*Bombay*
Male over 18			10	12 ½
Female over 18			10*	11 ½
Persons between 14 and 18			10*	12 ½
Do.	Do.	12 and 14	5*	12 ½
Do.	Do.	10 and 12	5*	12 ½
Do.	Do.	7 and 10	not at all	9*

Those marked with an asterisk (*) being regulated by law.

1 Letter from W.W. Drew, Inspector of Factories, Bombay to the Under Secretary to the Government of Bombay, 10 July 1888, in Proceedings April, Nos. 223–278, Home Department, Judicial Branch, 1889, National Archives of India (NAI), New Delhi.

was more desirable for British interests. For instance, Mr Stuttard of the Manchester Chamber of Commerce argued in 1888: 'Surely it will be better for the physical welfare of the Hindoo [sic] to remain in agricultural employment and give us plenty of cotton, rather than be attracted to the ranks of mill operatives.'[8]

Ironically, the pressure from British (metropole) capital ensured that while the resolutions of the 1890 Berlin International Labour Conference were thwarted in Britain,[9] the government in Britain applied ample pressure on the Governor-General of India to adopt the higher minimum age resolution. Indeed, the interests of English manufacturers were eloquently expressed by stalwarts of 'protective' legislation in Britain. One such noted advocate of 'protective' legislation was Lord Shaftesbury, who argued in a speech at the House of Lords:

> We must bear in mind that India has the raw material and cheap labour; and if we allow the manufacturers there to work their operatives 16 to 17 hours and put them under no restrictions, we are giving them a very unfair advantage over the manufacturers of our own country, and we might be undersold even in Manchester itself by manufactured goods imported from the East.
>
> (Hansards Parliamentary Debates, House of Lords, 30 July 1875, Vol. 226, Cols. 209–14)

By 1875 the Arbuthnot Commission was constituted by the Bombay Government (Arbuthnot Commission Report, 1875). It was a move deeply resented by the Bombay mill owners. Expectedly, pressure applied by the mill owners through overseers ensured that child witnesses did not speak about their long hours and the tediousness of their work (Ibid.: 2). Despite this obstacle, the Commission concluded that the children on an average put in 11 to 13 hours of work and were generally of the age 8 years and above (Ibid.).

Debates continued to rage in India as talk of effective regulatory legislation grew. The report of the Arbuthnot Commission was succeeded by similar commission reports in 1890, 1908 and 1931. In defence of their employment of child labourers at much lower wage rates than adult labour, mill owners posed several arguments in favour of existing practices of child employment. Many employers in India saw state intervention through factory legislation, especially to regulate child labour, as partisan action that favoured metropole capital. For example, the Chairman of the Chamber of Commerce, Madras, in response to the first Factory Bill unequivocally stated:

> The introduction of limited hours of labour in England was, the Chamber believe, in great measure due to the necessity for the children's receiving education at schools; such necessity has *not as yet been recognized by the Government of India* as applying to the children of this country, *nor*, so far as

> the Chamber are aware, *is it intended that the reduced hours of labour shall be enforced for the purpose of devoting more time to education.*[10]

Apart from questioning the intention and timing of factory legislation, employer lobbies in India justified the use of child labour in terms of the industriousness and disciplining effect factory employment carried. Importantly, employers' arguments justifying the use of child labour in factories were strongly indicative of the desire to tap cheap labour and to ensure a steady supply of labour for factory work. Here, they played up the argument of imparting productive knowledge and skills to children by projecting the utilization of child labour as beneficial not only to employers but also society at large. The productivity of child labourers was constantly contrasted with beggary, homelessness and juvenile crime (Report of the Bombay Mill-owners' Association for the Period Ending 31st October 1879: p. 113).

Some employers when arguing against factory legislation projected factory employment as beneficial when compared to other forms of employment in which children were bound to unfree contractual agreements. This line of argument gelled well with the general tendency of employer lobbies to posit their employment of labour as an expression of free contract. In fact, we come across references where Indian labourers employed in the mills were projected as freer than other labourers. According to F.B. Skrine, Senior Magistrate and Inspector of Factories, 24 Parganas, 'the mill operatives [are] the master of the situation ... the hands command their own terms, are excessively independent, and at the least attempt at coercion they migrate at once to another establishment.'[11] Of course, such claims were historically inaccurate. Once the contractual agreement was initiated, labour's withdrawal from the work commitment amounted to a penal offence under laws like the Workmen's Breach of Contract Act.[12]

Mill owners and other employers were not the only ones to play up the issue of the poverty-stricken condition of working-class children and their families when questioning the need for 'protective' labour legislation. Hailing such legislation as premature, local government officials also raised similar arguments. This was especially true of officials positioned in centres of industrial development where foreign capital dominated factory production, such as in the case of Bengal where the jute industry was controlled by Dundee capital.[13] Such opinions among government officials refused to see the blindness of one's own insight, in that much of the colonial *difference* – pauperization identified as fuelling child labour stemmed from consolidation of colonial rule in India.

Factory legislation and its pretentions

A crucial limitation of legislation regulating the age for employment and hours of work for child labour was the apparent focus on *factories.*[14] Plantations, mines and seasonal factories were kept out of the 'protective' ambit of early factory legislation. Furthermore, the Indian Factories Acts merely sought to regulate child labour on certain terms without changing the larger structure of the factory regime. It is here that the paradox of factory legislation is most evident.

While the 'protective' component of factory legislation indicates that labour was beginning to gain a new and distinct status within the larger rubric of colonial policy, this legislation was limited to regulating the *externalities* of work relations or *general* work conditions and *not the work contract itself.* Until well into the late 1920s, the colonial state expressed an unwillingness to meddle with the internal logic of the work contract, i.e. wages, renegotiation of wage, etc. For most part of the colonial period, factory legislation evolved *outside* the logic of the contract of employment and upholstered the contract of employment as a *private domain* of the employer. And so, while the state imposed shorter working hours for certain components of the factory workforce, employers continued to impose long factory shifts on the remaining workforce and in their private domain (the factory) the employers continued undeterred to enjoy punitive powers to enforce contractual obligations.

The paradoxical focus of factory legislation was well reflected in the first Factory Act of 1881, which identified a child worker as an employee between the age of 7 and 12 years who could be employed for a maximum of 9 hours a day. Given that adult labourers worked 12½ to 14 hours, the 9-hour clause was highly misleading when attached to the 'half-timer' and reflected the superficial transplantation of the category from England. As noted by W.O. Meade King, Inspector of Factories, Bombay:

> [M]anagers have told me time and time again, that in the present state of the law it is utterly impossible to employ children without running a daily risk of violating the Act. ... The fact is that being neither 'half-timers' nor 'full-timers', there is nothing to mark their time of commencing or finishing work, nor the intervals to be allowed to them.[15]

Not surprisingly, managers of factories, such as in Bombay's textile mills, kept objecting to the clause as it failed to fit in with the given factory regime of 12-hour shifts; the rationale being that if children work for 9 hours it was impossible to get people to supply their place for the remaining 3 hours.

Given that factory shift timings came to clash with the prescribed work hours of half-timers, labouring children increasingly fell prey, either to unemployment or to the corrupt practices of jobbers and factory owners.[16] Typically, jobbers found plenty of ways to evade the law. First, they did so by teaching the children to fear the factory inspectors. A well-known account of workers' conditions by A. R. Burnett-Hurst describes how children began to run helter-skelter whenever a factory inspector entered a department. If he chased them, the children often ran into machinery and hurt themselves badly (Burnett-Hurst, 1925: p. 54). The jobbers also evaded the law by using loopholes in the medical examination system and by (mis)using the practice of young children accompanying their parents to factories as an excuse to employ them.[17]

Subsequent Factory Acts included: (i) the 1891 Act, which fixed the minimum age limit at 9 years and the upper age limit as 14 years while stipulating 7 hours as the length of a child labourer's workday; (ii) the 1911 Act that stipulated 6 hours work for child labourers; and the (iii) the 1922 Act, which raised the upper age limit for defining a child labourer to 15 years. More often than not, these legislations proved ineffective in regulating child labour. As noted by W.C. Shephard, Collector of Bombay:

> There appears to be little doubt that a good *many children certified as half-timers really do a full day's work.* It seems probable that there are a good many more certificates granted than there are children employed, and this means that in some cases a child gets 2 certificates under different names enabling him to work at one mill for half the day and at another mill for the other half.[18]

Ultimately, the Factories Acts while specifying a legal maximum for the hours of work put in by a child, continued to emphasize a large stretch of the day during which child labour could be extracted. For instance, by specifying that children could be employed for a stipulated number of hours *between* 5 a.m. and 7 p.m. in a factory, the laws created the space for employers to find ways to keep children *within the factory premises* for longer than the number of hours they were shown as working. None of the Factories Acts fixed that child labourers could be employed only in the morning or only in the evening for the stipulated number of hours. Instead, the Acts spoke in terms of the usual work day (sunrise to sunset) in which children could be employed for a certain number of hours.

With this scope created by the law, it was not impossible for managers and jobbers to extract longer hours from the children while they were in the factory premises. In fact, factory schools became another convenient mechanism through which children were kept within the factory premises and could be called on, depending on immediate needs of production. The functioning of factory schools will be later elaborated.

As discussed earlier, the Factories Acts also helped bifurcate interrelated issues of wages and work conditions; thereby, maintaining a policy approach that conveniently sought to address concerns regarding child labour *in isolation from the larger question of precarious working-class family incomes.* These laws were based on the assumption that the state could regulate child labour and facilitate its gradual withdrawal from harsh manufacturing work *without* taking any measures to fix higher wages for adult labour. Such 'protective' legislation proved to be an immediate loss for working-class families. Such legislation proved to be a loss *even in the long run* as desperate families pressed children into alternative, unregulated forms of employment.

Considering the neglect of adult wage regulation by the state, it is not surprising that child labourers expressed wariness when it came to the expansion of their rights via legislation. The approach of child labourers to the granting of holidays is a telling example of how they perceived 'protective' legislation as a threat to their earning capacity. For example, the response of children to the Bombay Factory Commission's question on whether they would like four holidays in a month instead of two was initially positive. However, on being asked if they would avail of these if their salary were reduced, the children's response was 'then we would not like any holidays' (Arbuthnot Commission Report, 1875: Q. 947 and evidence of Nusserwanjee Dadabhoy in response to Q. 293).

Disconnected from the question of a family wage for the working class, factory legislation clearly reflected a bureaucratized misrecognition of the necessity of child labour for the sustenance of working-class family budgets. This essential fact is well reflected in the half-hearted colonial education project that facilitated expanding surveillance on child labourers and the mere reproduction of future workers.

Half-time work/half-time education *or* full-time reign of employer?

The hypocrisy embedded in and disciplinarian nature of the discourse that unfolded on the practice of child labour, both in the case of its supporters and critics, is worth noting. In the case of both supporters as well as critics of child labour, the idea that the child was a *future worker* remained very much intact. For those who spoke against reform and regulation the child labourer was essentially a worker, or was training to be one, and was entering a free contract. Intervention through regulation of this free contract was projected as a loss for the child labourer since it either meant loss of employment or the imposition of fewer hours of work and, consequently, lower remuneration. Often enough, the argument tilted towards the 'faster maturing' of children in the given climate and social conditions of India. Such a position clearly reflected a distinction made in the anti-regulation discourse with respect to an abstract universal notion of childhood and an 'Indian childhood', which was supposedly of a 'different duration'.

Even the discourse in favour of reform and regulation of child labour worked towards perpetuation of child labour and, at the most, prescribed *certain limits for its use*. This is evident when we examine the connection between regulation and education of the child worker.[19]

Talk of imparting basic education, i.e. writing, reading, mathematics and technical skills, to child labourers developed within circles of social reformers and such education was also advocated by individual employers and certain employer lobbies.[20] Of course, both reformers and employers focused on *technical* or *vocational* education. Such education, according to them, inculcated greater industriousness in the child worker; the only difference being that reformers spoke more in terms of children working and studying together so as to lessen the alienation brought on by mechanical industrial activity and employers spoke in more direct terms of the need to create a competent manufacturing class from within existing half-timers.[21] In the case of the latter, industrial classes were sometimes perceived as inculcating the 'dignity of labour' among the children – an opinion based on the presumption that children came from families that did not know the value of work![22]

At a time when laws for reducing work hours of child labourers were being introduced, some employers used factory schools to enforce greater surveillance and to keep child labourers easily accessible for factory work. Their effort was geared towards using factory schooling to *blur or keep flexible the distinction between work hours that were open to regulation, and the extra hours in which the children could be made to stay on under the pretext of education.* As noted by W.O. Meade King, Inspector of Factories (Bombay):

> On taking 12 children out of a mill at 6 o'clock one evening, and questioning them separately, each one said that he had been in the mill since the machinery was set in motion at about 5-30. A.M. and had attended no school in the meantime, though I was assured that all the children in that mill were compelled to attend school in the mill for 3 hours each day. I saw 2 children sitting on a form in the lodge, and was told that was the school.[23]

In this light, Bombay's mill districts saw the coming up of 17 factory schools by 1911, which met with varying degrees of success.[24]

Similarly, a school was opened in 1904 for the sons of workers and for workers belonging to two mills owned by Binny and Co. in Madras. In this school, the children were taught the basic skills of reading, writing and arithmetic, as well as technical skills to make them 'efficient' mill hands. According to the mill management, the half-timers spent half the day at school and the rest of the day acquiring practical knowledge in one of the mills.[25] Clearly, the paternalistic attitude of the Binnys towards their child workers was typical of certain individual capitalists who sought to build a competent workforce that would enhance productivity through efficiency and, hence, the firm's profit. Through their school which trained the half-timers in the proper use of machinery, the Binnys also sought to reduce the influence of the interpreter or *arkatti*, whom the management believed incited workers. Not surprisingly, by 1918 most of the Company's labour supply was drawn from the sons of employees in the mill school.[26]

The instrumentalism involved in churning out efficient workers from the factory schools was often asserted repeatedly despite falling attendance. In fact, we come across instances where attendance to such schools was made compulsory by the management in the context of their unpopularity. For example, in 1893, Dr Saisse of the East Indian Railway Company made attendance to the company's schools compulsory. Lacking teaching appliances, furniture and even paper these 'schools' came to stand out more as disciplining centres than truly educational ones. This should come as no surprise since education in colonial India was a contentious issue and was for a significant part of colonial rule restricted to local elites or upper classes. The introduction of free and compulsory primary education was continuously stalled by the colonial state until 1918 when the first Primary Education Act was passed by the provincial government of Bombay. The

Act was the outcome of a private Bill that was circulated and lobbied for by Vithalbhai Patel, an Indian legislator. This was not a pan-Indian legislation and only a few other British India provinces passed a similar legislation. Although some higher colonial officials believed enhanced literacy was a crucial tool for good administration, mass primary and higher education was viewed with suspicion.[27]

In the larger scenario of delayed efforts to expand education, as well as the tendency for schooling to reproduce caste and class hierarchy (see John, 2016a, op. cit.: pp. 277–280), the education of labouring children remained a half-hearted measure. Overall, the provision of such technical, elementary education for half-timers was a truncated process. Mill schools remained few in number and, thus, many half-timers had no schools to attend even if they wanted to. As noted by W.C. Shepherd, Collector of Bombay: 'The education of factory children cannot be said to be satisfactory. On 30th March out of 3,090 children employed in Bombay [factories] only 532 were receiving instruction" (Annual Factory Report of the Presidency of Bombay, 1916: para. 4).

The piecemeal nature of education policy, in turn, paved the way for factory schools and industrial schools to become yet another tool in the hands of employers to enhance their exploitation of child labourers. As discussed above, these schools often helped employers *to blur production time and education* time. They also *tied down child labourers to a future of manual work – a life no different from that led by their parents.*

Given the piecemeal nature of the colonial educational system, the stricter implementation of the Factories Acts and consequent retrenchment of child workers did *not* translate into the movement of working-class children into existing schools. If they were barely trickling into the school system before stricter enforcement of factory legislation took off after WWI, then it was too much to expect them to gravitate to schools once they were unemployed.[28]

Unfortunately, as retrenchment of children and women workers eventually took off due to employers' resistance to regulation of factory labour and with concerted rationalization and mechanization across industries from the 1920s, children and women moved into informal sector jobs in large numbers. Either they returned to their villages in search of non-industrial jobs that could help them sustain their families or they took low-paying work in cities. Child labourers were increasingly absorbed in jobs like that of *pankha* pulling, drudgerous work in eateries, domestic service, etc.

Abstract temporality and the resistance by child workers

In contrast to the discourse of employers seeking to justify their exploitation of child workers and the paternalistic reformist discourse on rescuing hapless child labourers caught between 'ill-informed' decisions of their 'wage-hungry' parents and devious jobbers, we do find evidence of labouring children asserting themselves against the factory regime.

On the one hand, powerful employer lobbies, as in the case of the Bombay Millowners Association, justified more than a 10-hour work regime for child labourers on the ground of the 'leisurely manner' of work (see Report of the Bombay Mill-owners' Association ...1879: p. 92). In reality, employers used the combination of per unit time with the amount of work performed in each such unit of time to channelize production towards profit maximization. This coinciding of time rate with piece work, on the other hand, meant that every act of opting out of work time by a child labourer constituted a loss for the employer. For the child labourer, of course, it constituted as reclaiming time from work for 'life'. In such context, absenteeism from work so as to attend fairs, festivals, weddings, etc. was equivalent to an act of defiance and was, as a result, cracked down on by a merciless system of factory supervision revolving around fines, wage cuts, physical violence, etc.

Apart from individual acts of defiance, resistance by child labourers also took the form of collective action. Participation of children in collective action was particularly spectacular as concerted efforts to retrench them took off in various industries in the early 20th century.[29] One interesting reference to strike activity involving children relates to the 1920–21 strikes in the Buckingham and Carnatic Mills in Madras where the Binnys determinedly sought to break a strike of the Buckingham mill workers through a prolonged lockout. This period witnessed enhanced efforts by the Binnys and employers across the board to discipline workers via a system of heavy fines, issuing of notices for absenteeism and the forfeiting of wages for late coming. These consequently became key issues for resistance by adult and child labourers. Workers, especially child labourers, complained of intense exhaustion and fatigue and demanded grace time for late coming, recognition of festivals as holidays and the provision of casual leave for their personal purposes.[30] On 1 April, four boys who had absented themselves from work in the Buckingham Mill were issued a one month's notice. In response to the crackdown, young men and children fought back, especially as more and more disciplining measures came to light. When an *adi-dravida* (lower caste) child labourer was dismissed for absenting himself so as to attend a wedding, 900 children employed in the Carnatic Mill struck work on 19 April.[31] It was a period when caste tensions were acute and employers often used lower caste labourers to break strikes, but still the issue was such that it galvanized the support of all and pushed workers to rise above caste distinctions.

Similar short-lived strikes kept breaking out in the month of May among the child labourers of the spinning department in Buckingham Mill and in the carding department of the Carnatic Mill.[32] In the case of the latter, we get ample evidence of the half-timers' heightened consciousness when we consider the fact that, among their demands for wage increases and extension of leave privileges, the carding boys struck work for the reinstatement of dismissed union members. These incidents and the child labourers' demands also reflect that they did not necessarily always accept their lot within the factory system.

In the 1930s in the Bombay textile mill industry we again come across several instances of strikes by adult and child labourers against the persisting system of fines for late coming and absenteeism and the rationalization schemes perpetuated by mill owners. One such strike was reported from the Phoenix Mills where an iconic incident was recorded by Kanji Dwarkadas, the labour officer of the E.D. Sassoon textile mills (Bombay). Dwarkadas discussed it as a showdown between adamant mill owners backed by the local government and charismatic communist trade union leaders (Dwarkadas, 1962: pp. 53–57). The said incident involved the wife of the legendary communist labour leader, S.A. Dange. In order to stop lorries filled with strike breakers from entering the compound of the Phoenix Mills, Utsa Dange placed her infant daughter in front of the gate. In doing so, she dared the strike breakers to walk over her daughter and then enter the mill. Not surprisingly, the lorries entered the mill compound without any workers in them. Those brought in to replace the strikers joined the picket line. The news of this incident spread like wildfire across mills and workers' neighbourhoods.

The same incident is recounted by Annabhai Sathe, a worker-turned-intellectual who later joined the Communist Party (see Sathe, 1993: p. 563). In his reminisces, Sathe recalls his days as a child labourer brought in as a blackleg during the heydays of the 1930s' strikes and how radical trade union politics and leaders succeeded in influencing many child labourers to fight against the injustices of the factory regime. His reminiscence offers a valuable insight into the world of a child labourer as *it captures the subjectivity of the child worker*. Here, the desperation with recurrent unemployment and fleeting anger against circumstances can be seen to conjoin with the child labourer's angst to fight back like other workers against the tyrannies of factory production.

Clearly, many of the workers' struggles revolved around the issue of time, which became a highly contested one between employers and workers. The earliest strikes to break out in the colonial period revolved around the issue of hours of work and provision of leave (Das, 1923b: p. 190; also see Sukomal Sen, *Working Class of India*, pp. 78–79. Sen discusses the interesting case of railway workers' strike in 1862 in Howrah for an eight hour working day. For an account of early strikes on the issue of Sunday as a holiday, see F. De Souza, *The House of Binny*, p. 88). As regulation of factory labour took off with the introduction of Factory Acts, the resistance by workers persisted on the issue of time and this was true for the entire span of the colonial era. Such resistance was expected, given that factory laws intertwined with evolving work rhythms in the factories in a manner that facilitated the co-production of oppressive work time/work regimes with regulation. The intense tussles that emerged around absenteeism, leave, intensification of work, fines, wage cuts, etc. eventually compelled the colonial state to enact laws such as the Payment of Wages Act, which sought to regulate the system of fines, wage deductions for absence from duty, wage for leaves, among other things.[33]

Notes

1 For a historical account of the half-time system in England, see McMillan, 1986.

2 It is worth noting that 'childhood' itself is a much debated concept. In 1960, Phillipe Ariés in his important work, *Centuries of Childhood*, argued that childhood far from being a biological concept was a historically determined *social* construct that emerged

after the 17th century. Despite many methodological and historiographical shortcomings, rightly highlighted by his detractors, his overall position is well sustained. The concept of childhood as a modern construct can be further strengthened if we consider the historical context in which large numbers of children were pushed out of declining household production for work.

3 For elucidation, see E.P. Thompson, 2016.

4 Evidence by A.C. Green, *Royal Commission on Labour in India (RCLI), 1931*, Vol. VII, Part I, p. 264.

5 Also see 'Labour in Travancore', *Planting Opinion*, 1 February 1896, pp. 18–19.

6 By 1925 with two half-timers counted as one full-timer, the average daily wage of child labourer came to Rs. 0-12-3, whereas the corresponding wage for male adults was Rs. 1-7-2. See Sedgwick, 1925: p. 36.

7 See Q. 947, *Arbuthnot Commission Report, 1875*, op. cit.

8 Quoted in observation, Das, (1923a): p. 41.

9 For Britain's non-compliance with the minimum age resolution passed in the Berlin Conference in 1890, see Shotwell, 1934: p. 247. For an account of the pressure applied on the Government of India to pass a new factory legislation on minimum age, see *Hansards Parliamentary Debates*, House of Commons, 12 March 1891, Vol. 351, Cols 747–748.

10 Note from Hon'ble A. Mackenzie, Chairman, Chamber of Commerce, Madras to the Acting Chief Secretary to the Government of Madras, dated 31 January 1879, in Proceedings January, Nos. 9-94, Home, Revenue and Agricultural Department, Judicial, 1880, NAI. Emphasis added.

11 Letter from F.B. Skrine to Magistrate of 24-Pergunnahs, File No. Judicial A, Nos 137–241, Home Department, Judicial Branch, September 1883, NAI.

12 For elucidation, see John, 2016a.

13 See the response of J. O'Kinealy, Superintendent and Remambrancer of Legal Affairs in Bengal, on the draft Factory Bill. Letter No. 1212, dated 17 January 1879, Home Department, Judicial Branch, Judicial A, 9-94 and K.W., January 1880, NAI.

14 The 1881 Factory Act applied to workplaces of 100 or more workers. See Section 2, clause (*b*) of Factory Act 1881, http://lawmin.nic.in/legislative/textofcentralacts/1881.pdf, accessed 3 April 2017. This clause was amended to include workplaces of 50 workers by the 1891 Factory Act. See Section 20 (2), of Factory Act 1891, http://lawmin.nic.in/legislative/textofcentralacts/1891.pdf, accessed 3 April 2017.

15 Letter from W.O. Meade King, Inspector of Factories, Bombay to the Secretary to the Government of Bombay, dated 24 June 1882. Proceedings October, Nos. 79A-91, Home Department, Judicial Branch, 1882, NAI.

16 Jobber was an intermediary between mill/factory agents and workers. He was instrumental in finding jobs for workers and also undertook supervisory work for the employers.

17 Personating of younger children by older ones and holding duplicate medical certificates were common right from the time the first Factory Act was enforced into the early 20th century. For an account of how pervasive duplicate certificates were, see *Annual Factory Report of the Presidency of Bombay*, 1912: paras 3–4.

18 Quoted in a letter dated 3 August, *Annual Factory Report of the Presidency of Bombay*, 1916: para. 4. Emphasis added.

19 'Protective' legislation in India was in many ways influenced by debates in Europe on child labour. Legislative action in the colony was influenced, for example, by certain reformist positions that saw child labour as an object of regulation and reform due to embedded concerns regarding juvenile crime arising from poverty. For example, Mary Carpenter, a renowned reformist and critic of penal laws used for purpose of social reform in England, spoke of the necessity industrial training and useful labour for checking criminality in working-class youth – a popular opinion that won many advocates across industrializing

countries. See Carpenter, 1851: p. 20. Not surprisingly, even in the Indian context, the question of educating working-class children within the workplace emerged almost simultaneously as the efforts to regulate child labour.

20 The Bombay government in 1913, for example, constituted a committee on factory education, which comprised prominent mill owners. The government accepted the recommendation of the committee. See Resolution No. 1238 of 14 February 1916, General Department, 1916, Maharashtra State Archives (MSA). We also find evidence of the fact that the Bombay Mill Owners Association (BMOA) was itself in favour of factory education. See *Report of the Bombay Mill Owners Association for the Period Ending on 31 October 1912*, p. iv.

21 The leather factory Cooper, Allen and Co., for example, opened a factory school in Cawnpore in 1908. For details, see *Report of the [Young] Committee on Educational Hygiene, 1913.*

22 For such an opinion, see Biss, 1921: p. 35. Here the opinions of the East India Railway Company are discussed with respect to the industrial school set up at the collieries in Giridih.

23 Letter from W.O. Meade King, Inspector of Factories, Bombay to the Secretary to the Government of Bombay, dated 24th June 1882, Proceedings October, Nos. 79A-91, Home Department, Judicial Branch, 1882, NAI.

24 However, many of these mills schools closed down by 1924 due to poor attendance.

25 Submission by Binny and Co., *RCLI*, Vol. VII, Part I, Evidence, pp. 138–40.

26 Statement by J. Hargreaves, Manager of the Carnatic Mill, *RCLI*, Vol. II, Part II, Evidence, p. 171.

27 For details, see John, 2016a.

28 See concerns expressed by J.P. Brander. Letter no. F.I. 5774, dated 29/31 May 1924 to the Secretary to the Government, General Department, in *Annual Factory Report of the Presidency of Bombay for the Period Ending 31 October 1923*: para. 5.

29 In cities such as Bombay, women mill workers fought militantly against their retrenchment, especially in the 1930s when they developed and popularized the practice of sit-in strikes. Their children were often an important part of these sit-in strikes.

30 Evidence by Madras Labour Union, *RCLI*, Vol. VII, Part I, p. 165.

31 Statement of the union representative in *The Hindu*, 24 May 1921, p. 5.

32 Letter from the union to the editor, *The Hindu*, 12 May 1921, p. 3.

33 See Payment of Wage Act, 1936. http://lawmin.nic.in/legislative/textofcentralacts/1936.pdf, accessed 5 April 2017.

Bibliography

Anderson, M. (1993). 'Work Construed: Ideological Origins of Labour Law in British India to 1918', in *Dalit Movements and the Meanings of Labour*, edited by Peter Robb. New York, London, Toronto, New Delhi: Oxford University Press, pp. 87–120.

Annual Factory Report of the Presidency of Bombay. (1912, 1916 and 1923), Bombay.

Ariés, P. (1962). *Centuries of Childhood: A Social History of Family Life.* New York: Vintage Books.

Biss, E. (1921). *Report on the Expansion and Improvement of Primary Education in Bengal.* Calcutta: Bengal Secretariat Book.

Burnett-Hurst, A.R. (1925). *Labour and Housing in Bombay: A Study in the Economic Conditions of the Wage-Earning Classes in Bombay.* London: P.S. King & Son, 1925.

Carpenter, M. (1851). *Reformatory Schools for the Children of the Perishing and Dangerous Classes and for Juvenile Offender.* London: C. Gilpin.

Das, R.K. (1923a). *Factory Legislation in India*. Berlin: W. de Gruyter & Co.

———. (1923b). *Factory Labour in India*. Berlin: W. de Gruyter & Co.

De Souza, F. (not dated). *The House of Binny*. Associated Printers.

Dwarkadas, K. (1962). *Forty-Five Years with Labour*. Bombay: Asia Publishing House.

Hansards Parliamentary Debates, House of Commons, 12 March 1891, Vol. 351. London.

———. House of Lords, 30 July 1875, Vol. 226. London.

Home Department. (1881–90). *National Archives of India (NAI)*. New Delhi: Home Department.

Home, Revenue and Agricultural Department. (1880). *NAI*. New Delhi: HRA Department.

John, M. (2016a). *Development of Indian Labour Law (1923–48): Repercussions on the Trade Union Movement and Workers' Responses'*. Unpublished PhD thesis, University of Delhi, New Delhi.

———. (2016b). '(De)skilling Caste: Exploring the Relationship between Caste, State Regulations and the Labour Market in Late Colonial India', in *The Vernacularization of Labour Politics*, edited by Sabyasachi Bhattacharya and Rana P. Behal. New Delhi: Tulika Books, pp. 267–293.

McMillan, M. (1896). *Child Labour and the Half-time System*. Pamphlet No. 15, London: Clarion Press.

Myers, C.A. (1958). *Labour Problems in the Industrialization of India*. Cambridge, MA: Harvard University Press. *Planting Opinion (newspaper)*.

Report of the Bombay Mill-owners' Association for the Period Ending 31st October 1879. (1880). Bombay: Times of India Steam Press.

Report of the Commissioners Appointed by the Governor of Bombay in Council to Inquire into the Condition of the Operatives in the Bombay Factories, and the Necessity or Otherwise for the Passing of a Factory Act. (1875). Bombay: Government Central Press.

Report of the Indian Factory Labour Commission. (1890). Calcutta: Central Press.

Report of the Indian Factory Labour Commission. (1908). Vol. II, Evidence, Simla: Central Press.

Report of the [Young] Committee on Educational Hygiene, 1913. (1913). Naini Tal.

Royal Commission on Labour in India (RCLI). (1931). *Minutes of Evidence*. Vol. VII, Madras Presidency and Coorg, pt. 2, Oral Evidence, London.

———. *Report of RCLI*, Vol. II, Part II, Evidence, London.

Sathe, A. (1993). 'Dange the Litterateur', in *S.A. Dange. Politicial Thinker of Modern India*, edited by Verinder Grover. New Delhi: Deep & Deep Publishers.

Sedgwick, L.J. (1925). *Report on an Enquiry into the Wages and Hours of Labour in the Cotton Mill Industry*. Bombay: Government Central Press.

Sen, S. (1977). *Working Class of India: History of Emergence and Movement, 1830–1970*. Calcutta: K.P. Bagchi & Co.

Shotwell, J.T. (1934). *The Origins of the International Labour Organization*. Vol. 1, New York: Columbia University Press.

Thompson, E.P. (2016) (reprint). 'Time, Work-Discipline and Industrial Capitalism', *Customs in Common*. New Delhi: Aakar Books.

9 Work-time technology and unpaid labour in paid care work

A socio-legal analysis of employment contracts and electronic monitoring

L.J.B Hayes[1]

Employment contracts and systems of electronic monitoring act as technologies of time in the UK homecare industry. They impact on paid care workers' temporal consciousness such that time is 'made' differently through practices of care. The data I explore is drawn from research with homecare workers in England; 30 women who each provided community-based care and support to older and disabled people living at home.[2] Through attention to evidence of workers' internal notations of time, we can observe how time materialises in working life as the disciplinisation of working habits and how both the state and employing organisations have shifted a large proportion of the economic cost of caregiving onto the shoulders of individual care workers. This focus on labour temporalities in homecare also goes some way to explain how the benefits of statutory employment protection are often inaccessible to homecare workers and how it is that much of their labour is unpaid. The analysis in this chapter is grounded in a Husserlian understanding of time since I argue that time materialises through human consciousness and I look for indications of the objective qualities of time in the subjective qualities of lived experience (Michalski and Dodd 2001:115–116).

Since the inception of UK welfare state provision in the late 1940s, social care services have been distinctively constituted. Whereas health services have been made available free at the point of delivery, social care has been subject to means testing and therefore some people are invoiced for part of the costs of their care and other people are not.

My point is that social care has never been fully 'socialised' and while the state discharges legal duties to ensure adults in need of care are in receipt of such care, it has historically sought to do so at minimal cost to the public purse. The UK was the first state in Western Europe to develop markets in social care, to privatise public sector provision and to constitute citizens in need of care as 'clients' (Lewis and West 2014). Nevertheless, the private sector homecare industry continues to be overwhelmingly state funded because local authorities contract with private sector organisations for the delivery of services. Following the financial crisis of 2008, successive governments have imposed sustained and severe public spending cuts and adult social care has been more harshly impacted than any other statutory sphere of local authority activity (ADASS 2016). The labour cost savings achieved by privatisation and outsourcing are no longer sufficient on their own to keep up with the cost pressures imposed by central government austerity policies.[3] Terms and conditions of work in homecare have deteriorated substantially and are classified in research findings as 'among the worst of any', 'illegal' and 'shoddy' (Kingsmill 2014:3; Koehler 2014:5). This is the context in which technologies of time manifest as integral to the working lives of homecare workers.

The term technology is typically understood to signify the work of machines and data, however, technologies are more broadly identifiable as the application of techniques to produce a product, structure relationships or organise a material or medium (Drengson 1995:30; Suchman 2003:97–101). Technologies of time are those that create temporal paradigms and materialise time as a technical accomplishment (see Grabham 2016a:7). The materiality of time is mediated by temporal consciousness but it is open to technological adaptation, revision and reinvention. To understand changes in homecare under conditions of marketisation, we need to appreciate how technologies of time transform worker consciousness. Between 2012 and 2014, I undertook ethnographic research with homecare workers employed in a single city in the south of England. All were women who provided hands-on-care to older and disabled people. In keeping with the demographic of the UK homecare workforce outside London, the vast majority were of white British ethnic origin, three were migrants to the UK and two were British born and of dual Pakistani/English heritage (see Hayes 2017:16–20). Of the 30 participants in my research, eight were about to be made redundant from the local authority for which they had worked for many years, 11 were employed by private companies that contracted with the same local authority, a further eight were self-employed with a customer base comprised of the older and disabled people for whom they cared and four were either working for a labour agency or employed in multiple, very part-time, homecare jobs of different types.

Central to the discussion advanced in this chapter is the narrative of a research participant to whom I have given the pseudonym "Debbie". I draw on Debbie's account to show how technologies of time in the homecare industry transform the ways in which workers apprehend time and the material impacts of such transformations. Debbie worked for a private sector care company and of the many work experiences she shared with other participants in my study, three are especially salient. First, Debbie's wages were low and irregular. Indeed, tens of thousands of homecare workers in the UK are paid wages that fall below the legal minimum (HM Revenue and Customs 2013; Hayes 2015; Pyper 2018). Second, in common with the vast majority of homecare workers in the UK (and all those in my study who were working in the private sector) Debbie was employed on a zero-hours contract (Gardiner 2014). Several studies have connected employment insecurity and low wages in homecare with the use of zero-hours employment contracts (see, for example, Rubery et al. 2011; House of Commons Scottish Affairs Committee 2014; Kingsmill 2014; Koehler 2014). This form of contracting is now standard within the industry and its 'zero hours' status means that the contract avoids any legal obligation for work to be provided by or performed by employers or employees respectively. The equality between parties that is suggested by a mutual lack of obligation in law belies the profound inequalities of power in practice where employees need paid work for survival while employers have access on demand to a plentiful supply of labour. Third, and in common with all the workers in my study who were either employed by the local authority or by private sector contractors, Debbie was required to use a telephone-based electronic monitoring system to track her arrival and departure times when she attended each of the clients scheduled on her daily rota. Because Debbie worked for a private sector contractor, the resultant data generated invoices between her employer and the commissioning local authority and it also interacted with her zero-hours contract by demarcating periods of time for which Debbie would receive wages.

The electronic monitoring of working time in the UK homecare industry has risen rapidly over the past decade and, while not universally implemented, is widespread and typical. Electronic monitoring has increased the capacity for local authorities and care companies to extract unpaid labour from homecare workers by targeting the organisation of their working time (Hayes and Moore 2017). For example, by requiring homecare providers to operate electronic monitoring systems, Hampshire County Council saved in excess of £1million in 2013/2014; Devon County Council and South Gloucestershire similarly reported savings equivalent to 10 per cent of their entire purchasing budgets for adult social care (CM2000 2014). These large cost savings accrue principally because electronic monitoring makes it possible for employers to pay homecare workers for fewer of the hours in which they work and this 'efficiency' is passed on to commissioning local authorities (Moore and Hayes 2017b). Hence, savings to the public purse come out of the purses of homecare workers. Private sector contractors are frequently required to adopt electronic monitoring as a condition of their service delivery contracts and the electronic monitoring of state-funded homecare services is not unique to the UK. For example, in the USA, where state funding is channelled through the Medicaid programme, contractors have tried in vain to injunct states seeking to impose electronic monitoring of visits as a cost reduction measure.[4]

When I spoke with Debbie, she expressed anger at her low pay and at her inability to provide her clients with the quality of care to which she aspired, yet she did not lay blame with her manager or with the care company for which she worked. Rather, Debbie targeted her ire at the zero-hours contract through which she was employed and the impact of electronic monitoring. In this chapter, I seek to understand these two non-human factors as technologies of time in the homecare industry. I follow categorisations of 'clock time', 'nature's time' and 'merchants' time', which were devised by E.P. Thompson in his exemplary scholarship on industrial temporalities (1967). Thompson established that historic shifts in workers' temporal consciousness were key to processes of industrialisation in the eighteenth and nineteenth centuries. The findings of my study suggest that the processes of industrialisation that have engulfed social care work in the twenty-first century rely on a distinctive temporal fluidity.

I show how the contemporary commodification of care relies on zero-hours contracts and systems of electronic monitoring to fragment clock time and to economically subordinate worker's internal notions of caregiving according to nature's time. The result is that labour apprehended in nature's time materialises as unpaid work and labour in clock time materialises as partially paid work. Hence unpaid labour in the UK homecare industry is established by contractual and monitoring technologies that impose merchants' time into the previously uncommodified location of an older or disabled person's home. This also creates a challenging temporal environment for labour law. Legal protections frequently accrue by a measure of clock time, according to a single dial, which is also presumed to measure paid time. Examples include the UK's statutory minimum wage formula, which calculates minima by the hour; periods of continuous service by which the ability to lay claim to employment rights is qualified (Grabham 2016b); and working-time regulations, which use clock time to limit the duration of a working day and establish the legal relationship between hours worked and paid holiday entitlements. Clocks are the traditional centrepiece of working life and symbolise the social ordering of time external to the home. For many people (and especially for many of those who are hourly paid manual workers), the clock dictates and constrains living standards. Labour law operates on a presumption that clock time disciplines the rhythms of working life, commands its subject to be 'at work' and dictates for how long they must 'stay' there. Technologies of time in homecare transform how time materialises in circumstances where 'home' is a site of paid employment. The resultant impact on care workers' temporal consciousness disrupts labour protections afforded in law and establishes unpaid labour as a material fact of their working lives.

Time and paid care work

There is a tendency for scholarship to assume that the labour of caregiving has a fixed relationship with time. For example, it is argued that productivity gains in paid care work are especially difficult to achieve because the work is labour intensive and technology cannot be applied to the labour tasks of care (Baumol 1993; Himmelweit 2007). Put simply, the urgency of care is understood to be fixed to the 'natural' rhythms of human bodies and a task such as helping a person walk to the toilet cannot happen in a shorter period than can be accommodated by that person's mobility. Indeed, it has been judicially accepted in equal pay law that care workers are unable to control the pace of their work.[5] Consequently, is not necessarily unlawful discrimination if employers deny (female) care workers' access to a productivity bonus scheme that they nevertheless make available to manual workers in roles predominantly undertaken by men that are controlled traditionally by the discipline of clock time.[6]

The non-productive characteristics of paid care work have also been explored as an example of 'cost disease', an economic term that seeks to explain the presence of wage cost pressures in sectors where labour cannot be replaced by technology (Fudge 2014). Accordingly, even in the absence of sectoral productivity gains, 'cost disease' forces employers in social care to raise wages because they must compete for labour with employers in sectors such as retail where wages increase because technology makes labour more productive (Baumol and Bowen 1966). It seems that caring labour is theoretically divorced from established understandings of productivity by a presumed fixity of care to natural paces and rhythms and its concomitant incompatibility with clock time.

However, feminist economists recognise that in practice, caring labour is traded as a commodity that is compartmentalised into clock time and they seek to account for its undervaluation on that basis (Nelson 1999; Folbre 2001). Scholars have argued that care can never be fully commodified because its true relational and qualitative value is not captured by the quantitative clock time measurements typical of service delivery contracts. Care cannot be adequately measured on a 'time is money' basis and is rendered subordinate and undervalued within a capitalist market economy by the patriarchal logic of capitalism (Stone 2005). The commodification of care presumes its masculinisation (Rasmussen 2001, 2004) and compartmentalises caregiving into tradable units of clock time. The relational substance and symbolically feminine qualities of care are erased from economic exchange in order to produce surplus value from labour extracted as unpaid work.

Taking together the productivity focus of equal pay law and cost disease literature to combine it with the critique of commodification advanced by feminist scholars, we can discern that the labour of care has a fixed relationship with the 'natural' timing of human needs. Its incorporation within market schemas of clock time is a reductive and gendered process in which large parts of its value are easily lost. The analysis of time and paid care work that I set out in this chapter is distinctive because I define zero-hours employment contracts and the electronic monitoring of service provision as technologies of time, i.e. as tools applied to the time in which care takes place (rather than to the labour of caregiving).

Time as consciousness

The importance of worker consciousness to the study of industrial temporalities was set out by E.P. Thompson in a ground-breaking sociological text on time and work discipline written in the late 1960s. Thompson adopted a historical materialist approach to show that changes in workers' apprehension of time were key to industrialisation. He elaborated variously on 'nature's time', 'clock time' and 'merchants' time' as temporal schemas that were materially embedded in working practices through changes in workers' consciousness. Different work situations gave rise to different notations of time and there were different ways in which those notations related to 'natural' rhythms. The crowing of the cockerel exemplified his vision of worker consciousness of labour in nature's time; it was seasonal, agrarian and materialised through a work rhythm that attended to tasks as evident necessities. Irregular moments of perception in which labour engaged with and responded to observable needs meant one time moment was unlike the next but each connected fluidly in the passing of time.

The displacement of nature's time by clock time, as a mode of workers' consciousness, was historically necessary for the synchronisation of labour in employment and facilitated the advance of industrialisation. Thompson perceived of clock time as sidereal time moved from the 'heavens into the home' and as communicated in the turning of the hour and minute hands on a clock face, the ringing of church bells and sounding of factory horns (1967:57). Clock time materialised in workers' consciousness as a strong demarcation between time as 'work' (which was harnessed to an employer) and time as 'life' (which was the workers' own). Internal notations of clock time extracted self-discipline from workers according to the objectivity of the dial and set the waged labourer apart from those engaged in unwaged subsistence farming and domestic work. Clock time also materialised in new productivity-orientated incentives, new working habits and new disciplinary regimes.

Thompsons' third schema was that of merchants' time, a consciousness through which time could be redeemed as riches, where it was 'owned' and consequently bought and sold. Merchants' time was a temporality that drew opportunity from nature's time (for example the opportunity of tides and winds) and was orientated towards a capture of 'nicks of time' set to work in order to move the merchant forward apace in an alignment of time with degrees of 'favourability' (1967:87). Merchants' time could be appropriated and used for accumulation and it was culturally symbolised through textual and pictorial images of time as a currency.

Thompson's account observed industrialisation in the temporalities of masculine, productive, paid labour yet he also included an assessment of care work, the unwaged labour of wives and mothers, as a counterpoint. Care work exemplified a task orientation that was free of the constraints of clock time, it was reminiscent of worker consciousness in pre-industrialised society and 'more humanly comprehensible than timed labour' (1967:61). This was nature's time in the home and women's'' apprehension of it gave rise to modes of self-discipline in caregiving which were similar to that of men's unwaged labour in the fields, based on a temporal self-governance that accorded with the perceived needs of animals, plants and human reliance on the wind, rain and the setting of the sun. Thompson argued that task-orientated temporalities pointed to a separation of 'work' from 'life' that was barely evident because 'social intercourse and labour are intermingled' (1967:60). However, the question of task orientation became much more complex when notions of employment were introduced into the mix. When time was located within a relationship of employment, it was prone to be measured as money – the employer's money. Employment marked the shift from task orientation to timed labour and apprehension of clock time marked the shift in consciousness from task to timepiece. Yet the measurement of labour as clock time was, according to Thompson, relationally constituted:

> Those who are employed experience a distinction between their employer's time and their 'own' time ... time is not passed but is spent.
>
> (1967:78)

This meant that in waged labour, workers exhibited a temporal consciousness of time as a finite resource utilised within the employment relationship. Once spent, the time was gone and could not be replenished until the next shift or working day. The employment relation centred around employee and employer cognizance of a bank of clock time that was cyclically filled and emptied through the interaction of both parties. Thompson argued that in contrast, labour occurring within a care relation was disclosed by the logic of necessity and inevitably disregarded clock time because there was no need of external imposition. The rhythms of women's work in the home were not easily attuned to the measurement of the dial.

In the following section, I turn to my research data to examine how workers' consciousness of time is expressed in the accounts of homecare workers. Therefore, I relate Thompson's temporal modalities to an aspect of the labour market that was non-existent at the time in which he was writing: that of industrialised waged care work. Industrialised care work arises from the commodification of social care. The precarious and gendered forms of waged labour that accompany it are characteristic of advanced capitalist societies that have engaged in a neoliberal restructuring of state welfare provision (Hayes 2017:2–3).

Contracts and electronic monitoring as technologies of time

The ways in which homecare workers discussed their daily routines and the challenges of doing their job well provided evidence of their temporal consciousness. I found that when they talked about 'care', they were often talking about 'time'. My analysis suggests that the contemporary commodification of care relies on the economic subordination of nature's time and a re-engineering of clock time. Technologies of time achieve this by cementing workers' apprehension of labour in nature's time as a labour of unpaid work in the home and by splitting clock time across a series of divergent and disparate clock dials so that labour in clock time is fractured and materialises as partially paid work.

Homecare work, as accounted for through a temporal consciousness of 'nature's time', pays primary attention to tasks associated with getting a person 'ready' for the day ahead, even if that person is bed bound. An erudite example of this was offered to me by a homecare worker who participated in my research, she worked for a private sector contractor and responded thus when I asked her to describe her daily work routine:

> Getting people up; showering or personal care; incontinence care; emptying leg bags; getting them clean; putting on fresh clothes if they want it; breakfast, cup of tea; medication ... One lady I go to is in a wheelchair, diabetic, she can't walk. Every manoeuvre she needs, you've got to do it for her. You get her up in the morning; it's all ceiling hoists; all sling work. Hoist her to her chair; wheel her to the bathroom, which again is a hoist job to get her on the toilet. Then she will want her breakfast sat on the toilet. She can't hold things very well enough in her hands, so cups of tea you've got to feed her fingers

> through the handle. She wants her medication sat on the toilet, and that'll be her tablets and her insulin, I inject her. And then it's hoist into the shower. Get her dressed in the bathroom and then put her back in the wheelchair and put her splints on her hands to keep her hands straight.
>
> (Homecare worker, Esther)

Here, the task orientation that Thompson associated with the unwaged care work of wives and mothers is evident in paid industrialised care work. The homecare worker, Esther, describes her labour as unfolding in tandem with the needs of her client, at the client's pace. She is conscious of her labour materialising in nature's time. If we were to measure this work according to clock time it would expand or contract on a day-by-day basis according to her variable interactions with her client and the fluctuating needs that accompany human bodies and desires. However, Esther worked within an employment relationship and she was paid her wages on a clock time basis fixed by her employment contract. The care that Esther provided was transacted in the care market on a nominal and fixed measure of clock time according to the service-delivery contract between her employer and the commissioning local authority. While Esther was conscious of labouring in nature's time, she was employed in clock time.

A lack of fit between the nature's time temporality of care work and the clock time temporality of employment has real world impacts on homecare workers within a system of marketised care. Combined with legal permissions set out in the NHS and Community Care Act 1990, the expression of care work in clock time was a historic development that facilitated the privatisation of public sector care services and the development of a homecare industry trading in care as a commodity. In Thompsons' account, the industrialisation of labour was accompanied by a shift in workers' consciousness from a dominant temporality of nature's time to that of clock time. In my study however, the accounts of care workers suggest that the rise of industrialised care (a process in which they were deeply immersed) has not erased 'nature's time' from their temporal consciousness or eclipsed it with internal notations of clock time. Homecare workers appear to continue to apprehend their working time in a modality of nature's time even though the industry in which they work operates on a clock time basis.

Set out below, Debbie's story is indicative of the extent to which homecare workers apprehend clock time as an intrusion on their work with clients. Her account illustrates that nature's time and clock time are simultaneously present as temporal modalities in the consciousness of homecare workers. Debbie was in her early 40s, of white British ethnic origin, she was living in rented accommodation and had worked in the homecare industry for about eight years. Two of Debbie's three children were old enough to have finished school but her youngest was just two years old. Employed on a zero-hours contract, Debbie was caught between her employers' refusal to provide her with either regular hours or a secure volume of work and the impossibility of finding reliable and affordable childcare which could be accessed on an ad-hoc basis. Hence Debbie was struggling to cope and when I asked if she considered herself to be 'poor' she replied, 'I am poverty, me'. I was struck by the fact that Debbie spoke as though her financial impoverishment defined her personhood. Debbie assigned a significant proportion of her woes to her zero-hours contract and her employers' introduction of electronic monitoring. These technologies controlled a considerable proportion of her life and had substantially reduced her wages. Debbie's account alerted me to the many ways that homecare workers seemed to engage in a dialogue with time as they attempted to translate one modality into another and tried to accommodate the inconsistencies.

In Debbie's view, the most credible and accurate measure of the quantity of the time she was 'at work' was the duration of her wearing of company uniform. Throughout the entire period of her 11 or 12 hour 'shifts' Debbie wore a green tabard. It served as a signal to her two year old son that someone else would be looking after him and Debbie told me that when he saw her in uniform he started to cry. Consequently, Debbie never returned home during periods of a working day when there was no paid work for her because: 'I upset my little son, so it's better to stay away. I don't even see him in a morning when I go to work because he is still in bed, so to come home, it just upsets him.' Debbie's internal notation of what we might call a 'uniform-wearing clock' measured her temporal separation from her own family. This was a measure that served to demarcate her personal from her working life and thus suggests a true fit with the consciousness of clock time described in Thompson's schema where clock time separated working time from workers' apprehension of life time.

However, Debbie understood that the zero-hours nature of her employment relationship meant she had 'signed a contract but it isn't guaranteed to get work'. Debbie was therefore aware that a day's work could never be assured by her contract, but her experience of the contract in practice gave rise to a very different kind of uncertainty: even when time accrued on the 'uniform-wearing clock' she never knew in advance the proportion of her time which would actually be recognised as 'work' for the purposes of pay:

> I am out on a Sunday for 11 hours, I only get paid for about seven, so four hours of my time it's just travelling and sat around waiting.

Here, Debbie divides her notion of working time between the attention of three clocks: a 'paid-time clock', a 'travelling-time clock' and a 'waiting-time clock'. She is conscious that each carries distinct social and economic meaning. For example, from the short quote above we can ascertain that Debbie diminishes the value of the working time measured on the 'travelling-time clock' by her preface 'just' and she submissively refers to working time measured on the 'waiting-time clock' as if it manifested in her adopting a sedentary posture, even though she remained on duty and was bridging variations and interruptions in her work programme. It was evident that Debbie measured her working day, one in which her contract was engaged, by reference to a series of dials. If, as per Thompson, worker consciousness of clock time manifests in a shift in apprehension from task to time-piece, the technology of the zero-hours contract appears to modify worker consciousness such that segments of working life are apportioned to a 'paid-time clock', a 'travelling-time clock' or a 'waiting-time clock'. Accordingly, clock time is temporally fractured. The time that Debbie consciously assigns to either the 'travelling-time' or 'waiting-time' clock is unpaid and direct links between clock time and understandings of 'work' for the purposes of pay are broken.

However, disciplines of clock time undoubtedly materialised in Debbie's work habits. She pointed to the absurdities that arose from the imposition of clock time into a caregiving relationship that otherwise depended on the meeting of observable, and fluctuating needs. Debbie pejoratively described one of her clients as a 'nit-picker' and claimed, 'if any carer was to leave a couple of minutes early he would report you to management. He will argue about it: 'I paid for 45 minutes, I want 45 minutes!' In this vignette, we learn of her client using clock time as a literal measurement of care with which Debbie's behaviour is controlled and her attention commanded. It seemed absurd to Debbie because other visits in her day would take longer than anticipated and a lack of flexibility was detrimental to the quality of care she was able to provide. The instincts of homecare workers' that arose from their labour in nature's time were subordinated to the discipline of clock time represented as a measure of clients' money. Although labour was disclosed in caring relationships by the logic of necessity, Debbie could not disregard the rhythms of clock time, which defined her employment relationship and rendered her accountable to the clock-based discipline of management.

Yet the ability of clients' to impose temporal control over homecare workers was limited by the extent to which clock time served employers' interests. A hierarchy of clock time over nature's time was evident in situations where Debbie recognised that her employment relationship 'forced' her to remain with clients for far longer than she was welcome. If workers' consciousness of nature's time extracted self-discipline according to client needs, a simultaneous consciousness of clock time diminished personal autonomy to the self-discipline of abiding by working habits which could become emotionally uncomfortable and counter-intuitive to a credible relation of care:

> We have clients where you go in and once you do your job they don't want you in their house anymore, but I have to stay.

Occasionally, Debbie would find that she was not needed at a client's home because a family member had visited, the client was engrossed in watching TV or they had chosen to refuse the bath that Debbie was scheduled to provide. This collision of clock time and nature's time led to considerable friction between Debbie and her manager, as well as with her clients. If a client had asked her to leave after 10 minutes, Debbie's employer would insist: 'We are supposed to be there for half an hour!' Debbie's recount of the collective term 'we' reflected her consciousness of clock time as the temporality that bound her within the employment relationship and disciplined her to literally sit out her stay in a corner of the client's home. This time spent waiting, however, was not assigned to Debbie's internal notations of a 'waiting-time clock' but rather to the 'paid-time clock'.

The example illustrated that Debbie's psychological compartmentalisation of time did not intuitively correspond with her physical behaviour. She would abide by her manager's instructions throughout the period she measured on her 'uniform-wearing clock' and hence some forms of waiting materialised as work on the 'paid-time clock' while other forms clocked up as unpaid labour. To understand how this happened requires an appreciation of electronic monitoring as a technology that imposed merchants' time into Debbie's working life as a spatial temporality; by which I mean a temporality that is sensitive to place and materialises by location.

Under conditions of electronic monitoring, homecare workers interact with software that tracks their location and arrival/departure times through data entered into clients' landline telephones or a GPS-enabled mobile. Workers dial their own unique identification number at the beginning and end of each visit to a client and this connects into the electronic monitoring providers' call processing centre, logs the time of their calls, location and calculates their correspondence with the worker's pre-programmed roster of visits. Electronic monitoring made measurements that prevented Debbie's labour from equating with clock time and failed to recognise the labour in which she engaged in nature's time. Viewed as a temporal technology, electronic monitoring was overriding clock time and imposing behavioural discipline through worker apprehension of merchants' time in the home. Debbie explained:

> When you go in, each visit we get a time limit to go in. To get our pay, if we are on a half hour visit we've got to stay in there a minimum of 23 minutes. If we go in for a 45-minute visit we've got to stay a minimum of 38 minutes and for an hour we have to stay a minimum of 53 minutes.

Failing to meet these time targets would mean Debbie was penalised by being paid for less time than she had worked in a client's home. For example, if she had to sign out of a 15-minute visit after 10 minutes she would receive pay for only five minutes of her time and if a planned visit of 30 minutes lasted for 22 minutes Debbie would receive just 15 minutes' worth of pay. Electronic monitoring introduced opportunities to shave labour cost-savings from the incompatibility of nature's time and clock time that are reminiscent of the 'nicks of time' that Thompson identified in his concept of merchants' time. Debbie's employer and the commissioning local authority could make financial gains by speculatively framing the temporal space and geographic place in which Debbie's labour was captured as a vehicle for enterprise.

Similarly, if Debbie stayed in a home past the time limit measured by the electronic monitoring system (which, in some instances, meant staying for too long and in other instances meant exceeding the point in clock time when she was supposed to leave regardless of the visit duration) she would not be paid for her additional labour. Rather, her employer instructed her to 'catch up on the next visit' or asserted that 'staying longer is your personal choice and it's not our business if you want to hang around chatting.' The labour of care in nature's time is discursively constructed here as being without value because the task of maintaining social intercourse is set up to equate with 'non-work' that lies outside of the employment relation. Nevertheless, the prospect of Debbie being able to 'catch up' on her schedule was frequently impossible because the care needs of her next client did not diminish. Meanwhile, if visits were completed more quickly than scheduled, longer term consequences could ensue. Merchants' time was in evidence when Debbie identified that reducing her attention to the needs of her client could be seized as opportunities for organisational gain:

> When I'm rushing to try and fit everyone in, if I left a person 10 minutes early, they [management] will say oh great! Then the next day they change the rota to put me down to leave earlier. So all of us carers know they're pinching minutes from people all the time.

Debbie's encounters with the electronic monitoring system reveal the impact of temporo-spatial collisions between notions of 'home' (as a place of care) and those of 'enterprise' (as a place of industry). Such collisions are integral to the contemporary organisation of the UK homecare industry[7] and exacerbate the discordance between a temporality of caring relations and a temporality of employment relations, which was discussed earlier in this chapter. Awareness of social care as a public service (albeit privatised in its delivery) should not diminish our awareness of care as a commercial industry valued at over £5billion per annum (Francis 2013:7; Holmes, 2015:10). By considering Debbie's experience of electronic monitoring we can observe how merchants' time is set into the homes where she worked. Merchants' time is notated as a currency and the opportunism of merchants' time is not coterminous with clock time because exchanges at some points in clock time are more profitable than at others.

Electronic monitoring encouraged homecare workers to perceive of their work as a labour of clock time rather than as a labour of care since it communicated that clients were to receive limited parcels of time in place of the meeting of their care needs. However, electronic monitoring did not record data about homecare workers' visits according to a true measure of clock time; this was a technology with the capacity to generate time and to eradicate it. When talking about the electronic monitoring system, Debbie was quite clear: 'The system is awful ... the money and the time you have to put in.' She indicated that clock time was the input she gave to her employer but she regarded as 'awful' the way in which she was required to deploy, divide and ration her input. It was especially evident that Debbie's temporal consciousness of merchants' time meant that in practice she responded to client's needs outside of the electronic monitoring system:

> We need to watch our clocks when we go in there [a client's home] but I don't always, it depends what you get ... if someone has fallen then you don't really want to be looking at your clock, you forget to clock in. If I go in and someone needs my help then my first main priority is to that person, not ringing in.

This hierarchy revealed how temporal inconsistences were negotiated. The clock time it took to do the job well and to respond to eventualities could not be measured in merchants' time, instead it was apprehended in a modality of nature's time and homecare workers were conscious that nature's time materialised as unpaid labour. As Debbie explained:

> I don't agree with the time limits we get . . . you haven't got enough time. You are being rushed all the time. If you go over it causes trouble. I'm the kind of carer, the old fashioned carer, where I think, tough, if I go over I go over. I'm not rushing them. Some of them can barely walk and then you're being told, if you go over the time we will lose the contract with the council, which I think is diabolical. All they want from us carers is to sit down and have a chat. You're not allowed to do that. It is terrible.

Debbie assigns the notion of 'time limits' to the electronic monitoring of her working time. Clocking in and out using the telephone technology is a manifestation of merchants' time in the domestic location of a client's home. Her experience of being rushed is evidence of the temporo-spatial collision of 'home' and 'enterprise'. As a consequence, homecare workers are highly attuned to the risk of 'trouble' from either and both unsatisfied clients and disgruntled managers. When Debbie described herself as 'old fashioned' she was seeking to justify her desire to refuse to pass the consequences of temporal collision onto her clients. She invoked notions of a pre-technological era in which it was apparently possible to defeat the disciplinisation of clock time with an appeal to the higher moral value of nature's time. Her complaint that she did not have 'time to chat' revealed her consciousness of care as a labour in nature's time, where life and labour are intermingled. In asserting that she would not rush her clients, Debbie was indicating her preparedness to resist acting on the panic she experienced when she herself was feeling rushed by the temporal pressures induced by technologies of time. Engaging in unpaid labour was how workers' consciousness of care in a modality of nature's time materialised.

Concluding discussion

Debbie's account sheds light on how homecare workers' apprehend and internally notate caregiving as time. It appears that electronic monitoring and zero-hours contracts are doing something to the nature of time itself within caregiving relationships. In an era of unprecedented reductions in public spending it would seem essential to the viability of the homecare industry that homecare workers exhibit a dual-consciousness of labour in the nature's time of caring relationships and the clock time of employment. I have illustrated how clock time is re-engineered to produce partially paid labour and how nature's time materialises as unpaid work. Clock time and nature's time are temporalities that are simultaneously evident in marketised homecare work and represent the ever present spectre of unpaid work within the spatial location of 'home'.

Zero-hours contracts enable employers to contract for the services of individual workers without providing any commitment whatsoever about the volume of clock time that will be measured as paid work. Such contractual arrangements are also 'law light', by which I mean that they are depleted of the benefits of many statutory rights because the contract is not fully recognised in UK law as being a contract of employment. As scholarship examining the impact of zero-hours arrangements in the homecare sector has noted, workers bear the risk of a loss of work or pay when a client is admitted to hospital or a care home and employers can insist on irregular working hours, resulting in episodic and unpredictable working time (Rubery et al. 2015). However, in this chapter, I have focused on the contract as a technology of time and have considered what the zero-hours contract is doing to transform time or to alter how time is materialised through labour.

In the absence of a legally meaningful temporal commitment, zero-hours contracts are activated when the employer periodically makes working time available that the worker accepts. Contra Thompson (1967) the homecare workers in my study who were party to zero-hours contracts did not comprehend working time as a resource measured by the cyclical depletion and replenishment of clock time. They were unable to rely on the temporal security of known start and end points within which working time was contained. There was no singular or predictable end time that separated working time from 'life' and there was no pre-existing bank of time that was available to be spent through the employment relationship. Rather, the temporal consciousness of homecare workers was of working time measured in a modality of fractured clock time in which 'what comes next' was unknown. Thompson's observations of clock time suggested a measurement of labour that was relationally constituted. What was hidden from view in his account was the contractual nature of this temporal relationship and the role of the employment contract as a technology of time.

Evidence of the contract as a technology of time was also apparent in the treatment of workers' time when engaged in travelling between clients. The job of homecare requires labour to be mobile within local communities so that service provision can move from one home to another to deliver a bespoke programme of individual care. It is not possible to have homecare work without worker movement yet the technology of zero-hours contracting has reconfigured understandings of movement into a consciousness of time measured by a dial that is not that of the 'paid-work clock'. As the care worker performs her duties the 'paid-work clock' is ticking. When the visit is complete her productive capacity for a repeat performance travels between one home and another. This is 'travelling time', a measurement of the temporal space that opens between one place and another. Across the homecare industry, most travelling time is unpaid and research suggests that homecare workers forfeit an average of 19 per cent of their wages due to time measured on the 'travelling-time clock' (UKHCA 2014). The undervaluing of commodified, caring labour is in part made possible by the capacity of zero-hours contracting to fracture clock time into paid and unpaid forms.

By drawing attention to paid care workers' inward notation of time, my observations suggest strong links between the specific temporal disciplinisation of work-time technology and the precarity that defines their labour. Thompson's account of clock time implied the synchronised regularity of a singular clock face. I have argued that, in the context of industrialised waged care work, the technology of zero-hours contracts locates clock time variously across four distinct dials: a uniform-wearing clock, a paid-time clock, a travelling-time clock and a waiting-time clock. The purpose is to re-engineer clock time as a temporality that is only partly paid. This observation fractures the singularised account of clock time offered by Thompson. Furthermore, the technology of electronic monitoring represents merchants' time in the consciousness of homecare workers and affirms that labour apprehended in nature's time is a measure of unwaged labour that resides within a caring relationship but is unrecognised within a relation of employment. As Thompson suggests, merchants' time draws opportunity from nature's time and in homecare work does so by aligning commodified care with times of favourability. The labour of care in merchants' time is a labour that is unencumbered of the risks associated with interacting with aging and ailing human bodies. It draws opportunity from nature's time by capturing care needs as moments of potential enterprise. To do so, the social and economic cost of responding to observable needs in nature's time, needs that are uncertain, unpredictable and unprofitable, is placed on the shoulders of individual homecare workers who apprehend labour in nature's time as unpaid work.

Thompson's attention to the shifting construction of time in the consciousness of working people is highly pertinent to my analysis of the accounts of homecare workers. His scholarship emphasised that the understandings of paid work around which our contemporary societies are organised grew from a social capacity for time to materialise from the consciousness of working people and to be captured for economic gain. Through industrial temporalities work is concretised as paid labour and my findings illustrate that care workers within the homecare industry have indeed been transformed into time workers. I have shown how time is materialised through caring labour and how technologies of time impact on care workers' temporal consciousness. Clock time is fractured across four separate dials and materialises as partially paid work. Caregiving as a labour in nature's time is economically subordinated and materialises as unpaid work. As technologies of time, zero-hours employment contracts and the electronic monitoring of service provision produce a temporal environment in which the legal entitlements of homecare workers are opaque and minimum labour standards are frequently overlooked.

By considering that homecare workers are labouring simultaneously in different modalities of time we can more richly understand the time work of care workers as a labour of time translation and negotiation. Clock time has been widely accepted as a hegemonic regulator of labour markets and a lynchpin around which entitlements and claims in employment law are organised. The labour of caregiving is considered by many as work that can never be fully commodified. My discussion of the multi-dimensional nature of time as manifest in homeworkers' temporal consciousness reveals how time, rather than care, is transformed under conditions of marketisation.

Notes

1 Lecturer in Law, Cardiff University, Wales, UK.
2 The research is the basis of a monograph, *Stories of Care: A Labour of Law. Gender and class at work* Palgrave (2017).
3 Remuneration in the private sector is about half the value of that in the public sector (taking into account hourly wages, pension costs, sick pay and other benefits; see Hayes 2017:58, 98).
4 See, for example *Companions and Homemakers v State of Connecticut Dept of Social Services*, Superior Court, District of Hartford, 23 January 2017.
5 Justice Elias in *Cumbria County Council v Dow (No.1)* [2008] IRLR 91 (EAT): 'A care worker who works properly is subject to the demands and requirements of the patient and cannot sensibly dictate the speed of working.' [145].
6 See also *Gibson v Sheffield City Council* [2010] EWCA Civ 63; [2010] IRLR 311.
7 For a detailed discussion, see Hayes 2017:189–193.

Bibliography

Association of Directors of Adult Social Services (2016), *ADASS Budget Survey 2016 Report.* London: ADSS.

Baumol, W. (1993), Health care, education and the cost disease: A looming crisis for public choice. *Public Choice* 77: 17–28.

Baumol, W. and Bowen, W. (1966), *Performing Arts, The Economic Dilemma: A study of problems common to theater, opera, music, and dance.* Michigan: MIT Press.

CM2000
(2014), Customer Case Studies, http://www.cm2000.co.uk/Success-Stories. Accessed 31 May 2018.

Drengson, A. (1995), *The Practice of Technology: Exploring technology, ecophilosophy and spiritual disciplines for vital links.* New York: SUNY Press

Folbre, N. (2001), *The Invisible Heart: Economics and Family Values.* New York: New Press.

Francis, J. (2013), *An Overview of the UK domiciliary care sector.* UK Homecare Association, Version 33. Wallington: UKHCA.

Fudge, J. (2014), Feminist reflections on the scope of labour law: Domestic work, social reproduction, and jurisdiction. *Feminist Legal Studies* 22 (1): 1–23.

Gardiner, L. (2014), *Zero-Hours Contracts: The latest figures and analysis.* London: Resolution Foundation

Grabham, E. (2016a), *Brewing Legal Times: Things, form and the enactment of law.* Toronto: University of Toronto Press.

Grabham, E. (2016b), Time and Technique: The legal lives of the 26 week qualifying period, *Economy and Society* 45 (3–4).

HM Revenue and Customs. (2013), *National Minimum Wage Compliance in the Social Care Sector*, Evaluation Report November. London: UKRC,

Hayes, L.J.B. (2015), Are the minimum wage rights of homecare workers at risk under the Care Act 2014? *Industrial Law Journal* 44 (4): 492–521.

Hayes, L.J.B. and Moore, S. (2017), Care in a time of austerity: The electronic monitoring of working time in homecare. *Gender, Work & Organization* 24 (4): 329.

Hayes, L.J.B. (2017), *Stories of Care: A Labour of Law. Gender and Class at Work.* Basingstoke: Palgrave Macmillan.

Himmelweit, S. (2007), The prospects for caring: Economic theory and policy analysis. 31 *Cambridge Journal of Economics* 31 (4): 581.

Holmes, J. (2015), An overview of the UK domiciliary care sector. UK Home Care Association. Wallington: UKHCA.

House of Commons Scottish Affairs Committee. (2014), *Zero Hours Contracts in Scotland: An Interim Report* (Tenth Report of Session 2013–2014). London: House of Commons.

Jacobs, A. and Padavic, I. (2015), Hours, scheduling and flexibility for women in the US low-wage labour force. 22 *Gender Work and Organisation*: 67.

Kingsmill, D. (2014), *The Kingsmill Review: Taking Care* (an independent report into working conditions in the care sector). London: Labour Party.

Koehler, I. (2014), *Key to Care* (Report of the Burstow Commission on the future of the home care workforce). London: Local Government Information Unit (LGIU).

Lewis, J. and West, A. (2014), Re-shaping social care services for older people in England: Policy development and the problem of achieving 'good care'. 43 *Journal of Social Policy*: 1.

Michalski, K. and Dodd J. (2001), *Logic and Time*. Boston Studies in the Philosophy and History of Science. Kluwer Academic: Dordrecht Netherlands.

Moore, S. and Hayes, L.J.B. (2017a), Taking worker productivity to a new level: Electronic monitoring in homecare: the (re)production of unpaid labour. *New Technology Work and Employment* 32 (2): 101.

Moore, S. and Hayes, L.J.B. (2017b), The electronic monitoring of care work. The redefinition of paid work, in Moore, P., Upchurch, M. and Whittaker, X. (Eds.) *Humans and Machines at Work: Monitoring, Surveillance and Automation in Contemporary Capitalism*. Basingstoke: Palgrave.

Nelson, J. (1999), Of markets and martyrs: Is it okay to pay well for care? *Feminist Economics* 5 (3): 43.

Pyper, D. (2018), *National Minimum Wage: Sleep-in Care*. House of Commons Library Briefing Paper, 8243, 8 May.

Rasmussen, B. (2000), Home-based care as a greedy organisation. Power and responsibility in decentralised organisations. 41 *Tidsskrift For Samfunnsforskning*: 38.

Rasmussen, B. (2004), Between endless needs and limited resources: The gendered construction of a greedy organization. 11 *Gender, Work & Organization*: 506.

Rubery, J. and others. (2011), The recruitment and retention of a care workforce for older people. Manchester: European Work and Employment Research Centre, University of Manchester.

Rubery, J., Grimshaw, D., Hebson, G. and Ugarte, S. (2015), 'It's all about time': Time as a contested terrain in the management and experience of domiciliary care work in England. *Human Resource Management* 55 (5): 753.

Stone, D. (2005), For love nor money. The commodification of care, in Ertman, M. and Williams, J. (Eds.) *Rethinking Commodification: Cases and Readings in Law and Culture*. New York: New York University Press.

Suchman, M. (2003), The contract as social artefact. *Law & Society Review* 37: 1.

Thompson, E.P. (1967), Time, work-discipline and industrial capitalism. *Past & Present* 38: 56–97.

UKHCA. (2014), *A Minimum Price for Homecare. Version 2.1*. Wallington: United Kingdom Homecare Association.

10 Standards in the shadows for everyone to see

The supranational regulation of time and the concern over temporal pluralism

Kevin Birth, Department of Anthropology, Queens College, City University of New York

Several years ago, some of those involved in the leap second debate (which I shall discuss later) approached me to conduct anthropological research on the cultural impact of global time policies. Since then, I have also been studying the leap second controversy, how time policy decisions are made, and the cultural impacts of these decisions. In the debates about time I have witnessed, the issue of the proliferation of timescales has been a concern among those who create, manage, and disseminate Coordinated Universal Time (UTC), the global time standard. The point of this chapter is to explore some of the causes and legal consequences of currently emerging timescale pluralism.

Whether it is in the architecture of computer systems in which every action receives a timestamp, or in the documentation of sequences of events, the recording of time is part of the backbone of accounting, governance, and legal practices. The legitimacy of any particular timestamp is a matter of documentable traceability to an authoritative time source—what Judah Levine of the US National Institute of Standards and Technology calls "legal traceability" (2001).

The adoption of international standards in combination with a growing consciousness of cultural pluralism and nationalism results in the issues of legal traceability and temporal pluralism becoming intertwined. With regard to time, there are several sources of timescale pluralism. Local solar time was a source that was addressed by the creation of universal time and time zones in the late 19th century (see Bartky, 2000). The proliferation of new technologies of time distribution, such as satellite navigation systems, and the growing availability of high quality clock technology is resulting in more and more institutions using timescales that are simulacra of UTC, but not directly sourced to a time service involved in the production of UTC. In addition, the coexistence of different cultural systems of reckoning time was suppressed by the emergence of the global time system managed by international institutions such as the Radiocommunication Sector of the International Telecommunication Union (ITU-R) and the International Bureau of Weights and Measures (BIPM), but with decolonization and growing postcolonial resistance to Euro-American dominance over time, there are indications that these alternative timescales may again be asserted.

Most clock users, including the courts, are unaware of these debates and concerns. For them, clock time is naturalized and unquestioned. This is because clocks are cognitive tools that almost completely mask how they mediate the expert knowledge of those who create and manage UTC for clock users (Birth, 2012). Indeed, many clock users only have a primary school level knowledge about time. So as the issue of timescale pluralism is salient for those involved in time metrology, it is largely hidden from view for those who rely on accurate timestamps for legal purposes.

Today's representations of time emphasize uniform timescales. A timescale is a conceptualization of time that allows its users to orient themselves in relationship to time. A uniform timescale achieves this through the use of units of standard length that extend into the past and the future. The current global time standard, UTC, is a timescale based on the precise measurement of *Système International* (SI) seconds using atomic clocks, and these measurements are compiled by the International Bureau of Weights and Measures (BIPM) in order to calculate Coordinated Universal Time, a timescale by means of which the accuracy of all clocks is evaluated and regulated.

The SI second and UTC are among the international standards that enable forms of calculation important to modern markets (Callon and Muniesa, 2005). Time standards are also part of the foundation for what Foucault describes as governmentality (Foucault, 2008). These standards are a form of power-knowledge that is mediated by technology in a way that structures and organizes many behaviors—including biological functions such as sleep. As Loconto and Busch point out (2010, 509), such standards achieve their power not through overt governmental action, but through individual self-governance. Clock users do not believe the time on the clock and structure their lives by the clock because of a consciousness of time policy; instead, clock time is naturalized, and, because of this, it is used by individuals to self-regulate their behavior, such as in the mundane behaviors of setting an alarm clock or meeting an appointment time. As such, these standards are a type of "soft law" (Abbott and Snidal, 2000) that emerges from an interaction of international agencies established by treaties and professional organizations that are largely outside the consciousness of those who rely on the standards. Most clock users do not know, or take for granted, the current cultural values that guide time standards, namely, the desire for stability, reproducibility, uniformity, and ubiquity. The first three of these values are frequently stated in discussions of time metrology (see Audoin and Guinot, 2001; McCarthy and Seidelmann, 2009; Quinn, 2012), whereas the last value, which indicates a desire for global hegemony, often remains tacit.

This chapter describes the choices behind the current globally ubiquitous timescales, how the leap second debate raises the issue of temporal pluralism, and how such pluralism gets related to the legal traceability of time.

Timescales as cultural choices

Clocks and calendars mediate cultural choices about time and its representation (Birth, 2012), and once a particular style of time reckoning shapes a mass-produced design, the cultural reproduction of that style of time reckoning is ensured, even as the logic behind the choice becomes forgotten to most users. Hence, the material distribution of clocks and calendars plays an important role in the self-regulation of behavior according to culturally and artifactually reproduced standards. The currently dominant time standards associated with these ubiquitous artifacts, namely 24-hour days with hours of uniform duration and the Gregorian calendar, are derived from European and American efforts to manage and coordinate government affairs over large distances, such as in colonial empires or the global economy.

The present globally distributed and managed time system is not the result of a unilinear evolution of time concepts, but is instead the result of the ascendency of certain standards over others in the service of power or convenience. In Europe, until the Enlightenment, there were several timescales that were used. For instance, with regard to the measurement of the day, in many parts of Italy, the hours were counted from one to 24 starting about 30 minutes after sunrise; in Nuremberg, there were separate counts for daytime and nighttime hours; and the canonical hours that structured the liturgical day varied in length depending on seasonal differences in daylight. Most of these alternatives had disappeared by the end of the 19th century as national time standards supplanted local practices and time zones came into existence, and as the power of the Spanish and Holy Roman empires waned in relationship to the ascendency of British global hegemony—in terms of both colonialism and global trade.

The acceptance of the European timescale in its present form is not because of its consistency or superiority, then, a fact not as recognized in the West as among those with alternative time-reckoning traditions, such as those found in Islam, South Asia, and China. In fact, unlike most metrological scales, the European timescale is not scalable from the smallest unit to the largest. The SI second is the building block of the timescale. Even using the SI second, days are not of equal length. Since 1972, there has been a policy of adding a second to a preannounced day in order to reconcile the atomically generated timescale with Earth's slowing rotation. This second, known as the leap second, produces a day that is 86401 seconds long whenever it is implemented, in contrast to a normal day of 86400 seconds. With regard to the unit of the year, there are two different definitions used. The Julian year has an average length of 365.25 days, which is achieved by adding a day to the month of February every four years—a leap year. The Julian year is preferred by scientists measuring long durations into the past because it is a continuous, unbroken timescale. When the Gregorian calendar was implemented in 1582, it removed 10 days from that year in order to reconcile the calendar with the solar year, thereby making the Gregorian chronology a discontinuous timescale. The Gregorian year also has an average length of 365.25 days, which is achieved by having a leap year every fourth year except for years that are divisible by 100 but not by 400 (the year 2000 was a leap year, but 2100 will not be a leap year). So, it is not always the case that 86400 SI seconds equals a day, or that 365 days equals a year, or that every century is of equal length. There is only precise scalability from the second to smaller units, not from the second to larger units.

The currently dominant European timescale is a hodgepodge of ideas including the 24-hour day (an ancient Egyptian idea), the 60-minute hour and 60-second minute (a Babylonian idea), the decimalized increments of less than a second (an inheritance from the French Revolution), the Roman calendar adjusted by a pope, and the use of leap years and leap seconds to keep it all reconciled with the foibles of Earth's rotation and orbit. This system is what it is through the reproduction of cultural knowledge that has produced a sedimentation of ideas about time measurement embedded in and reproduced by timekeeping artifacts, not by a deliberative process to invent coherent standards like those that produced metric units of measure. In contrast to our historically sedimented and cobbled together inherited timescales, the metric system is a product of metrological deliberation that involves units that are easily scalable with absolute precision into larger and smaller units.

To those who produce and distribute timescales, the choices behind the creation of the representation of time are recognized, as well as the awareness that the representation could be different. While I was in the process of writing this chapter, National Geographic posted a video on the Internet that featured comments by Demetrios Matsakis, the head of the Time Service at the United States Naval Observatory, and consequently the person in charge of overseeing many of the world's most accurate, precise, and important atomic clocks. In this video, Dr. Matsakis reflects on his own ideas of time: "I've never liked to carry watches: I don't really want to confine my concept of time to the measurement. If I'm too obsessed with the measurement, I could lose track of the big idea, and also lose track of my own innate sense of time" (2015). He is not alone among time scientists in his distinction between the idea of time and the measurement of time. Claude Audoin and Bernard Guinot, two important time metrologists, with Guinot once having headed the Bureau International de l'Heure, write: "Let us admit that we do not know what time is. We know only that we need a temporal coordinate and three spatial coordinates to represent physical phenomena and invent mathematical models for them. Why these 4 independent coordinates and not 5, or more? It is quite simply because 4 are enough to ensure that no measurable inconsistency occurs in our physical model" (2001, 6). The great mathematician Henri Poincaré wrote: "[T]here is no way of measuring time that is truer than all others. The one that is generally adopted is merely the most convenient" (1907, 30).

Legal traceability of time

Among the sedimented legacies of metrological choices is the decision to choose the uniformity of atomic transitions rather than the variability of Earth's cycles as the foundation for the current timescale, UTC. In effect, time measurement is no longer directly tied to solar cycles. Guinot observes that the difference between true solar time and the time displayed on local clocks and watches can be on the order of hours (Guinot, 2011). As a result, there is no way to check one's clock against the position of the Sun to determine the clock's accuracy. Instead, the global timescale is a calculation that is made by the International Bureau of Weights and Measures (BIPM) and distributed by national time laboratories and private enterprise time services. In other words, the currently dominant timescale is a mathematical *product*, not a direct *observation* using measurement. By implication, there is no single clock that represents the global time standard, and no means by which an individual can verify the precision and accuracy of a clock representing UTC as time passes—one has to wait until the BIPM announces the results of its calculations in *Circular T* (see http://www.bipm.org/jsp/en/TimeFtp.jsp?TypePub=publication) to know how well a clock has been performing.

In light of metrology's creation of timescales, as Judah Levine notes: "[T]he legal and technical definitions of time are not precisely the same" (2001, 52). This leads Levine to concentrate on the idea of legal traceability of time. By legal traceability, Levine means the ability to determine that a representation of time is derived from a reliable time source. Since most clocks are of poor quality, with the clocks of most desktop and portable electronic devices wandering by up to 30 seconds per day without synchronization, the time source for synchronizing such devices is important in demonstrating their accuracy, and consequently the accuracy of the timestamps they generate.

Time metrologists pay great attention to managing the UTC timescale to ensure its precision, accuracy, and stability. In contrast, governments and courts pay far less attention to the relationship between law and the best time metrological practices. Indeed, for most judges, legislators and heads of state, the tendency is to take the time indicated by a clock for granted without concern about its origin or reliability. The common question of "When did an event take place?" is rarely, if ever, followed by the questions, "What is your timescale? What is your time source? And how reliable is your clock?"

There was a place and period in which there was greater awareness of legal traceability of time. As Rooney and Nye (2009) have shown, this was particularly an issue for those selling liquor in late 19th century Britain, since liquor licenses stipulated that such establishments must close by a particular time. Apparently, an inaccurate clock was not an excuse for escaping legal trouble if one were caught serving liquor after the legally defined established closing time. As a result, pubs sought to have reliable clocks with legally defensible times, which, in turn, led them to be among the most numerous of subscribers to the Standard Time Company's telegraph time service, which provided a time set to GMT.

The notion of pubs taking a leading role in raising awareness of the legal traceability of time seems odd, yet the recent history of timescales is not one of governments deliberating and creating time standards through law, but of particular groups seeking means to mitigate civil or criminal liability. This includes railroads that desired to coordinate train schedules in order to avoid collisions (Bartky, 2000); the aforementioned pubs seeking to avoid being charged with violating licensing laws (Rooney and Nye, 2009); and, most recently, high-frequency traders seeking to have timestamps of high precision (as much as at the nanosecond level) that are acceptable as accurate by regulatory agencies (Angel, 2014; Birth, 2016).

When it comes to actual laws about time standards, the usual sequence of events, then, is for timescale practices to precede legal codification by a generation or more, with legislation reflecting practice long after the fact. For instance, the current global timescale of UTC was adopted in the 1960s by the regulatory bodies responsible for time metrology (the General Conference on Weights and Measures) and time signal dissemination (Comité consultatif international pour la radio, now the Radiocommuncation Sector of the International Telecommunication Union), but it was only formally accepted by the United States in the America Competes Act of 2007. Yet, all the times recorded in UTC before that law was passed were legally accepted. UTC is still not the official time of the United Kingdom. Instead, the UK uses Greenwich Mean Time (GMT). GMT and UTC are synchronized presently, so their coexistence creates no confusion. Because the history of time policies of the last 60 years has involved ongoing debates and policy changes, however, the future synchronization of GMT and UTC cannot be assumed. Indeed, the current proposal to eliminate the leap second policy would decouple GMT and UTC, creating a problem not only in the UK, but also in other countries that officially recognize GMT and not UTC (see Seago et al., 2011; Gabor, 2013).

The power of global standards

Who makes these choices that then get imposed on the world? In the ancient world, control over time was an important component of political power (Stern, 2012). The Julian calendar was a reform promulgated by the emperor Julius Caesar himself. The current dominant calendar, the Gregorian calendar, was the result of a reform of the Julian calendar decreed in 1582 by means of a papal bull that enshrined the new calendar as ecclesiastical law to be followed by all Roman Catholics (Gregory the XIII, 2002; see also Ziggelaar, 1983).

While heads of state have played critical roles in developing or adopting timescales, current practice involves technocrats and scientists making recommendations that then are followed internationally. This was played out at the International Meridian Conference of 1884. This conference was called by the American government to settle global issues of mapping and timekeeping. It was held in Washington, DC, and was attended by delegates from the major independent nations of the time. As Barrows describes it, this conference was not merely scientific, but involved "the problematics of imperial control and global conceptualization" (2011, 4). Globalization of travel, trade, and information created pressure for global standards (Krislov, 1997; Quinn, 2012), and the forging of a global time standard was one part of this movement.

The conference addressed the issues of where to place the prime meridian for purposes of mapping and how to define "universal time"; a global time standard tied to the prime meridian. The scientists there emphasized that their decisions were nonbinding, such as on the second day when there was a cascade of delegates following the lead of Juan Valera, the delegate from Spain, who "announced that he had no power to pledge his country on this subject; that his authority merely extended to the power of recommending to his Government such resolutions as this Conference might adopt" (International Meridian Conference, 1884, 31).

In this gathering of distinguished scientists declaring that they had no power to decide anything for their respective nations, a prime meridian running through Greenwich, in England, was approved by all the delegates except those from San Domingo, France, and Brazil. Even though the vote was nonbinding, its quick adoption in navigational practice and chart making forced dissenting nations into a de facto, but not de jure, acceptance of the prime meridian as running through Greenwich.

After settling the prime meridian question, the conference dealt with more contentious matter: the universal day and universal time. There was widespread agreement for the need of such an idea, but disagreement about which meridian should be chosen for the start of the universal day. After much debate, a resolution passed that began the universal day at midnight at Greenwich's meridian. The support for this resolution was not as great as the support for defining the prime meridian—while there were 15 votes in favor, there were seven abstentions and two votes against, including France.

The choice was based on British global influence and US support for the UK's position. Many of the "international" delegates had close ties to the UK and the US. For instance, the representative for Colombia was the superintendent of the US Naval Observatory, and the representative of Paraguay was Scottish. Moreover, in 1884 time standards were still closely tied to astronomical observation, and there was nothing about Greenwich as a smoggy, foggy suburb of London to make it the ideal location for such observations other than the presence of the Royal Observatory there, but there *were* other equally advanced observatories at the time, such as the Paris Observatory.

The 1884 conference also showed Eurocentrism in how the world was imagined. Inherent in the prime meridian and universal day decisions was global prominence being given to Europe for purposes of time and cartography. This was manifest in the tone of British apologists for the policies. In the journal *Nature*'s summary of the conference, the English astronomer William Ellis wrote: "[T]he change of universal date occurs at an hour well away from business hours. Only in New Zealand would there be inconvenience, the change of universal date occurring at civil noon" (Ellis, 1884, 10). In 1886, the British Astronomer Royal Christie wrote: "The advantage of making the world day coincide with the Greenwich civil day is that the change of date at the commencement of a new day falls in the hours of the night throughout Europe, Africa, and Asia, and that it does not occur in the ordinary office hours (10 a.m. to 4 p.m.) in any important country except New Zealand" (Christie, 1886, 523).

Today, office hours have expanded, and midnight UTC now corresponds to the beginning of the business day in East Asia. While nobody today argues that East Asian countries are not "important," Christie's logic of the relative importance of nations for purposes of defining time remains at the foundation of the globally distributed timescale, and it continues to manifest itself not only in the definition of UTC, but also in policies for implementing leap seconds to reconcile the atomically determined timescale with Earth's slightly variable rotation. For instance, on June 30, 2015, at 11:59:59 PM UTC, a leap second was inserted, but in Japan, this UTC time was the local time of 8:59:59 AM on July 1—a midweek business day on the first of the month, one second before the opening of banks and stock exchanges.

Imposition of standards

The decisions of the International Meridian Conference of 1884 left the legal issue of the relationship of local time to universal time unresolved. In many nations, the local meridian still determined legal time, with every degree difference in longitude resulting in a three-minute time difference (see Ellis, 1884). The problem of different times associated with different meridians had already arisen in British law in the case of *Curtis v. March* (157 Engl. Rep. 719). In this case, the local municipal time differed from the official court time in Dorchester, resulting in a defendant missing his trial. On appeal, a decision was made in favor of the defendant who, in using the local time, was using the time determined by the sun, whereas the court had erroneously used the time at the Greenwich meridian (see also Parrish, 2002). This precedent did not last long in the UK, for in the creation of the first legally defined time zone, the time at the Greenwich meridian was made the official time for the whole of Britain in 1880. This relieved confusion, for, as one barrister wrote: "Formerly, the justices were not bound to follow Greenwich time, but followed the medium time of the place, as in *Curtis v. March* ... But now, whenever any expression of time occurs in any Act of Parliament, deed, or other legal instrument, unless it is otherwise specifically stated, this shall mean in Great Britain Greenwich time: 43 & 44 Vict. C. 9, s. 1" (Patterson, 1889, 151).

In contrast with the UK, in 1890, Wilhelm Nordling documented ongoing confusion in continental Europe. He pointed out that Portugal and Spain had adopted Greenwich time as their official time (1890, 135). Switzerland, by way of contrast, had adopted three different time standards—the German, the Austrian, and the Italian (1890, 136). France was still holding on to its national time as determined by the Paris meridian, but Nordling urged France to join the same time zone as England (1890, 137). In Hungary, the railroad spanning the Austro-Hungarian Empire had adopted a single time that differed from Budapest time, despite Hungarians' "jealous" attachment to Budapest time (1890, 134). From Nordling's account, it is clear that governments were slow to catch up to what was happening in the regulation and distribution of time. Business, and particularly railroads, were adopting times different from the national times, but because of the importance of the railroads, their times were becoming the de facto official times.

In the US, there was also ongoing confusion. The case of *Salt Lake City v. Robinson* in 1911 is an example. In this case, a saloon owner was prosecuted for selling beer after midnight. As the case reads: "The policeman who made the arrest, and who apparently apprehended the appellant while in the act of selling the beer in question, testified in substance that the sale occurred 'at twenty or twenty-five minutes after twelve,' midnight; that he looked at his watch at the time, and that it was regulated according to the time that is generally observed in Salt Lake City" (State of Utah, 1913, 264). In response, the saloon owner argued that midnight was when the sun was at its "nadir," which is opposite the sun's "zenith"—in effect, that midnight is defined by the sun's relationship to the local meridian and not according to the clock. The court was forced to consider which time applied to the statute: the time of the standard mountain time zone as used by the city of Salt Lake City, or the apparent solar time. The court decided in favor of clock time. The dissenting opinion pointed to the ambiguity generated by the fact that the city statute had not specifically mentioned whether the term "midnight" meant solar midnight or standard mountain time midnight.

Such temporal pluralism was untenable, and eventually law caught up to the time standards that railroads, mapmakers, and telegraph companies had adopted after 1884. Their practices became the de facto standards that governments were eventually compelled to accept.

For instance, even though France was resolutely against accepting the prime meridian being the Greenwich meridian, and against the universal day starting at that meridian, participation in international commerce compelled France to reconcile itself with GMT. By 1911, France legally adopted a workaround that would retain a distinctive French meridian while at the same time reconciling that meridian with the prime meridian the rest of the world was using. This law decreed that for timekeeping purposes the prime meridian ran through the Paris Observatory and that the time tied to it would be adjusted by nine minutes and 25 seconds. This resulted in official French time coinciding with the time of the Greenwich meridian. In a bit of pique about metrological politics, the legislation also decreed that France would only officially recognize the prime meridian as running through Greenwich once the United Kingdom adopted the metric system (see *Le Figaro*, 1911, 1). As a result, France officially acknowledged the prime meridian in 1978 without fanfare or even much public awareness.

The leap second

Now, in 2018, the idea of global time is undergoing another extralegal transformation with legal consequences. Since the 1990s there has been a debate about whether or not to keep the leap second policy. This policy was put in place to reconcile extremely precise atomic timekeeping with the foibles of Earth's rotation. Since Earth's rotation is slowing down at an unpredictable rate, when its rotation is projected to deviate from the atomic timescale by. 9 of a second, a second is added to the atomically generated timescale of UTC.

With the increased use of networked computing in the 1990s, the leap second began to pose a problem. Computers do not care about Earth's rotation and function best with an unadjusted timescale. Adding a second at irregular intervals requires ad hoc patches to ensure smooth computer functioning.

Without the proper implementation of the patches, computer networks crash as they send and receive unexpected timestamps.

The leap second debate has dragged on since 2001, when the ITU-R first proposed eliminating the policy. The ITU-R is a United Nations agency responsible for global telecommunications. The history of its jurisdiction is associated with the distribution of precision timing. In the early 20th century, precision timing was broadcast by radio and used for the tuning of radio frequencies. This clearly placed the dissemination of timescales and their use under the governance of agencies concerned with broadcast signals. This led to the formation of the Comité Consultatif International pour la Radio (CCIR) in 1927. In 1932, it merged with another body involved in the distribution of global time signals, the International Telegraph Union, and it became known as the International Telecommunications Union (ITU), with the CCIR existing as a subsection concerned with radio communications. In 1992, the CCIR was renamed the Radiocommunciation Sector of the ITU (ITU-R). As timescale distribution shifted from telegraph to radio, and later to computer signals, the CCIR/ITU-R continued to manage global discussions over timescale distribution. Like the International Meridian Conference of 1884, resolutions of the ITU-R are nonbinding but have a way of becoming international standards for telecommunications that then force all governments to comply.

While the ITU-R has jurisdiction over the distribution of time signals and what time signal is to be distributed, it does not produce a timescale. Instead, the BIPM calculates UTC with a weighted algorithm using input from atomic clocks around the world. Its monthly report, *Circular T*, includes tables indicating the accuracy of time produced by the time laboratories that contribute to the calculation of UTC. The BIPM and ITU-R are independent but intertwined: the BIPM defers to the ITU-R on policies about timescale dissemination, and the ITU-R defers to the BIPM on issues of timescale maintenance and creation.

The most widely accessed source of time information is GPS—a timescale not emanating directly from the BIPM. GPS is a US military technology made available for civilian use in the 1990s. While it is known as a navigational tool, it consists of clocks in orbit that send time signals. GPS receivers synchronize with the orbiting satellite network, and then record time signals from multiple GPS satellites in known positions. The time the signal takes to arrive at the receiver is used to indicate the receiver's distance from that satellite's location. By using time signals from multiple satellites, it is possible to triangulate one's position with great precision.

GPS time is not UTC, and as a system of distributing time signals, it is not regulated by the ITU-R. Instead, it has its own timescale that GPS receivers then convert to UTC (Levine, 2001, 56). GPS time is steered to maintain its accuracy, and because GPS signals are available in most parts of the globe, GPS is, in fact, the most easily accessed source of accurate time for most of the world.

This has led to a question about whether GPS-generated time should be legally recognized as equivalent to the official global time standard of UTC. Levine's argument about the legal traceability of time is meant to address this concern. He points out that the BIPM only publishes what UTC *was* and the difference between UTC and time laboratories once per month, so that, in fact, the real-time source of time is not the BIPM, but these time laboratories. Moreover, these laboratories steer their clocks to synchronize it with UTC as reported by the BIPM (2001, 53). Because of this concerted global effort to maintain a precise, accurate, and stable timescale, since 1999 there has been an agreement among many time laboratories to accept one another's measurements as equivalent (Levine 2001, 54). Since GPS time is derived from time laboratories in the United States, its source of time is globally recognized and, therefore, according to Levine, GPS time is a legally traceable time. This begs the question of whether GPS or UTC takes precedence when there is a difference between them. Until now, since such a difference would be only a few nanoseconds (ns), it has not been a significant concern, but as the frontiers of precision are pushed to finer and finer units, a difference of a billionth of a second becomes more relevant. This is particularly true as big data sets, such as the NASDAQ data feed TotalView-ITCH, timestamp trades to the level of a nanosecond (NASDAQ, 2014, 2; Birth, 2016).

New frontiers

GPS as a de facto but not quite de jure global standard traceable to accepted global standards is fostering a new frontier in time regulation that threatens to proliferate private and proprietary timescales. It is currently possible for institutions to afford their own precision timekeepers, and the manufacturing and sale of both high-quality crystal oscillators and atomic clocks sustains several companies such as Symmetricon and Meinberg. With this development has come a new time protocol for generating timestamps and synchronizing local computer networks that takes advantage of the new levels of precision that are commercially available. This time protocol, IEEE 1588/PTP, uses local high-precision clocks synchronized to GPS satellites and keeping a timescale that is a simulacrum of International Atomic Time (TAI). When the local network must deal with another network, the local version of TAI is converted to UTC by adding the known offset published in *Circular T*. This local TAI is not TAI, however. The BIPM does not distribute TAI, only its offset from UTC.

The GPS-synchronized pseudo-TAI converted into UTC that is the timescale used by PTP systems produces timestamps acceptable to auditors and regulators. The legitimacy granted to these timestamps by such officials keeps their users from getting prosecuted (Angel, 2014). Yet, in a world where timestamps with ns precision are increasingly common, and in which billions of dollars can be gained or lost in milliseconds, the possibility of fraudulent timestamps in the millisecond to nanosecond range, in order to alter in the official record the actual sequence of events, must be considered as a very real possibility and as something that would be impossible to prove much less prosecute. This is because the range of accepted variability for any timestamp has to take into account that no clock is perfect, and that even the best performing time laboratories are often several ns off the official UTC as calculated by the BIPM. As a result, fraudulent timestamps in the range of a few ns can be hidden because they are within the range of accepted variability (Birth, 2016).

Even now, those in the computer science and engineering fields find themselves having to develop their own standards for computer hardware and software. As a result, the Institute of Electrical and Electronics Engineers (IEEE) has created a set of standards known as POSIX that contains time protocol standards that deal with how timestamp information is represented in binary, how computer time is synchronized, and the legitimacy of timestamps. Timescale practices are the result of politicized scientific and technological processes. They involve cultural assumptions about time and science, as well as conflict and competition between national interests. Decisions by these institutions are viewed as legitimate even though they are not enshrined in law or legal precedent. In a sense, legally, they are common time.

Yet, there is another level of activity that muddies the waters of law, policy, and practice. There are many systems administrators of computer networks who see their role as primarily to avoid trouble. A consequence of this is that their relationship to timekeeping is not always at the highest level of knowledge, much less participation in how timescales are developed and implemented. Instead, to them, the leap second is a challenge—even a problem—to be addressed with a fix. Since leap seconds do not come at regular intervals and are announced six months before their implementation, the fix involves developing a patch or other strategy to implement the second without causing a network failure caused by the generation of unacceptable timestamps. For some computer programmers, this is a worthy challenge that they relish meeting (see Main, 2013; Stenn, 2013); for others, it is a nasty problem, such as when the Qantas airline reservation system crashed because of incorrect leap second implementation in 2012.

The 2015 leap second was an example of how divergent practices are becoming. The leap was announced for midnight on June 30, 2015. There is no nation that legislates how the leap second is to be implemented. Instead, the standard practice, as reflected in Network Time Protocol, and based on ITU-R recommendations, is to insert the extra second after 11:59:59 UTC. In past leap second implementations, this insertion of an entire second has created problems. As a result, several notable entities, such as Japanese stock markets and Google, adopted what has come to be known as a leap smear. Instead of implementing the leap second all at once, they implement it in small increments leading up to 11:59:59 UTC, so that by 12:00:00 UTC, the leap second has been fully inserted. In the case of Japan, this leap smear was done in order to ensure stability for the opening of the Japanese business day, since 12:00:00 UTC was, in fact, nine in the morning in Japan and the time of the opening bell on the Tokyo stock exchange.

Postcolonial dimensions

Time metrologists worry about a proliferation of timescales to meet local needs of stability and precision, but there is another set of issues that would add a yet another dimension of temporal pluralism to the issue of legal pluralism. The structures that reproduce Euro-American domination over time standards are coming under increased scrutiny. While UTC is calculated from clocks distributed around the world, *Circular T*'s list of time laboratories is clearly skewed in favor of Europe and North America, with fewer contributors from the southern hemisphere or Pacific Rim nations. The implementation of leap seconds at midnight UTC occurs at a time that is difficult and disruptive for many Pacific Rim countries. GPS is a US military technology that serves as a de facto time source for much of the globe. The prime meridian is in the UK because of colonialism, not because Greenwich was the best place on the globe to make astronomical observations from. UTC is not the time of the world, but is the time the West has used to manage global affairs. How long can this last?

Examples of "anti-imperial" time are starting to increase. One form has been nations that define time zones unique to themselves, which Venezuela did in 2007. Another form has been representation, such as when Bolivia made the clock on its legislative palace run counterclockwise in 2014. Probably an even greater threat to the maintenance of globally uniform standards is the proposal suggested by Dr. Han Chunhao of China in early 2015, at a conference about the leap second. He put forth an argument that traditional Chinese time reckoning was as scientific as Western time reckoning. Consequently, if the leap second were abolished, and UTC were severed from rotational time, then there should be Earth orientation data transmitted globally to ensure that time systems such as that of China could be maintained. In effect, Western timekeeping logics should not be privileged over Chinese logics.

Conclusion

Current United States law only specifies the legal traceability of time to a reliable time source in few domains—telecommunications and securities exchange. In securities exchange, the time source must be the National Institute of Standards and Technology (NIST) and have a millisecond level of precision even though most high-frequency trading has the capability of timestamps at the level of nanoseconds. Many traders already technically deviate from this standard by using GPS and the time source for their PTP systems. GPS is traceable to the United States Naval Observatory (UNSO), not to the NIST. This is not a problem since both the USNO and NIST produce simulacra of UTC, and, consequently, are typically within a fraction of a nanosecond of one another. With regard to other elements of law that more people are likely to encounter, such as deadlines, there is no attention to legal traceability of time. In fact, even in securities trading, the users of timescales who are acutely concerned about the quality of their time often have standards far higher than those of regulators and the courts. Historically, it has been constituencies such as pubs, railroads, and securities traders that have been most concerned with legal traceability. Legal traceability, then, has not emerged to serve the legal system, but to serve those concerned about legal interventions. As business interests have come to transcend borders, so have the standards that permit legal traceability become supranational.

With current technology, computers can execute commands more quickly than the human brain can perceive them. In the case of high-frequency trading, we only know the sequence and amount of trades after they take place. The ontological status of these sequences is based on the quality and legal traceability of the timestamps that determine the sequence. If a case can be made that a timestamp is a legitimate UTC timestamp, then it is beyond question, yet the reality of clock drift and transmission delays and even relativity make the legitimacy of timestamps at the level of precision that is currently claimed dubious at best. The frontier of legal traceability and the construction of standards of dubious ontological merit that are legally unchallenged is the creation of illusions of precision over large distances. The theory of relativity suggests that a global absolute time is an illusion. Even so, at least one private equity firm has been public about its attempts to use PTP with its nanosecond timestamps across a global network (Estrela and Bonebakker, 2012).

This is occurring at the same moment that the Eurocentric hegemony structurally latent in time standards is becoming more widely recognized and challenged. The debate over the leap second indicates this complicated tangle of those seeking global precision timekeeping associated with computing and those challenging the influence of the United States over time standards. The elimination of the leap second policy was set to be voted on in 2012 at the World Radiocommunication Conference (WRC), but a behind-the-scenes straw poll indicated that the majority of delegates would abstain. Instead, a resolution was passed calling for further study of the leap second issue, even though the leap second issue is one of the most studied and discussed issues ever to come before the WRC. Based on the position stated by China's Dr. Han, even if the leap second were abolished, that would not stem the tide of the proliferation of timescales. To date, law has taken time for granted, but we may be entering a period in which temporal pluralism adds new and possibly confusing dimensions to legal pluralism.

Bibliography

Abbott, K.W. and Snidal, D. (2000). Hard and Soft Law in International Governance. *International Organization* 54(3), pp.421–456.

Angel, J. (2014). When Finance Meets Physics: The Impact of the Speed of Light on Financial Markets and their Regulation. *Financial Review* 49, pp.271–281.

Audoin, C. and Guinot, B. (2001). *The Measurement of Time: Time, Frequency and the Atomic Clock*. Cambridge: Cambridge University Press.

Barrows, A. (2011). *The Cosmic Time of Empire: Modern Britain and World Literature*. Berkeley: University of California Press.

Bartky, I.R. (2000). *Selling the True Time: Nineteenth-Century Timekeeping in America*. Palo Alto, CA: Stanford University Press.

Birth, K. (2012). *Objects of Time: How Things Shape Temporality*. New York: Palgrave.

———. (2016). While the West Sleeps: Deglobed Globalization and its Consequences. In Huebener, P., O'Brien, S., Porter, T., Stockdale, L. and Zhou, Y. R. (Eds.) *Time Globalization and Human Experience*. pp.109–126. London: Routledge.

Callon, M. and Muniesa, F. (2005). Economic Markets as Calculative Collective Devices. *Organization Studies* 26(8), pp.1229–1250.

Christie, W.H.M. (1886). Universal or World Time. *Nature* April 1, pp.521–523.

Curtis *v.* March. (1916).*The English Reports*, v. 157: 719–720. Edinburgh: W. Green and Son.

Ellis, W. (1884). The Prime Meridian Conference. *Nature* November 6, pp.7–10.

Estrela, P.V. and Bonebakker, L. (2012). Challenges Deploying PTPv2 in a Global Financial Company. In *2012 International IEEE Symposium on Precision Clock Synchronization for Measurement Control and Communication*. http://ieeexplore.ieee.org/stamp/stamp.jsp?arnumber=6336634.

Foucault, M. (2008). *The Birth of Biopolitics*. New York: Palgrave Macmillan.

Gabor, P. (2013). Diplomacy of Legal Translations. In Seago, J.H., Seaman, R.L., Seidelmann, P.K. and Allen, S.L. (Eds.) *Requirements for UTC and Civil Timekeeping on Earth*. pp.51–62. American Astronautical Society, Science and Technology Series, 115.

Gregory the XIII. (2002). *Inter Gravissimus*. http://www.bluewaterarts.com/calendar/NewInterGravissimas.htm.

Guinot, B. (2011). Solar Time, Legal Time, Time in Use. *Metrologia* 48: S181–185.

Han C. (2013). Space Odyssey: Time-scales and Global Navigation Satellite Systems. *ITU News* 7, September.

International Meridian Conference. (1884). *International Conference Held at Washington for the Purpose of Fixing a Prime Meridian and a Universal Day: Protocols of the Proceedings*. Washington, D C: Gibson Bros.

Krislov, S. (1997). *How Nations Choose Product Standards and Standards Change Nations*. Pittsburgh: University of Pittsburgh Press.

Loconto, A. and Busch, L. (2010). Standards, Techno-economic Networks, and Playing Fields: Performing the Global Market Economy, *Review of International Political Economy* 17, 3, pp.507–536.

Le Figaro. (1911). L'Heure Anglais. *Le Figaro* March 11, p.1.

Levine, J. (2001). GPS and the Legal Traceability of Time. *GPS World* January, pp.52–57.

Main, A. (2013). Programming Persepctive on Time Scales. In Seago, J.H., Seaman, R.L., Seidelmann, P.K. and Allen, S.L. (Eds.) *Requirements for UTC and Civil Timekeeping on Earth*. pp.235–257. American Astronautical Society Science and Technology Series, 115.

Matsakis, D. (2015). Maybe Time Doesn't Even Exist. *National Geographic Society*. http://video.nationalgeographic.com/video/news/150722-time-clock-matsakis-observatory-vin.

McCarthy, D. and Seidelmann, P.K. (2009). *Time: From Earth Rotation to Atomic Physics*. Weinheim: Wiley-VCH.

NASDAQ. (2014). NASDAQ TotalView-ITCH 4.1. www.nasdaqtrader.com/content/technical support/specifications/data products/NQTV-ITCH-V4_1.pdf.

Nordling, M.W.de. (1890). L'unification des heures. *Bulletin de la Société de Géographie* (Paris) 11 (7th series), pp.111–137.

Parrish, J. (2002). Litigating Time in America at the Turn of the Twentieth Century. *Akron Law Review* 36, 1, pp.1–47.

Patterson, J. (1889). *The Intoxicating Liquor Licensing Acts, 1872, 1874* (seventh edition). London: Shaw &Sons

Poincaré, H. (1907). *The Value of Science*. George Bruce Halsted, trans. New York: Science Press.

Quinn, T. (2012). *From Artefacts to Atoms: The BIPM and the Search for Ultimate Measurement Standards*. Oxford: Oxford University Press.

Rooney, D. and Nye, J. (2009). 'Greenwich Observatory Time for the Public Benefit': Standard Time and Victorian Networks of Regulation. *British Society for the History of Science* 42(1), pp.5–30.

Seago, J.H., Seidelmann, P.K. and Allen, S. (2011). Legislative Specifications for Coordinating with Universal Time. In Seago, J.H., Seaman, R.L. and Allen, S.L. (Eds.) *Decoupling Civil Timekeeping From Earth Rotation*. pp.29–48. American Astronautical Society (AAS) Science and Technology Series, 115.

State of Utah. (1913). *Reports of Cases Decided in the Supreme Court of the State of Utah, Volume XXXIX, March 1911 to December 1911*. Chicago: Callaghan & Company.

Stenn, H. (2013). Time, Timestamps, and Timescales. In Seago, J.H., Seaman, R.L., Seidelmann, P.K. and Allen, S.L. (Eds.) *Requirements for UTC and Civil Timekeeping on Earth*. pp.259–268.American Astronautical Society Science and Technology Series, 115.

Stern, S. (2012). *Calendars in Antiquity*. Oxford: Oxford University Press.

Ziggelaar, A. (1983). The Papal Bull of 1582 Promulgating a Reform of the Calendar. In Coyne, G.V., Hoskin, M.A. and Pedersen,O. (Eds.) *Gregorian Reform of the Calendar*. pp.201–239. Vatican: Pontificia Academia Scientiarum.

11 Energy governance, risk and temporality

The construction of energy time through law and regulation

Antti Silvast, Mikko Jalas and Jenny Rinkinen

Introduction

Over the past decade, scholarship on time, temporality, and law has made significant progress. Different studies on various areas – from global financial markets (Riles, 2011) to employment laws (Grabham, 2016), social theory (Greenhouse, 2014), and biosciences (Brown & Beynon-Jones, 2012) – have unpacked mundane technicalities of law, the specific temporalities that they enact, and their wider effects on politics and governance. These critical and detailed analyses have shown specific impacts that legal techniques have on social time and experiential time (Greenhouse, 2014; Grabham, 2016), and discovered wide gaps between the "reactive" time of policy cultures and the "day-to-day" time of activities such as scientific practice (Brown & Beynon-Jones, 2012). Temporalities are shaped together with laws in myriad often hidden ways. For example, global financial markets – seemingly imbued by real-time trading and just-in-time decisions – would not function in the same manner without the ongoing and routine work of specialized legal technicians (Riles, 2011). Our chapter complements, and advances these discussions by covering a closely related topic that has not often been explored in scholarship on law, regulation, and time: the governance of the energy infrastructure by national law and systems operating today on international electric power markets. Using energy infrastructures and power markets in Finland and Scandinavia as an exemplar, we discuss how state law and regulation of the energy infrastructure has changed historically, especially in reaction to critical policy events and risks; how these legal practices have enacted very different temporalities of energy; and how they may generate specific social and economic effects among energy companies and end users more widely in so doing.

The relationships between infrastructure and temporality (e.g. Star, 1999; Edwards, 2003; Bowker, 2015; Karasti et al, 2016) and between infrastructure, law, and regulation (e.g. Hughes, 1983; Hirsh, 1999; Darby, 2012; Breslau, 2013) are well-established in Science and Technology Studies (STS), energy anthropology, history of technology, and infrastructure studies literature. However, very few studies have brought together infrastructure, temporality, and law and regulation under one scope (see Ialenti, 2014, for a notable exception). Our chapter develops work on this intersection and builds on our earlier analyses on the rhythms of infrastructure (Jalas et al, 2016). It contributes to an understanding of the temporalities of governance in a variety of ways. First, the chapter introduces a new topic by adopting the study of law and time and exploring these themes among mundane legal technicalities of governing infrastructure. Second, by detailing these technical arrangements, we aim to show what may be original and specific about infrastructure governance in relation to the more general advances in temporalities and law literature (see also Grabham, 2016: 382). Third, our chapter discusses interconnections between this legally based energy time and everyday life. Here, we argue that the technicalities of energy law are not merely abstractions, but can create tangible conditions for how everyday folk and energy company staff manage and use energy, act on its risks, and are compensated or have to compensate for disruptive events such as electric power failures, as the chapter demonstrates.

Our method of addressing these concerns builds on earlier mainly anthropological and urban geography literature on critical infrastructure protection (Collier, 2008; Collier & Lakoff, 2008) and public and market logics in infrastructure provision (Graham & Marvin, 2001). Like these studies, we situate an interest in how experts enact infrastructure risks by using specialized *techniques of governance* (O'Malley, 2004). Typical examples are statistical and probabilistic calculations, foresight technologies, and the construction of scenario models. These enact the temporality of future hazards in distinct manners: probabilistics foresee uncertain future events via calculations of past events, scenarios enact the future by present imaginative thinking (Collier & Lakoff, 2008). A topical energy-related example is weather forecast technology: emerging "smart" electricity grids try to integrate weather forecast technology with electricity markets, hence combining the temporality of markets with the temporality of foresight through specialized techniques of governance.

This focus on governance requires an approach that does not stop with the question of which procedures are necessary to reach energy policy goals effectively (cf. Froggatt & Hadfield, 2015). Instead, we pay more particular attention to the rationales for control, and the subjects, that techniques of governance produce: including expectations about the characteristics and actions of energy sector actors and energy consumers; how they should govern themselves and anticipate unforeseen events; and how their behaviors can be sustained and changed. To understand these issues, we further draw from the earlier studies by taking a longitudinal, historical view and present a comparative analysis of two distinct historical periods in governing Finnish electricity provisions.

The first period starts from the oil price crises of the 1970s, an often acknowledged disruptive event to the energy sector. As we show, this event shifted the previous expectations of expanding energy systems over space and gave much more attention to the temporality of energy supply, especially attempts at securing its future stability. The oil crises in Finland led to centralized control of energy, from 1979 to 1995, when a temporality of prior preparedness was deeply inscribed in national laws. These laws sought to anticipate future electricity needs and infrastructure investments and design robust energy systems by society-wide planning procedures. Their overarching goal was to maximize society's electricity security – while still maintaining economically and technically feasible systems.

The second period starts in 1995 when the Finnish electricity provision was liberalized and opened to competitive entry. From then until around 2013, electricity law and regulation mainly concerned ex facto reactions, such as real-time energy pricing and trading on more or less real-time energy markets. This was done to mitigate the effects of incidents such as peak energy demands, threats to functioning systems, and intermittent power generation after they had already occurred.

These issues of differing temporality suggest wider themes from social science literature on risk and society. While risk strengthened as a social science topic several decades ago, over the past 15 years more nuanced literature on this area has burgeoned. Scholars today distinguish between the governance of future calculable *risk* and incalculable *uncertainty* (O'Malley, 2004) and between diverse forms of anticipatory risk strategies from *precaution* to *preemption*, and *preparedness* (de Goede & Randalls 2009; Anderson, 2010). While these nuances are insightful and highly relevant, our chapter suggests another fundamental temporal distinction lies behind energy law in the Finnish and Scandinavian case. Drawing from Sweden's energy policy and its interpretation by energy scholar Björn Wallsten (2014; see also Berglund, 2009), we name the first temporality as *anticipation* of known threats and the second as *resilience* to both known and unanticipated threats. We focus on the tensions and complementarity of the two temporalities that are also recognized in longstanding debates on risk assessment and perception (e.g. UK Royal Society 1992: 155–157). By discussing the figurations of this debate in law and regulation, we contribute to wider social and ethical viewpoints on socio-technical systems and fairness in risk management.

The materials of our inquiry are mainly legislative documents from Finland, supplemented with respective laws in the European Union (Finland became a member in 1995) and energy regulations across Scandinavia (Finland shares with Sweden, Norway, and Denmark a market for trading in electricity generation). Additional materials are taken from historical research into energy systems, especially from Finland but also from Scandinavia, to a lesser extent.

The chapter begins by reviewing the role of temporality in earlier research in infrastructure studies and large technological systems, placing these perspectives alongside the subjects of law and time. We then briefly outline the history of Finnish electricity prior to its centralization in 1979 and describe the temporalities that law helped to enact during this period of a planned infrastructure. The last empirical part recounts how the infrastructure was liberalized after its centralized control and outlines key temporalities in the laws and regulations, including European and Scandinavian-wide arrangements, that have sought to increase the resilience of the electricity infrastructure operating on liberalized transnational energy markets. We also highlight how the temporality of anticipation found renewed importance after major national electric power failures in Finland, raising possible tensions with the more or less real-time temporalities of the free market. The concluding section discusses the differences between anticipation and resilience in the electricity infrastructure, asking whether the two temporalities form a continuum or whether their clearly differing goals should be made more explicit in energy policy discussions.

Infrastructures, time and law: Advances in science and technology studies

As technology histories have shown, large-scale systems such as electricity supplies are intrinsically tied with law. The earliest electricity operators were characteristically local, serving only small areas, and regulated mainly at this scale. Expanding electricity networks (capable of serving a city and larger regions) became not mere inventions or local technologies, however, but evolved into something systemic, a large socio-technical system. This definition implies that systems are composed of parts that can be managed and steered – frequently centrally (Hughes, 1983). For example, the electric grid is composed of physical infrastructures such as transformers and transmission lines, but also laws and regulation, organizations such as utility companies, scientific components such as university education and research programs, as well as natural resources such as mines (Hughes, 1989: 51).

Such large technologies shape many other parts of the society and adjust to them: it is, for example, feasible to think that laws and regulations emerge and are shaped together with those technologies that they aim to govern. Recent years' advances in "smart" energy metering have opened up new possibilities (e.g. real-time energy pricing, remote disconnection of customers), but also created new issues (e.g. privacy, fairness) that the European Commission expects to legislate at large (Darby, 2012). Hence, energy laws and regulations – rules with quasi-legislative powers – are reshaped by new technologies but also shape the infrastructure back: legislation remains among the key mechanisms for codifying energy market rules (Breslau, 2013) as well as for protecting certain parts of electricity networks from market competition (Hirsh, 1999).

The research on large-scale technical systems also addressed time, but in a very particular meaning; mainly as historic time (van der Vleuten, 2004). This research has focused on the gradual emergence of technical systems through invention, diffusion, and standardization, and on the eventual disappearance of the same system (Edwards, 2010: 10). In contrast, the way that large systems affect everyday rhythms has received less interest (cf. Jalas et al, 2016). Among the key exceptions is research in the field of infrastructure studies situated within wider STS scholarship. Some years ago, scholar Paul N. Edwards (2003) stated that infrastructures, although inconspicuous, affect the experience of time in fundamental ways:

> [I]nfrastructures possess the power to shape human time, shaping the preconditions under which we experience time's structure and its passage ... Societies build infrastructure, of course, but because of their endurance in time, infrastructures then become the more important force in structuring society.
>
> (Edwards, 2003: 195)

The intention here is not to reify time or to suggest that time is technologically determined by certain infrastructures and their effects. Rather, the patterning of time is an effect of coevolution and mutual adjustment of infrastructures and everyday life practices (Star, 1999). The infrastructure of private mobility is, for example, tied to the patterns of work and systems of food provisioning. As novelties are gradually integrated into everyday life and novices turn into routinized users of technology, infrastructure begins to act as a set of self-evident coordinates of the everyday. Stable, existing, and taken-for-granted infrastructures hence demand and reproduce routines, and structure the use of time.

Insofar as the service is uninterrupted, relatively cheap, and produced remotely, infrastructures can become opaque (Graham, 2012). If and when the infrastructure service is reliable enough, it can assert effects on other system parts and become elementary for the normal procedures of everyday life (Collier & Lakoff, 2008). Fast communication networks, for example, contribute to more mobile patters of work if, and only if, the service can be expected to be available. Reliability of universal infrastructure provision is hence a key political concern (Darby, 2012).

Once again, however, this is not meant as an inevitable modernization story of infrastructures expanding and changing social and experiential time in so doing. The development stories of infrastructures – and by implication, the temporalities that they shape – tend to be intricate and difficult to foresee (Bowker, 2015). The power infrastructure, for example, is re-emerging as a coordinating infrastructure as intermittent power production changes the availability and price of electricity. Infrastructure studies summarize by stating that infrastructures have a dual temporality: they are long-living and durable technologies, but also real-time projects in the making through continual design, maintenance, repair, and coordination (Star, 1999; Silvast & Virtanen, 2014; Karasti et al, 2016).

All infrastructures, and particularly infrastructure that is plagued with failures and interruptions, co-exist with alternative systems of provision and related alternative patternings of time (Trentmann, 2009). Hence, even if modern households are increasingly electrified and depend on uninterrupted delivery, practices of making do without also exist (Trentmann, 2009; Rinkinen, 2013; Silvast, 2017). It is, therefore, feasible to think that there are two temporal structures depending on whether a service is available or not, even if the service is at the same time "critical" and has many implications on other aspects of everyday life (Jalas et al, 2016). During electricity blackouts, normal divisions of, for example, work and leisure, break, as humans orient themselves to coping with the interrupted delivery. Previous studies have shown such alternative patterns in everyday life – exposing normally hidden routines and skills. In this chapter, we complement this focus by highlighting how also energy law and regulation builds alternative temporalities to functioning systems – such as prior preparedness planning or compensations for power failures after they have occurred – to reduce uncertainties in the energy infrastructure.

Many aspects of energy are shaped by major public controversies and possible disruptive change, from sustainability transitions to nuclear disasters and the siting of onshore wind farms (Silvast et al, 2013), but energy law is a seemingly less conspicuous research subject. While clearly part of socio-technical energy systems as mentioned, laws of energy supplies, as anthropologist Vincent Ialenti (2014: 30) points out in the case of siting nuclear waste, "have long remained largely uncontroversial, undisputed, and unanalyzed within relevant literatures in STS (Science and Technology Studies), anthropology, and related fields." Similarly to Ialenti, who also situates an interest in risk and energy time, we seek to make hitherto neglected electricity laws more visible for scrutiny and draw on a STS approach that views legislation and energy time in practice alongside their specific potential effects on everyday life (Shove et al, 2012). Ialenti's (2014: 27) research on nuclear waste concerned "unique regulatory horizons that extended millennia into the future." The legal and regulatory horizon we will look at is the next decades of infrastructure planning and the more real-time competition on free power markets.

In this first analysis of a new research subject, we attain this aim by placing electricity legislation in Finland in historical context and detailing how the temporality of threats to functioning infrastructure was enacted in two periods. As manifest in laws and regulation, the legislation in these periods compromised between guaranteed system security and market competition in distinct ways (O'Malley 2004); by relying more on centralized planning, in the first instance, and liberalized electricity supplies a few decades later, although, as we also show, the balance has continued to shift both ways.

Centralized infrastructures and certainty over time

From the 1950s to the 1970s, the development story of Finnish electricity infrastructure could be summarized as gradual expansion confronted by a sudden surprise: the 1970s oil crises. Compared with the Scandinavian countries, Finland was electrified relatively late (Thue, 1995). While its first electrified factories and electricity in cities appeared in the late 19th century, the key expansion of Finnish electricity infrastructure began after World War II (Myllyntaus, 1991). Over the decades that followed, the prices of fossil fuels dropped, Finland established a number of new water power plants, electricity imports were initiated first from Sweden in 1959, and then from the Soviet Union in 1961, and in 1969, there was a decision to build a Finnish nuclear power plant that became operational in 1977 (Jahkola, 1993: 67). The large part of Finnish electricity networks was built in the 1960s and the 1970s (Energiavirasto, 2011) and at this point electricity was mainly a spatial issue: the aim was spreading the electricity grid and the related energy services. By the 1970s, the increasingly electrified country had become critically dependent on imported oil, gas, and coal.

Finnish energy industries and users were strongly affected by the 1973 energy crisis due to the oil embargo by OAPEC. The oil price crisis triggered an interest in more diverse and dynamic energy markets, through which energy companies could not depend only on a single provider lest they became vulnerable to supply disruptions (Ruostetsaari, 1998: 29). By the same token, the crisis also emphasized the importance of long-term cooperation between electricity producers and public interventions to safeguard energy security. The Finnish Electricity Act of 1979, which replaced the former Act on Electricity Utilities from 1928, leant more towards public planning than the free markets, just like the Swedish energy policy from 1975 (Kaijser, 1994: 224).

The 1979 Finnish legislation enacted a statutory planning system of electricity supplies. It divided Finland into 20 *cooperation districts for electricity supply*, larger than any single city and managed by a regional committee of utilities, sellers, and producers (Sähkölaki, 1979: Section 4). The remit of these committees was producing a standardized plan for the purchases of electricity and for its distribution regions, which was annually approved by the Finnish Ministry of Trade and Industry. The nationally significant electricity production and transmission had its own respective planning arrangements by the government, the industries, and energy users, also annually confirmed, this time by the Finnish Government (Sähkölaki, 1979: Section 3).

The temporality in this centralized planning emphasized that a single actor took responsibility for electricity provision for an extended period at any one time. Only a single organizational actor could provide electricity: the *electricity utility*, "a company or an establishment that produces or distributes electricity or provides it for other than its own use" (Sähkölaki, 1979: Section 1). Requiring a ministerial permit from 15 to 40 years, the permission for operating an electricity utility could only be given to a Finnish citizen, a domestic community, or a domestic establishment (Sähkölaki, 1979: Section 2). The national and regional planning requirements were rarely well-defined in years, although the regional plans were required to address the next 5 years *at minimum* (Section 21). The national-level electricity supply negotiation board was nominated for 3 years at a time (Section 15), which was (and is) only 1 year less than the parliamentary political cycle in Finland.

Generally, this law's temporalities were oriented to future systems and how they would serve expected national, regional, and environmental needs. As the law's third section defined:

> The purpose of united action and planning in electricity supply is to maintain and develop an electricity production, transmission, and distribution system that acknowledges the needs of the state and the country's different parts and the environment and is economically and technically adequate.
>
> (Sähkölaki 1979: Section 3)

Notably while these practices aimed at attaining a robust electricity system in the future, the topic of supply security and risk remained almost absent from the Electricity Act of 1979. Implicitly, security seems to have meant purposing a robust national system that would withstand external shocks like import disruptions. Concrete electric power failures would later become a central factor behind the development of Finnish electricity legislation, as will be seen, but were only loosely referred to at this point.

In one section (12), a utility was required to guarantee that those needing electricity would receive it for their usual purposes, unless the circumstances were "exceptional or difficult." That this was the only point mentioning failures, blackouts, was perhaps understandable from the point of view of infrastructures, routines of use, and reliability: if the large part of Finnish electricity infrastructure had not yet been completed, its failures would not pose a key problem, legally or otherwise. In other words, electricity infrastructure had not yet become critical in a sense of uninterrupted power supply – the government first defined energy as a basic supply system in 1984, albeit even then they called it a "secondary support system" (Silvast, 2017). Hazards caused by electrical equipment failing and causing harm were clearly the main future risk anticipated in the 1979 legislation. This corresponds with the observation that when an infrastructure is being built, its equipment failures can be riskier to the users than disruptions that concern the whole system or its subsystems. The context for Section 12 provides a clear case of socio-technicality (Hughes, 1989); electrical technology interacted with emerging energy legislation.

Because the centralized planning was based on consensus between industries and the government (Ruostetsaari, 1998), it also allowed real-time competition to exist and even to thrive. In 1990, 5 years before energy market liberalization, Finland already had the most competitive, private, and profit-oriented electricity sector of the Nordic countries, according to some (Thue, 1995: 14). Part of its high-voltage transmission network was privately owned and private manufacturing companies produced around 35–40 percent of Finnish electricity. If anything, the 1979 law had tilted the balance to guarantees of future robustness more than competition between energy companies – which seems to have nonetheless continued in areas such as manufacturing and energy production. For various reasons, the balance turned the other way soon, but not neglecting the public issues that had figured in the earlier law. Rather than a radical privatization, this was more akin to a reprogramming of the infrastructure through microeconomic devices, as anthropologist Stephen Collier (2011) has shown, and which the law and its temporalities aptly demonstrates.

Private competition, public risks

It is a common conception that liberalization commits societies to the rhythms of international capitalism, with its clear focus on more or less real-time competition (de Goede, 2004). However, as scholarship on law and time has shown, liberalization programs are also attached to more old-fashioned, slower tempos such as personal responsibility, eligibility for support, and improvement of legislation (Greenhouse, 2014: 144). An empirical description of how liberalization works becomes a key concern to appreciate its temporalities and their implications.

The liberalization of financial markets had begun in Finland in the early 1980s, the commissions from the sales of petrol and diesel were deregulated in Finland in 1984, and the public oversight of electricity prices ended in 1988 (Ruostetsaari, 1998: 10). Further deregulation of other sectors including trains and postal services was envisioned by the government of the liberal conservative Prime Minister Harri Holkeri (1987–1991). Finnish electricity market liberalization, in its turn, was initiated in 1990 by the Finnish Ministry of Trade and Industry by founding an Electricity Utility Commission, followed by an Electricity Act Working Group in 1993. According to official designations, this policy work was started so that the ownership structures, organization, and functions of electricity utilities would be reconsidered and more competition would be created in the electricity distribution (Ruostetsaari, 1998: 41).

By the late 1980s investors had a rising interest in electricity utilities and several electricity utility sales and acquisitions had already been experienced (SENER 2000: 6). All Finnish electricity utilities were legal monopolies, most of them in a municipality, and sales became problematic: "the monopoly position raised the possibility of making the customers pay for the costs of electricity utility sales" (ibid). One issue closely related to that of acquisitions was vertical integration, i.e. the possibility that large electricity producers would acquire local electricity distribution and start providing as well as generating electricity (Kaijser, 1994: 231). Such integration was seen not to benefit users tied to monopolistic utilities and pricing; hence, the liberalization of electricity markets would be needed to engage consumers, again, by allowing competition between electricity suppliers (Ruostetsaari, 1998: 42; Summerton, 2004).

Starting from these different considerations, the Finnish policy bodies recommended that local electricity networks be opened to competitive entry by all energy generators and that retail sales of electricity be no longer a monopoly or subject to permit. Additionally, the Ministry of Trade and Industry suggested the regulation of the free electricity markets through a specific Energy Authority – resembling US energy markets, their private corporations, and utility commissions monitoring these companies (Hirsh, 1999). The two co-existing Finnish high-voltage electricity transmission companies would be given a legal system responsibility, which meant maintaining the stability of the national electricity transmission system (SENER, 2000: 7). Here, one begins to sense how the advent of free markets is actually what gives more prominence to the governance of security and risk (Collier, 2011), but codes them and their temporalities in new ways. The aforementioned 1979 Act did not mention responsibility for security other than in the context of centralized planning for *future* infrastructure. In the 1995 Electricity Market Act that opened electricity to competition in Finland, the temporality of security turned real time and created visible new present intervention possibilities to energy companies for the sake of reliability: "[T]he electricity market authority orders one or more grid operators to be responsible for the technical operability of Finland's electricity system. A grid operator who has systems responsibility may impose conditions on the use of the power plants and other network connected to the electricity transmission network." (Section 16, quotes checked from the most recent translation, Electricity Market Act 2004.)

In addition to these national-level grid operators, local *distribution system operators* were tasked with operating local electricity networks, placing the system at the disposal of anyone against payment, and making it possible to transport electricity from one "trade participant to another" (Section 1). Amid the commercial terminology, this arrangement remained permit based and a regional monopoly, but allowed operation for an open term, and with no requirement of being Finnish by the energy market authority rather than the ministry (Section 2). An *electricity seller*, in its turn, a person, community, or establishment, could either perform bulk sale of electricity to retailers and large consumers or retail sale of electricity directly to electricity consumers (Section 1). As the law required, these new actors also were to unbundle the electricity systems from trade by separation of "any electricity system operations from other electricity trade operations and the electricity trade operations from its other trade operations" (Section 28).

In terms of temporality, it seems at first that there was very little activity oriented to the future in this Act. The law contained several sections and clauses on financial arrangements, contracts, pricing, and open-ended permits, but all decisions happened seemingly in real time, among commercial and independent decision makers. This atemporality, however, was only partially the case. The Electricity Market Act set electricity distribution as a regulated network business, which was allowed a profit margin, which in its turn was meant to guarantee future infrastructure investments – a temporally tied concept.

Hence, the market legislation incorporated security in a specific manner as mentioned above. Similarly, it should be recalled that the earliest European electricity market legislation noted that market mechanism attains aims in an infrastructure including efficiency, security, competition, and environmental protection: "[T]he internal market in electricity is particularly important in order to increase efficiency in the production, transmission and distribution of this product, while reinforcing security of supply and the competitiveness of the European economy and respecting environmental protection" (European Parliament & Council, 1996: 4).

Since liberalization the balance has tilted both ways in terms of markets, security, and their temporalities. In a 1998 amendment to the Finnish Electricity Market Act (1998), the national electricity *systems responsibility* (Section 16) was added with the maintenance of a more financially framed *national balance responsibility* (Section 16b): hence, the responsibility for a national infrastructure was no longer merely about technical operability and reliability, but also about transparent and fair "terms of trade." By way of contrast, however, in 1999, the Act incorporated several new consumer protection considerations about electricity distribution's errors, responsibilities, and compensations (Sections 26c, d, e), one year after allowing small-scale consumers to choose their electricity supplier.

In 2001, two exceptionally strong storms (Pyry and Janika) struck Finland and doubled the yearly number of electricity supply interruptions compared to the whole previous decade (Kauppa- ja teollisuusministeriö, 2006: 29). An evaluation about these interruptions (Forstén, 2002) recommended that Finnish energy end users receive compensations from all blackouts that lasted longer than 12 hours, and this became operational in the electricity market act in 2003 (Section 27f). The aim was to "motivate electricity distribution owners to act in a manner that shortens the duration of interruptions" (Forstén, 2002, 31–32), and to this end the report also suggested a maximum duration of 6 hours for an electricity interruption "even in exceptional conditions" (ibid, 2). A few years later, the

Finnish Ministry of Trade and Industry suggested that customers or "entrepreneurs" critically dependent on electricity purchase their own private emergency power generators (Kauppa- ja teollisuusministeriö 2006, 56), although a similar idea had been afloat since 2002:

> Uninterruptable electricity distribution cannot be guaranteed. If the customer's production or other activities do not tolerate reasonable electricity distribution interruptions, then the customer should personally secure the electricity supply.
>
> (Forstén, 2002, 35)

But as unattainable as risk-free electricity distribution may be, since 2008, Finnish electricity network companies have been penalized financially for each electricity blackout according to market regulation – the longer the failure, the greater the penalty (Energiamarkkinavirasto, 2007). In all of these examples, the public common effect of a blackout has been transformed into a calculable risk in order to create a fair, transparent, and market-based way of distributing harms across all energy consumers.

The main temporalities that result from such measures consist of maximum durations for failures, leading to monetary compensations that are paid when these limits are not met and hence the programming of acceptable risk levels into legislation. Importantly, maximum durations and financial penalties do not attempt to prevent accidents from happening. Rather, the rationale is that these techniques of governance make electricity systems – and energy consumers – bounce back as fast as possible in a *resilient* manner after a ubiquitous infrastructure breaks down. The Scandinavian common power market, Nord Pool, offers a similar example: earlier the market was simply framed as means of profit (Nord Pool, 2010), now it is increasingly aimed at reducing financial impacts of unanticipated incidents, such as wind power intermittency, in real time (Nord Pool Spot, 2016). This focus on the real time suggests that risk and risk management are at the heart of energy markets and their activities, similarly to other financial areas: "The legitimacy of modern financial instruments and increasingly complex risk management techniques is provided by the argument that these developments provide security in the face of an uncertain (business) future" (de Goede, 2004: 213).

On a more critical note, one could argue that such mechanisms not only manage risk, but also create new possibilities for the social "sorting" of customers. When power failures are assigned a cost, however high that cost is, power companies may start to prioritize their repairs according to customers' willingness to pay for good-quality energy – a concern that some in the energy industry in Finland have had (Silvast, 2017). Such calculations of risk are based on a logic where infrastructures are not merely universal services, but also market commodities whose demand is controlled by their price (Graham & Marvin 2001; Darby, 2012). However, this more or less real-time price mechanism could generate new inequalities with people living in the margins of consumption behind expensive prime time.

These temporalities became entrenched and did not change drastically before the Finnish Electricity Market Act was overturned in 2013. In Finland, a major storm on Boxing Day 2011 initiated a blackout that momentarily affected 570,000 customers and lasted for days for tens of thousands of customers – at a potentially critical time of the year when electric heating can experience high demand. Provoking worries and critical comments in the media and by the Finnish government, the blackouts stressed the necessity of preventing similar storm damages in the future by burying electrical cables and considerably increasing monetary compensations for customer damages from blackouts. Hence, government policies seemed to assume that private companies could not be altogether trusted to prepare for a crisis. The biggest Finnish national newspaper summarized its similar impression just a few days after the storms: "[I]t is pointless to imagine that profit-seeking (electricity) companies would maintain any higher level of preparedness than what is absolutely necessary" (HS, 30 December 2011).

This was not the first major national electrical blackout in Finland initiated by storms and the winter weather – incidents like that had been experienced in the early 2000s and before and have continued to occur since. What was crucial, however, was the discussion in the media and the government, which switched the temporality of the issue. Rather than the Electricity Market Act and the Nordic energy markets, which had been vying for real-time *resilience* once the system needed to bounce back from disruption, in emerging commentaries the issue of power failing was again about *anticipation* of breakdowns. The new Electricity Market Act (2013), passed by the Finnish government, closely followed this risk rationale.

The new Act from 2013 stipulates that electricity network operators must make plans and prepare for non-normal situations. Moreover, they have to provide instructions to their customers in the event of an interruption to the electricity supply. Suppliers of electricity services are now required both to take precautionary measures in order to build robust systems that enable an uninterrupted supply and to build capacity for quickly restoring services in the case of failure. End users can be variously engaged in this emergency preparedness. Housing permits may, as in Finland for example, require that detached houses have to have auxiliary heating systems (Jalas et al, 2016). In other cases, end users are only advised to take more modest measures of preparedness such as having bottled water in the house and battery-powered communication devices.

As minor as these plans and measures may seem – the network operators, for example, are usually required to update their plans only once every 2 years – they indicate an important wider policy trend. Rather than the state retreating from the electricity markets and letting market actors participate in resilient actions, it is revealing that the government and its branches are getting back to setting the frame of how electricity operators prepare for future hazards – just like they did in 1979 in Finland, though the perceived risk is different now (power failures rather than modernization and safety of power grids). In these ways, the findings resemble other commentaries of how governments are committing to energy policies and identifying its drivers again after a decade of absence in their faith in free enterprising (Winskel & Radcliffe, 2014). As critical security and human geography scholarship suggests, this shift also lines up energy with catastrophic visions over "total threats", where the key temporality is of disruption or surprise – an uncertain or indeterminate future calls for burgeoning techniques of precaution (e.g. moratoriums), preemption (e.g. geo-engineering), and preparedness (e.g. emergency planning) (de Goede & Randalls, 2009; Anderson, 2010). Rather than the more visible conflicts and controversies around energy innovation and energy transition, energy legislation and its temporalities provides ample new materials to study these shifts in government priorities in action.

Discussion and conclusion

This chapter set out to elaborate on the way that laws reflect and can be used to study the relations between infrastructures and their users. The particular focus of this chapter has been the temporalities of electricity provision and use. Our analytical methods have stemmed from literature on governance, particularly its focus on *governing techniques* – the various tools that make governing aspirations operational and sometimes reveal new policy problems in so doing, such as preparedness planning, foresight, and economic modelling (O'Malley, 2004).

This analysis of Finnish electricity laws has indicated that during different periods and among overlapping but different phases in the development of the infrastructure, legislation tilted towards different temporalities of risk; central planning and anticipation of future needs to guarantee security in the earlier period of 1979–1995, real-time activities on the free markets to maximize competition and resilience roughly between 1995 and 2013. More recently, the two temporalities of anticipation and resilience and the relevant governing techniques have begun to intertwine. We argue this is at least partially because blackouts which have lasted from hours to a few days have affected the way that providers and distributors need to anticipate the future and plan long-term investments.

At the same time, the role of privatization and liberalization in the changes of temporalities has not been clear cut. Early in the period, government actors were strongly involved in building up and electrifying the nation. Concerns about coverage and general availability of power supply overrode those of uninterrupted power supply. The liberalization of power generation and supply certainly changed this setting. However, liberalization was far from perfect. Local transmission and distribution grids continued to act as monopolies, and a market logic was thus never really tested and put into use in order to achieve reliable supply. Rather this remained as a task of socially embedded, trusted license holders. While these companies had limited interest in long-term network stability, the sanctioning of blackouts, and the simultaneous growing reliance of uninterrupted power supply, came to change this. Regulators, and laws in very concrete form since 2013, enforced new long-term temporalities over the actors of the liberalized electricity providers and distributors.

These problematics take us back to the governmental aspirations for *anticipation* and *resilience*, a relationship that underpins a classic debate in risk management and governance (UK Royal Society, 1992). Traditionally, anticipation in risk management prompts advance detection of potential threats, whereas resilience argues that complex failures are not wholly predictable and emphasis should be laid on capacities to cope with the unexpected incidents that are thus provoked. While the two goals clearly appear to be in tension, they are not always one another's alternatives. For decades, risk practitioners have sought to deploy both approaches by combining "lessons learned" with "foresight," for example (UK Royal Society, 1992: 156). The form of the legislation studied in this chapter exemplifies such blurring: while an analyst can unpack strategies of anticipation and resilience in them, the laws themselves rarely speak in such terminology. In our case, exploring the temporality of law requires scholarly reconstruction, and is not a given fact. To a different interpretation, the laws might also suggest continuum between anticipation and resilience: energy law even when it stresses resilience could be seen a means of building capacity for anticipated future resilience.

Nevertheless, we believe there is merit in emphasizing the difference between anticipation and resilience in energy policy discussions. Our results show that, in Finnish electricity infrastructure development, and the legislation that accompanied it, anticipation-based strategies and resilience-based strategies practically did function as alternatives for several decades and have only recently begun to be intertwined. Finnish history of electricity regulation also suggests the pragmatic difficulty of reconciling the long-time span of central planning with real-time market competition. When market mechanisms appropriate risk and promise to manage it, this easily shifts the temporality back to real-time resilience (de Goede, 2004). If risks are expected to be managed by markets and price mechanisms, this can practically undermine energy companies' efforts in creating preparedness planning: for example, market prices are not easy to foresee or simulate with any exactitude as ethnography of power trading has shown (Silvast, 2017). Perhaps making these two risk strategies more distinct adds to those situations where only one is present or stronger than the other. Another topical example is local decentralized electricity grids. While appreciated by many energy policy programs as a means of adding redundancy and resilience, most also admit that the decentralized electricity grid would not stay afloat without anticipatory actions, such as building robust infrastructures and backup capacities, which require a certain degree of centralized activity such as national laws or wide regional electricity capacity markets (Breslau, 2013).

When studying law and temporality in the energy case, it is important to stress that the temporalities of resilience and anticipation are not born in legislation. Although we could not show the link here for lack of space, legislation draws these temporalities from a variety of other sources; from practices of government planning to economic theories, research works, and mathematical tools such as operations research (see Silvast, 2017, for more details). Laws, regulation, and their temporalities matter for energy infrastructure, as we have tried to show, but remain underexplored in the literature on infrastructure and temporality. They create new conditions for thought and action among experts and laypeople, which seems pertinent especially because energy is widely considered to be a liberalized industry. As such, law and regulation help codify those patterns, activities and tempos that society expects of the energy infrastructure. Future research could pay more attention to the effects – for example, via ethnography or historical statistics – that law and regulation has on temporalities of maintaining and using infrastructures.

Bibliography

Anderson, B. (2010). Preemption, precaution, preparedness: Anticipatory action and future geographies. *Progress in Human Geography*, 34 (6): 777–798.

Berglund, B. (2009). *Svarta svanar och högspänningsledningar – om försörjningstryggheten i det svenska elsystemet ur ett teknikhistoriskt perspektiv* (*Black Swans in the Power Grid – How Critical Events Has Affected the Security of Electricity Supply)*, dissertation.

Bowker, G. (2015). Temporality: The infrastructure toolbox. *Cultural Anthropology* website [online]. Available at: https://culanth.org/fieldsights/723-temporality. [Accessed 17 Mar. 2017]

Breslau, D. (2013). Designing a market-like entity: Economics in the politics of market formation. *Social Studies of Science*, 43 (6): 829–851.

Brown, N. and Beynon-Jones, S. (2012). "Reflex regulation": An anatomy of promissory science governance. *Health, Risk & Society*, 14 (3): 223–240.

Collier, S. (2011). *Post-Soviet Social: Neoliberalism, Social Modernity, Biopolitics.* Princeton, NJ: Princeton University Press.

Collier, S. and Lakoff, A. (2008). The vulnerability of vital systems: How critical infrastructures became a security problem, in Dunn Cavelty, Myriam Kristensen and Kristian Søby (Eds.) *Securing 'the Homeland': Critical Infrastructure, Risk and (In)security*, New York: Routledge, pp.17–39.

Darby, S. (2012). Metering: EU policy and implications for fuel poor households. *Energy Policy*, 49: 98–106.

De Goede, M. (2004). Repoliticizing financial risk. *Economy and Society*, 33 (2): 197–217.

De Goede, M. and Randalls, S. (2009). Precaution, preemption: Arts and technologies of the actionable future. *Environment and Planning D: Society and Space*, 27 (5): 859–878.

Edwards, P. (2003). *Infrastructure and Modernity: Force, Time and Social Organization in the History of Sociotechnical systems*, in Thomas, Misa, Brey, Philip and Feenberg, Andrew (Eds.) *Modernity and Technology*, Cambridge, MA: MIT Press, 185–225.

Edwards, P. (2010). *A Vast Machine: Computer Models, Climate Data, and the Politics of Global Warming*. Cambridge, MA: MIT Press.

Electricity Market Act. (2004). 386/1995, amendments up to 1772/2004 included. Unofficial translation by the Finnish Ministry of Trade and Industry.

Energiamarkkinavirasto (Finnish Energy Market Authority). (2007). *Sähkön jakeluverkonhaltijoiden hinnoittelun kohtuullisuuden arvioinnin suuntaviivat vuosille 2008-2011* (*Guidelines for Evaluating the Reasonableness of Pricing of Electricity Distribution Network Owners for 2008-2011*). Dnro 154/422/2007. Helsinki: Energiamarkki- navirasto. Available at: http://www.energiamarkkinavirasto.fi/files/ Sahko_jakeluverkko_suuntaviivat_154-422-2007.pdf. [Accessed 3 Jun. 2013]

Energiavirasto (Finnish Energy Authority). (2011). *Keski-iän huomiointi sähköverkon nykykäyttöarvon laskennassa.* (*Acknowledging Average Age when Calculating the Current Use Value of the Electricity Network*). Muistio (Memo). 22.11.2011.

European Parliament & Council (1996). *Directive 96/92/EC of the European Parliament and of the Council of 19 December 1996 concerning common rules for the internal market in electricity.*

Forstén, J. (2002). *Sähkön toimitusvarmuuden parantaminen* (*Improving the Reliability of Electricity Distribution*). Report for the Finnish Ministry of Trade and Industry. Available at: http://www2.energia.fi/myrsky.pdf/toimitusvarmuus.pdf. [Accessed 17 Mar. 2017]

Froggatt, A. and Hadfield, A. (2015). *Deconstructing the European Energy Union: Governance and 2030 Goals*, UKERC (UK Energy Research Centre) & University of Exeter Energy Policy Group Working Paper: EPG 1507. Available at: http://www.ukerc.ac.uk/

publications/deconstructing-the-european-energy-union-governance-and-2030-goals.html. [Accessed 17 Mar. 2017]

Grabham, E. (2016). Time and technique: The legal lives of the 26-week qualifying period. *Economy and Society*, 45 (3–4): 379–406.

Graham, S. (Ed.). (2012). *Disrupted Cities. When Infrastructure Fails*. New York, London: Routledge.

Graham, S. and Marvin, S. (2001). *Splintering Urbanism: Networked Infrastructures, Technological Mobilities and the Urban Condition*. New York: Routledge.

Greenhouse, C. (2014). Time's up, timed out: Reflections on social time and legal pluralism. *Journal of Legal Pluralism and Unofficial Law*, 46 (1): 141–153.

Hirsh, R. (1999). *Power Loss: The Origins of Deregulation and Restructuring in the American Electric Utility System*. Cambridge, MA: MIT Press.

HS (Helsingin Sanomat) (30 December 2011a). *Kehitysmaatouhua*. (*Developing Country Standard*). Editorial. Available at: http://www.hs.fi/paakirjoitukset/ Kehitysmaatouhua/a1305552354993. [Accessed 17 Mar. 2017]

Hughes, T. (1983) *Networks of Power: Electrification in Western Society, 1880–1930*. Baltimore, MA: Johns Hopkins University Press.

Hughes, T. (1989). The evolution of large scale technological systems, in Bijker, Wiebe, Hughes, Thomas and Pinch, Trevor (Eds.) *The Social Construction of Technological Systems: New Directions in the Sociology History of Technology*, Cambridge, MA: MIT Press, 51–82.

Ialenti, V. (2014). Adjudicating deep time: Revisiting the United States' high-level nuclear waste repository project at Yucca Mountain. *Science & Technology Studies*, 27 (2): 27–48.

Jahkola, A. (1993). Energian tarpeen kehitys ja siitä laaditut ennusteet. (The Development of Energy Need and the Forecasts that Concern it), in Keskinen, Risto (Ed.) *Suomen energiatekniikan historia: teknis-historiallinen tutkimus energian tuottamis-esta ja käytöstä Suomessa 1840–1980*. (*The History of Finnish Energy Technology: A Technological-Historical Investigation of Energy Production and Use in Finland 1840–1980*). Tampere: Tampere University of Technology Publications, 115.

Jalas, M., Rinkinen, J. and Silvast, A. (2016). The rhythms of infrastructure. *Anthropology Today*, 32 (4): 16–19.

Kaijser, A. (1994). *I fädrens spår: den svenska infrastrukturens historiska utveckling* och framtida utmaning (*In the Tracks of the Fathers: The Historical Development and the Future Challenges of the Swedish Infrastructure*). Stockholm: Carlsson.

Karasti, H., Millerand, F., Hine, C. and Bowker, G. (2016). Knowledge infrastructures: Part III. *Science & Technology Studies*, 29 (3): 2–9.

Kauppa- ja teollisuusministeriö (Finnish Ministry of Trade and Industry). (2006). *Sähkönjakelun toimitusvarmuuden kehittäminen: Sähkön jakeluhäiriöiden ehkäisemistä ja jakelun toiminnallisia tavoitteita selvittäneen työryhmän raportti*. (*Developing the Supply Security of Electricity Distribution: The Report by the Working Group that Explored the Prevention of Electricity Supply Failures and the Practical Targets for the Supply*. Available at: http://www.tem.fi/files/17096/Sahkokatkostyoryhman_ raportti.pdf. [Accessed 3 Jun. 2013]

Myllyntaus, T. (1991). *Electrifying Finland: The Transfer of a New Technology into a Late Industrialising Economy*. Helsinki: ETLA.

Nord Pool Spot. (2010). *The Elbas market*. [online] Available at: http://www.nordpoolspot.com/trading/The-Elbas-market/. [Accessed 10 Nov. 2010]

Nord Pool Spot. (2016). *Intraday market*. [online] Available at: http://www.nordpoolspot.com/How-does-it-work/Intraday-market/. [Accessed 17 Mar. 2017]

O'Malley, P. (2004). *Risk, Uncertainty and Government*. London, Sydney, Portland, OR: Glasshouse Press.

Riles, A. (2011). *Collateral Knowledge: Legal Reasoning in the Global Financial Markets.* Chicago, IL: University of Chicago Press.

Rinkinen, J. (2013). Electricity blackouts and hybrid systems of provision: Users and the reflective practice. *Energy, Sustainability and Society*, 3 (25): 1–10.

Ruostetsaari, I. (1998). *Energiapolitiikka käännekohdassa. Järjestöt ja yritykset vaikut-tajina vapautuvilla energiamarkkinoilla.* (*Energy Politics at a Turning Point: Associations and Companies as Stakeholders in the Liberalizing Energy Markets.*) Tampere: Tampereen yliopisto (University of Tampere).

Sähkölaki (1979). 319/1979. Available at: http://www.finlex.fi/fi/laki/alkup/1979/19790319. [Accessed 17 Mar. 2017]

Sähkömarkkinalaki (1995). 386/1995. Available at: http://www.finlex.fi/fi/laki/alkup/1995/19950386. [Accessed 17 Mar. 2017]

Sähkömarkkinalaki (2013). 588/2013. Available at: http://www.finlex.fi/fi/laki/alkup/2013/20130588. [Accessed 17 Mar. 2017]

SENER (Finnish Electricity Association). (2000). *Vapaan sähkön lyhyt historia: Suomen sähkömarkkinoiden avaus ja kipupisteet.* (*The Brief History of Free Electricity: The Opening and the Pain Spots of Finnish Electricity Markets*), a discussion paper by the Finnish Energy Industries, then Finnish Electricity Association.

Shove, E., Pantzar, M. and Watson, M. (2012). *The Dynamics of Social Practice. Everyday Life and How it Changes.* London: Sage.

Silvast, A. (2017). *Making Electricity Resilient: Risk and Security in a Liberalized Infrastructure.* New York: Routledge.

Silvast, A., Hänninen, H. and Hyysalo, S. (2013). Energy in society: Energy systems and infrastructures in society. *Science and Technology Studies*, 26 (3): 3–13.

Silvast, A. and Virtanen, M. (2014). Keeping Systems at Work: Electricity Infrastructure from Control Rooms to Household Practices. *Science & Technology Studies*, 28 (2): 93–114.

Star, S.L. (1999). The Ethnography of Infrastructure. *American Behavioral Scientist*, 43 (3): 377–391.

Summerton, J. (2004). Do electrons have politics? Constructing user identities in Swedish Electricity. *Science, Technology, & Human Values*, 29 (4): 486–511.

Thue, L. (1995). Electricity rules: The formation and development of the Nordic electricity regimes, in Kaijser, Arne and Hedin, Marika (Eds.) *Nordic Energy Systems: Historical Perspectives and Current Issues*, Canton: Science History Publications, 11–30.

Trentmann, F. (2009). Disruption is normal. Blackouts, breakdowns and the elasticity of everyday life, in Shove, E., Trentmann, F. and Wilk, R. (Eds.) *Time, Consumption and Everyday life. Practice, Materiality and Culture*, Oxford, New York: Berg, 67–84.

UK Royal Society. (1992). *Risk: Analysis, Perception and Management – Report of a Royal Society Study Group.* London: Royal Society.

van der Vleuten, E. (2004). Infrastructures and societal change: A view from the large technical systems field. *Technology Analysis & Strategic Management*, 16 (3): 395–414.

Wallsten, B. (2014). Review of the thesis "Anticipating interruptions: Security and risk in a liberalized electricity infrastructure" by Antti Silvast. *Nordic Journal of Science and Technology Studies*, 2 (2): 41–43.

Winskel, M. and Radcliffe, J. (2014). The rise of accelerated energy innovation and its implications for sustainable innovation studies: A UK perspective. *Science & Technology Studies*, 27 (1): 8–33.

12 Doing times, doing truths

The legal case file as a folded object

Irene van Oorschot, University of Amsterdam

Introduction

The study of time and temporality has drawn attention to the active and partial ways legal practices *take* and *make* time. Statutes of limitations are instruments of periodization, legal norms themselves technologies that stabilize expectations with regards to the future (Luhmann, 2004), specific legal rules structure both the legal regulation of time (e.g. time spent working and time spent 'off') and our experience of time (Grabham, 2011, 2014). Moreover, legal practices *take* time: procedure, as well as the slow or fast pacing of everyday legal work practices, introduce in our appraisals of the relationship between time and the law a diachronic dimension (Latour, 2010). In this contribution, however, I wish to draw attention to a rather recalcitrant, if relatively understudied, temporal actor in these everyday work practices: the legal case file. Translating and transporting a potentially punishable event in space and time (van Oorschot and Schinkel, 2015), legal case files are as much technologies of recording and memory, as they are instruments of forgetting. Drawing on the notion of the temporally folded object (M'charek, 2014), I show how the legal case folds within itself multiple temporalities. Not only does it record and trace both 'the facts' and its own procedural history, it also makes its own histories of production partially invisible. Tracing how precisely these 'invisible' histories are mobilized and used in court, I show legal practices of truth-finding to be intimately tied up with the folding and unfolding of the case file's multiple histories. Emphasizing the relationship between truth-finding and the making of multiple temporalities in legal practices, this piece offers a discussion of the temporal agency of legal case files. As such it is an effort to materialize our understanding of the relationship between law and time, in that it aims to show how different temporalities are made in and by the legal case file and how these are made to matter to the legal decision at hand.

By way of an introduction into this problematic, let's place ourselves in the middle of things. The following is an account of a moment in which the legal case file's multiple histories were mobilized in fact-finding in a Dutch court.

In medias res

Our defendant, Harry Jackson,[1] is accused of breaking and entering his ex-girlfriend's house; and in addition is charged with the destruction of some of her property. According to the prosecutor's version of the events in question, Harry climbed into his ex-girlfriend's house through a rooftop window in the summer of 2013, when she was on vacation abroad. While residing there for a couple of days, he stole some of her personal belongings and damaged some of the electronic appliances in her kitchen. Harry's lawyer has prepared an elaborate closing argument. His lawyer begins his plea:

> I will start by saying that there is only one witness to the breaking and entering, and it [the witness statement] is far from sufficient. This witness does not describe any of my client's defining [physical] characteristics. So how can we be sure that it was indeed my client who was seen entering this apartment? The police never organized a line-up either, so we can't quite identify the person who was seen breaking and entering yet. Then there is this other statement, that statement made by the affected party. Well, this statement is completely contradictory: she [the victim] mentions different time periods in which she would have been abroad, for instance. And some of her statements are simply incorrect: for instance, she has told the police she did not know that my client, her ex-boyfriend, had been under electronic house arrest. But she did know, because she has previously assisted with the electronic surveillance of my client, that is, when they were still together! [...] Besides, when we look at the process-verbal of the interrogation with my client, I see, typed down, in the middle of one of my client's questions, the phrase, 'theft, unqual.', which arguably stands for 'theft, unqualified'. But my client would never express himself this way, nor would other defendants, presumably. So who is speaking here? The police officer of the defendant? Furthermore, the victim has told the police, and I quote, that 'all the neighbours have seen it'. So why was their testimony not taken? I think the police have indeed talked to these neighbours, but that they [their statements] are not present in the case file. My last point is that the police suggest, in the file, that they would further investigate the site for traces of my client's presence, but the results of this investigation are curiously lacking from the case file. It seems to me that exculpatory evidence has been excluded from the file, so that the evidence is wafer-thin.

Referring, again and again, to the evidentiary materials in the legal case file, Harry's lawyer aims to cast doubt on the public prosecutor's version of the events in question. Can we rely on the identification made by the affected party's neighbour, if this neighbour – who is supposed to remember and know the defendant, who lived together for a while with his now ex-girlfriend – tells the police that he has *recognized* the defendant, but has not explicitly *described* the defendant's physical characteristics? Can we trust the statement made by the victim, considering the fact that she denies any knowledge of her ex-boyfriend's previous conviction while she must have known very well he had been convicted earlier? And was she not caught lying about the period she spent abroad? Seen in this light, can her statements be considered trustworthy enough to merit conviction of the defendant? What can these statements tell us about what really happened?

However, the lawyer's plea does not only offer an interpretation of the stories present *in* the file; he also tells us a story *about* the file. This lawyer first challenges the neutrality of the written transcription (process-verbal) of the interrogation with the defendant: he suggests that the police officials have been so set on shaping and rewriting his client's words that it has now become unclear who precisely is speaking. If police officials complement his client's words with words such as 'unqual.', then how can we be sure that the rest of the client's statements in this process-verbal are truly his – and not added by overzealous police officials? Second, this lawyer suggests that the case file offers only a partial rendering of the full police investigation: the police, he suggests, have indeed spoken with more witnesses but these statements never made it to the legal case file. Police officials also mention additional investigation into traces of his client's presence in the house, yet he cannot find the results of such testing anywhere in the file. Does this imply that the prosecutor failed to exercise due diligence?

All in all, a smooth transportation from the here-and-now of the court session towards the time and space of the offence is barred: not only because the individual witnesses are unreliable (although according to Jackson's lawyer, they are that, too), but also since the case file is the product of specific modes of translating oral statements into written evidence and of practices of partial inclusion and exclusion. In other words: the case file itself has a history and it is that history that Harry's lawyer mobilizes in his attempt to thwart conviction.

In this chapter, I am interested precisely in the case file's status as both a neutral transporter and carrier of evidence and a non-innocent, perhaps treacherous, object that inevitably transforms reality, an object with a complex history. This chapter asks the question, first, *how* the case files manages to build a bridge between offence and court session and, second, how *traces* of its own disavowed histories allow actors – most notably defence lawyers – to question the validity of the facts it presents. It is interested in the relationship between legal procedure and fact-finding, yet refrains from treating legal procedure as an unproblematic 'legal context' to practices of fact-finding. Instead, it highlights how both 'factuality' and 'procedure' are enacted in and through the case file. The notion of the 'folded object' (M'charek, 2014) is particularly useful in doing so: offering a vocabulary within which to begin to understand the multiple and dense temporalities of objects, it is especially suited to inquiry into the relationship between law, time, and truth.

Law, times, truths

In its concern with the histories and uses of the legal case file, this chapter is meant as a respecification of dominant approaches to the relationship between legal procedure and legal truth-making and a contribution to the study of law and time more generally.

'Guarded by procedure': Procedure as a frame

First, there is, of course, a clear connection between procedure and legal modes of truth-making, especially so in Dutch (inquisitorial) criminal law. Cleiren (2001: 16) for instance notes that 'the criminal process is aimed at finding truth in order to punish those guilty. Verification of the facts of which the accused is charged is therefore a prime goal of the criminal process.' But because there is a real danger of convicting innocent suspects, such 'verification' must be safeguarded procedurally:

> [T]he function of criminal law is to be formulated hybridly: on the one hand, it is the finding of truth in order to punish transgressions of material law, and on the other hand, the protection of citizens against far-reaching governmental breaches of their constitutional rights, understood to include the prevention of the punishment of those innocent'.
>
> (Cleiren, 2001:18)

On the one hand, then, the truth of the matter is carefully guarded by procedure – not *all* facts may come to bear on the matter at hand, for instance when evidence is attained by illegitimate means. On the other hand, it is not entirely up to the affected parties to deliver the facts and agree, among each other, on the delineation of the case: it is the judge, in Dutch criminal law, who decides on both the facts (their admissibility and relevance) *and* the law. The 'material' truth matters and precisely because it matters so much its establishment is guarded by procedure.

It is tempting, within this rather general mode of addressing the relationship between legal procedure and the production of legal facts, to treat procedure as an unproblematic 'context' to the production of legal facts. Procedure then functions as a 'frame': something that both *structures* and *contains* practices aimed at the truth of the matter. Such an approach effectuates several things at once. First, it glosses over the question how 'facts' with regards to the specific offence in question are made and made to matter to the decision at hand. In other words, it treats the 'facts' as already established and of equal relevance and weight to the decision at hand. In doing so such an approach fails to address the question *how and where such facts are made* and *how these are made to matter to the decision at hand.* This question, crucially, is precisely the question Jackson's lawyer raises with regards to the case file as a producer of facts: how is the case file made? What is lost? What is distorted? Second, and vice versa, treating 'procedure' as a context risks treating that same context as similarly 'already there' as a stable frame and container for practices of legal truth-telling. However, did not Jackson's lawyer precisely implicate a concern with procedures of evidence-production in his plea? That is: is not 'procedure' drawn on, evoked, made consequential within and to the decision it is supposed to merely 'enframe'? Procedure, then, does not enframe 'the truth' in any straightforward matter: it is a 'moving horizon' (Scheffer, 2010: 45). Both truth and procedure, then, have to be done somehow, somewhere.

Procedure and time

Taking the simultaneity of 'doing procedure' and 'doing truth' seriously positions this effort, second, in relation to questions about legal temporalities more generally. As such it draws inspiration from approaches to legal temporalities that treat temporality not as a backdrop or temporal container of practices – in which legal events happen 'in' time – but rather as something that is effectuated within practices, giving rise to multiple and specific ways of making pasts, presents, and futures. Latour (2010) points for instance to law's strange 'timelessness'. The law, he states, never fundamentally changes. Law-making, among the counsellors of state, is always understood as a practice of *finding* law, not *creating* it. Law only evolves – but it does so always with reference to precedent, that build-up of past decisions. But taking place in reference to precedent does not quite make law a historical being itself: as something that can be found, it was *always already there*, a timeless totality that places itself outside of chronological time. Law knows no beginning or end; only a perpetual now. Yet this sense of timelessness, of ahistoricity, contrasts with the slow pacing of the counsellors' work practice, Latour notes (2010): there, predictability is ensured through doubting, through hesitations: that is, by not *hurrying*. Luhmann's efforts resonate to some extent with those of Latour. If Latour emphasizes the production of predictability, Luhmann (2004) emphasizes normative expectations. Legal norms, according to Luhmann, presuppose an unknown future. In relation to this unknown future, they make the promise that whatever may happen, the legal norm will hold. As such legal norms allow for the stabilization of expectations in an operation of 'time-binding' (Luhmann, 2004). Grabham (2011, 2014), in taking seriously the temporal *products* of legal regulation, instead turns her attention towards specific modes of analogizing of time spent working and time spent off work in work-life legislation (2011, 2014). Legal practices, then, both *take* and *make* time.

The case file: A folded object

With procedure and facts, we hence enter the relationship between the case file and *legal temporalization*: the way pasts, presents, and futures are made and remade in legal practices. In other words, I am interested in unpacking what role is played by case files in such practices of legal temporalization. In so doing, I follow up on M'charek's (2014) crucial contribution to the study of temporality: that is her suggestion that objects are not to be understood solely in spatial terms, but in temporal ones. With the help of three narratives on the history of the first genetic map of human beings – the Anderson sequence – M'charek illustrates how objects fold time within themselves. Folded into them are their histories, which, in turn, are entanglements of places and times: 'the essence of the folded object [...] lies in the intricate ways in which it gathers heterogeneous spaces and temporalities together' (2014: 33). This Anderson sequence is unproblematically used in some practices, for instance in laboratory practices, where it allows comparison with other genetic sequences. At such moments, it hides the places and times that have become entangled within it, and have been folded into it: 'Once made, they appear to be independent of human action, "thrown at us" and assuming an allegedly stable state' (ibid: 30). M'charek (2014) further argues that the times and places folded into objects remain, however, present – perhaps absently present. A folded object 'indexes and enacts its history' (29), even though that history may not be immediately visible. M'charek's analytical work consists precisely of attempting to unfold this object and trace the times and places within it. Where and how is this object made? In what precise ways have various times and places become entangled? But also: where and how does this object make its own history invisible, and where and how does it inadvertently betray itself by showing traces of its past?

Treating the legal case file as active in practices of legal temporalization, this contribution suggests that neither procedure nor time is to be understood as containers of or for action; instead, it suggests that time and procedure are themselves the outcome of specific modes of 'sorting time' (Serres and Latour, 1995). In doing so my efforts diverge somewhat from Latour's treatment of temporalization: while he concentrates on law's 'timelessness' and contrasts it with the diachronic pacing of file-work, I am interested instead in the way the case file *itself* folds time – and how such folds create the very possibility of unfolding and refolding in other sites, in other times. In contrast with Luhmann, furthermore, I aim for a materialized understanding of legal practices, i.e. one that incorporates the materials of the legal trade – case files, briefs, arguments – rather than a dematerialized emphasis on communications (see van Oorschot and Schinkel, 2015; Philoppopoulos-Mihalopulos, 2014).

With the folded object, then, we are closer to understanding the relationship between the sorting and folding of time and the making of legal truths. Drawing on this notion, I am interested, first, in how the legal case file folds within it multiple histories in its effort to render history – the offence in question – available; and, second, how the case file may itself become the object of un- and refolding practices in the making and remaking of that same historical event. After briefly elaborating on the ethnographic data on which this piece is based and zooming on some methodological conundrums that attend to the study of temporality in this specific context, I will follow up on legal actors' local concerns with the case file's temporalities. This exercise first requires an understanding on how legal case files are folded in the first place, which discussion I will focus in particular on the ways it hence ends up mediating epistemic access to 'what really happened'. Then, I describe how the case file may be refolded in court by judges, lawyers, defendants and prosecutors. In a concluding discussion, I will further elaborate on the implications of this discussion for our understanding of truth-finding in legal settings.

Tracing truth-making and time-making: An ethnography

The observations on which this particular account of legal time- and truth-production is based are grounded in an ethnographic study of a criminal court in the Netherlands. In this project, I have aimed to depart from judicial self-descriptions that locate the activity of judging in the neutral and unbiased (and human!) judge. Rather, I have approached judging as a local practice that is distributed over both human and non-human actors. This ethnography is hence less concerned with 'hard cases', highly publicized cases or cases in which legal and non-legal knowledges intersect. Its focus is rather on the most basic of operations and as such has instead concentrated on rather simple and common cases, effectively making up the large majority of criminal court cases in the Netherlands. These cases are dealt with by so-called 'police-judges' (*politierechters*) – an awkward nomer as these judges are firmly entrenched in the judiciary. The large majority of criminal court cases – around 85% in 2010, for instance – is dealt with by these police judges, who usually deliver their verdicts orally, *in situ*.

Having requested formal permission to do fieldwork, I received access to the criminal law section of this particular Dutch court in the spring of 2013. The fieldwork consisted of two phases: in the first phase, I focused on studying case files and getting to know administrative personnel and court clerks, as well as people in strategic positions, e.g. the head of the administrative offices and the heads of the two criminal law teams. In the second phase, I have traced cases as they unfold; this has meant that I have selected specific court sessions – in which around 15 cases are usually decided on – and read these case files myself, after which I observed judges' preparatory file-work, and accompanied them to these court sessions. This method of 'shadowing' individual judges has also allowed me to ask questions during their file-work or between cases in court. Clerks and prosecutors – who remain seated in the same room while defendants and lawyers exit and are called in – were also participants in some of the more informal conversations I would have regarding individual cases and defendants. In total, I shadowed 14 individual judges and traced about 250 cases this way.

My concentration on the everyday practices that constitute 'judging' renders phenomena visible that otherwise go unnoticed: for instance, the 'messiness' and materiality of these everyday practices, their distribution over various kinds of workers in the court and the production of an operative understanding of the case, elsewhere called the 'story-before-the-trial' (van Oorschot, 2014). With venturing 'backstage', to the offices and hallways of the court, comes simultaneously an appreciation of the centrality of the legal case file. While the court session is rather 'phonocentric' (Derrida, 1967), these backstage work practices take place in reference to the written words in the legal case file. However, it is a mistake to treat legal case files as texts only: not only do case files have a material existence (see van Oorschot, 2014), they are also, as I will demonstrate in this contribution, objects that fold together multiple times and places. The concerns with the case file's histories and futures are very much of local concern to those involved in working with case files. Indeed, once one ventures 'backstage', it is difficult not to be struck with the various ways in which court workers engage themselves with the case file's histories and futures. While the study of the law and temporality may present unique challenges depending on one's research interests and field, in this case the question of time and history quite readily presented itself as an object of study. As we will see, time, like much like truth, is a local topic of concern.

The case file as folded object: Time and selective in/visibilities

Making materials traceable

'We weren't there when it happened, right?', a public prosecutor tells me over a quick coffee in between cases. 'And because we weren't there, we *press the world onto paper.*' Playing with the two meanings of the Dutch verb *persen*, the public prosecutor speaks of the activity of *printing* something on paper, but the Dutch 'op papier persen' also has connotation of reducing something, of transforming something into something else. And this is precisely the first way the legal case file starts folding places, times and actors within itself. The case file is not in the last place a *paper* object: it translates heterogeneous entities, e.g. spoken words, observations, traces of blood, plastic bags of weed, video materials and even decisions made by police officials and prosecutors, into sheets of paper. Transporting evidence means here: to transform it. Case files are hence 'comprehensive recording devices that register everything in the medium of writing', or, it must be said, photographic materials, 'even that which is not writing. They register events, voices, gestures, appearances (Vismann, 2008: 10).

However, sheets of paper are not quite documents yet, that is, 'evidence in support of a fact' (Briet, 1951, cited in Buckland, 1997). To refer to a reality out there, the case file cannot simply transport evidence – it also has to carefully trace it. Tracing consists of two activities. On the one hand, correspondence between the evidentiary materials itself – a spoken word, a trace of blood on a curtain, bags of weed – and its paper double needs to be carefully traced. The legal case file ensures such correspondences by tracing precisely where, how and by whom the piece of evidence was found, elicited, or investigated. Tracing these 'chains of reference' is key to ensuring the 'chain of custody' (Lynch and McNally, 2005): the case file must ensure these small correspondences between, for instance, that trace of blood on a curtain, a numbered sample of this trace and a report of the Dutch Forensic Institute that matches this trace with a known offender (see also Toom, 2010).

A second kind of tracing is geared to ensuring and accounting for authorship. Sheets of paper become *evidence* through autographs of the various (human) actors contributing to the file: witnesses, defendants, victims, police officials. Stamps, furthermore, meticulously trace the dates documents were sent, received or filed. Copies of original documentation are similarly stamped with 'copy conform original' and, in rare cases, these stamps themselves need to be authorized with a signature. The case file as such participates in 'a specific social economy, an economy of law' (Kozin, 2007: 195), which revolves around the attribution of statements to authors, and in doing so qualifies these utterances as legally relevant (Pottage, 2012: 177).

The case file as a whole also traces its own development: within it are not only primary documents testifying to the case at hand, but also documents that offer official notification of decisions made throughout the investigation. And on its paper surface, the case file's travel through the legal-bureaucratic networked is traced by, again, stamps, signatures, and stickers (see Figure 12.1): 'Signs of its history are continuously and deliberately inscribed upon the artefact itself' (Hull, 2003: 296). As such, the case file is a 'chronicle of its own production, a sedimentation of its own history' (ibid: 296). In doing so, the case file the legal case file participates in the 'machinery of sameness' (M'charek et al, 2013) that characterizes jurisdictions with a focus on procedural fairness. Through these techniques, which allow decisions to always be traced back in time and place, the case file also becomes compatible with its anticipated future use in court. Only if it has carefully traced small correspondences

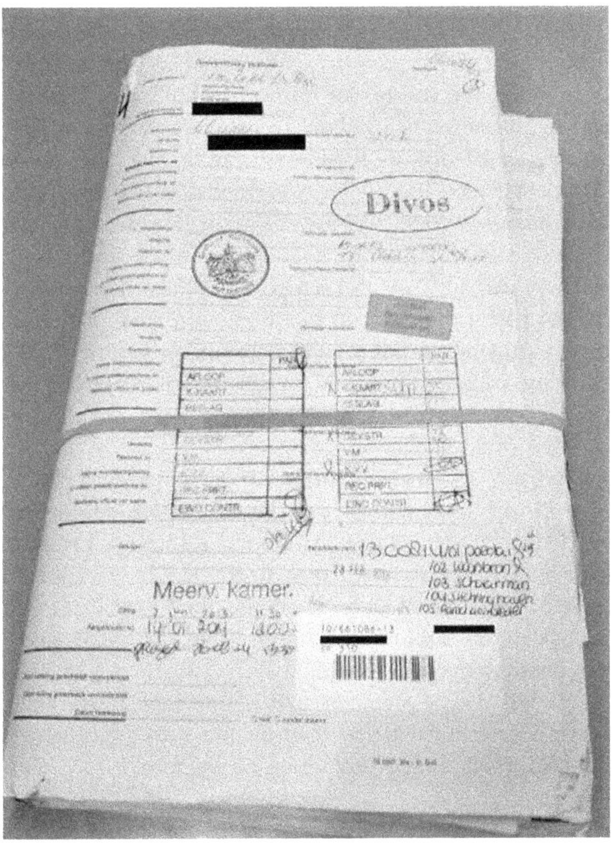

Figure 12.1 A file from the Court's archive.

NB: A file that, in anticipation of a judicial decision on the execution of a suspended sentence, has been taken out of the Court's archive, in which autographs, stamps and stickers make its history traceable. The names of the defendant and the judge(s) on the sleeve of this case file have been anonymized.

and attributed accountabilities it can be employed in the investigation in court. This way, it folds both history and future within itself.

Writing up in anticipation of the future

However, the case file has another existence, too: '[I]t is [both] an object and a story' (Kozin, 2007: 195). And in the stories it tells it similarly anticipates its future and similarly produces its own visibilities and invisibilities.

Take the processes-verbal in the case file: the documents, composed by police officials, which report on the police's findings, witness statements, or interrogations with defendants. These processes-verbal are written in a field of tension: on the one hand, victims, witnesses and defendants are required to tell their stories in 'their own words'. Only if the document permits no doubt as to *who* precisely said, saw or witnessed what, can it be used in court. On the other hand, these documents make clear how precisely the event in question – 'what really happened' – can be related to one (or more) of the formal description of illegal activities found in the letter of the law. In other words: these processes-verbal must anticipate the legal operation of subsumption, i.e. the question whether 'what really happened' can indeed be subsumed under a description of illegal activity in the criminal law code (see, for this point, Komter, 2002, 2003, 2006). Precisely this question is of course at stake in the future (inquisitorial) proceedings in court. These demands are also temporal: the processes-verbal must report on the facts of the past – the event in question – and anticipate its future use in court. These two demands produce very particular visibilities and invisibilities. Take the following fragment from a process-verbal reporting on a criminal complaint, lodged by Nancy Carr, female victim of domestic abuse:

> I wish to lodge a criminal complaint of assault against my ex-boyfriend, named Stan Dwyer. I will tell you exactly what happened this afternoon. This afternoon, Thursday the 3rd of May, around 3:15 p.m., I was at the TileStor shop on Regent Street number 70 in Rotterdam. [...] I went outside and saw that Stan was indeed in front of the door. [...] Stan said he really wanted to talk to me. I told him I did not want that. Stan asked me if it was really over between us. I told him that I thought it had been over for a while. [...] I heard that Stan repeated to me that it was really over then. Subsequently I saw and felt that Stan hit me with a flat hand on the right side of my face. I felt an enormous pain on my face.

Reporting on her story this way, the process-verbal anticipates the criminal charge of physical assault with criminal intent, this being defined in the Dutch criminal code as the 'intentional infliction of pain or injury or other physical harm or suffering onto the body of a person'. First, the victim reports that it was *Stan* who hit her (and not someone else); she reports that she *felt* his hitting, which she felt on the right side of her face (the hit was hence directed against her body); and she reports having felt pain. Indeed, Stan's indictment reads as follows:

> [T]hat he in **Rotterdam** on or about the **3rd of May 2012**, intentionally abusing a person (namely **N. Carr**), has **(forcefully) hit/slapped in/on/ against the face multiple times or at least once**, as a result of which this person has suffered injury and/or pain.

Note how the bold text refers to the particulars of the event in question: they refer to the time, place, name of the victim and the specifics of the event, which here covers slightly different accounts. The questions whether it was hitting or slapping, or whether the defendant hit Nancy once or more times, are, of course, up to the judge. As such this indictment weaves together both event and criminal code.

Now, this process-verbal has effectuated a couple of things. A dialogue taking place at the police station has been translated into a written, first-person narrative. The dialogue itself however has been rendered invisible: we only know *that* it took place, but the particular ways police officials elicit this story have been rendered inaccessible. These prompts and suggestions, of course, are precisely how the story becomes formatted to anticipate the criminal assault charges (see, for this point, Komter, 2002, 2003, 2006). Komter (2006) hence argues that 'considering the way in which this text has emerged, it will be clear that the interrogator's activities are "noticeably absent".' Or perhaps: *absently present*. In this translation of talk into text a certain history has been written – a particular story about 'what really happened' on the 3rd of May, 2012 – but another history, at first sight, erased. But is it lost?

Working towards the time and place of the court hearing and the text of the law while tracing actions and times in its past: this is how the case file mediates access to 'what really happened'. Making the event in question 'judgment compatible' (see Latour, 2010) here consists of rendering histories visible as well as invisible. It is precisely these temporal in/visibilities that allow the case to proceed, that is: move forward in time and space. Yet all its histories – even the 'invisible' ones – are not lost: 'history', we will see in court, 'can strike back capriciously' (M'charek, 2014: 31).

The file on trial: Unfolding practices

The case file folds within itself multiple histories: a historical occurrence which is potentially a criminal event; the time of legal acts; and the times and places in which written and graphic materials are made. If all goes well, these temporalities are kept separate and partially invisible, so that the time of procedure functions smoothly as a frame, the time of the file's production is conveniently glossed over and the historical event of the alleged offence becomes an object of concern. The question, then, is how to keep these temporalities separate; how, in other words, to trace some histories while forgetting others. Within the court, such practices are distributed over various court workers.

When a case file arrives in the court building, administrative workers will check whether the file, and the documents within the file, meet a set of procedural requirements, after which they register the file. Only if the case file and the documents within it has correctly traced its procedural path can the file be used in court. Administrative workers' activities are hence 'both logistical and legal' (Latour, 2010: 79).

It is, however, on the court session I wish to concentrate here, as it is there that the case file becomes implicated in a complex *intertextual field* (Scheffer, 2006; Lynch and Bogen, 1996). In this field, written and photographic evidence are woven together with the spoken accounts of the defendant, as well as those of witnesses and expert-witnesses. Written testimony here structures the interaction between prosecutor, defendant, lawyer and judge in a practice that Lynch and Bogen have termed 'documentary methods of interrogation' (1996). It is in this setting that the case file sometimes remains folded – and is employed as a neutral container of evidence – while at other moments, it is unfolded, that is, employed as a material object with a complex history. At such points its 'truth-function' (Vismann, 2008) is endangered in the here-and-now of the court session.

Histories of production

Take yet another case, that of Martin Galloway. A private security guard of a night club, Galloway has been charged with the physical assault of a young woman, which offence he allegedly perpetrated in his capacity as a security guard. This woman, Miss Starr, had been quite drunk and rowdy and had resisted Galloway's attempts to isolate her from the small crowd outside the night club. In the brief, physical struggle that ensued, Galloway allegedly hit her in the face, which would qualify as assault. The case file includes some contradictory accounts of various eyewitnesses: two accounts of bystanders and two accounts of a colleague of the accused. Galloway himself strenuously denies that he hit the victim: in the struggle that ensued, he argues, she tried to hit him, while he tried only to ward off her assaults.

The statements made by Galloway's two colleagues are briefly touched on in the prosecutor's closing remarks when she argues that:

> Yes, your colleagues tell us that they didn't see anything untoward in your conduct. Well, I've seen things like this before, where people in your business stick up for each other. Bearing that in mind I can't say that these are, strictly speaking, exculpatory accounts.

Here, the prosecutor expresses her reservations with regard to the truth-value of these two documents by casting doubts on the impartiality and hence reliability of the two witnesses. Of course, Galloway's lawyer draws on precisely the same two documents in arguing the opposite: these two statements clearly contradict the victim's account. While both know that the processes-verbal are not 'exact representations' of what was said to the police, the prosecutor and the lawyer nevertheless treat these documents as 'at least [...] reflection[s] of what has been said in the interrogation room' (Komter, 2006: 222). And precisely because these processes-verbal are relatively truthful reflections of 'what was really said', they enable the production of potentially competing, but ideally plausible and coherent accounts of 'what really happened'.

Yet this kind of use of the file does not exhaust its possibilities. The case file itself can become implicated in lawyers', defendants' and even prosecutors' truth-telling activities. In such cases, these parties do not concentrate on the stories *in* the file, but rather tell stories *about* the file, bringing to life its partially invisible histories. Galloway's lawyer leverages precisely this strategy when he commences his concluding plea, which concentrates on the eyewitness account of the victim's friend:

> My client insists that he has only warded off her attempts to assault him. One of the Miss Starr's friends says here [pointing to the process-verbal] that she saw the movement of my client's arm, but it must be said she did not see that Mister Galloway indeed hit Miss Starr. Things like these have to do with the way police officials write things like this down, you see. They will ask, 'did you see the accused hitting her?' and then the eyewitness might say 'no' or something else. But the police will write down, 'did not see whether the accused hit the victim'. Which makes the statement neither an exculpatory, nor an incriminating statement: this way, it just seems that the eyewitness simply didn't see anything. But it could have been an exculpatory statement: maybe the eyewitness did see that something or other did not happen, and then we would have ended up with an exculpatory statement.

Here, the interrogation of the accused about the events in question shifts to an interrogation of the document itself (cf. Lynch and Bogen, 1996). Placing us in the interrogation room, where police officials are busy translating talk into text, the lawyer suggests that the statement can be read in two competing ways: either the eyewitness saw *that* Galloway did not hit the victim or the eyewitness did not see *whether* he hit the victim. In this case, the exploitation of this ambiguity works: the judge, 'unwillingly' (sic) declares the defendant not guilty. The process-verbal reporting on the conversation with the eyewitness is no longer successful in corresponding to 'what was really said', so that it can neither tell us something about 'what really happened' at that nightclub some months ago.

How police officials write things down: Institutional writing in a bind

Galloway's case casts 'the way police officials write these things down' into sharp relief. As we have seen, these writing practices take place in a zone of tension: on the one hand, police officials must aim to retain people's 'own words' and 'own observations'; on the other, these processes-verbal need to render the event in question judgment compatible. This is their conundrum: emphasizing the naturalist portrayal of interaction as it actually took place risks not only including swaths of irrelevant material; the risk is also that parts of the charges cannot be substantiated. Focusing, contrariwise, on massaging the text to be able to meet legal rules and definitions may lead the document to betray its own history of production. Judge Fielding comments ironically:

> Some things they can't seem to write down anymore. They never say [write], 'I felt I was being hit', but rather say something like, 'I saw and felt I was apparently receiving a blow to my body.' It's a kind of fear – after all, they know how we work.

The problem is magnified, for judges at least, when police officials write down their *own* observations in the '*ambsthalve*' process-verbal (*process-verbaal van bevinding ambsthalve opgemaakt*). These kinds of process-verbal tend to be used more widely as indications of what the police officials in question observed when arriving at the scene of the alleged offence, but may also be used to write down observations of what they heard (or overheard) the defendant say after the offence. Aside from the obvious legal implications of such 'overheard talk' committed to writing, judges tend to comment largely on the *practical* difficulties that accompany reading, evaluating, and using such processes-verbal. For instance, as police officials tend to work in pairs, such processes-verbal tend to be signed by two persons. Of course, the question is whether both or merely one of the two officials saw an incriminating act – a question that that may come up in court. At the same time, police officials are to be believed at their written word, even if that written word does not specify the observations individually: the relationship, Judge Jamison suggests, is one of necessary and 'institutionalized trust'.

Unaccounted histories: The decisions not to

As the court scene described in the introduction suggested, unfolding practices may also focus on the *delineation* of the legal case file. While the case file always traces its growth – by attributing authorship to and hence accounting for every step in the criminal investigation – it does not similarly account for the decision to stop the criminal investigation. In other words, the case file accounts for the evidentiary materials present in the file, it does not similarly explain their absence. These unaccounted decisions, inaccessible to the parties in the courtroom, may come to 'haunt' the proceedings in court when lawyers suggest that police officials have failed to exercise due diligence or have composed the case file in a prejudiced way. For instance, the lawyer in the introduction of this piece suggests that the police have actively barred competing and exculpatory eyewitness accounts from the case file. Defendants, too, may level similar objections to the judge, like, for instance, a young man accused of stealing a mobile phone in a bar arguing that the police should have judged security camera footage and check the phone he allegedly stole for his fingerprints: 'They didn't bother! All this seriously hurts my defence!'

Faced with files like this, lawyers commonly request that additional witnesses be heard or that security camera footage be collected. Here, the case file's histories are again inserted into the intertextual field of the courtroom; case files appear as objects that are far from 'finished' and complete. As files become inserted into the intertextual field of the courtroom, their supposed completeness may, however, be cast into doubt. A partial file inexplicably missing crucial pieces of potentially exculpatory evidence, for lawyers, is proof that the prosecution has failed to exercise due diligence. Sometimes, lawyers couple this line of reasoning with a request for additional witnesses to be heard or security camera footage to be collected. These appeals are, at times, successful in that they lead judges to require additional evidence to be gathered. However, lawyers may also be quick to point out that hearing additional eyewitnesses is not going to help the defendant in his or her defence much: after all, (*chronological*) *time* has passed since the offence, human memory is fallible and witness testimony is likely to become less trustworthy over time.

When judges grant requests like this, concerns with the correct 'folding methods' take centre stage again: not any document can be folded into the case file. Decisions like these are recorded by assisting clerks and later expanded into a formal document testifying to the reasoning behind these decisions. Having been signed by the presiding judge, these documents will be added to the file while the file itself will await additional documentation, like authorized reports drawn up by police officials or expert witnesses. The case file is then kept 'open' and 'alive', that is, until the newly appointed date. Unfolding and refolding the case file is hence a play with its temporality: it consists of leveraging invisible and inaccessible histories to thwart a guilty verdict in the here-and-now or, at least, to adjourn the case, that is: to allow the case file to proceed further into a deferred and uncertain future.

Un/making cases and temporal interferences

This chapter has been an attempt to start accounting for the intricate relationship between law, time, and truth. In the preceding pages, I have attempted to show how struggles over 'what really happened' in courtrooms do not simply draw on the stories present 'in' the file, but that such interpretative struggles are extended to the file itself. Understanding how and why this happens is assisted by a conception of the legal case file as an object that has folded times, places and actors within itself that nevertheless may come to 'haunt' the procedures in court: '[H]istory can be can be recalled in objects. History is never left behind' (M'charek, 2014: 3). A focus on these histories – either explicitly accounted for, or made absently present – allows one to carefully trace the way the case file mediates epistemic access to the event law seeks to judge. That is, it takes seriously the way the case file builds correspondences with 'what actually happened', while it simultaneously underscores how this particular way of building correspondences and trace histories offers the parties to the case unexpected possibilities to make or unmake a case. As such, this chapter has made problematic a rigid distinction between 'procedural context' or 'frame', on the one hand, and legal modes of arriving at the 'material truth', on the other. 'Observing procedure' is a practice of *enacting* procedure; 'acquiring the facts' is similarly a practice of folding statements and utterances into legal space-time. Highlighting, furthermore, precisely the *connections* between 'doing time' and 'doing truth', this chapter has refused to treat one as a context for the other. The case file, transporting and transforming evidence, is a crucial object doing both legal and truth-telling work. This contribution has also shown that the 'process' that precedes, in chronological time, the 'event' of the court is itself always already *oriented towards* that event: process and event, past and present, are difficult to tease apart a priori. Indeed, it is only through the spatial and temporal enactment of a 'cut' (Barad, 2003, 2007) that process and event are separated: only then it makes sense not to speak of an unfolding process but an event with a before and after; only then can both 'procedure' and 'investigatory process' appear as 'context' to the event in question (Scheffer, 2010: 186–188).

Temporal interferences

In emphasizing the making of multiple temporalities, this chapter has paid specific attention to moments we could refer to as *temporal interference*: the moments at which the time of procedure, the time of the file's production and chronological time cannot be neatly kept apart but rather interfere with one another to produce barriers to truth-making. In each of the cases drawn on in this chapter, the time of procedure, the time of the production of the file and the time of the offense are evoked and 'brought to life' simultaneously, producing a situation both propitious (for the defendant and lawyer) and challenging (to prosecutor). These moments of temporal interference demonstrate that, even though while great care is taken to set the procedural stage for truth-making – to make procedure into a *context* – such efforts do not necessarily succeed. 'Procedure', as well as the times and places of the case file's production, can be evoked to bar access to the truth. To speak with Barad (2003), processes of mattering – of something becoming material to and consequential for, of making differences that make a difference – have, then, both spatial and temporal dimensions. Or rather, spatiality and temporality are *themselves* the product of 'ongoing open process of mattering through which "mattering" itself acquires meaning and form in the realization of different agential possibilities' (2003: 817). Both 'temporality and spatiality emerge in this processual historicity' (ibid: 817–818). The case file's multiple temporalities play a crucial role in these practices of translating between the there-and-then of the offence and the here-and-now of the court session. By folding, ordering, and sorting different temporalities, the case file is both what allows procedure and facts to be "kept apart" as much as it presents the possibility of such temporal interferences and, with these, the undoing or unmaking of a case.

In so doing, this chapter can be read, perhaps, as a few inquisitive steps into a direction of research that takes seriously how and where presents are made, histories are written and futures anticipated in legal settings. Where and how, to speak with Bakhtin (1981: 84), do perhaps multiple temporalities 'thicken' and 'take on flesh'? Memorizing and forgetting, recording and erasing, making visible and rendering invisible: these are operations crucial to the temporal agency of the legal case file touched on in this chapter. In its emphasis on court workers' and especially lawyers' concern with forgotten, erased histories, it treats time and temporality as a local matter of concern. The notion of the folded object (M'charek, 2014), together with an emphasis on unfolding practices in court, has been a crucial step in this direction.

Acknowledgements

This piece was made possible with help of funding from two sources: the Dutch Fund for Scientific Research (NWO) and the European Research Council (Race-Face ID research project, principal investigator: Amade M'charek).

Note

1 In order to ensure confidentiality and anonymity, all the names of defendants, lawyers, judges, prosecutors and places have been changed.

Bibliography

Bakhtin, M. (1981). Forms of Time and of the Chronotope in the Novel: Towards a Historical Poetics. In *The Dialogic Imagination: 4 Essays.* Austin: University of Texas Press.

Barad, K. (2003). Posthumanist Performativity: Toward an Understand of How Matter Comes to Matter. *Signs: Journal of Women in Culture and Society* 28.3: 801–831.

———. (2007). *Meeting the Universe Halfway: Quantum Physics and the Entanglement of Matter and Meaning.* Durham, NC: Duke University Press.

Briet, S. (1951). *Qu'est-ce que la Documentation ?* Paris: EDIT.

Buckland, M. K. (1997). What is a Document? *Journal of the American Society for Information Science* 48.9: 804–809.

Cleiren, C. P. M. (2001). Waarheid in het strafrecht: niet tot elke prijs. In Cleiren, C. P. M., Bock, R. H. de, Klaassen, C. J. M. (Eds.) *Het Procesrecht en de waarheidsvinding.* Den Haag: Boom Juridische Uitgevers.

Derrida, J. (1967). *Of Grammatology.* Baltimore, MA: Johns Hopkins University Press.

Grabham, E. (2011). Doing Things with Time: Flexibility, Adaptability, and Elasticity in UK Equality Cases. *Canadian Journal of Law and Society* 26.3: 485–508.

———. (2014). Legal Form and Temporal Rationalities in UK Work-Life Balance Law. *Australian Feminist Studies* 29: 67–84.

Hull, M. S. (2003).The File: Agency, Authority, and Autography in a Pakistan Bureaucracy. *Language and Communication* 23.3: 287–314.

Komter, M. (2002). The Power of Legal Language: The Significance of Small Activities for Large Problems. *Semiotica* 131.3/4: 415–428.

Research on Language and Social interaction 39.3: 201–228.

———. (2003). The Interactional Dynamics of Eliciting a Confession in a Dutch Police Interrogation. *Research on Language and Social Interaction* 36.4: 433–470.

———. (2006). From Talk to Text: The Interactional Construction of a Police Record.

Kozin, A. (2007). The Legal File: Folding Law, Folded Law. *International Journal for the Semiotics of Law* 20.1: 191–216.

Latour, B. (1999). *Pandora's Hope: Essays on the Reality of Science Studies.* Cambridge, MA: Harvard University Press.

———. (2010). *The Making of Law: An Ethnography of the Conseil d'Etat.* Cambridge: Polity Press.

———. (2013). *An Inquiry into Modes of Existence.* Cambridge MA: Harvard University Press.

Law, J. (2009). Actor Network Theory and Material Semiotics. In *the New Blackwell Companion to Social Theory*, 3rd ed., edited by B. S. Turner, 141–158.Oxford: Blackwell.

Luhmann, N. (2004). *Law as a Social System.* Oxford: Oxford University Press.

Lynch, M. (1993). *Scientific Practice and Ordinary Action.* Cambridge: Cambridge University Press.

Lynch, M. and Bogen, D. (1996). *The Spectacle of History: Speech, Text, and Memory at the Iran-Contra Hearings.* Durham, NC: Duke University Press.

Lynch, M. and McNally, R. (2005). Chains of Custody: Representation, Visualization and Accountability in the Processing of DNA Evidence. *Communication & Cognition* 38.3/4: 297–318.

M'charek, A. (2014). Race, time, and folded objects: The HeLa error. *Theory, Culture and Society* 31.6, 29–56.

M'charek, A., Hagendijk, R., and De Vries, W. (2013). Equal before the Law: On the Machinery of Sameness in Forensic DNA Practice. *Science, Technology and Human Values* 38.4: 542–565.

Otte, R. (2015). *Het Proces. Strafrecht in de praktijk.* Amsterdam: Boom.

Philoppopoulos-Mihalopulos, A. (2014). Critical Autopoiesis and the Materiality of Law. *International Journal of Semiotics of Law* 27.2: 165–177.

Pottage, A. (2012). The Materiality of What? *Journal of Law and Society* 39.1: 167–183.

Scheffer, T. (2005). Courses of Mobilisation. Writing Systematic Micro-histories on Legal Discourse. In *Theory and Method in Socio-Legal Research*, edited by M. Travers and R. Banakar, 75–89. Oxford: Hart Publishing.

———. (2006). The Microformation of Criminal Defense: on the Lawyer's Notes, Speech Production, and the Field of Presence. *Research on Language and Social Interaction* 39.3: 303–342.

———. (2007). File Work, Legal Care, and Professional Habitus: An Ethnographic Reflection on Different Styles of Advocacy. *International Journal of the Legal Profession* 14.1: 57–81.

———. (2010). *Adversarial Case-Making. An Ethnography of English Crown Court Procedure.* Leiden: Brill.

Serres, M. and Latour, B. (1995). *Conversations on Science, Culture, and Time: Michel Serres Interviewed by Bruno Latour*, Ann Arbor: University of Michigan Press.

Toom, V. (2010). *Dragers van Waarheid: Normatieve Aspecten van 20 Jaar Forensisch DNA Onderzoek in Nederland.* PhD disseration. Amsterdam Institute for Social Science Research.

Van Oorschot, I. (2014). Seeing the Case Clearly: File-Work, Material Mediation, and Visualizing Practices in a Dutch Criminal Court. *Symbolic Interaction* 37.4: 439–457.

Van Oorschot, I. and Schinkel, W. (2015). The Legal Case File as Border Object: On Self-reference and Other-reference in Criminal Law. *Journal of Law and Society* 42.4: 499–527.

Vismann, C. (2008). *Files: Law and Media Technology.* Stanford. CA: Stanford University Press.

13 Topological time, law, and subjectivity

A description in five folds

Sameena Mulla, Marquette University

This chapter describes my approach to the emergent framework of topological time as I have developed and deployed it to go beyond the enmeshing of time and space,[1] and set forth a temporality that also characterizes subjectivities under conditions of anticipating violence. Anticipation is itself contingent; it is not to be mistaken with certainty of the future. My interest in thinking about time as topological is also conditioned on the ethnographic. In my book, *The Violence of Care: Rape Victims, Forensic Nurses, and Sexual Assault Intervention* (2014), I examine the rapidly changing world of sexual assault forensic intervention in the U.S., particularly as it is mediated by the relationship between law and medicine in formal emergency room-based programs. The book traces the complex of care that emerges from the interpenetration of legal and therapeutic practices. Based on ethnographic research in a Baltimore, MD, emergency room, a milieu I entered as both anthropologist and rape crisis advocate, my work argues that the sexual assault victim is recruited into the world as both patient and legal victim. In my ethnography, I attend to the ways that distinct, incongruent, and divergent configurations of space and time mark the nexus of clinic and courtroom, reshaping the relationship of care to investigation, and projects of healing to projects of justice, which are at times closely attuned and other times disparate.

While I briefly introduce the notion of topological time in *The Violence of Care*, I breezily move past the introduction to focus on three distinctive temporal modalities observed within the course of my fieldwork: 1) forensic time; 2) criminal time; and 3) biographical time (Mulla, 2014, 57). These three modalities represent time figured metrically, and are differently privileged, or even structured as existing in tension with one another. Their gathering together is what characterizes my ethnographic descriptions of topological time, which I complicate by demonstrating how patients struggle to assert their own meaningful time frames and events into the forensic framework. In this chapter, I want to revisit the underpinnings of topological time as a particularly productive approach to violence and the law, and to linger over how thinking with topology might offer us insight into the temporality of subjectivity in the aftermath of sexual violence.

One of the key temporal configurations of forensic intervention is its particular structure of anticipation. Namely, the forensic intervention anticipates the trial, regardless of whether the trial comes to pass. In fact, the trial rarely comes to pass.

The courtroom is a privileged site and destination, so much so that it is present in the clinical space as an agency that structures the examination. In my book, I suggest that the courtroom is in fact one of many actants breathing life into the form that suffering, healing, and justice may take in the forensic intervention (Law and Lodge, 1984). My past work develops a focus on the structure of anticipation as it was present for each case, regardless of the actual trajectory of these cases, which were most likely to end with no follow-up investigation, charges, or prosecution.[2] Feminist engagements with theories of anticipation and indeterminacy call for approaches to such temporal configuration that account for both structure and power (McNay, 2003). The temporal modalities of forensic intervention into sexual assault are embedded within the structures of gender, sexuality, race, and law. Rather than give an account for each of these axes of experience, I set forth a theory of topological time through which such structures are enfolded and sutured together to constitute the subject.

Approaching time as topological, I build on the work of Michel Serres, which I found very useful as I contemplated the operations of time in the forensic intervention. Thinking of a large technically complex interdisciplinary intervention such as sexual assault forensic examination lent itself to thinking with Serres, with his dedication to sprawling networks of science and technology. Serres's *Conversations on Science, Culture, and Time* (1995) posits an approach to time as topological. One key passage in which he describes his approach to time in conversation with Bruno Latour reads as follows:

> SERRES: An object, a circumstance, is thus polychromic, multitemporal, and reveals a time that is gathered together, with multiple pleats.
>
> LATOUR: You are explaining here a sentence I was going to ask you to explain from your book *Le Tiers-Instruit*, which speaks of precisely these nonmetrical diversities: "I have always used a process of abstraction like this, which could be called topological, and whose principle consists of describing nonmetrical diversities—in this case the network."
>
> SERRES: Yes. If you take a handkerchief and spread it out in order to iron it, you can see in it certain fixed distances and proximities. If you sketch a circle in one area, you can mark out nearby points and measure far-off distances. Then take the same handkerchief and crumple it, putting it in your pocket. Two distant points suddenly are close, even superimposed. If, further, you tear it in certain places, two points that were close can become very distant. This science of nearness and rifts is called topology, while the science of stable and well-defined distances is called metrical geometry. (Serres, 1995: 60)

The temporal description he sets is not merely a meshing together of spatial-temporal coordinates, but a figuration of temporality as it is enmeshed with subjectivities in contexts of suffering. I invoke suffering here because Serres opens his interview with Latour with talk of his being of "the war generation," situating his philosophical projects as against war (2). My point here is that Serres's thinking emerges under conditions of war, and that he is describing a form of temporality that maps onto the wartorn landscapes of his childhood and early adult life. In what follows, I model Serres's approach to topological time by drawing together biography, ethnography and philosophy. In particular, I excavate two other topological figures within the work of Ludwig Wittgenstein and Maurice Blanchot, further developing a temporal topology of contingent anticipation. This framework is particularly well suited to analyzing law when it takes up the adjudication of violence, and for analyzing the law as violence itself. My own research on the medico-legal investigation of sexual assault and rape is concerned with both the adjudication of violence, and the violence of the law, which imposes and normalizes a burden of pain, suffering and humiliation on the complaining witness (Cover, 1983; Mulla, 2014). What is more, the sexual assault victim finds herself the object of the state's foundational violence (Benjamin, 1986; Derrida, 1992; Mulla, 2014).

Building on Serres's description of time as folded, contingent, and heterogeneous, I conceptualize time as topological for two purposes: the first is to provide a notion of time that is confluent with space, and the second is to give a sense of temporally inflected subjectivity. These concepts are particularly useful for theorizing subjectivities shaped by the shock of violence, and are furthermore applicable in the realm of law, a violent force itself that requires its subjects to imagine themselves at various temporal junctures, and to anticipate a future that may or may not arrive.

First fold: Welcome to the doughnut world

My own disciplinary orientations in anthropology predispose me to think through topological time philosophically, ethnographically, and biographically. In a sense, my reading of various texts, moments, and anthropological analysis is topological in nature, bringing into proximity texts that were born at both temporal and geographical distance from one another but intersect and are enfolded in my own subjective experience of them. I begin with a snippet of biography that seemed germane as Serres's introduction of topology invited me to think about what I knew about topology prior to my reading of *Conversations on Science, Culture, and Time*. Topology captured my imagination as an undergraduate student over 20 years ago. While I never took geometry in a university setting, as luck would have it, I attended a talk by mathematician Richard Schwartz, who deigned to introduce a group of (mostly) non-mathematics majors to topology. Most striking to me was his explication of the doughnut world. The doughnut world, he described, was, as one might intuit, shaped like a doughnut (or inner tube or bagel). In geometry, the figure is called a torus. Just as standing on a spherical planet like the Earth may give one the perspective of standing on a plane, the torus offers particular vistas that are dependent on both one's orientation, as well as the particular dimensions of the torus. One configuration Schwartz described had one standing on the torus, facing towards the hole in the center. Under the right conditions, standing in this way, Schwartz explained that one may see a person standing in front of you. Depending on the parameters defining your doughnut world, that person may be far in the distance, or she may be very close to you. Wondering who the person before you may be, and anticipating discovering their identity, you might reach out your hand to tap the person on the shoulder, Schwartz suggested, only to find that someone is tapping you on your shoulder at the very same moment. In fact, the person in front of you is you—you are staring at your own back.

Curiously, this description of a self on a toroidal planet who is both in front of and behind oneself, while very much being in one place, struck a deep chord. It reminded me, rather oddly, of my experience of nearly drowning. The summer of my seventh year, I became a sufficiently confident swimmer that I began routinely meandering into sections of pools in which I could not reach the bottom. At a public pool, my uncle encouraged me to swim my first length in one of the lap lanes. The pool was not overly deep, although it was deep enough that I could not stand with my head above water. Paddling across the pool, I began to tire, and only a few feet away from the far wall, I began to struggle and sink under the water. Once under the water, I noticed a girl flailing and gasping. I could not hear her. While I was calm and observant, she was clearly in distress. Her dark hair floated around her panicked face, while her fluorescent green and black swimsuit seemed oddly familiar. "That girl is in trouble," I remember thinking. "That girl is me."

At the very moment I recognized myself, I ceased to be in front of myself and instead felt the powerful tug of a lifeguard yanking me from the water. I coughed vigorously and with pain, expelling the water I had inhaled. I had been both beside myself and within myself. Or, per Schwartz's explanation, a perforation had been introduced into my world, and I was drowning in toroidal space. In that moment, I experienced the sharp pivot from life toward death, as water poured into my 7-year-old lungs and robbed me of my breath. I had watched myself drowning, beside myself and anticipating some conclusion to the plight of the drowning girl.

Second fold: Anticipating violence

My approach to developing a full sense of topological time is also rooted in the ethnographic. In addition to the aforementioned work by Serres, I return often to Pradeep Jeganathan's essay on the checkpoint in Sri Lanka (Jeganathan, 2004). In my own work writing about sexual violence as a question of law, I was attuned to the potential tension between the sexual assault victim as traumatized subject, and the needs of the law as it operates through the forensic modality. Trauma has, in my opinion, tended to be the most commonplace framework through which we understand sexual violence and rape. It also places victims in ontologically untenable positions in which the traumatized subject must not have access to memories of trauma, but as a legal witness, she must be able to narrate these events. One might characterize trauma as the return of the repressed, a type of haunting, in which the past intrudes on the present, what Cathy Caruth terms an "unclaimed experience" (Caruth, 1996). But diagnostically, trauma in its disordered form, if we were to rely on a diagnostic technology like the DSM, is unknown to the victim (in this case, patient), who reenacts the traumatic memory without recognizing it as such. In the context of the criminal justice intervention, however, the victim must recount, often in painstaking detail, the violence she has experienced. The traumatic memory must be recovered for the victim to become a witness. The clinical world would then cast the victim out of the category of trauma as syndrome without the key symptom of traumatic memory's repression (Young, 1995).

This conundrum, along with the fact that not every sexual assault victim is a clinically traumatized subject, was one of the main reasons I became skeptical of relying on trauma as a theoretical account of the temporalities at work in the forensic intervention. The trauma of rape is also stitched to the wound of sexism; gendered bodies traversing public space know viscerally the sensation of anticipating public comment, confrontation, and harassment. These wounding words may never come, but they have been volleyed before, and the dread one experiences in anticipating their return, from unseen voyeurs is discomfiting. One form of this anticipatory dread may well be the fear of rape. These structures of feeling (Williams, 1977), are not unrelated to the wound of racial animus. In the opening of his essay, "'Race', Time and the Revision of Modernity," Homi K. Bhabha begins by citing Fanon: "'Dirty n——!' Or simply, 'Look, a Negro!'" (1991, 193). Of these utterances, he says:

> Whenever these words are said in anger or in hate, whether of the Jew in that estaminet in Antwerp, or of the Palestinian on the West Bank [...]; whether they are said of the body of the woman or the man of color; whether they are quasi-officially spoken in South Africa or officially prohibited in London or New York, but inscribed nevertheless in the severe staging of the statistics of educational performance and crime, visa violations, immigration irregularities; whenever "Dirty n——!" or "Look a Negro!" is not said at all, but you can see it in a gaze, or hear it in the solecism of a still silence; whenever and wherever I am when I hear a racist, or catch his look, I am reminded of Fanon's evocatory essay "The Fact of Blackness" and its unforgettable opening lines.

Where Bhabha goes on to analyze Fanon's iconic account of what it means to belong to a marginalized category, and the temporality of emergence he ascribes to the "belatedness of the Black man," what I want to emphasize here is the description of anticipation within Bhabha's opening lines. This anticipation, rooted in the past, is both held in the racialized and gendered body, and reproduced through the gaze as it is embodied by silent and non-silent interlocutors. It is realized through individual and institutional agencies, and strikes the subject as she traverses the landscape.

For further instruction on structures of anticipation, I turned instead to other ethnographic accounts of living with violence. Jeganathan's account of the checkpoint in Sri Lanka, in the context of the civil war there, offered a compelling description of life in the wake of violence. He wrote of Colombo as "a map of targets, organized spatially, classified through some social logic. Such a map filters and flickers as implied targets do, for what might be subject to 'violence' shifts and the targets themselves move like shadows across the landscape of the city" (2004: 69). He continued, "targets are marked by checkpoints," talking of the many "basic and ordinary" checkpoints all across Sri Lanka, where officials "ask questions of those who pass by" (Ibid). These checkpoints are symbols of the state and its force, with the ability to question, detain, and arrest those passing through the landscape in which violence has once occurred and may yet occur again. As such, "if the logic of anticipation of violence creates a plethora of shifting targets that flicker and move like shadows across the landscape with each explosion or threat, then the checkpoint is an attempt by an agency of the state to control that flickering movement . . ." (Ibid). The "flickering movement" pointed to a lack of stability in which one could still anticipate violence, but would never truly know it.

Going on, Jeganathan continues:

> [T]he checkpoint configures practices of anticipation in a double way. On the one hand, to pass through a checkpoint is to remember why checkpoints exist—it is to recall the possibility of a bomb. The few who are, in fact, carrying or have some knowledge of a bomb would also, I imagine, anticipate its explosive impact. But, on the other hand, there is another kind of anticipation—that of the soldiers checking on the flow of traffic and people, asking questions, they are anticipating violence another way.
>
> (Ibid)

Anticipation is doubled in this account—it is not anticipation of a singularity, but of multiple possibilities that marks life in the wake of violence and under the auspices of a repressive regime.

In thinking about the location of violence in the lived world, Jeganathan produces an account embedded in the spatial landscape of the city of Colombo, also invoking the layered nature of anticipation that is instantiated, again and again, through the checkpoint. This contributes to the case for topological time, for the checkpoint is a moment of gathering together disparate experiences of anticipation, wrinkles in time that erupt at the same spatial location, in the same moment, and co-exist precisely in the space of the checkpoint as an intervention.

The checkpoint as the state's intervention, as it works to sort passersby into potential threats and non-threats, seemed to me to invite some comparison with the forensic intervention—a state-sponsored practice also emerging in the wake of violence, gathering various actors together who exist within a professional modality that anticipates violence, while seeking to respond to its eruption in a measured, routinized way. As with the checkpoint, the forensic intervention anticipates violence, while also guided by other forms of anticipation. To pass through forensic intervention is to remember rape—to recall its possibility and its actuality while anticipating a future of some kind. Jeganathan's reference to the ethnographic map of Colombo demonstrates his attentiveness to the reconfiguration of space and time by the reality and possibility of violence. Bombs have exploded and lives have been lost, harm perpetrated. Violence is destined. This is what it means to live in disaster's wake.

Third fold: Writing the disaster

My interest in Maurice Blanchot extends to his biography. A French journalist and literary theorist, Blanchot was almost executed by a Nazi firing squad, an experience he describes in the text *The Instant of My Death*. Blanchot's *Writing the Disaster* grapples with writing in the wake of violent upheaval, and the violent upheaval marking Blanchot's lifeworld was that of the rise of the Nazi regime and the ensuing Holocaust. While Jeganathan does not himself cite Blanchot's *Writing the Disaster*, the way in which Blanchot's book opens could just as easily describe Blanchot's disaster, as it could the anticipatory topologies of Jeganathan's checkpoint-laden landscape:

> We are on the edge of the disaster without being able to situate it in the future: it is rather always already past, and yet we are on the edge or under the threat, all formulations which would imply the future—that which is yet to come—if the disaster were not that which does not come, that which has put a stop to every arrival. To think the disaster (if this is possible, and it is not possible inasmuch as we suspect that the disaster is thought) is to have no longer any future in which to think it.
>
> (2004: 1)

The reference to edges, of our awareness of lacking awareness of them, recalls deep scholarly traditions around thresholds and limits. Edges are elusive in toroidal and folded landscapes. We are not always able to recognize them. Where Jeganathan figures the state as anticipating violence, Blanchot asks, "Would law be the disaster? The supreme or extreme law, that is: the excessiveness of uncodifiable law—that to which we are destined without being party to it" (1995: 2). This gives me an opening to think about what law anticipates, specifically within the auspices of forensic intervention, and how the anticipation of law structures anticipation itself. Once I have experienced violence, whether it be the violence of forensic intervention or the court of law or near-drowning, I am destined for violence.

What is more, "I" am multiple. Or, as Blanchot relates: "The disaster ruins everything, all the while leaving everything intact. It does not touch anyone in particular; 'I' am not threatened by it, but spared, left aside. It is in this way that I am threatened; it is in this way that the disaster threatens in me that which is exterior to me—an other than I who passively become other" (1995: 1). I watched myself drown, with concern and curiosity. I was both the other and the self.

Fourth fold: Gathering time

Even as I gather here snippets of biography, passages of text that illustrate time as topological, I attended to multiple temporalities in my earlier research on forensic intervention (Mulla, 2014). Criminal time is one of three temporalities I discussed, also highlighting what I call biographical time, and forensic time. These are not the only modes of working time in the forensic examination. The intervention's urgency is driven by the diminishing life of DNA. The problem of documentation is one of time itself. By the time a case goes to trial, the victim's wounds, psychic and physical, may have healed or taken some other form. Forensic technique captures wounds, fixing them in forensic time so that they may endure and extend into the time of the trial. This manipulation of time in order to overcome the problem of time's forward march is reflected within a particular investigative context in which the victim's narrative is clearly demarcated as having a beginning and an end. This timeline of victimization, plotted on criminal time, is determined by formal criteria derived from legal statutes. Once the timeline is determined, nurses work to uncover evidence that populates the timeline in dense increments. This process takes the form of the forensic interview, during which victims struggle to describe the event of victimization through their own meaningful frameworks. Victims' narratives of suffering do not have the same start and end points as the forensic narrative. The forensic interview becomes a series of interruptions in which victims tell their stories and forensic nurses ask questions. This struggle over the most meaningful way to relate a sexual assault is largely driven by the different anticipatory structures in which the participants are enmeshed. For the nurses, the court of law is the ultimate point of arrival, and for the victims, a return to the everyday (or a descent into the ordinary, as Veena Das might term it [2006]) is what forms the future horizon. Although this is not my chapter's focus, it is also important to note that therapeutic frameworks give forensic nurses recourse to different temporalities of pathology through the understandings of chronic and acute illness. It is clear that the forensic intervention closes off the understanding of sexual assault as a pathology with chronic etiology, producing it within the boundaries of the acute, which suits the criminal justice investigation, while potentially shorting the therapeutic processes of each patient in this context by not considering broader causes of risk, or long term repercussions of sexual assault.

Clinical practices and clinical ontologies are also part of the heterogeneous gathering that constitutes the forensic intervention—what is folded together in the topological temporality that characterizes time's multivalent and coincidental operation within forensic nursing practice. Returning to the passages from Serres's conversations with Latour, we see that Serres distinguishes between what he considers a metric time from topological time. Metric time is the clear delineation of a time that moves progressively forward and backward in "straight" lines. The "crumpled" version of time is the proximity of metrically distant points on the handkerchief as the fabric is folded in the hand or the pocket such that they become proximate. This is the model of time that perhaps best reflects the way violence is made meaningful within the lives of those who suffer it. For victims who render their experiences meaningful within the complex and autobiographical topologies of their own life circumstances, the soteriological narrative is one that may reach back to any number of events or moments in time, while its futures race ahead on many paths that flow from its anchoring into the heterogeneous biographical narratives. The institution, however, requires that the time of the sexual assault can be measured and plotted, resembling what Serres calls flat metric time, which he contrasts with topological time. For Serres, metric time is the way that an institution can impose its method (1995: 45). Because the institution, in this case the forensic practice and the criminal justice system in which it is embedded, must produce a narrative that can be investigated and assessed in a juridical process, the twists, folds, tears, and crumples of the topological narratives that sexual assault victims voice during the intervention are subsumed under the metric narrative solicited and preserved in the dialogical interaction between the nurse and victim.

Fifth fold: Topological figures

Although Serres's approach to time is developed in relation to his scholarly practices, and not necessarily in relation to experiential (or ethnographic) and embodied understandings of time, as an anthropologist myself, his formulation clearly struck a chord with me. Latour characterizes Serres as "absolutely indifferent to temporal distances," as willing to engage Pythagoras as he is La Fontaine, to which Serres's response is essentially, "all authors are our contemporaries" (1995: 44). Serres's appreciation for a wide array of thinkers from various historical periods models his skepticism of epistemological histories that emphasize rupture, and his genealogical approach to his subjects of analysis poses many possible continuities that co-exist with the ruptures stressed in many scholarly works that account for the history of scientific thought (1995: 48).

On the narratives of progress, newness and invention, Serres says:

> That's not time, only a simple line. It's not even a line, but a trajectory of the race for first place—in school, in the Olympic Games, for the Nobel Prize. This isn't time, but a simple competition—once again, war. Why replace temporality, duration, with a quarrel?
>
> (1995: 49)

Serres's dismissal of lines opens out into his characterizing of metric and topological time, and his clear relegation of metric as instrumentalized measurement of time. Mistake not measurement with a general theory of time, he admonishes. Law, so often requiring measurement, still exists within folded topological time.

Even as Serres wrote against war and proposed a topological understanding of time, I stumbled on a short passage describing an unusual geometric figure within *Writing the Disaster*: "The circle, uncurled along a straight line rigorously prolonged, reforms a circle eternally bereft of center," Blanchot wrote (1995: 2). Bereft of the center in the reconstituted circle, Blanchot asserts a practice of patience:

> Through patience, I take upon myself the relation to the Other of the disaster—the relation which does not allow me to assume it, or even to remain myself in order to undergo it. Through patience all rapport between myself and a patient self is broken.
>
> (1995: 14)

Two dyads are mentioned within this brief sequence: myself and the Other of the disaster; and myself and a patient self. Standing on the toroidal planet, I see the Other, and reaching for her, I come to know that the Other is me. If the dyads correspond to each other, the self is the Other of the disaster. Lost and separated from oneself, "the passion of patience, the passivity of a time without present (absent time, time's absence), had to be his sole identity, circumscribed by a temporary singularity" (Ibid). Blanchot describes the disaster's wake as the experience of being surrounded or circumscribed within a "circle eternally bereft of center." Are there other ways of understanding the state of circumscription without center? Thus surrounded, would the subject see the edge? Is the edge a lining?

In her explication of Ludwig Wittgenstein's complicated descriptions of the inner and outer as they relate to language, Veena Das suggests, "that the inner is not like a distinct state that can be projected to the outer world through language [...] but rather [it is] like something lines the outer," and, as such, "language and the world (including the inner world) are learned simultaneously" (Das, 1998: 190). Indeed, at a graduate seminar at Johns Hopkins University in 2001, Das once described the relationship between the inner and the outer as a Mobius strip, a continuous fused ribbon in which the ribbon has been twisted before being joined. This allows one to draw a continuous line on both the inner and outer surfaces of the loop without lifting one's pen. Or, if the Mobius were a vast planet, one could walk its paths eternally without ever reaching an edge, or even noticing the absent center. The center is not absent as long as one is (alive) on the planet; it is only a lack when one has been expelled from the Mobius and floats beside it (in death).

Several passages in *Philosophical Investigations* explore the relationship of the inner and the outer, perhaps most iconically, Wittgenstein's discussion of (and resistance to) private language, one formulation of which he works through as the ability to feel pain in the body of another (§256–257). Towards the end of the *Investigations*, returning to the original positing of one's knowledge of pain in the body of another, he adds: "I can know what someone else is thinking, not what I am thinking. It is correct to say 'I know what you are thinking', and wrong to say 'I know what I am thinking'" (222e). This approach to language is, of course, not simply about literal utterances, but philosophical descriptions of everyday life. In this description, the relationships between two subjects are posited, and full apprehension of one's inner state is approached with skepticism. Wittgenstein further elucidates these relations to the "I" with a thought experiment:

> If there were people who always read the silent internal discourse of others—say by observing the larynx—would they too be inclined to use the picture of complete seclusion?
>
> If I were to talk to myself out loud in a language not understood by those present, my thoughts would be hidden from them.

> Let us assume there was a man who always guessed right what I was saying to myself in my thoughts. (It does not matter how he manages it.) But what is the criterion for his guessing *right*? Well, I am a truthful person and I confess that he has guessed right.—But might I not be mistaken, can my memory not deceive me? And might it not always do so when—without lying—I express what I have thought within myself?
>
> (222e)

In these passages, the relation between the inner and the outer are interconnected (one lines the other) and the description of language that emerges reveals both our grammars and our subjectivities. To apprehend my inner self, I must trace the fold that is contiguous with another. Perhaps I call this the outer. I see another drowning, and recognize in her my own drowning.

Suturing

Here, I have drawn together five folds, but there are easily multitudes of folds that could follow, freshly relevant in different ethnographic contexts, settings or moments. In many respects, topological figures serve as spatial metaphors with which to think about time. Relying on ethnography and experience to project oneself into any one of the figures reveals a deeper understanding of how subjectivity emerges in topological time. A topological approach to time allows for the contingencies of experience, the intersection of the singular and the institutional, the routine and the critical, and the acute and the chronic. It accounts for the structures of anticipation that are generative of experience without privileging the metric over folding. Topologies connote densely intermeshed temporal and spatial relations that constitute bodies and subjectivities. Law, with its attendant force, its practice of patience, and anticipation (of violence), may appear to juxtapose various metrics of time even as it navigates topological temporalities.

Notes

1 Forman and Sowton's collection, *Taking Our Time: Feminist Perspectives on Temporality*, critiques patriarchal time, with a recurring theme of resistance to linear time connecting several of the chapters. Some of the authors in the collection assert embodied time as a counterpoint to linear time, and draw attention to the ways in which embodied time and the time of medical institutions, such as hospitals and clinics, collide and co-exist amid tension.

2 In my study, roughly three of every 10 cases in which a sexual assault forensic examination was conducted resulted in prosecution.

Bibliography

Benjamin, W. (1986). "Critique of Violence," in *Reflections: Essays, Aphorisms, Autobiographical Writings*. Trans. E. Jephcott. New York: Schocken Books, pp. 277–300.

Bhabha, H. K. (1991). "'Race', Time and the Revision of Modernity," *Oxford Literary Review* 13(1): 193–219.

Blanchot, M. (1995). *The Writing of the Disaster*. Trans. A. Smock. Lincoln and London: University of Nebraska Press

Caruth, C. (1996). *Unclaimed Experience: Trauma, Narrative and History*. Baltimore, MA: Johns Hopkins University Press

Cover, R. M. (1983). "The Supreme Court, 1982 Term—Forward: Nomos and Narrative," *Faculty Scholarship Series*. Paper 2705. Yale Law School. Available at: http://digitalcommons.law.yale.edu/fss_papers/2705.

Das, V. (1998). "Wittgenstein and Anthropology," *Annual Review of Anthropology* 27: 171–195.

———. (2006). *Life and Words: Violence and the Descent Into the Ordinary*. Berkeley: University of California Press.

Derrida, J. (1992). "Force of Law: The Mystical Foundation of Authority," in *Deconstruction and the Possibility of Justice*. Eds. D. Cornell, M. Rosenfeld and D. Carlson. New York and London: Routledge, pp. 3–67.

Forman, F. and Sowton, C. (1989). *Taking Our Time: Feminist Perspectives on Temporality*. London and New York: Pergamon Press.

Jeganathan, P. (2004). "Checkpoint: Anthropology, Identity and the State," in *Anthropology in the Margins of the State*. Eds. V. Das and D. Poole. Santa Fe and Oxford: School of American Research, pp. 67–80.

Law, J. and Lodge, P. (1984). *Science for Social Scientists*. London: Macmillan Press Ltd.

McNay, L. (2003). "Agency, Anticipation and Indeterminacy in Feminist Theory," *Feminist Theory* 4(2):139–148.

Mulla, S. (2014). *The Violence of Care: Rape Victims, Forensic Nurses and Sexual Assault Intervention*. New York: New York University Press

Serres, M. with Latour, B. (1995). *Conversations on Science, Culture and Time*. Trans. R. Lapidus. Ann Arbor: University of Michigan Press

Williams, R. (1977). *Marxism and Literature*. Oxford and New York: Oxford University Press.

Wittgenstein, L. (1953). *Philosophical Investigations*. Trans. G. E. M. Anscombe. Oxford and Malden: Blackwell Publishers.

Young, A. (1995). *The Harmony of Illusions: Inventing Post-Traumatic Stress Disorder*. Princeton, MA: Princeton University Press.

Index

Please note that references to Notes are indicated by the letter 'n' followed by the Note number.

For Product Safety Concerns and Information please contact our EU representative GPSR@taylorandfrancis.com
Taylor & Francis Verlag GmbH, Kaufingerstraße 24, 80331 München, Germany

www.ingramcontent.com/pod-product-compliance
Ingram Content Group UK Ltd.
Pitfield, Milton Keynes, MK11 3LW, UK
UKHW010957180926
475701UK00004B/412
9780367665302